Handbook of Psychotherapy and Jewish Ethics

Moshe Halevi Spero

HANDBOOK of PSYCHOTHERAPY and JEWISH ETHICS

Halakhic Perspectives on Professional Values and Techniques

FELDHEIM
Jerusalem/New York

First published 1986
ISBN 0-87306-406-2

Philipp Feldheim Inc.
200 Airport Executive Park
Spring Valley, NY 10977

Feldheim Publishers Ltd.
POB 6525 / Jerusalem, Israel

Printed in Israel

To
Miriam Rivkah,
Yisroel Nachman Halevi,
Yonina Yachad,
and Daniel Halevi

מי־שת בטחות חכמה
או מי־נתן לשכוי בינה?

איוב לח:לו

Who hath put wisdom in the inward parts?
Or who hath given understanding to the mind?
Job 38:36

Publisher's foreword

In our complex world of today, psychotherapy continues to rise in importance, as human beings seek to disentangle themselves and to find a better way of life than what their early years might otherwise allow them. One result, to be noted with astonishment perhaps, is that this field, which developed in Vienna at the turn of the century with a powerful bias against our age-old Jewish religion, now includes a respectable and growing number of practitioners and students of psychotherapy who seek to live in commitment and obedience to the Torah and its recognized authorities. Time, evidently, does not stand still.

The consequence has been an ever-increasing ferment and body of discussion on what has been termed the interface between therapy and authentic Judaism.

As a rule, the Feldheim imprint does not appear on any book intended solely for the professional psychologist and the serious, accredited student. In this instance, an exception has been made in the hope that something of value may be added to the above-mentioned interface. It should thus be noted that this collection of articles is published for the observant Jewish professional.

Let it be added, further, that this book represents only the author's views, for which he alone bears responsibility. It does not imply any consent by the publisher for opinions or conclusions in a field where we cannot claim any competence.

ACKNOWLEDGMENTS

Acknowledgment is made to the following in whose pages parts of this book first appeared:

"Modern Psychotherapy and Halakhic Ethics: An Approach Toward Consensus in Values and Practice," *Journal of Medicine and Philosophy 8*, no. 2 (1983): 81-110; "The Halakhic Status of *Hirhur Asur* in Psychotherapy," *Assia 7*, nos. 1-2 (1980): 52-64; "Psychiatric Hazard and the Halakhic Disposition Toward Birth Control and Abortion," *Journal of Jewish Communal Service 53*, no. 2 (1976): 155-162; "Postponement of Ritual Circumcision in Young Children for Psychiatric Reasons," *Assia 7*, nos. 3-4 (1980): 79-90 and *Intercom 19*, no. 1 (1980): 23-31; "Countertransference in Religious Therapists of Religious Patients," *American Journal of Psychotherapy 35*, no. 4 (1982): 565-575; "Further Examination of the Halakhic Status of Homosexuality," *Proceedings of the Associations of Orthodox Jewish Scientists 7* (1984): 117-126; "Halakhic Definitions of Confidentiality in Psychotherapeutic Practice," *Tradition 20* (1982): 298-326; "Toward a Halakhic Perspective on Radical Forms of Psychological Manipulation and Behavior Control," *Proceedings of the Associations of Orthodox Jewish Scientists 7* (1984): 91-116; *Judaism and Psychology: Halakhic Perspectives* (New York: Ktav/Yeshiva University Press, 1980); "Violating Shabbat for Suicide Emergency," *Journal of Halacha and Contemporary Society 2* (1982): 72-83.

List of Abbreviations

Scripture

Gen.	Genesis
Exod.	Exodus
Lev.	Leviticus
Num.	Numbers
Deut.	Deuteronomy
Josh.	Joshua
Judg.	Judges
1 Sam.	1 Samuel
2 Sam.	2 Samuel
Isa.	Isaiah
Jer.	Jeremiah
Ezek.	Ezekiel
Hos.	Hosea
Obad.,	Obadiah
Jon.	Jonah
Mic.	Micah
Nah.	Nahum
Chab.	Chabakkuk
Zeph.	Zephaniah
Chag.	Chaggai
Zekh.	Zekhariah
Mal.	Malachi
Ps.	Psalms
Prov.	Proverbs
Songs	Song of Solomon
Lam.	Lamentations
Eccles.	Ecclesiastes
Esth.	Esther
Ez.	Ezra
Nech.	Nechemiah
1 Chron.	1 Chronicles
2 Chron.	2 Chronicles

Midrash

Deut. R.	Deuteronomy Rabba
Eccl. R.	Ecclesiastes Rabba
Ex. R.	Exodus Rabba
Gen. R.	Genesis Rabba
Lev. R.	Leviticus Rabba
Mid. Tanch.	Midrash Tanchuma
Num. R.	Numbers Rabba
Songs R.	Songs Rabba

Talmud

Arkh.	Arakhin
ARN	Avoth de-Rabbi Natan
Avoth	Pirkei Avoth
A.Z.	Avodah Zarah
Ber.	Berakhoth
B.B.	Bava Bathra
Bekh.	Bekhoroth
Betz.	Betzah
B.K.	Bava Kamma
B.M.	Bava Metzia
Chag.	Chagigah
Chul.	Chulin
DEZ	Derekh Eretz Zuta
Eduy.	Eduyoth
Eruv.	Eruvin
Git.	Gittin
Hor.	Horayoth
Kallah R.	Kallah Rabbathi
Kallah Z.	Kallah Zutretha
Ker.	Kerithoth

Ket.	Kethuboth
Kid.	Kiddushin
Maksh.	Makhshirim
Mak.	Makkoth
Meg.	Megillah
Meil..	Me'ilah
Men.	Menachoth
M.K.	Mo'ed Katan
Naz.	Nazir
Ned.	Nedarim
Pes.	Pesachim
R.H.	Rosh ha-Shanah
Sanh.	Sanhedrin
Shab.	Shabbath
Shek.	Shekalim
Shev.	Shevu'oth
Sot.	Sotah
Suk.	Sukkah
Taan.	Taanith
Tem.	Temurah
Ter.	Terumoth
Yev.	Yevamoth
Zev.	Zevachim

Codes, etc.

BaCH	*Bayit Chadash*, by R. Yoel Sirkis
BaHaG	*Baal Halakhoth Gedoloth*
J.T.	Jerusalem Talmud
M.T.	Maimonides, *Mishneh Torah* (*Hil.=Hilkhoth*)
RaN	Rabbeinu Nissim ben Reuven Gerondi
Resp.	Responsa
ShaKH	R. Shabbethai ha-Cohen
Sh.A., Ch.M.	*Shulchan Arukh, Choshen Mishpat*
Sh.A., E.H.	*Shulchan Arukh, Even ha-Ezer*
Sh.A., O.Ch.	*Shulchan Arukh, Orach Chayim*
Sh.A., Y.D.	*Shulchan Arukh, Yoreh De'ah*
SMaG	*Sefer Mitzvoth Gadol*
SMaK	*Sefer Mitzvoth Katan*
TaZ	*Turei Zahav*, by R. David ben Shmuel ha-Levi
Tos.	*Tosafoth* (s.v.="under the heading")
Tur Sh.A.	*Tur Shulchan Arukh*

Contents

PREFACE

I am grateful to God for enabling me to bring to light this volume dealing with the intersect between psychology, psychotherapy, and Halakhah. In the forthcoming chapters, I will follow a pattern of analysis introduced in my earlier text, *Judaism and Psychology: Halakhic Perspectives* (New York: Ktav/Yeshiva University Press, 1980) and strive for the synthetic expression of psychological values and methodology in terms of their essentially halakhic form.

In undertaking to produce a "handbook" of so-called practical analysis and possible solutions to halakhico-psychological problems, I think it may be worthwhile to differentiate two meanings of practicality. On one hand, practicality is generally taken to suggest the study of actual technique—such as the therapeutic management of religious patients' resistances to psychotherapy—or the identification of distinctly Orthodox Jewish norms for psychometric or projective tests or the proposal of ways to intervene against the rising rate of alcoholism among Jews, and so forth. According to this first interpretation, then, practicality means assuming the basic acceptability of therapeutic technique and procedure and implementing it specifically against the unknown parameters of Jewish social and psychological problems.

According to the second possible interpretation of practicality, psychological technique and practice is itself the unknown variable. That is, when seeking to integrate psychology and halakhic ethics, practicality means focused analysis of how Halakhah informs, guides, and even constrains whatever one does when one engages in psychotherapeutic practice; and this analysis is with regard to all applications of such practice. From this second perspective, practicality is defined as the achievement of maximum identification of the inherently halakhic forms for therapeutic behavior, while classifying those techniques and professional behaviors which Halakhah does not consider legitimate expressions of its mandate, values, and norms. The scope of this second type of analysis of practicality, and its indices, shall be explicated in detail in the first chapter, and the subsequent chapters will represent applications of the synthetic approach.

I also wish to add a caveat necessary in approaching this handbook. I believe that the forthcoming halakhic analyses are valid ones—that is, they conform to specific and traditional rules and methods of halakhic research and present honest interpretations of halakhic principles. At the same time, none of the essays are intended as *halakhah le-ma'aseh* or as definitive rulings. Rather, these chapters present the directions and findings of my study, and not conclusive arguments for any final arbitration in Jewish law. My central intention is that the material presented here will serve to stimulate further research and will introduce the mental health professional to one possible and useful halakhic approach to his work and to the objects of his study.

I now ask forbearance from the reader, whose appetite to begin reading has been whetted, while I pause to express gratitude to those who so richly deserve it.

I am deeply grateful to publisher Philipp Feldheim and his son, Yaakov Feldheim, for accepting this text for publication and for their painstaking efforts to transform these many pages into a singular source of pride and satisfaction. I am indebted to Bernard Scharfstein of Ktav Publishing Co. for granting permission for the re-publication of three chapters from my earlier text (although these have all been substantively modified, amended, and updated) and for similar permission from the editors and publishers of the various scholarly journals in which many other of these chapters originally appeared. I again thank Mr. and Mrs. Gerald Spero for innumerable provisions which enabled me to write these chapters in a style to which I have fondly grown accustomed. Finally, I express my love and affection for my parents, my parents-in-law, and especially for my dear wife, Yehudit, without whose love and efforts at patience this entire product would surely have been an impossibility. I believe that these persons all have a justifiable share in whatever reward comes to those who make it possible to provide knowledge to others.

Jerusalem
March 1986/Adar II 5746

1
Modern Psychotherapy and Halakhic Ethics: Approaching Consensus in Values and Practice

I. Introduction: Ethics and Psychotherapy

The relevance of personal and professional ethics to the practice of modern psychotherapy is increasingly apparent to clinicians and ethicists alike.[1] This awareness in turn brings into focus two distinct problems: (1) the need to understand the particular ethical beliefs of the client and the ways in which these should be managed in psychotherapy, and (2) the need to resolve specific ethical dilemmas in the theory and practice of psychotherapy; e.g., the implications of the medical model in psychotherapy, the problems of coercive interventive models versus the commitment to libertarianism, and so forth.

The above realizations have made the problem of safeguarding ethical neutrality in psychotherapeutic practice significantly more complex. On the one hand, psychotherapists are attempting to include in their clinical scope the patient's ethnic uniqueness and ethical beliefs in order to minimize "strangeness" in the therapeutic alliance, and also in order to be able to deal in a holistic way with the patient's problems in living. But, on the other hand, therapists continue to adhere to the practice wisdom of maintaining a nonjudgmental rather than a guiding or educational attitude toward the patient's expression of valuational material.

It has indeed become apparent that the original policy of ethical neutrality does not necessarily preclude the development of value problems in psychotherapy. Even a theoretical commitment to valuelessness can affect the therapeutic endeavor, as suggested by writers like Beit-Hallahmi, for example, who maintains that the radical clinical model of behavior modification is the logical result of the "end of values" movement in clinical psychology, and leads to the reduction of moral questions in psychotherapy to technical ones.[2] The commitment to value-free practice is itself a value commitment which may present conflict to patients who view the selection and process of psychotherapy from the perspective of specific ethical constraints and proscriptions.[3]

The concern with ethical issues in psychotherapy is not only of philosophical significance. It has been demonstrated in the varied disciplines of social work, psychology, and psychiatry that clinicians' ideological and theoretical commitments influence in both subtle and conspicuous ways such variables as the selection of therapeutic goals, the directions of the process of psychotherapy, the type of material produced by the patient, and, in the long run, the actual outcome of psychotherapy.[4] Inasmuch as there are inappropriate as well as appropriate ways to manage these influences, the commitment to address the patient's ethical beliefs quite clearly has to be recognized as both an ethical *and technical* issue in psychotherapeutic practice.

The subcategory of *religious* beliefs of patients and therapists has also been related to specific types of management problems and therapeutic misalliances, some of which are particular to therapists and patients of different religious beliefs and others to therapists and patients of like religious beliefs.[5]

In one sense, the patient and psychotherapist generally may be assumed to have different religious attitudes toward religious belief or practice to the degree that the determination of the therapist's religious beliefs is relatively less pathological or dys-autonomous than the determination of the patient's beliefs. Of course, therapists who presume that this putative difference between therapist and patient as to religious belief is true in *all* instances, or who alternatively assume that like religious affiliation between patient and therapist is a guarantee of harmony, may be defending their own unconscious neurotic perceptions which often motivate counterproductive reactions during psychotherapy. In the case of the religiously oriented therapist who will not treat the homosexual patient who does not include his homosexual preference as part of his psychosocial difficulties, or of the religiously oriented patient who refuses to associate freely on sexual matters—both of whom ascribe the rationale for their behavior to ethical commitments rather than to resistance—one again sees that ethical commitments impose certain constraints on therapeutic technique, whose acceptance and management, or rejection, are necessarily legitimate objects of technical consideration.

Thus, it is evident that the ethical commitments of the therapeutic participants bear directly on the successful outcome of practice. My concerns in this paper are the implications for practice of the religious Jewish psychotherapist's commitment to Halakhah (Jewish law and ethics), the constraints these commitments impose upon practice, and halakhically appropriate alternative approaches to dealing with such constraints.

II. The Problem of Consensus Between Halakhic Ethics and Modern Psychotherapy

Despite the burgeoning attention to ethics and values in psychotherapy, and in dramatic contrast to the creative productivity in the application of halakhic ethics to general medical practice, halakhic examination of the practice of psychotherapy is still in its infancy. One cause of this discrepancy may be that psychotherapy, unlike general medical practice, has not been subjected to centuries of rabbinic examination. Simply put, the subject matter under study has not been brought forward for halakhic study as frequently and consistently as have the objects of medical study.

Psychotherapeutic practice also is of a much more fluid and less objectifiable nature than medical practice. This has partially reinforced the field's confusing assortment of ideologically and theoretically inspired approaches (as well as the troublesome persistence of approaches the efficacy of which cannot be amply demonstrated). Such variance in understanding a single reality seems to discourage the ready application of halakhic values inasmuch as this task has traditionally been conceived as the fitting of tight halakhic guidelines to scientific or technical constants. Psychological science on the main cannot yet provide the halakhist with bound or constant data. However, I shall try to show that this does not mean that Halakhah lacks useful models which would allow for the variable nature of psychotherapy while also subsuming the practice under appropriate prescriptive and proscriptive norms.

An additional contributor to this conspicuous lack in halakhic application is the fact that Judaism is afflicted by a disorganized and undetailed metapsychology, by which I mean its assumptions about human behavior and personality development rather than assumptions about the soul and so forth.[6] Theories about the soul represent a limited use of the prefix "meta," yielding a collection of isolated rabbinic statements about phenomena truly "beyond" psychology that have little relevance for the contemporary ego psychologist or psychotherapist.

The psychotherapist's interest in more directly observable (or inferable) and manipulable aspects of human personality does not, of course, require the repudiation of traditional metapsychologies, nor does it imply the ascription of qualitative supremacy to modern psychological tenets in the overall analysis of human development and creativity. Rather, the psychotherapist's *change-oriented focus* demands more narrow attention to variables that can be efficiently and consistently manipulated and linked with measurable change in behavior. This focus can, in fact, be synchronized with numerous halakhic writings which tend to address the *yetzer* of man, or the behavioral and cognitive manifestations of human striving, rather than the more distant *n^eshamah* or soul of man.[7] This domain of *yetzer* is the legitimate object of both halakhic and psychological *change models* and can be profitably expanded by modern psychological understandings to the point where it is analogous to the objects of current modificatory foci.[8]

To be sure, halakhic literature does discuss select legal and moral implications of mental states which are directly akin to psychopathology, or which include this characteristic, such as *kordiakus*, *ruach ra'ah*, *teiruf da'ath*, and *sh^etuth*. Yet there are few discussions of anything that approaches a theory of modification of psychiatrically disturbed behavior.

The awareness that there are specific halakhic reservations about modern psychotherapy, however, has not led to the adequate development of halakhic solutions to these problems. Five recent, halakhic texts dealing with medical ethics have invited halakhic examination of modern psychology, but have produced disappointingly naive responses.[9] The select rabbinic responsa and scattered sources in halakhic literature which have important implications for modern psychotherapy have not been explicated, organized, and disseminated.

As I have stated elsewhere, the failure of Jewish psychologists and halakhists concerned about the role of Jewish thought in this field to develop a unified model for Halakhah and modern psychotherapy has also contributed to the disarray in this bioethical endeavor.[10] If there has been a consistent "approach" to the relation between psychotherapy and halakhic values, it has been the advocacy of retaining certain "approved" psychological techniques, while rejecting allegedly disagreeable philosophic underpinnings (e.g., determinism, libido theory) or actual techniques (e.g., free association, psychosurgery).[11]

This "approach" is the direct consequence of the absence of a unitary model and is inadequate for several reasons:

(1) It is generally advocated on the basis of unlettered explications of the philosophic foundations of psychotherapy and on popular rather than professional understandings of technique.

(2) It has discouraged approaches to the synthesizing of apparent differences between psychological and halakhic values which can in fact be resolved without doing violence to either set of tenets, and without having to substitute "Torah psychology" for "secular psychology."[12] For example, previous writers have emphasized an insuperable conflict between halakhic commitment to free will versus psychological determinism. This conflict actually results from assuming stricter definitions of determinism than are accepted by most theoreticians in psychiatry and of not considering seriously the softer definitions of determinism which are in fact compatible with the halakhic conception of voluntary behavior. Indeed, careful examination reveals that Jewish law and ethics maintains numerous deterministic notions within its basically libertarian ethic; e.g., *chazakah* (behavioral presumptions), *rov* (universal or particularistic norms), *umdana* (expectations or estimates), *n^edarim* (vows), the laws of *ha-ba b^e-machtereth* (that one has permission to kill an intruder who appears to be intent on murder), and so forth.[13] Similar compatibility can be found among allegedly conflicting Judaic and

psychological views on useful and dysfunctional levels of anxiety and guilt, and so forth.

(3) It gives the false impression that rejecting objectionable philosophy or theory somehow liberates practitioners from the influence of metaclinical assumptions. This belief is false because (a) technique is rarely employed in the absolute absence of intuitive or theoretical assumptions which guide the therapist through the chaos of interpersonal transactions which occur during psychotherapy, and (b) the need to link therapeutic outcomes with antecedent procedures necessitates generating theoretical schemes.[14]

(4) The practitioner who rejects theoretical or philosophic underpinnings (e.g., methodological determinism) is obliged to present an alternative theoretical approach through which he claims to guide his practice and communicate his professional behaviors and observations, or he risks weakening the scientific quality of his professional endeavor. None of the authors who advocate the haphazard bifurcation of practice and ideology have offered an adequate theoretical alternative.

Some writers, pinning their hopes of purifying modern psychotherapy on language substitution, have attempted to supplant concepts of ego psychology with reference to the vicissitudes of the "evil inclination" or the *n^eshamah* or other metaphysical concepts. This has rendered psychotherapy no more precise. In fact, this attempt risks hubris by implying greater adeptness at observing and manipulating the *n^eshamah* than the ego or observable behaviors. Thus, simple-minded language substitution is at worst a gross "category mistake" and at best a venture into uncharted territory.

(5) Finally, the lack of a unitary model has distracted attention from real halakhic problems of psychotherapeutic practice which are in no way resolved merely by rejecting extant philosophical views or techniques of psychotherapy. *As we shall see, these practical problems demand the development of a halakhic model which supports the intrinsically halakhic nature of psychotherapeutic beliefs and techniques when they are carried out following certain parameters, rather than the wholesale rejection of technique on the grounds of isolated incompatibilities or alleged malpractice.*

There is yet another reason for the religious psychotherapist to resolve halakhic problems confronting his practice. I believe it is true that the halakhically oriented therapist is in a position to influence positively the ethical and spiritual as well as psychological well-being of the patient,[15] but precisely for this reason he is also in a position to confuse these outcomes and their sequence, and to mismanage both. It may appear paradoxical, but, while it is not the psychotherapist's goal to arbitrate his patients' ethical beliefs, short of liberating these from pathogenic determinants, nonetheless such liberation represents a step forward toward authentic choice of autonomous religious beliefs and ethical values. However, a unitary halakhic model would resolve this paradox by indicating that liberation of ethical and spiritual strivings from pathogenic forces is itself a religiously prescribed endeavor and a positive influence on the patient's life. It would also be consistent with standard therapeutic procedures for dealing with valuational material in psychotherapy, thereby also safeguarding the therapist's obligation to refrain from directly arbitrating specific moral values for the patient.

III. A Unitary Halakhic Model: Toward Consensus

The underlying premise of the unitary approach to psychotherapeutic and halakhic ethics is that no aspect of reality is without some essential or intrinsic halakhic form, implied in the halakhic-aggadic belief that Halakhah is an *a priori* "blueprint" for reality.[16] Halakhic forms are realized through appropriate prescriptive norms and can be distorted through violation of these norms. Typically, these halakhic prescriptions are specified in Biblical writings and are made more specific through subsequent talmudic interpretation (e.g., how to slaughter an animal, how long to mourn, what not to do on the Sabbath, that one may heal), but often such models must be expanded upon through precise methodology to fit novel needs and developments (e.g., is electricity the equivalent of fire, is "brain death" truly death, is transsexual surgery halakhically valid).

It is desirable that one determine an appropriate halakhic model or paradigm for every aspect of human endeavor. For example, the psychotherapeutic endeavor (which we will return to later), as a subspecies of the overall medical endeavor, may be underwritten by several Biblical imperatives: the obligation to heal;[17] the obligation to return lost goods—which the Talmud renders "And you shall return *him to himself*";[18] and the obligation to maintain equilibrium and to restore it whenever it is absent.[19]

In some instances, existing halakhic principles can be directly applied to the psychologist's professional behavior; e.g., halakhic parameters of confidentiality and occasions for revelation of professional secrecy, the halakhic sanctions against transsexual surgery, or the halakhic attitude toward homosexuality. In instances such as these, both the halakhic principles and psychological applications are known variables. In numerous other areas, however, the psychological applications cannot be readily defined in terms of existing halakhic categories. For example: (a) May one discuss in psychotherapy material of illicit sexual content given that the prohibitions against *hirhur davar ha-asur* or *hirhur arayoth* are incumbent despite an appeal to the standard "healing model" (*v^e-rapo yerapeh*)? (b) How can one do reconstructive, historically oriented insight therapy when there is a prohibition against verbally reminding an individual of his previous ethical or social deviance? (c) How would Halakhah view involuntary modification of psychopathology, through a radical technique like psychosurgery, given Halakhah's commitment to free will? To simply retort in these cases that "we're doing *therapy*!" is neither an intelligent nor necessarily valid response to our dilemma (e.g., problem (a)) *since Halakhah does not* specifically *speak of* psychotherapy *as a unique modality of change.*

Thus, in order for psychotherapy to achieve status as a halakhically modulated set of behaviors, it is necessary to develop analogies between certain definitive characteristics of the psychological applications and particular halakhic principles. These analogies, expressed in abstract form as halakhic models, would allow the extension of halakhic norms to the specific applications which fit these models. This approach has been utilized in the forthcoming chapters, such as in the reinterpretation of the halakhic efficacy of "psychosocial anguish," and in viewing the psychotherapeutic endeavor as a form of *vidduy* or *t^eshuvah* or as an agency of *beth din.* These models are neither fanciful nor contorted. Rather, they represent ways to incorporate psychological realities into a unique halakhic framework wherein certain prescribed norms for professional behavior can be derived. By appealing to such models, we do not mean that psychotherapy is *identical* to confession or to ethical rebuke or that the therapist is an agent of *beth din*. Rather, the unitary approach maintains that certain psychological and halakhic processes and values are different but related perspectives on the human endeavor—the halakhic project emphasizing the possibility of general ethical growth but also including psychological modification, and the psychotherapeutic project emphasizing psychological growth but also enabling ethical modification. Second, this framework does not render the phenomena or processes under examination any less "psychological," nor is it yet broad enough to include every therapist-patient behavior. But it does emphasize how halakhic Judaism defines professional psychological behavior, transforming psychological behavior into halakhic behavior and, at the same time, transforming halakhic models into psychological ones.

The unitary approach has several additional values. (1) It brings to light common characteristics in psychological and halakhic process and belief. (2) It allows the coordination of these two systems, leading to the halakhically appropriate execution of therapeutic practice. (3) It presents a parsimonious mediating structure for attaining these goals. (4) It enables the psychotherapist to better safeguard the patient's halakhic obligations which devolve in seeking out and electing psychotherapy. (5) It enables the therapist to fulfill his incumbent religious obligation to confront his fellow with the latter's erroneous religious behaviors or beliefs (the precept of *hokhachah* and the prohibition against standing idly by as one's fellow errs), while preserving his therapeutic role and identity.[20] (6) It validates the therapist's professional role as *mumcheh* (expert) in instances where psychologic or psychiatric input is required by halakhists, promoting more meaningful communication between these two communities. (7) Finally, it would help reduce the attitude of suspicion with which the mental health professional is regarded in some Orthodox Jewish communities. The development by halakhically oriented psychologists of a high level of competence in dealing with frequently encountered halakhic problems would reduce the perception of distance between patient and therapist, the opportunity for the emergence of potentially disruptive fantasies and counterproductive doubts, and the difficult-to-manage complication of the patient's demand for third-party rabbinic approbation of psychotherapy and of the psychotherapist.

I will digress here to discuss the "crisis in confidence" between some circles in the Orthodox Jewish community and the Orthodox Jewish professional. In one sense, this crisis involves the accusation of oversimplification hurled between the professional and consumer communities. There has indeed been no paucity of criticism of psychology's occasionally oversimplified views toward religious belief and the potentials of spirituality—from Jewish and non-Jewish critics alike. Critics within the Jewish community contend that the mental health professional is unskillfully tampering with the unfathomable domain of the *nefesh* or the soul. This criticism assumes that the laws of psychology are not equivalent to "laws of the soul," and considers reductionist any attempt to merge the object of psychotherapy and the object of religion.

Rabbi Y. Weinberg, who generally dispenses with the obligatory belittling attitude toward psychoanalysis, has it that "Freud denied the existence of spirituality and tried to reduce it to the level of the psyche."[21] Even Lifschitz, after writing,

> The spirit too has its own structure, goals and values. These do not contradict that of the mind. Even to the Mystics, the experience of the soul does not contradict that of the mind,

concludes:[22]

> If you turn this upside down, and place the spiritual somewhere else in the scheme of things—and not at the base—confusion and frustration results . . . I don't believe psychologists working in this framework can resolve the fundamental problems of human behavior. The major difference between Jewish and non-Jewish psychologies is that they see the spiritual as the expression of the psycho [sic], and we see the relationship exactly the opposite.

From here derives the cautious attitude taken to goals and techniques of psychological manipulation which seem to give primacy to the needs of the psyche over the soul.

In response to this, it is equally reductionistic to believe that the staunchest of *mussar* authorities failed to grant that cognition, emotion, and, ultimately, all behaviors represent at least *varied routes* to the soul. Indeed, it is a halakhic and ethical axiom in Judaism that the soul "follows" or expresses itself in "the murmurings of the heart." The heart, or psyche, is the sense receptor, if you will, of the soul—"*Lev yode'a marath nafsho.*"[23]

The *nefesh*—as an all-good spiritual endowment—may in fact bear the same relationship to the *yetzer*, man's purposive strivings, as Eros and Thanatos bear to autonomous ego functions. That is, their relationship is attenuated by a multiplicity of instinctual, emotional, social, perceptual-motor, and other variables. In the truest sense, then, even man's religious behavior is multi-determined. The ultimate relevance of the *nefesh* is that it is *affected by* human behavior; it is an investment to which Judaism holds man responsible. Individuals fulfill this responsibility within the realm of behavior and motivations subsumed under the category of man-as-*yotzer*. It is at this level that Maimonides frequently interpreted the relevance and function of law and ritual.[24]

To support this approach, consider two talmudic examples. In order to induce an obstinate individual to fulfill his vows, or to execute a writ of divorce, the rabbis instruct, "We force him until he exclaims, 'I am willing!' "[25] The obvious contradiction this dictum poses to the need for voluntary execution of vows and of granting a divorce is resolved by commentaries who suggest that all persons desire on a deeper level—the level of the *nefesh*—to fulfill the commandments. The Jewish court only removes obstacles which stand in the way of such voluntary fulfillment. In a second instance, we learn that an individual possessed of the desire to engage in illicit sexual relations is advised to "dress in black, travel to a town where he is unknown, *and do what his heart desires.*"[26] Commentaries immediately reject the obvious interpretation of this advice and explain it to mean that after one has thus debased oneself, one will be able to suppress the unethical desire and thereby fulfill what the soul *truly* desires. Both cases indicate that the *nefesh* is not the object of direct, corrective manipulation. Rather, the object is the behav*er*, his manifest behav*ior*, and his unexpressed motivations. Ultimately, the *nefesh* is redeemed, but psychological dynamics, or man's *y*ᵉ*tzarim*, represent the point of access.

Psychology and Jewish law address this realm of *yetzer*. While the religiously committed psychologist would not be satisfied to view the *objects* of religious belief in general merely as manifestations of *psychological* reality, religious beliefs, feelings, and struggles are psychological as well as spiritual experiences. When we say that psychotherapy is one route to the soul, we mean that it expands upon the subject of analysis—the very same subject dealt with in *mussar*—the same way that *mussar* sought to elaborate upon the vagueness of moral law.[27] *Mussar* deepened the analysis by focusing on the complexity and the vicissitudes of ethical behavior as *manifestations of* the spiritual.

Psychoanalysis originally attempted to supplant the concept of spirit with more detailed examination of the directly observable or inferable psychological mechanisms of behavior. Yet, as psychoanalysis broadened its exploration of the mechanisms and dynamics of inter- and intrapersonal life, it quickly accepted that such mechanisms might also *manifest* ethical and spiritual strivings.

It is only a short jump, then, to understand psychological theory and practice as providing additional schemata and techniques through which the spiritual goals of *k*ᵉ*vishath ha-middoth* and *tikkun ha-middoth* could eventually be obtained. Thus, there is little to be gained in wholesale rejection of psychology's useful contributions to the study of the self, the development of object relations, theories of learning, and so forth, which are involved in the elevation of the soul. These can be integrated as *additional* perceptions and adjuvant processes with our religious belief in the primacy of the *nefesh*. With a proper commitment to religious goals, psychotherapy can also contribute to the modification of the psychological facets of the *nefesh*. From this perspective, the circumscribed targets or objects of psychotherapy are not necessarily antithetical to the commitment to *nafshiuth*; they merely presuppose it (just as readily and even with greater reason than some earlier, uncritical forms of psychological doctrine rejected *nafshiuth* out of hand).*

* The similarities between the philosophy of *mussar* and modern

IV. The Application of Halakhic Models to Specific Therapeutic Problems

It is important for any symbiosis between Halakhah and psychotherapy that the identity and roles of the psychotherapist fit

---

psychotherapeutic values have been emphasized by several authors. It is quite clear that *mussar* has positively influenced psychosocial and interpersonal behavior in the Jewish community; it has certainly been successful in raising ethical sensitivity. Primarily, *mussar* attempted to give meaning to human suffering by pointing out that the source of man's sins and hurts is his own *yetzer*. It is doubtful, on the other hand, whether *mussar* is a successful alternative to psychotherapy where full-fledged psychotherapy is necessary, as opposed to religious counselling or education. This is because the study of *mussar*—even when undertaken in a "therapeutic" fashion within an intimate dyadic relationship (the so-called *chaver* approach)—remains an essentially didactic, conscious, and rather behavioral approach to human suffering, highlighting ethical perspectives on human strengths and weaknesses. The bulk of truly pathogenic suffering, however, stems from unconscious tributaries, expressed through character traits or discrete acts which have long since become autonomous from their source and which represent derivative rather than core expressions of intrapsychic conflict. In the case of true psychopathology, the deep psychological force of personal dis-ease is completely untouched by conscious appeal to ethical "insight," although this is often denied both by the community which recommends "*mussar* therapy" and by the hopeful beneficiary.

There are cases where preoccupation with *mussar* as a "treatment" approach has actually exacerbated symptomatology, leading in one case to deeper depressive trends in a borderline psychotic patient, and in another case to frank depersonalization. Some yeshivah students initially turn to *mussar* as a route to self-discovery, only to further lose themselves in ruminative and compulsive preoccupation with ideas of Jewish metapsychology (soul *vs.* spirit *vs.* *nefesh* *vs.* *n*ᵉ*shamah*, etc.) and masochistic self-flagellation. In other cases, the "flight into *mussar*" may satisfy a need to confirm self-abnegatory wishes and to reinforce a debased and shame-ridden self-image. No less than skimming through a textbook of abnormal psychology, the student of *mussar* texts will never fail to find his "ethical pathology," but will fail to become aware of the deeper and inadmissible motives for true psychological disturbance. Even in the normal to neurotic range of personal suffering, *mussar*'s stress on identifying the *yetzer ha-ra* or other impulses as the ultimate source of sin often has the effect of reinforcing externalization and projection of guilt. Rarely will *mussar* produce its beneficial effects when the cognitive and emotional avenues through which it achieves its influence are independently constricted by deeper conflicts. One basic clue to such misuse of *mussar* is the individual's consistent failure to successfully achieve the truly adaptive goals of *mussar* or any other *hashkafah*-oriented educational program or system of belief.

comfortably into some halakhic model. Two candidates might be the Biblical imperatives to heal and to return lost goods, which Halakhah accepts as the basic models for the medical healing endeavor.[28] Adapting the healing model to psychotherapy lends to our endeavor the norms attendant to the general medical interventive endeavor; e.g., that the psychotherapist must indeed heal, that he must not provoke destructive changes in the patient, that it is incumbent upon persons with psychiatric problems to present themselves for modification, that the therapist may legitimately charge fees for his time even though the actual source of all cure is God, and so forth.[29]

There are problems, however, with the analogy between psychotherapy and the halakhic healing model.

First, the healing model for psychotherapy may require the acceptance of a "psychological disorder as sickness" or "disease" conception precisely when many modern practitioners are seeking to disavow such an approach toward mental disorder and its modification.[30] I have dealt with some of the philosophical implications of the healing model elsewhere and wish here to make the following response.[31]

The mental disorder as "illness" or "disease" issue is to a large degree a sematic one.[32] Popularized criticisms notwithstanding, it is important to adopt operationally the assumption that all emotional states, including so-called functional disorders, have physiochemical correlates, even though such correlations have not all been demonstrated or are not yet measurable. Both Halakhah and modern psychology can accept this unitary approach to mind and body although each may have occasion to discriminate qualitatively between mind and body (e.g., for philosophical and theological reasons, one may not wish to say that minds are *identical* with brains). Generally, emotional disturbances can be correctly viewed as illnesses of a unique sort.[33] At the very least the alternative concepts of mental *disorder* or *deviance* advocated by militant psychologists and psychiatrists do not alter, save by semantic substitution, either the above physiochemical principle or, more importantly, the useful therapeutic implications of the healing model.[34]

To the charge that the illness concept implies a clear-cut discontinuity between health and unhealth which is not always demonstrable in psychological disorders, one can respond that halakhic ethics, in its tendency to view psychological deviance or illness in terms of spiritual impropriety, does seek sharp demarcation between states which require modification and states which do not. While psychotherapy may, because of its commitment to ethical neutrality, have more difficulty in applying a strict disease model to psychosocial disorder, halakhic ethics can readily employ this model in terms of its normative categories. By extension, a psychologic-halakhic healing model would seek to classify such demarcations and to impose modification when appropriate.

Finally, holistic and adaptational perspectives which seek to enhance rather than discard the medical model,[35] emphasizing not only psychological conflict or physiological abnormality but also other factors basic to man in relation to social systems, are also compatible with the halakhic healing model.[36] While the disease-healing model has historically been limited to biomedical categories, it can and should be expanded to reflect social categories and man's judgments about adaptation and personal fulfillment.

The second problem with the healing model is that it would require psychotherapists to contend with the limits this halakhic model imposes upon their practice. For example, it is a halakhic axiom that all prohibitions in the area of ritual and observance, including the strictures of Sabbath observance, are waived in the interests of preserving life, even where there is merely a possibility of danger to life (*safek sakanath n^e^fashoth*) or merely a possibility of saving life (*safek pikuach nefesh*). This is expressed in a general principle: *Chamira sakanta me-isura*, "Danger to life is more stringent than prohibitions."[37]

However, there are exceptions to this principle: prohibitions involving the three cardinal sins of idolatry, illicit sexual relations, and bloodshed are never waived even in the presence of *sakanath n^e^fashoth* (danger to life). This subordinating principle is expressed as *yehareg v^e^-al ya'avor*, "Be killed rather than transgress."[38] Each of these three cardinal sins is fenced in by numerous Biblical and rabbinic prohibitions which designate certain behaviors or thoughts which merely approximate these three sins as *abizraya* or appurtenances of sin, and which are equally inviolable (rabbinic levels of *abizraya* may not be as inviolable).

Included in the prohibition against illicit sexual relations (and also based on other Biblical sources), for example, are masturbation, acting-out of homosexual impulses, and even thought or fantasy about illicit sexual acts. Applying this ethic, psychotherapeutic techniques which require and encourage the patient's uncensored association to fantasy of "illicit" sexual content, or which include masturbation in the presence of heterosexual or homosexual audio-visual stimuli as part of a therapeutic regimen to modify sexual orientation, would not be condoned by mere appeal to "saving life"—and certainly not by appeal to merely enhancing the quality of mental health. This is because, as noted, the halakhic healing model cannot waive prohibitions guarding such actions or thoughts even in the presence of *sakanath n^efashoth*. Thus, the healing model may not be adequate in many modern and effective psychotherapeutic applications.

The third problem with the unmodified healing model relates specifically to the halakhic definition of *sakanath n^efashoth*. While the definition of *physical* threat to life has enjoyed consensus in halakhic codes and responsa, it has been difficult to define *sakanah* of *psychosocial* nature with similar consensus. Suicidal tendencies, on the one hand, have been considered bona fide *sakanah*—yet not by virtue of recognition of any distinctly psychological quality of suicidal ideation per se, but rather because of the obvious threat to physical existence such tendencies portend.[39]

However, it is desirable that the concept of *sakanah* be understood as including uniquely psychological or psychiatric characteristics, with the same attendant power to waive prohibitions that is wielded by physical definitions of *sakanah*—or to redefine the gravity of prohibitions—in instances of severe threat to psychological equilibrium or well-being *where there is no threat to physical existence*. For example, Halakhah does allow under certain circumstances a lenient attitude toward contraception and abortion—such as in situations of life-threatening maternal distress caused by certain physical conditions, and also in some cases where severe emotional distress is imminent, even without evidence of potential loss of life.[40] In this application, the psychological examiner or social worker are often consulted with regard to psychosocial forms of maternal distress of grave but not necessarily life-threatening nature; e.g., pregnancy due to rape, maternal anxiety about a fetus known to be afflicted with genetic disease, or even maternal distress concerning the possibility of becoming pregnant with yet another child in the presence of various familial crises, failing ability to manage her current children, etc.

The medical healing model *could* allow for an expanded definition of *sakanah* which would subsume the above factors, and evidence of this possibility already exists in the halakhic literature. Notwithstanding the hesitancy on the part of halakhic authorities to broadcast this possibility—in partial fear of reinforcing an inhospitable attitude toward increasing Jewish population growth—the relevant parameters of an expanded definition of *sakanah* must at least be explicated to those professionals who will in specific instances be consulted for their expert opinion.

Before proceeding to specific applications of the unitary approach to Halakhah and psychotherapy, a final comment is in order. Note that in resolving specific halakhic-psychotherapeutic dilemmas through the use of halakhic models one simultaneously expands the halakhic definition of the role and identity of both therapist and patient. An example of this is Linzer's approach which also seeks halakhic "exemplars" for the behavior of the therapist and his professional identity.[41]

Linzer postulates *chesed* (loving-kindness) as a model or exemplar for the psychotherapist-as-helper, emphasizing an ethic of voluntarism which does not preclude egocentric satisfactions, and *tzimtzum* (the halakhic-mystical idea of contraction or synthesis) as a model for the professional self, advocating containment, self-control, and self-analysis as prelude to therapeutic creativity. While of heuristic value as an indigenously Jewish perspective on the role of the psychotherapist, Linzer does not apply these models directly to resolve specific practical dilemmas. That is, the halakhic parameters of *chesed* and *tzimtzum* are not usefully applied to analogous technical problems in modern practice.

Of course, Linzer's *chesed* model can be used to address a metaclinical dilemma. From the halakhic viewpoint, the therapist's involvement with his patient is essentially the fulfillment of a Biblical demand for acts of loving-kindness. If so, must the therapist's motivation be so selfless as to willfully forego the narcissistic gratifications and neutralized voyeuristic satisfaction which are considered healthy rewards of his strenuous efforts and restraint? This would follow given some interpretations of the ultimate value of *chesed* or from a strict interpretation of the general imperative to perform *mitzvoth* (commandments) with a conscious attitude of *lishmah*, i.e., solely for the sake of fulfilling the word of God rather than for any reward.[42] However, once one broadens the analogue of *chesed* with the halakhic qualifications that one *is* allowed to obtain satisfaction from acts of *chesed*—that by acting with *chesed* one becomes a *chasid* (pious)—and that motivations which might be termed *lo lishmah* are acceptable means to an end, then libidinal and object-relational satisfactions may also be considered legitimate rewards of the therapist's involvement, especially since they maintain the optimum quality of his work.

V. Specific Applications of Halakhic Models to Psychotherapy

An adjuvant model for numerous applications in psychotherapy is the halakhic process of *t^eshuvah* (repentance), which includes the corrective mechanisms of *hokhachah* (ethical rebuke) and *vidduy* (confession of sin). That is, we will seek to compare the psychotherapeutic process with aspects of the *t^eshuvah* process and *vidduy* process, and the therapist's role with that of the *mokhiach*, or ethical mentor, in the sense that therapy and therapist are in the position to initiate or facilitate through psychological techniques a corrective process which can be linked with the patient's ability to achieve ethical growth and development.

Several practical implications emerge from these analogies.

(1) Psychotherapy as *t^eshuvah* suggests that the modification of psychopathology on an individual or group level is as religiously desirable as the modification of behaviors or traits which are deemed inappropriate from a wholly secular ethical standpoint. This implication is valid within a halakhic world view that considers certain types of psychopathology deviant from an ethical viewpoint (e.g., homosexuality, or pathologic narcissism inasmuch as this condition precludes autonomous fellow love). Maimonides reinforces this conclusion when he considers the "sick of soul" who deny insight into the cause of their pain as sinners,[43] and

when he rules that the obligation of *t^eshuvah* applies both to outright transgressions as well as to destructive personality traits (*de'oth ra'oth*).[44] This conclusion is also supported by numerous talmudic aphorisms and axia, e.g., "One who is [quick to violent temper] is likened to an idol worshiper," "Do not be evil in thine own eyes," and so forth.[45]

(2) Specific elements of the *hokhachah* and *vidduy* processes can be applied to the psychotherapeutic process. Consider, for example, the initial danger of establishing the analogy between ethical modification and psychotherapy. Here there is the danger of developing a pseudo-therapeutic approach which is primarily remonstrative, didactic, or pastoral in nature—as if psychotherapy were merely *hokhachah* or *vidduy*! But, this danger is mitigated precisely by adhering to the halakhic guidelines of *hokhachah* and *vidduy*.

(a) "Flail yourself before you flail others."[46] That is, the therapist must be cognizant of his own unconscious and conscious attitudes and tendencies which may detract from his ability to listen productively to the patient.

(b) "Do not despise your brother *in* your heart," [which one may] read, "*with* your heart."[47] In other words, the therapist must distinguish the patient's perceptions and separate them from his own projected feelings and attitudes, and must not protest against the expression of desires, vices, or pathology simply because of his own personal reaction to such material, ethically justifiable or not. The patient must be allowed to achieve his own autonomous understandings of the disordered nature of his cognitive, verbal, and behavioral products, rather than have such understandings imposed upon him from an outside source.

(c) "Just as there is an obligation [in *hokhachah*] to say things which will be [accepted], so is there an obligation to not say things which cannot be [accepted]."[48] This principle expresses the idea that *what* is said by the therapist—be it an interpretation, question, or even the use of silence—the *content* of what is said, and its timing, are critical elements in the *hokhachah*–psychotherapy project.

(d) "All love that has not the elements of *hokhachah* is

not love."[49] This basic principle emphasizes that proper psychotherapy is not merely the offering of an unanalyzed transference relationship nor certainly a real friendship, but the gradual imparting of a critical attitude toward the positive and negative emotions and modes of relating which arise within the therapeutic relationship, their autonomous or dysautonomous qualities, and their influence upon current behavior. This does not mean that psychotherapy is merely an educational endeavor (i.e., *hokhachah* per se), but rather stresses that the above aspects of the process have a consensual halakhic nature.

(3) For Halakhah, thought and fantasy are subsumed under ethical and normative regulations. For Halakhah as for psychodynamic psychology, fact and fancy have little distinction from the perspective of psychological reality—"If we did not do it, we thought it; and if we did not think it, we saw others do it and we derived pleasure."[50] The ancient Zohar testifies to what modern psychoanalysis calls the dynamic nature of the unconscious, "All things follow thought and fantasy" (also, "Following the intentions of the heart are all things").[51] At least five passages are utilized to determine the parameters of the prohibition against *hirhur davar ha-asur*, thought or fantasy over forbidden acts in general, and *hirhur arayoth*, thought or fantasy over sexual matters in specific.[52] The "fences" augmenting these prohibitions are numerous, the most important of which is Maimonides' ruling that it is even forbidden to do anything which will bring about *hirhur asur*.[53] *Hirhur* is considered one of the experiences from which no individual is spared (certainly a psychological truth, given the Zohar's understanding of *hirhur*).[54]

Thus, a practical dilemma for psychotherapists, whose definition of behavior includes the domain of thought and fantasy, is the apparent conflict (1) between therapies designed to facilitate free association, the liberation of pathologic ideation and phobic thought patterns, and reinforcing positive emotional approaches to such material,[55] versus the general halakhic safeguards of the moral quality of thought and fantasy, and (2) between the therapist's listening and facilitative role versus the halakhic prohibition against being an audience to material of sexual content or of otherwise forbidden nature (e.g., disrespectful comments about parents, "slander," etc.). These conflicts represent significant obstacles to both the therapist's and the patient's behavior during psychotherapy. We will return to this problem in chapter 3.

VI. Additional Halakhic Models: A Definition of Psychiatric *Sakanah*

Halakhah considers certain physical conditions to represent *sakanath n^efashoth*, danger to life, endowing these with power to waive all prohibitions except the three cardinal sins. Does Halakhah grant an equivalent status to conditions which involve psychological distress irrespective of the existence of direct risk to physical well-being? The unitary approach to mind-body phenomena, which Halakhah accepts, logically should entail this extension, yet one often finds psychiatric disorders given halakhic efficacy only when such factors lean on present or probable danger to physical existence.

In fact, the uniqueness of psychiatric illness and grave forms of psychologic distress as forms of *sakanah sui generis* is emphasized in a responsum by Rabbi N. Z. Friedman.[56] The following illustrations will further demonstrate the halakhic efficacy of psychological disorder as a uniquely "mental" rather than "body" event.

(1) Specific instances are recorded in the Talmud, codes, and responsa where the danger of *teiruf da'ath*—which appears to range from gross psychological decompensation to forms of psychosocial anguish which are of far less grave quality than frank psychosis or decompensation—is deemed a valid reason for the waiver of Sabbath prohibitions. In these applications, there seems to be no risk of physical danger. The Talmud rules that disfiguring scabs may be removed on the Sabbath, even though this ordinarily falls under the domain of proscribed medicinal activities, if the individual suffers such embarrassment from these scabs that he is unwilling to be seen in public.[57] The operant emotion in this case is termed "*tza'ar*" (anguish) and clearly refers to pain of non-physical nature.

(2) The popularity of elective reconstructive ("plastic") sur-

gery for enhancing or modifying physical appearance in less-than-life-threatening instances (i.e., for cosmetic purposes) raises the following halakhic question: Can such surgery, which necessarily involves physical insult to body tissue, waive the incumbent prohibition against *chabbalah* (wounding)? Traditionally, *chabbalah* has only been waived for medical procedures which have been subsumed under the category of the *healing* model and which in some way involve the restoration of life or function to body and limb. Elective surgery for cosmetic purposes would not seem to fall under this category. Also, cosmetic preoccupations in the case of the male are considered by strict definition in violation of the rabbinic prohibitions against emulating cosmetic behaviors and habits normally associated with women (*lo yilbash gever*); e.g., dyeing hair, shaving underarm or pubic hair.[58]

However, precedent for waiving at least the prohibition of *lo yilbash* is found in the Talmud and codes which rule that a male may shave underarm hair if it causes him pain and is not done merely for cosmetic purposes.[59] Rabbi M. Klein argues that removal of a blemish, congenital or caused by accident, is not a violation of *lo yilbash* or *chabbalah*.[60] Rabbi Y. Y. Weiss permits dyeing white hair which causes an individual intense anguish, citing others who have been lenient in this regard.[61] Rabbi Y. Briesh specifically rules that cosmetic procedures would be permissible to alleviate "pain," which would presumably include psychological anguish.[62] Indeed, the availability of cosmetic surgical procedures for men as well as women—given the above halakhic distinction that the end result is not *merely* cosmetic—contradicts its characterization as a uniquely female preoccupation.[63] Thus, while cosmetic surgery is not permissible merely for reasons of vanity, it may be permissible when the need for such modifications is so intense as to produce psychological *tza'ar*. (Rabbi E. Waldenberg forbids such surgery, but does not at all consider this factor of psychological anguish.[64])

Given this definition of psychological pain, it is obvious that Halakhah could not grant equal status to such pain in a situation where its basis was a state or condition or impulse antithetical to halakhic values. Thus, a male transsexual patient's non-psychotic desire to cross-dress, which stems entirely from a desire to *be* a woman, would not seem to fall under the earlier categorization of psychological *tza'ar* which is capable of waiving the prohibition of *lo yilbash*. Indeed, sex-reassignment surgery—which is by no means yet a recognizable or bona fide "cure" for transsexuality although it may, in some cases, alleviate the patient's intense desire to cross-dress[65]—has achieved much popular acclaim as a novel treatment approach for transsexuality. And yet, in addition to the fact that the actual hormonal and surgical procedures involved violate the prohibitions against castration (*seirus*),[66] the very end-product of such surgical transformation may also violate the principle of *lo yilbash*.[67] On the other hand, according to the lenient view which accepts that the prohibitions against castration do not devolve upon a minor (whose genitalia are, strictly speaking, not yet generative), an *androgynos*, or an individual with ambiguous gonads,[68] there may also be room to argue that the prohibition of crossing sex-role norms cannot be applied to such individuals.[69] But even this last possibility would not apply to the transsexual—who is physically if not psychologically clearly a male or, in the case of a female transsexual clearly a female—both by halakhic as well as psychological definition.[70]

(3) The Talmud elsewhere permits lighting a candle on the Sabbath if requested by a pregnant woman in order to spare her such *teiruf da'ath*.[71] This permission is extended for a similar request by a blind pregnant woman, since she will be calmed by the knowledge that her attendants can work more effectively with adequate lighting. Maimonides codifies this principle, and in two additional applications permits otherwise forbidden activities in order to prevent *teiruf da'ath*.[72] This principle is further reinforced in select responsa which waive prohibitions in order to forestall such psychologic distress. Rabbis Duran, Ibn Zimra, Unterman, Waldenberg, and Weiss permit violating the Sabbath prohibitions to prevent *teiruf da'ath* even when such *teiruf* is not specifically related to the actual course of medical treatment.[73] Also, Rabbi M. Briesh and Rabbi M. Feinstein permit the violation of the Sabbath in the presence of significant prodromes to suicide.[74]

(4) In a recent responsum, Rabbi Moshe Feinstein permits taking psychoactive medication on the Sabbath in a situation where failure to follow the prescribed regimen on a consecutive basis may lead to the recrudescence of psychological symptomatology on the Sabbath, thereby destroying the spirit of Sab-

bath observance as well as the patient's psychological well-being.[75] Although Rabbi Feinstein adds that he does not believe that a single day's interruption of the therapeutic regimen will have ill effects, he has underscored through this lenient ruling the halakhic efficacy of psychological anguish of a non-life-threatening nature (at least as a type of dis-ease which would fall under the category of *michush she-mitzta'er mimenu kol gufo*—pain which irradiates throughout the patient's body—which allows the violation of rabbinic prohibitions on the Sabbath).

(5) In a little-known responsum attributed to *Rashba*, the author considers the following case. An individual publicly swore to abstain from playing games of chance and subsequently became deranged ("*nitr^efah alav da'ato*").[76] It happened that he passed some persons who were gambling, and he somehow experienced temporary surcease of his symptoms. He then claimed that he could be cured if he were able to play such games again. The specific question presented is whether he would be permitted to nullify his oath under the circumstances (the question presumed certain halakhic difficulties in nullifying public vows which render them practically impossible to nullify). The responsum concludes that one may nullify one's vow in such a case since sparing the individual from *teiruf da'ath* is tantamount to sparing him *sakanath nefesh*.

(6) Halakhah requires that *vidduy* (a confession prayer including the *Sh^ema*) be recited prior to death. There is also an obligation upon bystanders to the moribund patient to urge the patient to recite *vidduy* as soon as death appears imminent.[77] Halakhah prudently asks that *vidduy* not be recommended too early in the course of illness as this may weaken the patient's struggle for life; and that when the time for *vidduy* is propitious (after three days of serious illness), it be recommended to the patient by means of a formula which reminds him that "many have died and not recited *vidduy*; many have confessed and not died."[78]

A practical problem in recommending *vidduy* to the moribund patient occurs in the following circumstance. The moribund patient is categorized as a *goses* (an allusion to the flickering instability of his life forces), at which stage Halakhah strictly forbids doing or even saying anything to the *goses* which may tip the balance against life. Indeed, the rationale of Halakhah's earlier recommendation that *vidduy* not be recited too early in the course of illness is that this may evoke *shivron ha-lev* (heartbreak), which may in turn weaken the patient. Given this, it would appear that recommending *vidduy* at the relatively late stage of *g^esisah* should be proscribed when it may evoke psychological decompensation or even fatal consequences.

In responding to this problem, one first notes that Halakhah defines the most appropriate time for recommending *vidduy* as the stage of *noteh la-muth* (is on the way to dying), or as the patient "turns for the worse." It can also be shown that *noteh la-muth* is identical in halakhic usage to the stage of *g^esisah*.[79] Thus, based on this factor alone it appears that Halakhah views the recitation of *vidduy* at *g^esisah* as a priority, which may presumably have been based on empirical observation of minimal untoward effects. Second, Rabbi Y. M. Epstein states specifically that *vidduy* be recommended at *g^esisah* in that while it may cause some "*tza'ar*" or anguish, it is more desirable that the patient confront death in a state of absolution from sin.[80]

In early stages of illness, then, the *shivron lev* that may be elicited by *vidduy* may conflict with the struggle to endure illness. However, at the stage of *g^esisah*, *vidduy* is viewed as evoking psychological and spiritual preparedness for death and would thus not be considered among the proscribed activities in the presence of the *goses*. *Shivron ha-lev*, in other words, does not have the same negative effect as full-fledged *teiruf da'ath*. At the same time, a patient who in addition to being a *goses* is *also* in a state of psychological turmoil—indicating that Halakhah does not consider emotional turmoil a general characteristic of *g^esisah*—is exempt from *vidduy* inasmuch as his psychological state is antithetical to the quality of intentionality (*kavanah*) necessary for meaningful *vidduy*.[81] In this instance, *actual* psychological decompensation waives the requirement of *vidduy*. In this application, one again sees that psychological distress or risks are dealt with through consideration of their unique characteristics.

(7) It is appropriate to end this section presenting evidence of the distinct status of psychological *sakanah*, with an application that touches upon the optimistic aspirations of psychotherapists.

Halakhah requires that a blessing of gratitude (known as

birkath ha-gomel) be recited upon release from four prototypes of danger: one who safely traverses an ocean, or a desert, one who is redeemed from prison, and one who recovers from grave illness.[82] With regard to recovery from illness, rabbinic authorities debate the definition and necessary duration of grave illness. The consensus is that this *birkath ha-gomel* is recited (1) following recovery from life-threatening illness (general *sakanath nefesh*), (2) upon *remission of symptoms* of illness which characteristically "comes and goes," and (3) even upon recovery from a relatively less serious illness or *michush* which nonetheless is of such nature as to render the patient bed-ridden for at least three days, or is of that nature whether or not the patient actually remained confined to his bed.[83]

It would seem that psychiatric illnesses which include threat to life require upon their alleviation the recitation of *ha-gomel*; e.g., suicide and suicidal depression,[84] psychoses, alcoholism (and perhaps even the symptomatic withdrawal state of *delirium tremens*). Second, psychiatric disorders which are as yet not curable, but whose disturbing symptoms can be effectively relieved for significant periods of time through specific procedures, also require the recitation of *ha-gomel* once this remission state is achieved; e.g., following lithium treatment of manic-depression, electroconvulsive therapy of schizophrenia and depression, and perhaps even following some future efficacious forms of psychosurgery.

It is more difficult, however, to classify the neuroses and character disorders under extant halakhic categories of illness. At the same time, even such mental disorders can elicit functional and organic losses of physical ability, and other debilities; e.g., bronchial asthma, ulcerative colitis, prolonged amenorrhea, and so forth. Recovery from such symptoms would also seem to warrant the expression of *birkath ha-gomel.*

In all of the above three categories, the argument in favor of reciting *birkath ha-gomel* upon their abatement is fortified by the preceding evidences that mental disorders are given equivalent status to general *sakanath nefesh* or extreme *tza'ar*. Support can also be drawn from two additional sources.

First, in an essentially aggadic commentary, Rabbi S. Edels interprets the common denominator of the four paradigms of danger for which one recites *ha-gomel* as the negative effect of being unable to live or pursue a spiritually invigorating existence.[85] Thus, even when actual threat to life is absent, which is the case in the neuroses, there may still be sufficient impairment of the autonomous functions of the ego and of the ability to freely and satisfactorily fulfill spiritual requirements, to justify the need to recite *ha-gomel* upon recovery from such states. Second, an interesting responsum is cited by Rabbi D. Trini[86] which presents the question of whether one who emerges unscathed from the mystical realm of *Pardes* (as did Rabbi Akiba in the incident cited in *Hag.* 14b: In this story, R. Akiba and three colleagues transcended into the mystical realm of *Pardes.* While R. Akiba was able to enter into and depart from this state unharmed, one colleague died, another went berserk, and the third became an apostate.) needs to recite *birkath ha-gomel*? Trini responds affirmatively, reasoning *a fortiori* that if one must recite *ha-gomel* following relief from physical danger, surely one must express gratitude following relief from psychical danger! Practically, this perspective would include emerging unharmed from chemically-induced hallucinogenic stupor or psychotic delusional states, inasmuch as these represent severe alterations in reality testing and sense of reality, with the potential for untoward consequences. *Birkath ha-gomel,* then, is seen as a requirement upon recovery from *sakanath nefesh* in the literal sense.

Conclusion

I have examined a number of introductory examples of actual and potential consensus between Jewish ethics and the practice of modern psychotherapy, psychology, and psychiatry. I have also introduced the reader to a unified halakhic approach which posits specific halakhic models representing analogies to modern psychotherapeutic principles and practices, and which through analogy lend specific halakhic guidelines to modern practice. The unitary halakhic approach presented here is both heuristic—in that it seeks to demonstrate the ways in which psychotherapeutic processes are essentially halakhic ones—as well as practical—in that it facilitates professional behavior informed by halakhic norms.

Through this approach, psychological theory and practice have been brought into intimate contact with the ethical requirements of the halakhically committed mental health practitioner and his or her patient, filling an inexcusable void in halakhic application to modern technology and setting a direction for future work in this area.

Notes

1. Beit-Hallahmi, B., "Salvation and its Vicissitudes: Clinical Psychology and its Political Values," *Am. Psychol., 29* (1974): 124-129; E. Erwin, *Behavior Therapy: Scientific, Philosophic and Moral Foundations* (Cambridge: 1978); Greenbaum, H., "Human Values and Psychoanalysis," *J. Amer. Acad. Psychoanal., 8* (1980): 353-368; Halmos, P., *The Faith of the Counselors* (New York: 1970); Levy-Suhn, M., "The Role of Ethics and Religion in Psychoanalytic Theory and Therapy," *Int. J. Psychoanal., 27* (1946): 110-119; London, P., *The Modes and Morals of Psychotherapy* (New York: 1964); Pattison, E., "The Role of Religion in Psychotherapy," *Int. Psychiatr. Clinic, 5* (1969): 72-92; Pattison, E., "Psychiatry and Religion: Analysis of a Decade," *Past. Psychol., 27* (1978): 119-141; Wile, P. "Ideological Conflict Between Therapist and Patient," *Am. J.Psychother., 31* (1977): 437-449; Hobbs, N. "Science and Ethical Behavior," *Am. Psychol., 14* (1959): 217-225; "Special Issue: Values in Psychotherapy," *Psychother.: Theory, Res. & Prac., 17*, no. 4 (1980): 369-471.
2. Beit-Hallahmi, B., op. cit.
3. Cohen, R."Socially Reinforced Obsessing: A Reply," *J. Consult. and Clin. Psychol., 45* (1977): 1166-1171; Cohen, R. and Smith, F., "Socially Reinforced Obsessing: Etiology of a Disorder in a Christian Scientist," *J. Consult. and Clin. Psychol., 44* (1976): 142-144; Halleck, S., "Discussion," *J. Consult. and Clin. Psychol., 44* (1976): 146-147; London, P., "Psychotherapy for Religious Neuroses?" *J. Consult. and Clin. Psychol., 44* (1976): 145-146.
4. See Ford, D., and Urban, H., *Systems of Psychotherapy* (New York: 1967).
5. Beit-Hallahmi, B., op. cit.; Novey, S., "Utilization of a Social Institution as a Defense Mechanism," *Int. J. Psychoanal., 38* (1957): 82-91; Novey, S., "Considerations on Religion in Relation to Psychoanalysis and Psychotherapy," *J. Ner. Ment. Dis., 130* (1960): 315-324; Pattison, E., "The Role of Religion in Psychotherapy," 1969; Pattison, E., "Psychiatry and Religion: I," 1978; Pattison, E., "Psychiatry and Religion: II," 1978; Pruyser, P., "Assessment of the Patient's Religious Attitudes in the Psychiatric Setting," *Bull Menn. Clin., 35* (1971): 272-291; Pruyser, P., "The Seamy Side of Current Religious Beliefs," *Bull. Menn. Clinic, 41* (1977): 329-348.
6. Cf. Hirsch, W., *Rabbinic Psychology* (London: 1947); Levi, L., "Toward a

Torah-Based Metapsychology," *Proceedings AOJS, 2* (1969): 81-114.
7. See Prov. 14:10; *Kid.* 80b; *Yoma* 83a, *R.H.* 6a, *Yev.* 106a; *M.T. Hil. Gerushin* 2:20; *Malbim* to Ps. 51:7.
8. Spero, M., *Judaism and Psychology: Halakhic Perspectives: Vol. I* (New York: 1980), chap. 5.
9. Abraham, A., *Lev Avraham* (Jerusalem: 1979); Lifshitz, H., "*Yachas ha-Halakhah la-Psychologia ha-Modernith*," in I. Warhaftig, ed., *Techumim: Kovetz Halakhti* (Jerusalem: 1979); Rabinowitz, G., "*Takanath Banim ha-Mukim al-Y'dei ha-Horim*," in M. Hershler, ed., *Halakhah U-Refuah* (Jerusalem: 1980); Stern, M., *Ha-Refuah le-Or ha-Halakhah* (Jerusalem: 1980); Wislicki, L., *Madrikh Refui Lefi Masoreth ha-Yehudith* (Jerusalem: 1977).
10. Spero M., "Discussion of 'On the Conflict Between Applied Psychology and Judaism': Continued Confusion at the Interface Between Psychology and Judaism," *J. Psychol. and Jud., 4* (1980): 32-48; and *Judaism and Psychology* (1980), chaps. 1 and 2.
11. See Amsel, A., *Judaism and Psychology* (New York: 1969) and *Rational Irrational Man* (New York: 1970); Berger, J., "Why Should They be Permitted to Peddle their Filth?" *Intercom, 17* (1978): 28-30; Kahn, P., "Judaism and the Challenge of Modern Psychology," *Intercom, 16* (1976): 3-6; Klein, J., "On the Conflict Between Applied Psychology and Judaism," *J. Psychol. and Judaism, 4* (1979): 15-31; Lifshitz, H., "*Yachas ha-Halakhah la-Psychologia ha-Modernith*," 1980; Ury, Z., "Beyond Behaviorism," in J. Kaminetsky and M. Friedman eds., *Building Jewish Ethical Character* (New York: 1975). Catholics have also followed this approach, as in J. Marshall, *Medicine and Morals* (New York: Hawthorne, 1960), p. 136.
12. Spero, M., "Psychiatry, Psychotherapy, and Halakhah," in J.D. Bleich and F. Rosner, eds., *Jewish Bioethics* (New York: 1979); Spero, M., "Discussion," 1980; Spero, M., *Judaism and Psychology*, 1980.
13. Ahren, Y., "Remarks on Freud's Determinism," *J. Psychol. and Jud., 4* (1980): 222-227; Schimmel, S., "Free-will, Guilt and Self-Control," *Judaism, 26* (1977): 415-429; Spero, M., *Judaism and Psychology* (1980): chap. 3.
14. Ford and Urban, *Systems of Psychotherapy* (1967); Hall, C. and Lindzey, G., *Theories of Personality* (New York: 1957); Patterson, C., *Theories of Counseling and Psychotherapy* (New York: 1973); Wolberg, L., *The Technique of Psychotherapy* (New York: 1967).
15. See also Levy-Suhn, M., "The Role of Ethics and Religion in Psychotherapy," 1946, and Mermelstein, J., "Mental Health Problems of Orthodox Jews as They Relate to Children and Adults," *Intercom, 18* (1979): 28-39.
16. *Ramban*, "*D'rashath Torath ha-Shem T'mimah*" (in C. Chavel, ed. *Kithvei Ramban*); *Pes.* 54a (to Prov. 8:32); *Nid.* 73a (to Hab. 3:6); *J.T. Kel.* 1:7; *Mid. Gen. R.* 1:2; see also *Chiddushei ha-Ramban la-Talmud*: *Meg.* 31b.
17. Ex. 21:19.
18. *Sanh.* 73a to Deut. 22:2.
19. Prov. 4:26; and see commentary Vilna Gaon ad loc., *M.T. Hil. De'oth* 2:7.
20. Lev. 19:14, 16; *Sanh.* 73a.
21. Weinberg, Y.Y., *Seridei Esh* (Jerusalem: 1977), vol. 4, p. 338n.

22. Lifschitz, C., in M. Beck, ed., *Mussar and the Ethics of Education* (Jerusalem: 1976), p. 30.
23. Prov. 14:10; *Yoma* 83a; also "*Middoth ha-adam — mareh libo*," Shlomo ibn Gabirol, *Mivchar ha-P'ninim* 43:23, p. 466; "*ha-Sekhel — k*e*mo kaf maznayim la-regesh*," Yosef Ibn Tzaddik, *Ha-Olam ha-Katan*, p. 4; "*Ma'aloth ha-middoth kodmoth bi-z*e*man le-ma'aloth ha-siklioth*," Meiri, *Beth ha-Bechirah: Chibbur ha-T*e*shuvah*, p. 33; "*Tikkun ha-middoth hu refuath ha-nefesh v*e*-kochothehah*," *Rambam, Sh*e*moneh P*e*rakim* 1; "*Ezeh davar gorem be'adam: ha-teva o ha-sekhel o ha-mussar? Ha-Mussar yisron ba-sekhel, v*e*-ha-teva m*e*koram v*e*-nos'am*," A. Halevi ben Chasdai, *Ben ha-Melekh ve-ha-Nazir*, 26, p. 173.
24. See Spero, *Judaism and Psychology* (1980): chap. 5, note 75; see also *M.T. Hil. Gerushin* 2:20, "*. . . ela hu anas atzmo b*e*-da'ato ha-ra*."
25. *R.H.* 6a to Lev. 1:13; *Yev.* 106a; *Kid.* 49b-50b; *B.B.* 48a; *Arkh.* 21a; *M.T. Hil. Ma'asei ha-Korbonoth* 14:16.
26. *Kid.* 40a; *Chag.* 16a; *M.K.* 17a; see R. Chananel ad loc. and *Tos.* in *M.K.* and *Chag.*
27. See I. Salanter in S.Z. Hirshowitz, *Even Yisroel* (Vilna: 1912), pp. 16-17, 33-34 and also M. Gottleib, "Israel Salanter and Therapeutic Values," *Tradition, 15*, nos. 1-2 (1975): 112-129, and A. Rabinowitz, "Reflections on the Concept of the Unconscious in Judaism," *Journal of Psychology and Judaism, 4, no. 1* (1979): 49-57.
28. See *Rambam, Peirush Mishnayoth: Ned.* 4:41b.
29. *Sanh.* 73a, *B.K.* 85a.
30. E.g., Albee, G., "Emerging Concepts of Mental Illness and Modes of Treatment," *Am. J. Psychother., 125* (1969): 870-876; Szasz, T., *The Myth of Mental Illness* (New York: 1961), *The Manufacture of Madness* (New York: 1970); Werry, J., "Psychotherapy: A Medical Procedure?" *Can. Psychiatr. Assn. J., 10* (1965): 278-282.
31. Spero, *Judaism and Psychology* (1980): chap. 4.
32. Graham, D., "Health, Disease, and the Mind-Body Problem," *Psychosom. Med., 29* (1967): 52-71; Moore, M., "Some Myths About 'Mental Illness,'" *Arch. Gen. Psychiatr., 32* (1975): 1438-1497; Reiss, S., "A Critique of Thomas S. Szasz's 'Myth of Mental Illness,'" *Am. J. Psychiatr.*, 128 (1972): 1081-1085.
33. See also Akiskal, H. and McKinney, W., "Psychiatry and Pseudopsychiatry," *Arch. Gen. Psychiatr., 28* (1973): 367-373.
34. See Erwin, *Behavior Therapy* (1978): pp. 133-71.
35. E.g., Fabrega, H., *Disease and Social Behavior* (Cambridge: 1974), ——., "The Position of Psychiatry in the Understanding of Human Disease," *Arch. Gen. Psychiatr., 32* (1975): 1500-1512.
36. Spero, M., *Judaism and Psychology* (1980): chap. 4.
37. *Hul.* 10a; *M.T. Hil. Yesodei ha-Torah* 5:1-5; *Sh. A., Y.D.* 116, 157.
38. *Sanh.* 74-74b; *M.T. Hil. Isurei Biah* 21:1, *Hil. Yesodei ha-Torah* 5:6, and see *Or Sameach* ad loc.
39. E.g., *Resp. Igroth Moshe: O.H.*, vol. 1, no. 127; I. Unterman, "*Mitzvath Pikuach Nefesh u-G*e*darehah*," *Ha-Torah ve-ha-Medinah, 4* (1952): 22-29.
40. See Bleich, J.D., "Abortion in Halakhic Literature," In J.D. Bleich and F. Rosner eds.|, *Jewish Bioethics* (New York: 1979), ——. "*Hapalah M*e*lakhutith l*e*-*

Or ha-Halakhah," *Or Mizrach, 26* (1978): 185-193; ——. "Sexuality and Procreation," in I. Franck, ed., *Biomedical Ethics in the Perspectives of Jewish Teaching and Tradition* (Washington: 1980); Feldman, D., *Marital Relations, Birth Control, and Abortion in Jewish Law* (New York: 1974); Jakobovits, I., *Jewish Medical Ethics* (New York: 1965); Rosner, F., "The Jewish Attitude Toward Abortion," In M.M. Kellner, ed., *Contemporary Jewish Ethics* (New York: 1978); Steinberg, A., "*Hapalah M^e^lakhutith l^e^-Or ha-Halakhah*," *Assia*, vol. 1 (1972), 107-124.

41. Linzer, N., "A Jewish Philosophy of Social Work Practice," *J. Jew. Comm. Serv., 55* (1979): 309-317.

42. *Sot.* 22b, *Tos.*, s.v. *l^e^-olam; Ber.* 17a, *Tos.*, s.v. *ha-oseh.*

43. *Shemoneh Perakim*, chap. 3.

44. *M.T. Hil. T^e^shuvah* 7:3. This comparison between *vidduy* and the psychotherapeutic process is also stated definitively by Rabbi Y.B. Landau, "*Diyun bi-P^e^ratiyuth b^e^-Sugei Choli ha-Ruach v^e^-ha-Nirpa'in be-ha-Metzi'uth Terufah ha-Chaddashah*," in M. Amsel, ed., *Sefer She'eloth-u-T^e^shuvoth ha-Ma'or* (New York: 1966), p. 382.

45. *Pes.* 113b; *Avoth* 2:6, 13, 18; 4:24.

46. *Sanh.* 19a; *B.M.* 107b, citing. Zeph. 2:1.

47. Lev. 19:17; see *Sifra* to Deut. 1:27.

48. *Yev.* 65b.

49. Gen. R. 54:3.

50. *Shab.* 64a.

51. Zohar Gen. 155; *Meg.* 20a.

52. Lev. 11:44-45; 18:6, 20:7, 26; Num. 15:39, 40; 32:22; Deut. 32:10.

53. *Ber.* 12b; *A.Z.* 20a; *Kid.* 40a; *Ket.* 46a; *Tur. Sh. A., E.H.* 23; *M.T. Hil. Isurei Biah* 21:2, *Hil. Yesodei ha-Torah* 5:6, 9 to *Sanh.* 75a.

54. *B.B.* 164b, *Niddah* 13b, *Yoma* 29a, *M.T. Hil. T^e^shuvah* 4:2.

55. Wolberg, L., *The Techniques of Psychotherapy*, 1967; Watkins, J., "Psychotherapeutic Methods," in B. Wolman, ed., *Handbook of Clinical Psychology* (New York: 1965).

56. Resp. *Netzer Mata'ai* (1958): vol. 1, no. 8.

57. *Shab.* 50b, *Tos.*, s.v. *bishvil.* See also the distinction between "*tza'arah degufah*" and "*choli*" made by M. Hershler, "*Din Mitzta'er she-Hitiru bo Sh^e^vuth*," pp. 109-12, in his *Halakhah u-Refuah*, vol. 1 (Jerusalem: 1980).

58. Deut. 22:5; *Nazir* 59a; *Sh. A., Y.D.* 182:5.

59. *Nazir* 59a, *Tos.*, s.v. *gevul; Beth Yosef* (citing *Resp. Rashba*) to *Tur. Sh. A., Y.D.* 228:9; *ShaKH*(5) ad loc.
resp. Rashba) to *Tur. Sh. A., Y.D.* 228:9; *Shakh* (5) ad loc.

60. *Resp. Mishneh Halakhoth* (1970), vol. 4, nos. 246-247.

See also R. Moshe Feinstein's recent opinion that any surgery which is for constructive purposes—even cosmetic modification—and not merely *hezek* is not to be considered *chabbalah*. He thus permits cosmetic surgery for women, but does not discuss in this ruling the *lo yilbash* problem involved with such surgery for males (in "*Nituach l^e^-Na'arah l^e^-Yappoth eth Atzmah*," pp. 323-28, In M. Hershler ed., *Halakhah u-Refuah* [Jerusalem: 1980]).

61. *Resp. Minchath Yitzchak* (1973): vol. 6, no. 81; see also Y. Weinberg, *Resp.*

Seridei Esh, vol. 2, no. 81; *Resp. Shoel u-Meishiv, Mahadurah Kamma*, vol. 1, no. 210; see also *Sedei Chemed*, vol. 3, p. 319.

62. *Resp. Chelkath Ya'akov* (1956), vol. 3, no. 4, based on *Sh. A., Y.D.* 241:3 and Meiri to *Sanh.* 84b. See also R. I. Jakobovits, *Noam*, vol. 6, p. 273.

63. See also *Resp. Mishpetei Uziel: Tinyana, Y.D.*, vol. 1, no. 25. However, cf. *Resp. Igroth Moshe: Y.D.*, vol. 1, no. 82.

64. *Resp. Tzitz Eliezer* (1967): vol. 11, no. 41.

65. See J. Meyer, "Psychiatric Considerations in the Sexual Reassignment of Non-intersex Individuals," *Clinics in Plastic Surgery, 1* (1974): 275-283; N. Fisk, "Gender Dysphoria Syndrome," *Int. Symposium on Transsexualism* (Palo Alto: 1973); C. Markland, "Transsexual Surgery," *Obst. & Gyn. Ann., 4* (1975): 309-330; J. Meerloo, "Change of Sex and Collaboration with the Psychosis," *Am. J. Psychiatr., 124* (1967): 263-270; D. Leff, "Genes, Gender, and Genital Reversal," *Medical World News*, (April 18, 1977): 45-68.

66. See J. David Bleich, "Transsexual Surgery," in J. David Bleich & F. Rosner, eds., *Jewish Bioethics* (New York: 1979), pp. 191-96; D. Meir, "*She'eloth Halakhtioth le-Or ha-Refuah ha-Mithchadesheth*," *Torah she-be'al Peh, 18* (1976): 108-111; *Resp. Tzitz Eliezer*, vol. II, no. 78, rules that so long as the external organs of a hermaphroditic patient are female, there is no prohibition involved in hormonally castrating the internal vestiges of male genitalia.

67. Rabbi Meir Amsel, cited in Bleich, op. cit., 1979, p. 192 states the same opinion. The principle, again, is to prevent individuals from parading as and mixing with women, and *vice versa* (*Beth Yosef* and *BaCH* to *Tur Sh. A., Y.D.* 182), which is the intent of the transsexual.

68. See *Minchath Chinnukh* no. 291. See also *Resp. Chatham Sofer; E.H.*, no. 20 and in no. 17 who adds that although there is a stringency which states that *seirus achar seirus* is also punishable by flogging (*Sh. A., E.H.* 5:11), this does not apply where the original "castration" was congenital (i.e., "through the hands of heaven"). See also *Resp. Beth Yitzchak: E.H.*, vol. 1, no. 36 and *Resp. Chavatzeleth ha-Sharon: E.H.*, no. 12.

69. However, it seems that the *isur* of cross-dressing does indeed apply to an *androgenus* or a *tumtum*, although not punishable by flogging—see *Darkei Moshe*, no. 3 to *Tur Sh. A., Y.D.* 182 and *M.T. Hil. A.Z.* 12:4, 10.

70. See J. Meyer, op. cit., 1974 and J. Money & R. Gaskin, "Sex Reassignment," *Int. J. Psychiatry, 9* (1970-1971): 249-269, and D. Feinbloom, *Transvestites and Transsexuals: Mixed Views* (Boston: 1976).

71. *Shab.* 128b; *Tur Sh. A., O.H.* 330. Other examples are cited in I. Jakobovits, "*Tza'ar shel Adam be-Dinei Yisrael*," pp. 132-42, in M. Kasher, N. Lamm & L. Rosenfeld eds., *Leo Jung Jubilee Volume* (New York: 1962).

72. *M.T. Hil. Shabbath* 2:11, *Hil. A.Z.* 11:11, *Hil. Zekhiya u-Matanah* 8:2; see also *Kesef Mishneh* and *Lechem Mishneh* to *Hil. Shab.* 2:11.

73. *Resp. Tashbatz*, vol. 1, no. 54; *Resp. Radbaz*, vol. 4, no. 66; Unterman, "*Mitzvath Pikuach Nefesh u-G'darehah*" (1952); *Resp. Tzitz Eliezer*, vol. 8, no. 15; *Resp. Minchath Yitzchak* (1969), vol. 1, no. 115, vol. 3, nos. 25-26, vol. 4, no. 8.

74. *Resp. Chelkath Ya'akov*, vol. 1, no. 72; *Resp. Igroth Moshe: O.H.*, vol. 1, no. 127.

75. *Resp. Igroth Moshe: O.H.*, vol. 3, no. 53.

76. Cited in *Beth Yosef* to *Tur. Sh. A., Y.D.* 228 (p. 147).
77. *Shab.* 12a-b; *Sh. A., Y.D.* 337, 339.
78. *Sanh.* 43b; *Sh. A., Y.D.* 338; *S^emachoth* 1.
79. *Rama* to *Sh. A., E.H.* 121:7, *H.M.* 211:2, *Y.D.* 339:4.
80. *Arukh ha-Shulchan: Y.D.* 338.
81. See *Biur ha-Gra* to *Sh. A., Y.D.* 338.
82. *Ber.* 54b; *Sh. A., O.H. 219; M.T. Hil. Ber.* 10:8.
83. *Sh. A., O.H.* 219:8, *Rama* and *Magen Avraham*, loc. cit.
84. Regarding suicide, the following authorities rule that *birkath ha-gomel* be recited upon being saved: *Resp. Tzitz Eliezer*, vol. 12, no. 18 (8); *Resp. Lev Chayim*, vol. 3, no. 53; *Resp. Yechaveh Da'ath*, vol. 4, no. 14; however, cf. *Resp. Tzitz Eliezer*, vol. 10, no. 25 (23). See also *Nishmath Avraham: O.H.* 219 (10).
85. *Maharsha* to *Ber.* 54b.
86. *Ikrei Dinim* to *Sh. A., O.H.*, vol. 1, no. 10:22.

2
The Halakhic Status of Neurotically Motivated Religious Acts

I.

A perennial concern of halakhically oriented mental health professionals is the halakhic status of the neurotically motivated religious act. One widely accepted point of view has been that when psychopathology is evident within an individual's overall religious commitment, such commitment may and sometimes must be sacrificed in the interest of securing mental health. Aside from the disturbing generality of this position, certain religious objections arise in the face of this excessively sharp distinction between psychological and spiritual processes.

An equally extreme and no less erroneous position is maintained in some religious camps. This second view holds that religious acts as such retain their "religious" and incumbent quality, no matter what disruptive elements pervade the individual's life — with the exception of elements that would render an individual a *shoteh* (one who is mentally incompetent and hence generally exempted from religious obligations). Moderate points of view reject the conception of a necessary relationship between disturbed psychological functioning and religious beliefs and practices, but still tend to question the value of religious beliefs and practices upheld by neurotic or otherwise conflicted individuals.

It is relevant, both to the practice of psychotherapy and to the professional's ethical obligations to the religious patient, to understand exactly when religious acts must be considered sacrosanct *despite* the presence of unhealthy motivation and when such acts must be considered psychologically *and spiritually* undesirable and subject to modification. A halakhic guideline is needed.

A comprehensive analysis of the halakhic status of neurotically motivated religious acts must consider three aspects or characteristics of the type of religious act in question: (1) Is the act motivated solely by neurotic elements or are non-neurotic motivations mixed with neurotic ones? (2) How does the religious act measure against the category *mitokh she-lo lishmah ba lishmah* (literally, by fulfilling *mitzvoth* with motivations not oriented specifically toward religious observance one eventually achieves the proper motivations)?[1] (3) Does the motivation of the religious act conflict with the proper intention (*kavanah*) required during the performance of *mitzvoth*? In fact, these three elements are interrelated.

It would seem that neurotic motivations in fulfillment of *mitzvoth*—e.g., indulging in repetitive ritual as some sort of "undoing" mechanism, deprivation of bodily needs in obedience to self-punishing or guilt-ridden dynamics, over-attention to detail beyond the requirements of Halakhah and in concert with compulsivity or obsessiveness, and so forth—fall under the category of motivations that would be readily deemed *lo lishmah*, or not for the sake of the religious purposes of *mitzvah* observance. The Talmud itself considers "fear of punishment" and "desire for reward" psychical or emotional examples of *lo lishmah*.[2] Indeed, the Talmud is elsewhere sharply critical of the religious behavior of certain types of "pharisees," whom it describes as one who bloodies his head by bumping into walls because he, in false piety, keeps his glance on the ground so as not to gaze upon women, or as one who knocks his feet together from walking with exaggerated humility. Other talmudic discussions denounce the "pious fool" who refuses to save a drowning woman lest he defile himself.[3] In these instances, while the behavior imitates authentic religious piety, the pathological or "un-halakhic" motivations produce destructive consequences, rendering the act itself the antithesis of religious behavior.

However, the Talmud adds a significant qualification to its classification of pseudo-piety. In some instances, apparently disingenuous motivations should be tolerated if only because they tend eventually to develop into more mature, constructive motivations: *mitokh she-lo lishmah ba lishmah*. Thus, reasons the Talmud, perhaps some forms of immature motivation may be accepted. Yet, *Tosafoth*, a principal commentary to the Talmud, notes that the rabbis had elsewhere stated, "One who engages in Torah study *she-lo lishmah* would be better off not having been created."[4] There would seem, then, to be an apparent discrepancy in the rabbinic attitude to indirect or inappropriate motivations for *mitzvah* observance.

The *Tosafoth* resolves this dilemma by drawing an important distinction between two types of *lo lishmah*. One type, the object of the lenient view *mitokh she-lo lishmah ba lishmah*, while not pure, can in some way lead to proper and healthy fulfillment of religious observance. For, motivations aside, the individual in this case at least produces religiously prescribed behavior. "Fear of punishment" and "desire for reward" would be subsumed under this first distinction *so long as these motivations are not so extreme as to produce destructive consequences*. While these represent relatively immature motivations, more constructive development can be anticipated. On the other hand, motivations which are *antithetical* to the goals of *mitzvah* observance and which elicit destructive acts rather than religious ones are intolerable. This last category would include the self-destructive behavior of the "pharisee" or of the pietist who studies the law but behaves disrespectfully toward his parents or is hypercritical of others (*al m^{e}nath l^e-kanter*).[5] This latter form of motivation is not expected to be conducive to healthy religious growth.

At this point, it seems clear that some intensely pathological or antisocial motivations for religious acts merit censure: the religious act itself may not be redeemed merely by virtue of its "religious" overtones. This category would include religious observance which results in or reinforces physical or psychological injury or incapacitation, or which by unconscious design aggravates interpersonal and family conflict. These represent the fair game of psychological modification and psychotherapy. On the other hand, motivations which are more akin to the "developmental immaturity" highlighted in the *Tosafoth*'s first distinction may be acceptable, following the principle *mitokh she-lo lishmah ba lishmah*.

II.

I noted another element relevant to the halakhic status of neurotically motivated religious acts: *kavanah*. This element is critical since the issue of quality of motivation has bearing on the final value of religious acts only if motivation is in a position to either help or hinder the net quality of *mitzvah* observance. For if we accept that *mitzvoth* do not require *kavanah*—as many halakhic codifiers state—then even neurotic motivation cannot detract from the value of religious acts as long as they are performed in a behaviorally correct way.

Actually, there is debate among early halakhic codifiers whether or not *mitzvoth* require *kavanah*.[6] The outcome of this debate for our practical purposes is that while it is not critical that one have in mind the meaning and purpose of *mitzvoth* before fulfilling them, the biblical commandments require (with few exceptions) that a person maintain a minimal awareness that he is in fact executing a *mitzvah* and an elemental *kavanah* that with this act he is fulfilling the word of God. Thus, motivation reenters the discussion inasmuch as distractions from this required, elemental *kavanah* would render a religious act invalid. (In such cases, though the act would have to be repeated with the proper *kavanah*, blessings would not be repeated as these are rabbinic institutions and do not require *kavanah* according to all views.[7]) Even according to those halakhists who do not require any *kavanah* in certain *mitzvah* observances—such as *mitzvoth* which are fulfilled through eating—if the act is executed improperly, nothing has been achieved from the halakhic standpoint, e.g., one who wraps the *t^efillin* (phylacteries) around the neck as some sort of talisman rather than properly upon the arm and forehead. Indeed, it is germane that Halakhah specifically exempts one who is in a state of *tza'ar*—which includes psychological unease or tension as well as a broad spectrum of obsessional preoccupations—from the *mitzvah* of *t^efillin* or *sukkah*.[8] The basis for these exemptions is that such *tza'ar* is antithetical to the *kavanah* requisite for proper performance of *mitzvath t^efillin* or sitting in one's *sukkah* in the manner in which one usually sits in the comfort of one's home (*teishevu k^e'ein taduru*[9]).

One can also see why it is relevant whether a patient's religious acts are motivated wholly by destructive motivations or by an admixture of neurotic and more healthy ones. When neurotic motivations of the sort that detract from basic *kavanah* are unmitigated by healthy motivations, the resultant religious act will be of questionable value. Where a requisite and appropriate *kavanah* exists in addition to other, less wholesome ones, the resultant religious acts may be acceptable.

Finally, halakhic decisors note that religious acts which result accidentally from other pursuits or which are inevitable and indirect consequences of some other involvement are not acceptable even according to those who rule that *mitzvoth* do not require *kavanah*; e.g., acts which are of the category *mith'asek*, such as when an adult who has eaten a meal leads a child in the recitation of grace after meals, without attention to his own obligation to recite grace, resulting in effect in the adult's having pronounced the words of the grace for his own meal. By extension of this argument, some religious acts which are the indirect or accidental consequence of some other neurotic, phobic, or otherwise disorganized preoccupation would not be considered *mitzvah* fulfillments. One example of *mith'asek* would be meticulous cleaning of the house prior to Passover, where there is no intent to fulfill the Biblically required religious objective of removing all manner of leavening from one's domain (though, in this case, the patient would successfully avoid transgressing the passive aspects of *not having* any leavening in his possession [*bal yeira'eh u-val yimatzey*]). Another is a patient whose intense hate for a parent provokes flight from the family, where the resultant "lack of altercation and confrontation" is not intended as a fulfillment of filial piety. Instead, through this acting-out behavior, the situation is a continuation of the destructive interpersonal relationship.

Of course, few neurotic persons are so disturbed that they withdraw completely from the attention to the demands of the real world, or from the halakhic world in the case of our subjects. It is also not common that neurotic interference in autonomous thinking and emotional expression is so great as to invalidate all religious acts. There is, on the other hand, another range of less-than-psychotic personalities, such as the overideational obsessive or hysteric or the preschizophrenic, whose emotional liabilities or rigidity may and frequently does interfere with the necessary, free qualities of thinking and interpersonal relating. Such persons *are* religious, but in a disorganized and conflict-ridden way. In these cases, the therapeutic goal is not liberating the personality from his or her religion, but rather to liberate the autonomous and healthy aspects of the personality and the religious beliefs from their conflicted sources and pathologic qualities.

Notes

1. *Pes.* 50b; *Sanh.* 105b; *Sot.* 22b; 47a; *Hor.* 10b; *Nazir* 23b; *M.T. Hil. T*[e]*shuvah* 10:5, *Hil. Talmud Torah* 3:5.
2. *Sot.* 22b.
3. *Sot.* 21b.
4. *Sot.* 22b, *Tos.*, s.v. *l*[e]*-olam; Ber.* 17a, *Tos.*, s.v. *ha-oseh.*
5. *Ber.* 17a; See also the *Rosh* to *Pes.* 4:2, and also *Korban Nethanel* ad loc., who include in the second category of *lo lishmah* one who performs *mitzvoth* merely to avoid work or other responsibilities.
6. See *Ba'er Halakhah* to *Sh. A., O.H.*, 60:4 and also *Arukh ha-Shulchan, O.H.*, 690:19 who states that *mitzvoth* that must be executed orally have to be *lishmah* even if these *mitzvoth* are only rabbinic. Also see *Sedei Chemed*, vol. 4, pp. 125-45.
7. *Mishnah Berurah, Sh. A., O.H.*, 60:4.
8. *M.T. Hil. Tefillin* 4:13 and *Birkei Yosef* to *Sh. A., O.H.*, 472 (10); also *Sh. A., O.H.*, 38:6 and *Magen Avraham* ad loc.; also *BaCH to Tur Sh. A., O.H.*, 625.
9. *Suk.* 26a, *Tos.*, s.v. *holkhei d*[e]*rakhim*, and *Suk.* 28b; see also a discussion in *Menorath ha-Maor* of R. Yisrael al-Nakawa, vol. 2, p. 415

3

The Halakhic Status of *Hirhur Asur* in Psychotherapeutic Communication

I.

The realm of thought and fantasy is an active aspect of human psychology and is rightly considered as deserving of therapeutic attention. The Zohar testifies, in a sense, to what psychoanalysis calls the dynamic nature of the unconscious, "All things follow thought and fantasy"—*Kol milin d'almah azley bathar machshavah v^e-hirhurah.*[1] Rabbenu Bachaya (d. 1340) states in his commentary to Deut. 29:18, "It is well known that the heart of man is the central point of the organism, *and that thoughts are its branches, and that actions are its fruits.*... [Thus] one should not take lightly the relevance of thought since happiness, as well as woe, are dependent upon it." With this reference, as well as numerous others like it scattered throughout rabbinic literature, is an important early awareness of the continuum along which lie thought, affect, and action. Moreover, it expresses an early commitment to the reality of the *unobservable* in addition to the observable realm of human behavior, and a recognition of the influence of mental events on physical events.

However, a considerable ethical and clinical conflict would seem to exist between the demand of many forms of psychotherapy that patients' fantasies and verbalizations be expressed freely and without censorship and the carefully safeguarded halakhic domain of purity and sanctity in thought and speech. Traditionally, psychoanalysis has been considered the prime example of therapeutic technique whose success depends upon commitment to the "fundamental rule" of free association. A central tenet of the psychoanalytic process is that action and fantasy must be converted, uncensored, into verbal form. It is in this fashion that unconscious material, considered a vital focus for psychotherapy, becomes conscious and amenable to modification. Equally, many behavioral techniques require the expression of fantasy material for use in certain anxiety-reducing programs (e.g., reciprocal inhibition, thought-stopping). Almost all psychotherapies accept the notion—contributed by learning theorists— that "ventilation" of anxiety-provoking thought and speech within an accepting, nonjudgmental environment such as exists between therapist and patient serves to extinguish anxiety while reinforcing positive emotional approaches to the same material.[2]

While there is no doubt that therapists do accept certain social or clinical values on what types of thoughts and fantasies can be generally considered "normal" or "abnormal," there is equal commitment to the idea that the so-called dirtiness, licentiousness, primitiveness, or symbolic significance is conferred upon it rather than inherent. This is one aspect of the methodological relativism of psychology. Accordingly, energy expended on the upkeep of barriers around "taboo" fantasies or in the disposition toward rigid cultural norms governing the manner of verbal expression and thought is often construed as a defense mechanism. In fact, a religious patient's claim to be unable or not allowed to discuss certain topics or think certain thoughts may be a powerful resistance through which to prevent uncomfortable yet critical therapeutic progress.

To be sure, there is little credence in the view that all psychoanalysts, or psychotherapy, in general seek to totally eradicate the concept of guilt or anxiety or that it eschews the idea that some acts and thoughts are simply unethical and perverted while others are not. On the other hand, psychotherapists do not accept as their role to be moral arbiters for their patients inasmuch as the limited focus of psychotherapy is the removal of *disproportionate* guilt and anxiety, inappropriate levels of affect, rooted in past or present, which hamper an individual's ability to function, or obsessive attention to detail—as distinguished from authentic religious *dikduk*—with regard to thought and speech.[3] As K. Menninger noted, an individual upon the completion of psychotherapy may even have the same guilt and anxiety, but is considered healthy precisely because he or she has learned how to deal appropriately with such feelings and to calibrate their relative worth in the given circumstances wherein such feelings arise.[4]

Halakhah, however, is not formally a relativistic system. That is, Halakhah is a unified theory that ascribes intrinsic qualities to acts, speech, and thought. When circumstances necessitate a change in the halakhic position, Halakhah is not simply waived, but rather a new halakhic status must be afforded the circumstance necessitating the change. For an elementary example, though Halakhah forbids the consumption of non-kosher food, there arise medical emergencies requiring that such foods be consumed. Halakhah does not simply waive the prohibition against non-kosher food, but instead makes the consumption of food obligatory from the standpoint of the halakhic requirement to preserve life. Thus, a continuous balance is preserved between the intrinsic status of phenomena and modifications in the contexts wherein such phenomena occur.

The following review of halakhic literature will make clear the degree to which Halakhah requires purity of thought. Specific examples of how such carefully delineated halakhic requirements may conflict with psychotherapeutic tasks will be offered. Simply waiving these halakhic standards in the interests of mental health is not an intelligent halakhic response to the serious difficulties which exist, as we shall see. Rather, an alternative halakhic model, consistent with prior halakhic models,[5] must be considered which would transform the status of the therapeutic circumstance wherein occurs otherwise forbidden thought.

II.

There are Biblical imperatives which explicitly or implicitly govern the sanctity of thought. At least five passages are utilized to determine the parameters of the prohibition against *hirhur davar ha-asur*, thought or fantasies over forbidden acts, in general, and specifically, *hirhur arayoth*, thought or fantasies of sexual content. Specifically, "Do not come close to uncover [their] nakedness" (*lo thikrᵉvu*).[6] "Do not follow after your hearts and after your eyes" (*lo thathuru*).[7] "Sanctified you shall be" (*kᵉdoshim tihyu*).[8] "And you shall be perfect . . . before the Lord" (*vihyithem n^ekiyim*).[9] "And guard yourself from all evil things" (*v^e-nishmarta mi-kol davar ra*).[10] The passages *vihyithem n^ekiyim* and *k^edoshim tihyu* have been utilized extensively by authors of books of *mussar* to emphasize the degree of holiness necessary in thought and speech. *K^edoshim tihyu* substantiates a particularly powerful ethos, for the Talmud considers that all of man's behavior must be modeled after God: "As He is holy, so must you be holy; as He is merciful, so must you be merciful . . ."[11] However, the specific halakhic discussion of *hirhur averah* is based on the other three passages which, in turn, are the foundation for all subsequent *mussar* writings.

The clause *lo thathuru* is divided by the Talmud into two derivations, recorded by numerous halakhic codifiers.[12] " 'After your eyes,' refers to *hirhur averah*; 'To which you turn,' refers to *hirhur avodah zarah* [idol worship]." Thought preoccupied with idolatrous intent—which Halakhah assumes will eventuate in actual idol worship—is enumerated as one of the 365 negative Biblical precepts.[13]

More prevalent are the halakhic discussions of *hirhur asur*, which includes, according to some, *hirhur arayoth*. Based on *v^e-nishmarta*, R. Pinchas b. Ya'ir says, "Do not think illicit thoughts in the day and come to nocturnal emission of seed."[14] Here, opinion divides whether this exegesis from *v^e-nishmarta* is a *d^erashah g^emurah*, or merely an *asmakhta*, a hint to the impropriety of such thought but not carrying full Biblical status, yet serving as a basis for a strong rabbinic prohibition.[15] According to *Rambam*, though the specific passage of *v^e-nishmarta* alone serves only as an *asmakhta* for this prohibition, *hirhur asur* is still considered fully Biblical—based on *lo thathuru*.[16] In Rambam's *view, it is forbidden to experience* hirhur asur *and even to do anything which will bring about* hirhur asur.[17]

Hirhur over forbidden acts is considered as requiring a guilt offering: "If we stayed away from the commission of the forbidden act, we did not stay away from *hirhur*."[18] In additional rulings of the category of *s^eyag* or 'protective fence' around the basic prohibition, the rabbis prohibited staring at animals copulating, at women washing clothes, and any activity felt to dispose toward *hirhur asur*.

With specific regard to *hirhur arayoth*, one is dealing with the additional stringency of the Biblical interdict against incestuous relationships. Unlike all other commandments (except murder and idolatry), one must allow oneself to be killed rather than violate the prohibitions of *arayoth*. *Rambam* and many other authorities rule that meditation or thought about such forbidden relations represent *abizrahu d^e^arayoth* (appurtenances of the prohibition) and are also Biblically forbidden.[19] Even conversing in a sexually evocative context with a woman from behind a curtain—in the well-known case of *Sanhedrin* 75a—is specifically enumerated as one such forbidden *abizra*; a law which *Rambam* adds is in force "*l^e^-doroth*," forever.[20]

There are opinions that women are not subsumed under the prohibition of *hirhur* inasmuch as its basis is to prevent the occurrence of nocturnal emissions.[21] Others, however, do include women under this law by reference to another distinct Biblical prohibition: *lo thilbash*. R. Moshe Feinstein notes that while the prohibition for women cannot be derived from *v^e^-nishmarta* (with its specific goal), it is to be derived from the biblical *lo thathuru*.[22]

In a related, practical discussion of this halakhic category, the talmudic sages debate whether the *sotah*, a married woman suspected of adultery and brought before the *beth din* for trial by ordeal through the "bitter waters,"[23] should be entirely undressed in the presence of the young priests officiating as per the biblical command. The majority opinion is that since the emotional context of this ordeal is one of repugnance and sadness, there is no tangible fear of *hirhur asur* on the part of the priests.[24] Yet, in the case of taking a female criminal to be stoned, where there is a *mishnaic* requirement to undress the victim (so as to speed up the process of death), the same sages rule that she should not be undressed entirely as she has suffered sufficient disgrace. R. Judah, however, rules to the contrary in both instances. In the case of *sotah*, the woman should not be undressed because despite the melancholy climate, she may be found innocent and, at that moment, the young priests might become infatuated with a then lawfully married woman. On the other hand, a female criminal bound for inescapable doom may be completely undressed as this context will not elicit harmful fantasies in the onlooker's mind.[25] The law follows the majority opinion in both cases.[26] However, a general principle is retained from R. Judah's argument: Where there is a tangible risk of *hirhur*, one may even waive a biblical mandate (in this case, the requirement that the *sotah* be undressed prior to her ordeal).[27]

There is ample rabbinic reinforcement of the need for protecting the realm of thought. *Hirhur* is considered one of the experiences from which no individual is spared (certainly a psychological truth, given the Zohar's understanding of *hirhur*),[28] and, with excessive preoccupation, prevents repentance.[29] "All who stimulate themselves to evil thought do not enter the Divine presence."[30] "The beginning of sin is the murmuring of the heart" (*hirhur ha-lev*).[31] "The thought of sin is worse than the actual sin."[32] In one tradition, Ezekiel is praised as one who never experienced illicit *hirhur*.[33] In testimony to the ways man can actively or passively participate in the world of experience, the Talmud notes that one is not suspected of iniquity unless one actually commits a sin, or commits it partly, or thought of committing it, or saw others commit it while he experienced pleasure in that.[34] The Talmud forbids sexual relations with one's wife while thinking at the same time of another woman.[35] Finally, in explaining the gravity of *hirhur asur*, *Rambam* writes that to engage in sinful thought is to sin with the "noblest portion of the self" (. . . *b^e-mivchar she-b^emidothav*).[36]

It is clear at this point to what degree halakhah monitors wanton fantasy, sexually indulgent rumination, and even thoughts related to other forbidden acts. The clinician, however, works with the objective of having the patient grow out of infantile and primitive stages of regressed or arrested development by re-experiencing the turmoil of the past in the emotionally corrective atmosphere of the present therapeutic situation. Frequently, a patient's fantasy material is a critical tool for a full understanding of his or her psychological conflicts. The fantasy world of children is an area rich in significance for therapeutic focus. The treatment of homosexuality, for another example, is most successfully undertaken when there is evidence of heterosexual fantasy and desire in the otherwise homosexual personality. Even behavioral approaches need to deal with such material in the effort to extinguish the learned anxieties which occur together with heterosexual fantasies in the homosexual or, in other cases, to build up a viable heterosexual response to emotionally stimulating fantasy material. The discussion of incestuous wishes or the abreacting of past traumata having distinctly erotic themes is often part of psychotherapy in the treatment of, among others, homosexuals, incestuous families, and even child-abusing parents. Indeed, the therapeutic axiom here is almost the complement of the rabbinic one: "There is no sin without *hirhur*"—i.e., there is no behavior without its psychic, affective counterpart.

In other instances, casework with the *ba'al t^eshuvah*, who often attempts to resolve psychological or social (family) conflict through the mechanism of religious intensification or conversion with the effect that pre-existing psychic conflicts become inextricably interwoven with the proper function of religious beliefs and behavior,[37] is often hampered by the utilization of religious laws as defense tactics. A troubled *ba'al t^eshuvah*, or any other religious patient, may refuse to relate to erotic fantasies by an appeal to the types of prohibitions already discussed. Sexual dysfunctions may be difficult to treat in the religious individual who exercises unbending control over affective experiences felt to be sinful, and by resistance to expressive forms of treatment intended to moderate such rigidity toward halakhically acceptable standards. Yet, as long as pathological behavior is considered as unrelated to unconscious impulses and drives—and as long as a patient withholds relevant aspects of his inner world from scrutiny or seeks to keep them in check by obsessional taboos and symptomatic behavior—psychotherapy is prevented access to a critical determinant of psychological imbalance.

The halakhically-minded psychotherapist or counselor must consider this problem and the need for an alternative halakhic model which offers a unique status to *hirhur* in the treatment context. As previously stated, the concerned therapist cannot make an appeal to the halakhic "medical model"—that risk to life waives rabbinic and even Biblical prohibitions—since (1) most psychotherapeutic circumstances do not involve threat to life, and even more important, (2) even a medical emergency, it would appear, could not waive the Biblical injunctions attendant to the realm of *arayoth* and *hirhur arayoth*.

III.

There are two relevant factors which support the possibility of an alternative halakhic model for dealing with *hirhur asur* in the psychotherapeutic encounter. First, note the qualification that *abizrahu d^{e}arayoth* are so strictly forbidden only in a sexually provocative context. M'eiri notes that the prohibition against *hirhur arayoth* only concerns preoccupation with such thoughts.[38] Others note that the *isur* centers on *hirhur bederekh chibah v^{e}-nishuk derekh ta'avah*.[39] Further qualification appears in the analysis that *hirhur arayoth* is dependent upon the degree to which an individual truly reigns over his impulses.[40] Of course, all those who discuss the problem summarize their views with the warning that the type of self-understanding and self-control exhibited by certain rabbis in the Talmud are not common and that it is not for modern man to rule uncautiously on such matters.[41]

A related concern to this first factor stressing the context of *hirhur* is *Rambam*'s strict ruling that *yehareg v^{e}-al ya'avor* applies even to *abizrahu d^{e}arayoth* and, as in the case of *Sanhedrin* 75a, apparently even to rabbinic levels of *isur* (intercourse with an unmarried virgin). Others maintain that rabbinic levels of *arayoth* would not demand *yehareg v^{e}-al ya'avor*.[42] As for *Rambam*'s view, two alternative approaches can be suggested. The first is that to judge by the wording of this law in his *Mishneh Torah*, it would appear that *Rambam* intended it as a *halakhah v^{e}-ein morin kein*:

> He who sets his eyes upon a woman and becomes deathly sick-in-love with her . . . he should die rather than have intercourse with her even if she be a *p^{e}nuyah*. And even to talk with her from behind a wall *we do not instruct him to*, and he should die, *and do not rule for him to speak* with her from behind the wall.

A second approach, suggested by the *Even ha-Ezel*,[43] is that *Rambam* is strict here precisely because *this* individual lusted after the woman and now wishes to attempt again to obtain the object of his desire; but, in general, *abizrahu d^{e}arayoth* would not demand *yehareg v^{e}-al ya'avor*.

Thus, the context of *hirhur asur* is critical to establishing the gravity of its prohibition (*hirhur derekh chibah* . . .). The extension

sion of this is that individuals will differ with regard to temptation and the degree to which given erotic stimuli will elicit wanton fantasizing. It has been noted that Halakhah is less concerned about *hirhur* in circumstances where respect for authority, for example, would prevent forbidden thought.[44] Thus, for example, though the rabbis warned against holding the membrum while urinating lest this stimulate *hirhurim*, this concern was theoretically relaxed if one was urinating in the vicinity of a synagogue. In certain contexts, then, one can differentiate the *affective characteristic* of a behavior or thought—e.g., its erotic nature— from its *value characteristic*—e.g., its 'sinfulness' or 'perverseness.' Illicit motivation would lend a negative value to affective responses whether or not these responses were erotic in nature. Yet the reverse is not necessarily the case either, for there are erotic responses that are not illicit simply because they are erotic, given certain contexts.

The second factor suggesting an alternative model is the need for becoming a *gibor* or master over one's impulses. The consensus of talmudic opinion is that such mastery is not gained by repression of these impulses, but rather by rerouting them along acceptable lines.[45] A confrontation with such impulses, even "forbidden" ones, becomes part of the process of their productive neutralization. However, this alone would not require that one force such confrontation to the fore. Indeed, *Rambam* warns against seeking out situations of temptation so that one can wilfully succumb and then do *t^eshuvah*—the logic of *echtah v^e-ashuv* can actually hamper repentance.[46] Thus, an additional step is necessary before these two factors—the context of *hirhur* and the need for confrontation with one's *yetzer*—can be operationalized. This third step is the proposal of the alternative halakhic model for *hirhur* in the psychotherapeutic context: therapy as *vidduy*.

Vidduy, generally translated as confession, is a major component of repentance (*t^eshuvah*) and atonement (*kaparah*). Repentance from any sin, whether of interpersonal nature or between God and man, requires full recognition of all aspects of sin. Thus, *vidduy* must be both internal and verbal.[47] *Rambam* specifies in his general definition of *t^eshuvah* that the ultimate version of repentance includes a fully particularized and verbalized *vidduy* as well as the re-experiencing of the original situation of sin—while one is in full possession of equal temptation and willingness (and fantasies) to commit the sin ("... *v^e-hu omed b^e-ahavatho bah u'v^e-khoach gufo* ..."[48])—and resisting!

Inasmuch as *Rambam* also states that repentance is a model for the appropriate response to both the ordinary conception of sin as well as to flaws of personality (*de'oth ra'oth*),[49] it can be hypothesized that the modern tool of psychotherapy can be conceptualized halakhically as following the models *t^eshuvah* and *vidduy*. This is not to say that reciting *al chet* suffices where psychotherapy is indicated, but rather that the psychotherapeutic agenda is accepted into the halakhic world via its meta-psychological form as *vidduy* (a theory elaborated upon elsewhere[50]). If so, then the halakhic details of *vidduy*, its goals and mechanics, pertain with regard to the psychotherapeutic encountered as well. What was formerly to be hopelessly construed as *hirhur asur* now becomes a halakhic desideratum if it is therapeutically necessary for the successful modification of behavior—if it is something which should rightfully be confronted and dealt with in one's *vidduy* endeavor (if *vidduy* alone would not be sufficient). That is, *qua vidduy*, one deals with the affective nature of the thought-act divorced from its negative value, while, reflectively, one is aware that in other contexts the act has negative value.[51]

It is necessary to justify the therapist's involvement in this process, as Halakhah neither accepts the notion of a "confessor" nor would it appear that the therapy as *vidduy* model allows the *therapist* to experience verbalizations of forbidden content. In fact, the therapist's role is halakhically prescribed using a model of therapist as *mokhiach*. *Rambam*'s definition is explicit: "One who sees his fellow sin or that he is following an evil path [which surely can include a psychopathological path as an example of *de'oth ra'oth*], it is an obligation to return him to the good and to make him know that he sins *against himself*... as it is said, 'You shall surely rebuke your fellow.' One who so rebukes his fellow, whether on matters between themselves or on matters between him and God, *the matter should be discussed between themselves*."[52] Second, the therapist serves in a capacity emphasized by Ramban's didactic interpretation of the imperative to "remember that which

God did to Miriam" (which he, at least, considers a Biblical commandment): to facilitate a confrontation with the past, with repressed memories, despite the fact that it is generally forbidden to remind a convert or *ba'al t^eshuvah* (which, in a sense, is what the psychiatric patient can be likened to) of their past behaviors.[53] R. Moshe Sofer also accepts this thesis and views the interpersonal encounter as a unique opportunity for confronting the dynamic aspects of psychosocial conflicts.[54] Thus, if there is an actual demand to recall "forbidden material" where personal growth is vital, the therapist can also serve as a catalyst in this process.

Practically speaking, it becomes halakhically tenable to expect the fully religious patient to nondefensively probe, examine, and experience the realm of *hirhurim*. The value characteristic of *hirhur asur* stands as only temporarily suspended during therapy. Therefore, it becomes the onus of the psychotherapist to ensure that the atmosphere of the therapeutic encounter remains consistent with the halakhic guidelines noted above. Resistance beyond this point needs to be handled like any other resistance in psychotherapy, paying careful attention to the secondary gain such cultural standards can afford the neurotic or otherwise troubled individual. Viewed as such, this aspect of the psychotherapeutic process becomes an intrinsically halakhic one.

Notes

1. Zohar Gen., 155; and similarly, "*Achar kavanath ha-lev hen hen ha-d^evarim*," *Meg.* 20a.
2. See L. Wolberg, *The Technique of Psychotherapy* (New York: 1967), vol. 1, p. 50; J. Watkins, "Psychotherapeutic Methods," in *Handbook of Clinical Psychology*, ed. B. Wolman (New York: 1965), pp. 1143-67.
3. See also my "Clinical Aspects of Religion as Neurosis," *Am J. Psychoanal., 36*, no. 4 (1976): 361-365 and J. Mermelstein, "Piety, Psychopathology, and Parenting," *Intercom, 17*, no. 2 (1979).
4. K. Menninger and P. Holzman, *The Theory of Psychoanalytic Technique* (New York: 1973), p. 174.
5. In my *Judaism and Psychology: Halakhic Perspectives* (New York: 1980), chap. 1, 2.
6. Lev. 18:6.

7. Num. 15:39.
8. Lev. 11: 44-45; 20:7, 26; Num. 15: 40.
9. Num. 32:22.
10. Deut. 23:10.
11. *Shab.* 133b; *M.T. Hil. De'oth* 1:6.
12. *Ber.* 12b to Judg. 14:3.
13. *Sefer ha-Mitzvoth*, Neg. no. 44, 353; *SMaG*, Neg. no. 15; *SMaK*, no. 30; *Sefer ha-Chinnukh*, no. 387.
14. *A.Z.* 20b; *Ket.* 46a.
15. Viewing it as an *asmakhta*: Me'iri to *Chul.* 37b; and as a *d^erashah g^emurah*: *A.Z.* 20b, *Tos.*, s.v. *shelo*; *Ramban* and *Chiddushei ha-RaN* to *Chul.* 37b; *SMaG*, Neg. no. 126; *SMaK* no. 24; R. Yonah in *Orchoth Chayim*, vol. 2, p. 113.
16. *M.T. Hil. Isurei Biah* 21:2, 19 to *Niddah* 13b and in *Peirush ha-Mishnayoth*: *Sanh.* 54b; *Tur Sh. A., E.H.*, 23:2.
17. Ibid., and also *M.T. Hil. Isurei Biah* 21:3, 19; see also *Tzafnath Paneach*, vol. 1, 90 who holds that *hirhur* is forbidden as *g^eramah*, or a disposing variable.
18. *Shab.* 64a; *Kallah R.* 1, on Num. 31: 49-50.
19. *M.T. Hil. Yesodei ha-Torah* 5: 6, 9, *Hil. Isurei Biah* 21:1; *RaN* to Pes. 25b; *Rama* to *Sh. A., Y.D.* 157:1; cf. *ShaKH* to *Sh. A., Y.D.* 157:9.
20. *Sanh.* 75a; *M.T. Hil Yesodei ha-Torah* 5:6, 9.
21. See *Panim Yafoth* to Deut. 22:5; see also *Birkei Yosef* to *Sh. A., Y.D.* 335:5.
22. "*Lo yiheyeh k^eli gever al ishah* . . ."; see also *Resp. Igroth Moshe: E.H.*, vol. 1., no. 69 and *Sefer ha-Chinnukh*, nos. 128, 387.
23. The so-called bitter waters, Num. 5:11-31.
24. *Mish. Sot.* 7:1; *Sot.* 8a and cf. *Sanh.* 45a.
25. *Sanh.* 44b-45a.
26. *M.T. Hil. Sanhedrin* 15:1, *Hil. Sotah* 3:11; *Tos.*, s.v. *v^e-im*, *Sot.* 8b.
27. Ibid.
28. *B.B.* 164b.
29. *M.T. Hil. T^eshuvah* 4:4, *Hil. Isurei Biah* 22:18-20.
30. *Niddah* 13b to Gen. 38:10.
31. *TDE Zuta* 6.
32. *Yoma* 29a. *Rambam* (*Moreh*) seems to explain the sense of *hirhur kasheh me-aveirah* as that the punishment is, proportionately, worse than the crime. See also Rabbenu Bachaya's commentary on Deut. 29:18. Exceptions to the rule that an "evil thought" is not counted as action (*einah mitzarefeth l^e-ma'aseh*; cf. *Kid.* 40a) are *hirhur avodah zarah* and *hirhur arayoth* (see the *Rosh* to *R.H.* 17b). Medini explains (*Mikhtav l^e-Chizkiyahu*, pp. 60b-61a) that such thoughts are always considered *machshavoth she-osim peiroth*: hence, the fact that an individual did *not* actually commit the act is considered merely accidental.
33. *Chul.* 37b to Ezek. 4:14.
34. *M.K.* 18b, and similar to this, "*Ein ha-machshavah holekheth ela achar ha-oved*," *Zev.* 46b; *Meg.* 20a; *Kid.* 59b.
35. *Ned.* 20b; *Pes.* 112a.
36. *Moreh* 3:8. A non-Jew would seem in general judged equally for thought or act (*Tos., Kid.* 39b), and the complications discussed here may not be resolved in the case of a *ben Noach* through the models proposed here.

37. See note 5 *supra*.
38. On *Chul.* 37b, "... *mi she-margil atzmo li-d^{e}varim ha-m^{e}vi'im liy^{e}dei zeh* ...".
39. *Yam shel Shlomo: Kid.* 4:25; see also *RaN* to *Ned.* 20b, s.v. *u-k^{e}shelo*; Rashi to *Chag.* 56.
40. *Ritva* cited by *Yam shel Shlomo*, loc. cit.; see also *Pithchei T^{e}shuvah* to *Sh. A., E.H.* 21:3, "... *she-isur histakluth* ... *taluy l^e-fi mah she-adam makir b^e-atzmo im nikhnah yitzro o lo.*"
41. See also *Sefer ha-Chinnukh*, no. 188.
42. *SHaKH* to *Sh. A., Y.D.* 157:9; see also *Resp. Igroth Moshe: E.H.*, vol. 1, no. 56.
43. *Even ha-Ezel* to *M.T. Hil. Yesodei ha-Torah* 5:9. Rabbi Y.Y. Weinberg, *Resp. Seridei Esh*, vol. 2 (*O.H.*), no. 8, also discusses the qualification of *derekh chibbah* (citing *Rama* to *Sh. A., E.H.* 21 and *Tos.*, s.v. *ha-kol, Kid.* 82a).
44. *Ber.* 20a; *Ket.* 17a; *Niddah* 13a. *Ritva* mentions these exceptions as Halakhah. However, there are other contexts where it is unclear whether *hirhur* is blocked by extreme affects; *Sanh*, 20a, *Tos.*, s.v. *nashim*, suggests that *hirhur* does not occur in contexts of fear, yet it may overpower one even during bereavement (*Kid.* 80b, *Tos.*, s.v. *ki.*). See also *Niddah* 13a. The rabbis there note that in the context of fear, one need not be concerned about holding the membrum while urinating: "*hakhi nami kivan d^e-ba'ati lo ati l^e-hirhuri.*" Yet cf. *Tos.*, loc. cit., s.v. *ochez*, that the lenient majority view later accepted the individual, stringent view. The *Tur, Sh. A., O.H.* 3, does not mention these exceptions. *Beth Yosef* (s.v. *v^e-lo*) explains that we are no longer capable of discriminating these "fear contexts." *SMaK*, no. 292, however, retains the majority view, and *Magen Avraham* (no. 14) also notes that there are other instances where we differentiate types of fear, but perhaps one should still be stringent in this area.
45. *Shmoneh P'rakim*, end chap. 3 and chap. 6.
46. *M.T. Hil. T^{e}shuvah* 4:4.
47. *Yoma* 86b; *Beth Yosef* to *Tur Sh. A., O.H.*, 607:4.
48. Ibid., and also *Hil. T^{e}shuvah* 2:1-3.
49. *M.T. Hil. T^{e}shuvah* 7:3. See also S.R. Hirsch to Lev. 16:6 (*vekhiper*) and Num. 5:7 (*v^{e}hithvadu*), and also *Mikhtav Me'Eliyahu*, vol. 2, p. 55ff.
50. See note 5 supra.
51. Further difficulties exist regarding the treatment of homosexuality; see chap. 11 of *Judaism and Psychology*, op. cit., 1980.
52. *M.T. Hil. De'oth* 6:7.
53. See *Ramban, Esen ha-Nosafin le-Sefer ha-Mitzvoth*, no. 7 and his commentary to Deut. 24:9. *Rambam* accepts this basic premise in *Hil. Tumath Tzara'ath* 16:9, but does not enumerate this *z^{e}chirah* as a separate *mitzvah*. Cf. *Arukh ha-Shulchan: O.H.*, 60.
54. Introduction to *Mekor Chayyim: Shmirath ha-Lashon*, p. 6; see also R. Yonah ha-Chasid, *Igereth ha-T^{e}shuvah, Yom 2*, p. 195, and *Resp. Igroth Moshe: O.H.*, vol. 4, no. 118. A model of quasi-dynamic exploration of the sinner's (patient's) motives is found in the priest's attempts to secure a confession from the *sotah* (see *Sot.* 7a, *Mishneh*).

4

The Concept of Psychiatric Hazard and the Halakhic Disposition toward Contraception and Abortion

The observant Jew's actions and decisions for action in any specific regard are guided by the dynamic requirements of Halakhah. The observant Jewish mental health professional engaged in individual, family, vocational, or marital counseling, is equally bound by the valences of the halakhic process even when the actions in question fall under the aegis of therapeutic necessity. For example, assertiveness training must be instituted within the framework of the *halakhoth* of *derekh eretz l^ehorim u-morim* (respect for parents and teachers); sex therapy must be engaged in with respect for the laws of *taharath ha-mishpachah* (family purity); discussions of attitudinal and value change must take place in the light of Torah and the rabbinic understanding of Torah.

The understanding of Halakhah which bestows upon it such an all-encompassing power is that it is not a random collection of rules and rabbinic statements, but rather a system of thought and conduct based on the dialectic between the word of God and the latitude of personal initiative. As rabbinic scholar David S. Shapiro put it, "Halakhah is a vast system of thought which extends over the limitless ranges of human experience, subjugating them to its critical scrutiny in the light of the principles, regulations and laws revealed at Sinai and unfolded in the rabbinic literature of subsequent millennia."[1]

Implicit in the fact that Halakhah addresses itself to mundane reality is the notion that it must be conditioned to limitations and changes in that reality. Historical circumstances may determine the application of many *halakhoth*—commandments and practices.[2] Halakhic policies are not always absolute;[3] some laws are contingent on the vicissitudes of human desire, while individual personality factors can also affect halakhic decisions.[4] Moreover, there is a legitimate process of adaptation in the halakhic system, sensitive to both the exigencies of the individual and the fluid realities of changing times. To be sure, there is disagreement as to exactly how far Halakhah may bend to meet these needs and how fluid the process truly is. It suffices as an introduction to our topic in this chapter that a halakhic understanding of the client's needs surely plays a large role in determining the attitude taken by the observant counselor/therapist.[5]

This chapter will attempt to outline the parameters of "psychiatric danger" from the standpoint of Halakhah. It will be seen that Halakhah is sensitive not only to psychiatric risk of a life-threatening nature, but also to what can be called "psychiatric danger," designating a type of *tza'ar* or psychosocial anguish of a non-life-threatening nature. There are three reasons why such an analysis is important, two of them straightforward. First, I wish to delineate relevant halakhic perceptions which are not readily available to the Jewish (or non-Jewish) mental health professional. Second, I wish to emphasize that the halakhically observant client's desire to afford "mental adjustment" or "balance" will always be secondary to a primary concern—what one is halakhically obligated to do and to not do to achieve such psychological desiderata.

The third reason is perhaps an expansion of the first but needs to be stressed on its own. While halakhic decisions are primarily the concern of the rabbinic authority, consultation with trained experts in various professions is often required in order for the rabbinic ruling to be meaningful. Thus, for example, in determining the *kashruth* of certain synthetic foods, biochemical input is necessary; in arbitrating a euthanasia decision, medical and technical information is required. In all such situations, Halakhah recognizes the professional ability of experts in the field to provide relevant information on natural phenomena or processes which may bear on a halakhic decision. The Talmud states, "A judge can only rule on the evidence before his eyes,"[6] i.e., in view of the specific circumstances and contemporary understandings of the problem under consideration. This is often precisely the area for professional input.

To date, however, very little work has been done on the application of this process to the dilemmas which can occur, from the halakhic standpoint, in the socio-psychotherapeutic setting.[7] Several years ago one author stated, "The entire area of psychological problems and severe emotional disturbances and their bearing on halakhic questions has not as of yet been adequately explored,"[8] and the situation has not changed significantly since then. This chapter is concerned with one such concurrence of Halakhah and social work or psychological intervention: abortion and birth-control counseling. The issue at hand, pressing in terms of the high incidence of such cases currently brought before Jewish family service institutions, private-practicing caseworkers, and rabbis, concerns the determination of situations or circumstances when it might be halakhically appropriate to modify the normally strong prohibitions against birth control and abortion.[9] The urgency of this question is heightened by the increased availability of medically supervised abortion and prenatal disease testing (such as amniocentesis), and by the widespread fear of being a carrier of a Tay-Sachs, PKU, or otherwise genetically inferior fetus. Both of these factors have played no small role in weakening the formerly fervent anti-abortion stance of many young married couples, whether religious or nonreligious.[10]

While Halakhah does not recognize "social inconvenience" as sufficient grounds for relaxing the prohibitions against birth control and abortion, it very clearly recognizes threat to the mother's physical well-being, when caused by the pregnancy,[11] as a lenience factor in abortion (so long as the infant's head has not yet extruded into the world)[12] and, *mutatis mutandis*, in permitting birth control through acceptable means.[13] Physical dangers include general risk to the mother's life as well as specific medical catastrophes which could leave the mother's life permanently or temporarily endangered—again, where the cause is the *pregnancy* itself, if carried to term—such as deafness[14] or excruciating and debilitating (though not even life-threatening) pain.[15]

Ostensibly, the caseworker does not enter the decision-making process in this regard. It would seem to be solely the territory of the physician and the rabbi; and the final ruling is a halakhically composed ruling of the rabbi, who, from the practical standpoint, is the final arbiter of action.[16] There is, however, another leniency factor which enters into the rabbinic disposition toward birth control and abortion: *psychiatric* hazard. The rabbinic admission of the broad range of psychologically disordered states into the halakhic decision-making process requires that such states be gauged, measured, and described, and that analogies be sought between contemporary psychiatric nomenclature and the select terms used in the Talmud and codes which appear to describe psychiatric phenomena. And it is in these tasks that the caseworker/therapist as *mumcheh* (expert) plays a significant role in the halakhic process. With regard to the specific problem of when psychiatric danger is sufficient to permit contraception and abortion, one must be specific as to how psychiatric hazard is defined and by what criteria it is measured.

A brief overview of previous responsa literature should be taken into account. One considered body of opinion on the abortion issue is summarized by I. Jakobovits, the Chief Rabbi of Great Britain: "The [halakhic opinion on] the destruction of an unborn child is that it is not murder. But it is a grave offense, except where indicated by some hazard to the safety of the mother, whether for physical *or psychological* reasons" (emphasis added).[17] A second approach follows Maimonides' ruling that abortion is, in effect, an act of murder. Of course, there are occasions for leniency toward the act of abortion even according to Maimonides' interpretation of the grave offense involved in general circumstances.[18] The basic leverage for lenient rulings in the case of abortion rests upon (1) the fact that an unborn fetus is considered less than human by Halakhah, and (2) that in any circumstance of physical or severe danger to the pregnant mother, the fetus assumes the legal status of a *rodef*, a pursuer, which although innocent and not as yet a person, may be sacrificed when a halakhically valid warrant exists to save the life of the mother. After birth, however, the neonate gains full claim to life.[19]

The operative consideration where leniency can be allowed is not merely the *punishment of the aggressor* but the timely saving of the victim. One insightful commentary notes that when circumstances demand it, the concept of *rodef* implies that abortion is *required* rather than *permitted*, so that even if a mother, out of love for her unborn child, chooses to die so that it may live, her choice is not halakhically acceptable.[20] In such cases, the mother must act under the statute "Do not pity the pursuer,"[21] based on the Divine fiat: "Do not stand idly by your brother's blood."[22]*

The late Chief Rabbi of Israel, I. Unterman, viewed the killing of a fetus when necessary in a very stringent light, practically speaking. In a responsum-article he writes that the fetus *cum* pursuer loses its claim to our protection and to the status which would ordinarily make its killing murder. However, he adds, an "unintentional pursuer"—viz., one following the natural course of childbirth processes which always involves struggle—would not forfeit the status which makes its killing impermissible. Thus, only in absolutely life-saving situations could a fetus be aborted.[27] And yet, if we examine other of R. Unterman's responsa, we find his definition of life-saving circumstances to include "mental anguish *only if suicidal tendencies prevail*," since such tendencies obviously constitute an ever present threat to life.[28] Insanity alone, he opines, is not sufficient warrant for abortion, "for even the insane have an instinct for self-preservation." In relation to Tay-Sachs disease, Dr. F. Rosner writes, "If a woman who suffered a nervous breakdown following the birth (or death) of a child with Tay-Sachs disease becomes pregnant again, *and is so distraught with this knowledge . . . that she threatens suicide*, Jewish law can

---

* The matter of *rodef* is a difficult one. Maimonides rules that in certain circumstances the fetus may be sacrificed because it is "*like a rodef*," leading many glosses to ask: why may the child not be sacrificed even after its head has extruded since it is still a "pursuer"? Numerous answers on Maimonides' behalf have been offered. The central thesis of most of them is that Maimonides only intended to stress that the endangering fetus, *like* the real *rodef*, may be sacrificed; once born, however, it has full human status and therefore equal claim to life (given the absence of additional aggressive, homicidal tendencies on the part of the infant).[23]

The law of pursuit[24] is that a bystander is required to disable the aggressor, by a fatal blow if necessary, in order to save the victim. Some explain that this is why Maimonides likened the fetus to a *rodef*; i.e., even though ordinarily one should first try to disable the aggressor, the fetus may even be killed if necessary.[25] However, when intrauterine amputation of a limb would suffice to save the mother's life without recourse to an embryotomy, destruction of the fetus could not be sanctioned strictly from Maimonides' standpoint.[26]

allow amniocentesis . . . and rabbinic consultation should be obtained regarding the decision to abort" (emphasis added).[29] Obviously, Rosner has in mind the availability of permissive rulings such as R. Unterman's.

On the surface, this appears to be progress toward a definition of psychiatric hazard, yet closer reflection reveals that it reduces to no more than the standard leniency factor of "physical danger," inasmuch as the threat of suicide is the lever rather than the unique element of the mental anguish. Although Rav I. Unterman's ruling recognizes psychiatric phenomena ("suicidal tendencies," "attacks of hysteria"), the leniency in such cases emerges not from the *psychiatric* element but from the *physical danger* that may come about because of it. This is not yet a meaningful way to operationalize psychiatric hazard. Nonetheless, the appeal to the potentially life-threatening consequences of severe psychiatric disorder appears in several responsa in different applications. In order to prevent *teiruf da'ath*, mental damage or unbalance,* R. Moshe Feinstein permits eating on Yom Kippur[30] and permits a contraceptive,[31] R. Israel M. Mizrachi (18th cent.) permitted eating nonkosher broth,[32] and Rabbis Unterman, Eliezer Waldenberg, Y. Y. Weiss, and others have permitted the violation of the Sabbath in order to forestall a mental breakdown.[33] *Yet in all the cases cited here, apparently making use of some psychiatric-hazard principle, the psychiatric hazard is not considered as dangerous as the life-endangering acts which the affected individual might commit.*[34]

In order for the concept of psychiatric hazard to have full

---

* In earlier papers, I favored translating *teiruf da'ath* as what we call "psychological decompensation," or the virtual disorganization and disintegration of ego structure and reality testing. However, since "psychological decompensation" itself always requires further and more specific qualification (e.g., *Which* ego functions are involved? Have hallucinations occurred? Is reality testing totally impaired?), the same would apply when using the term *teiruf da'ath*. Thus, in view of the fact that *teiruf da'ath* is characterized in terms of gradients rather than as an absolute, the lenient rulings referred to here and elsewhere may be subsuming a very wide range of emotional states. Indeed, if even the *possibility* of causing *teiruf da'ath* is sufficient to favor a lenient ruling, then one is already talking of a less severe *actuality* than exists when one talks of the *presence* of severe psychiatric disorder.

meaning over the broad range of mental aberrations it encompasses, some precedent must be found which treats the psychological qualities of certain states of mind as a class in itself, as opposed to the potential *physical* threat which may come about because of them. *Prima facie*, it would appear that many of the emotional anxieties surrounding pregnancy or the desire to conceive are based on very rational, reality-oriented fears: fears concerning monster births and genetically inferior children, inability to truly balance economic demands with healthy emotional demands, delivering and raising a child resulting from rape, etc. Indeed, how would one classify the psychic trauma some persons may experience upon learning that they are disease carriers or are carrying a defective fetus?[35] While not everyone would become "insane" or suicidal under the influence of such fears, they may still have a disastrous emotional impact upon one's general *joie de vivre* and ability to lead a peaceful and productive existence. In such cases, it becomes invaluable to both caseworker and rabbi to be able to examine the case and formulate decisions through criteria which give evidence of Halakhah's sensitivity to just this type of "lesser" psychiatric distress as opposed to hazard and which recognize their legitimacy as a leniency factor in abortion and birth-control rulings.

Such precedent can be found. First, we note Maimonides' ruling that the psycho-physical pains of a nursing mother—e.g., her craving for certain food, despite her husband's protestation that eating what she desires may kill the child—come before all other considerations.[36] There is apparently no danger in the case upon which this ruling is based of the woman going insane. An innovative consideration was later formulated by R. Jacob Emden (d. 1776) who in his responsum uses the notion of "great pain" (*tza'ar gadol*). In a question of permitting abortion of a fetus resulting from an adulterous relationship, where the woman was now fully contrite, R. Emden finds numerous reasons to be lenient in principle, and then adds: "With a legitimate fetus too, there is room to allow abortion for 'great need,' so long as the birth process has not yet begun, *even if the reason is not to save her life—even if only to save her from the 'great pain'* it may cause her. But the matter requires further deliberation" (emphasis added).[37] Note, however, that the logic of R. Emden's ruling evolved in a case where, according to Biblical law, the woman would have the status of "bound for execution," and thus provides one with a very limited principle. Others who cite R. Emden's responsum typically seek to extract the principle of *tza'ar* as *sakanah*, and to use R. Emden's argument in conjunction with other arguments.

In response to a similar query, R. Yosef Hayim ben Eliyahu answers, "Evidently there is room to permit abortion: [quoting R. Emden and others] when disgrace [*nivul*] is involved which can be called a matter of 'great need.' But I have already said that I am issuing no ruling, merely placing the above before you for consultation with another rabbinic authority."[38] Indeed, the introduction of the additional factor of *nivul* or disgrace is significant because it expands our interpretation of *tza'ar*, especially according to authorities like *Or Sameiach* who opine that *bizyona*, or disgrace, is actually a more powerful factor than the unqualified term "*tza'ar*."[39]

Of great interest also are the responsa in which the late Chief Rabbi of Israel, Ben-Tzion Uziel (d. 1954), compares leniency in abortion for a contrite adulterous woman to the rabbinic law demanding the abortion of a fetus in a woman found guilty and about to be executed so as to prevent accidental extrusion of the fetus during the execution, thereby sparing her *nivul* (disgrace).[40] In other words, psychiatric *distress*, clearly not a threat to physical life or sanity, serves to legitimatize leniency.

Indeed, R. Uziel writes, "Abortion is not permitted in our law for no reason; that would be destructive of the possibility of life. But for a reason, even if it is a weak reason [*ta'am kalush*], such as to prevent a woman's *disgrace*, then we have precedent and authority to permit it."[41] R. Moshe Zweig, who rules permissively, agrees in principle with this line of reasoning.[42] And R. Moshe Feinstein, responding in a case where a mother who had already given birth to two deformed children would experience *great pain* and *anguish* if she were to bear more children (far more than the normal wear and tear involved in raising a family), notes that if a woman's anguish is indeed so great, then perhaps she is not so bound to her husband as to need to have intercourse in a fruitful manner. Thus, with a provisional limit of three years to his dispensation, he allows the couple to avail themselves of an acceptable method of birth control.[43]

Further examples exist. One rabbinic authority writes, in a case concerning a mother's fear that her unborn child might be epileptic, "How can we kill based on doubt? . . . whatever the author of the *Responsa Levush Mordekhai* wrote in order to permit abortion was only because of the mental anguish of the mother. But for a fear of what might be the child's lot, [we cannot permit]."[44] That is, leniency would have been forthcoming for the *mother*'s psychological distress. In yet another example, it is noted that a thalidomide baby cannot be aborted for the sake of protecting it from its fate. A concern, however, that continuation of the pregnancy would have debilitating psychological effects on the mother would justify an abortion.[45] Summarizing the tone of these rulings in the words of R. Moshe Sofer, "No woman is required to build the world through destruction of her own."[46]

The general halakhic position suggested by the examination thus far is that while the rabbinic authorities would tend not to permit abortion on the grounds of a mother's feelings or fears for the unborn child, psychiatric and medical hazards and the mother's *psychological* distress (due to fear or mental anguish) could stand as *bona fide* leniency factors.

II. ________________

Thus there is rabbinic precedent allowing psychosocial anguish (psychiatric distress) to stand as grounds for abortion and birth control. It remains to be seen, however, how "anguish" and "distress" are to be characterized and diagnosed.

R. Jakobovits has stated that "Psychiatric indication would be acceptable only if some *grave danger* to the mother is in fact anticipated to result from her fears or nervous condition as certified by a competent medical opinion" (emphasis added).[47] And there is little doubt that the caseworker/therapist is in the class of *mumcheh*, the expert, referred to by those who recommend consultation with a mental health professional prior to the issuing of a rabbinic ruling.[48] The caseworker in this sort of situation confronts two dilemmas: (1) his own discipline's limitations in predicting characterological reactions to stress and trauma, and (2) halakhic imprecision about exactly what constitutes "mental anguish," "great need," or "psychiatric distress." In an effort to enhance the psychologist's or caseworker's ability to interact with concerned rabbis, various elements constitutive of psychiatric distress from the halakhic standpoint must be delineated.

It should be remembered that evidence of a potential psychotic breakdown is superfluous to a definition of psychiatric *distress* because such disorder is severe enough to be subsumed under the rabbinic notion of *physical* danger and, as such, would readily bring about a lenient ruling. Definitions of psychiatric distress as due to extreme social disgrace (e.g., following rape), or which evoke "extreme shame," as noted by R. Zweig,[49] have crucial halakhic complications but do not satisfy the need for detail. Thus one must look elsewhere.

The Talmud forms a composite picture of the *shoteh*, or insane person, as one who exhibits a violent temper, breaks property entrusted to him, rips clothing, travels alone at night through cemeteries.[50] Maimonides notes, however, that these are to be construed as examples, and not as an exhaustive definition of the *shoteh*.[51] Thus, to speak more broadly, *sh^{e}tuth* (insanity) might denote one who has lost the ability to reason or make reality-based judgments. *Sh^{e}tuth* may also signify the loss of emotional control.[52] Indeed, the *mumcheh* must reckon with the unique halakhic status of *temporary* insanity. One authority has it that, in general, sadness, melancholy, and hyper-intense emotion eventually lead to insanity.[53] This suggests that when alerted to the presence or onset of such reactions in an individual, one is justified in assuming the significant possibility of danger. Others, however, differentiate between such extreme fears and true insanity.[54] Thus, one looks to other situations wherein Halakhah has more clearly operationalized the power of psychic distress.

Some assistance may be found in another halakhic arena: that of determining the psychiatric status of suicide victims (*m^e'abed atzmo le-da'ath*). In order for a suicide to be legally culpable for having sinned, he must have committed his self-murder while *compos mentis*. Any indication, however slight, that the death was the result of an unsound mind is mobilized in the interest of removing the stigma of suicide from the deceased. In fact, if the death resulted from an unsound mind, then halakhically it is *not* a suicide.

In this regard, the psychosocial element of "duress" is utilized to its full capacity—ranging from full-blown psychosis to depression—and this disposition enjoys majority halakhic support.[55] Duress has been defined by the existence of any one of the following in the personality of the individual in question: (1) compulsion—such as the necessity to kill oneself rather than surrender to an enemy or violate God's laws; (2) despair of life; (3) pathological identification with a loved one who has recently died; (4) self-inflicted punishment for real or imagined sinfulness or guilt (e.g., R. Chiya bar Ashi caused his own death by worrying about a sin he intended to commit and thought he had committed, but in reality did not—his pathological worry removed the stigma of suicide).[56] Most revealing are the words of the eminent authority on the subject, Rabbi J. M. Tukachinsky:

> Notice that the *Responsa Besamim Rosh* [no. 345] holds that all who kill themselves under the influence of their great anguish and despair are not considered *m^{e}abed atzmo le-da'ath* [suicides]. Yet I have already verified that his words cannot be taken literally, for if so, the concept of suicide would be obviated as all suicides come out of personal anguish. Nonetheless, when possible, one should try to utilize his [the author of the *Besamim Rosh*] theory when circumstances are even slightly indicative to allow for leniency.[57]

While halakhic categories, as a rule, do not flow readily across circumstances, there is in this discussion of suicide a good working description of psychiatric distress. It would seem probable that the same kinds of criteria can be applied in cases of abortion and birth control. In other words, the caseworker must evaluate for each individual whether becoming pregnant or carrying the pregnancy to term might result in (1) destructive self-inflicted punishment (e.g., due to introjected guilt for bringing an abnormal child into the world and thus ruining the lives of others); (2) despair of life, depression, and melancholia; or (3) any one of the so-called situational adjustment-reactions, *but only where* (a) the mitigating factor is the pregnancy or conception, *and* (b) the individual's premorbid state indicates general characterological inadequacy, personality disorder, mood lability, etc.[58] As has been noted, some intense forms of non-life-threatening *tza'ar*, or *bizyona*, are likened by R. Moshe Feinstein to the highly efficacious category of *michush she-mitzta'er mimenu kol gufo*[59] whose existence in the client's psychological profile deserves mention to the halakhic authority. If applicable, the caseworker should consider these as symptomatic of the type of psychiatric distress Halakhah considers significant and so inform the consulting rabbinic authority.

The caseworker must be on guard for inauthentic appeals to these principles as well. For example, one client harbored latent hostility toward her husband and, in extension, toward her unborn child. She claimed to be extremely concerned that the child was genetically defective. A battery of medical examinations and even amniocentesis revealed that there was no cause for such anxiety. In reality, she was subconsciously intent on punishing her husband. While it may be a genuine concern that the child might want for a better caretaker, should it be born to a woman so predisposed with hostility toward it, there was still insufficient warrant from the standpoint of her psychiatric profile to advocate the abortion. In this case, further psychotherapy focusing on marital issues was successful in eliminating the individual's "need" for abortion. To give another example, while psychoanalysis is generally not undertaken with pregnant patients, when it is, or when pregnancy occurs during on-going psychoanalytic therapy, a sudden claim of interest in an abortion may, in reality, be a transference ploy on the part of the patient.[60] In this instance the woman's interest in an abortion is an artifact of the dynamic relationship between patient and doctor and must be analyzed rather that acted upon. Thus, the caseworker must differentiate the pathological use of the psychiatric principle from its genuine usage and duly inform the rabbi.

Another concept which may significantly clarify the psychologist's role in determining the presence of psychiatric distress is *shalom bayith*, or marital or domestic harmony. *Shalom bayith*, besides its ethico-moral implications, has its own halakhic function in the justification of continued marriage while seeking marital counseling to restore a marriage's damaged union and balance, when contraception is made necessary, and even when childlessness is the lot of a couple. Based on the principle "Great is peace, for even God tampered with the truth to preserve it,"[61] the Talmud and later rabbinic responsa adduced *shalom bayith* as a leniency factor in various legal circumstances. For example, in a discussion of halakhic problems surrounding contraception, R. Feinstein concludes that the factor of preserving marital peace is at least one important factor in ruling leniently in select circumstances.[62] In yet another case, R. Feinstein considers the cause of peace so great as to allow an individual to marry, in the first place, a woman who for medical reasons would need to practice birth control temporarily.[63]

Another element of marital life crucial to *shalom bayith*, besides healthy interpersonal understanding and communication, is the quality of sexual satisfaction.[64] One sage considered his loss of sexual interest the cessation of the mechanism of domestic peace.[65] Moreover, *onah*, the marital aspect of sexuality in Jewish life, is halakhically distinct from the procreative aspect, *p^eru ur^evu*.[66] *Onah* deals directly with "the fulfillment of her yearnings."[67] So powerful is the *shalom bayith* factor that, when halakhic discretion warrants, it can obviate many difficulties inherent in the concept of birth control.[68] Indeed, the following is characteristic of the rabbinic viewpoint: "Not the physical hazard [*sakanath n^efashoth*] concept was needed to set aside the prohibition [against birth control]; it was annulled by the more important reason: not to separate the couple."[69]

The above establishes that a substantial threat to *shalom bayith* would be a strong consideration in the diagnosis of psychiatric distress. To be sure, halakhic authorities differ regarding what factors they will allow to play a role in their willingness to be lenient in the case of contraception as opposed to the case of abortion (although less so when dealing with abortion prior to the fortieth day of gestation). But it is the mental health professional's role to submit his or her judgment of the client's psychological status as revealed by standard methods of assessment and diagnosis. Generally, then, in cases of non-life-threatening psychiatric danger, the caseworker should consider: (1) what would happen to the relationship between husband and wife if said child was born or if future childbearing was not forestalled; (2) how deeply such a strain would extend; (3) what the effects would be, if any, on the mother's ability to meet both her needs as well as those of the rest of her family in an appropriate manner; (4) whether there could be an eventual adjustment to this strain in view of previous ability to cope with crisis; (5) whether a possible change for the better can be foreseen even when, at present, distress is highly indicated, or would relationships, etc., tend to get progressively worse? When the latter two factors are evident, the caseworker must consider whether the woman (or couple) in question would be able to develop different views on the need for abortion or birth control if there was an opportunity for immediate counselling on alternatives. In such cases, crisis counselling is more halakhically appropriate than contraception or abortion.

In this regard, the issue of permitting birth control for the sake of "spacing" children comes to mind. The rabbinic disposition here appears to be a cautious one, to say the least. There was a time when becoming pregnant while still nursing represented a potential hazard to the existing child, since hormonal changes brought about by pregnancy curtail the mother's milk production. Some authorities feel that this condition has changed.[70] Other authorities permitted an abortion in such a case because of the assumed physical risk to the existing child.[71] Of course, the availability of bottled formula generally makes this issue academic. R. Simon Pollak (d. 1919) of Rumania permitted birth control during the nursing period on the grounds that the woman was "weak" and the physician said she needed rest, regardless of the risk to the child.[72] On the other hand, R. Moshe Feinstein writes, "What you heard in the name of a rabbi in Lithuania that the rabbis there permitted contraception to women for two years after each childbirth, is simply not true . . . only danger legitimates the use of contraception."[73] Nevertheless, leniency in the application of spacing children for temporary periods of time has found advocates among halakhic authorities such as most recently R. Yosef Henkin (*Responsa Bnei Banim*, no. 30). And as throughout the preceding discussion, psychological factors must be considered as well.

Conclusion

In this chapter we have discussed the problem of determining parameters which might facilitate the use of the concept of "psychiatric hazard" as a leniency factor in rabbinic dispensations regarding birth control and abortion. A "psychiatric hazard" principle and a lesser "psychiatric *distress*" consideration are firmly grounded in the halakhic tradition but suffer from lack of definition and yet, despite this lack of definition, the caseworker may be called upon to assist the rabbinic authority in determining whether psychiatric distress exists, and may be unclear as to the relevant criteria for determining such conditions in accordance with Halakhah.

The difference between psychiatric hazard as a *threat to physical life* and psychiatric *distress* was pointed out, showing that "mental anguish" and "great pain"—where both are neither life-threatening nor psychotic in nature—are halakhic leniency factors. It was also observed that the psychiatric distress principle draws its legitimacy from concern for the mother and not from any probable pity for the child. Diagnostic clues to psychiatric distress were obtained from an analysis of "duress" in volitional suicide: (1) threat of self-inflicted punishment; (2) pathological despair of life; and (3) prior personality disorders or inadequacies. The element of severe shame or disgrace as a factor was also noted. Finally, by introducing the concept of *shalom bayith* and its preservation, the elements of marital and intrafamilial distress and the issue of future adjustment were added.

I believe these guidelines to be appropriate ones for the caseworker from the standpoint of mental health and adjustment as well as from that of the Halakhah. Guided in this fashion, the caseworker can contribute positively to both of these aspects of the client's life by virtue of the appropriate information about the client that the caseworker is able to transmit to the halakhic authority, and by further helping the client to come to terms with the eventual halakhic ruling. The warning given by Maimonides, however, remains critical in the task of establishing the definition of mental or emotional status: "The matter is dependent on the assessment of the *dayan* [judge] because it is not possible to give an exact assessment of the mind in writing."[74]

As mentioned above, a halakhically acceptable variation in halakhic norms is itself a halakhic mode of behavior. Thus, when the situation warrants opting for alternatives to birth and conception, such options may be assumed with clear conscience.

Only the pious fool is stringent where such strictness may lead to halakhically undesirable states or to conditions that are hazardous to mental and physical well-being. On the other hand, there is a strong counter-current: the timeworn and deeply etched tradition in Jewish life involving the acceptance of *yisurin*, pains, and *nisyonoth*, tests of faith, where such are deemed ineluctable aspects of the Divine-natural plan. Many deeply observant and knowledgeable Jews nurture an attitudinal instinct, if you will, that our faith in God the Provider must overcome any fears one has about the ability to support or care for children, no matter how apparently valid be the basis of the fear.

R. Moshe Tendler, a contemporary halakhic authority, notes for example, that the Malthusian specter of overpopulating the world is not a factor for the Jew to consider when debating the need for contraception.[75] True, insofar as the principle of "He who provided life will provide sustenance"[76] is concerned. However, when physical or psychological threats enter the discussion, a halakhically unique light is cast on "economic considerations," which are then to be viewed as physical or psychological first and economic only second. And here, I think, in view of the sometimes deep-seated and potentially destructive fears related to conception and pregnancy, one cannot appeal to faith alone—with all due respect to the proven wisdom of not promulgating generalized lenient rulings before the lay public.

It would certainly be well and good if Jewish educators and *rabbanim* could make successful efforts to deal with the weak psychological, existential, and religious frameworks which dispose many people today to be pessimistic about their ability to raise children "in quality surroundings and conditions." Yet this is preventative psychiatry and certainly is not the appropriate response in cases where all previous educational or spirit-fortifying discussions and other efforts have run their course unsuccessfully. One never truly rules out the possibility that a spiritual leader's or husband's or family's supportive role will somehow result in the type of fortitude that enables one to overcome apparent crises. But when a rabbinic authority has ultimately decided that more radical measures must be taken to deal with the crisis at hand, the mental health professionals who are asked to assist in this process must proceed forthrightly with an assessment of the current situation which will best inform the final halakhic decision. Halakhic latitude is being suggested here precisely for those whose acute crises are beyond the assistance of psychosocial and religious-attitudinal counseling.

Notes

1. D.S. Shapiro, "The Ideological Foundations of the Halakhah," *Tradition 9*, nos. 1-2 (1967): 100. See also the references to the all-inclusive and dynamic quality of Halakhah in Rabbi Joseph B. Soloveitchik, "*Ish ha-Halakhah*," *Talpiot* (1944): p. 665 and his "Sacred and Profane: *Kodesh* and *Chol* in World Perspectives," *Gesher, 3* no. 1 (1966).
2. *Eruv.* 29a; *Sanh.* 20b; *Kid.* 36b; *Sot.* 47a-b; *A.Z.* 8b; *Zev.* 112b.
3. *M.T. Hil. Mamrim* 2:1. Also consider the concept of *nishtaneh ha-teva: Magen Avraham* to *Sh. A., Orach Chayyim* 179:6, 173:1; *M.K.* 11a, *Tos.*, s.v. *kavra*; A.Z. 24b, *Tos.*, s.v. *parah.* Halakhah recognizes that the human personality is flexible, yet no personality change could ever obviate Sinaitic laws. See *Resp. Maharam Shick, Y.D.* no. 244 cited in *Sedei Chemed*, 1962, vol. 3, p. 8. Nor would it override a prevailing *chazakah* in a circumstance where we give priority to a *mi'ut*, such as in the case of danger (see *Sedei Chemed*, vol. 8, p. 237). Even where Halakhah seems to allow for situational latitude—implied by Deut. 6:18, 12:28, 26:17; Lev. 19:2; *Git.* 59b; *B.M.* 16b, 30b, 108a—such halakhic flexibility is based on prior, objective halakhic rules; see *Ramban*, Lev. 19:2. The realm of *derekh eretz* or *lifnim mi-shurath ha-din*—acting beyond the level strictly required by law—also falls within the scope of normative Halakhah. This last issue is further discussed by A. Lichtenstein, "Does Jewish Tradition Recognize an Ethic Independent of Halakhah," in *Contemporary Jewish Ethics*, ed. M.M. Kellner (New York: 1978), pp. 102-24, originally published in M. Fox, ed., *Modern Jewish Ethics: Theory and Practice* (Columbus: 1975), and in notes 44 and 60 of L. Kaplan's "The Religious Philosophy of Rabbi Joseph Soloveitchik," *Tradition 14*, no. 2 (1973): 43-64. Without citing more sources, the point is that there is a comfortable margin for so-called subjective phenomena, even within an objective, *a priori* system, which in no way alters the essential halakhic status of such subjective phenomena. Even the most subjective discrimination will ultimately be rooted to a highly formal halakhic structure—and thus even the subjective discrimination represents an ontic realization of Halakhah. Finally, for an excellent discussion of the role of novel input from outside reality in the creation of Halakhah, see Rav B. De-Pris, "*Ha-Uvdah k^e-Gorem l^e-Chiddush Halakhah*," in M. Kasher, N. Lamm, & L. Rosenfeld (eds.), *Leo Jung Jubilee Volume* (New York: 1962): 143-48.
4. Deut. 19:6, 12:20, 17:14; *Kid.* 21b; *Sanh.* 81b; *Suk.* 82a; *Ber.* 16b; *Sh. A., Orach Chayyim* 13:3, 25:1, 613:4, 639:1. See *Arukh ha-Shulchan*: *Y.D.* 116:15, 21, 24.

5. However, cf. R. Israel, "The Elusive Appeal to Authority in Rabbinic Counseling and Social Casework," *Journal of Jewish Communal Service 45* (1969): 303-11.
6. *Sanh.* 6b; *B.B.* 131a; see *Resp. R. Abraham ben ha-Rambam*, no. 97, pp. 147-48.
7. See above, chap. 1, and my "Critical Review" section of the *Journal of Psychology and Judaism*, vol. 1, nos. 1 and 2, vol. 2, nos. 1 and 2, vol. 3, nos. 2 and 3.
8. J.D. Bleich, "Abortion in Halakhic Literature," *Tradition 10*, no. 2 (1968): 101.
9. For a basic discussion, including ample references, of the prohibition against birth control and abortion when not halakhically permissible, see F. Rosner, "The Jewish Attitude Toward Abortion," *Tradition 10*, no. 2 (1968): 48-71, and in *Contemporary Jewish Ethics*, ed. M.M. Kellner (New York: 1978), pp. 257-69; Bleich, "Abortion in Halakhic Literature"; I. Jakobovits, *Jewish Law Faces Modern Problems* (New York: 1965) and *Jewish Medical Ethics* ("Abortion and Embryotomy") (New York: 1959); D. Feldman, *Marital Relations, Birth Control, and Abortion in Jewish Law* (New York: 1974); most recently, J.D. Bleich, "*Hapalah M^e^lakhutith l^e^-Or ha-Halakhah*," *Or ha-Mizrach 26*, nos. 2-3 (1978): 185-93; S. Raphael, "*Hapaloth M^e^lakhutioth*," *Torah she-ba'al-Peh* no. 18 (1976): 89-94, and A. Steinberg, "Induced Abortion According to Jewish Law," *Journal of Halachah and Contemporary Society 1*, no. 1 (1981): 29-52.
10. See E. Beck et al., "Advocacy and Compliance in Genetics Screening: Behavior of Physicians and Clients in a Voluntary Program of Testing for the Tay-Sachs Gene," *New England Journal of Medicine 291* (1974): 1166-70.
11. Mishnah *Oholoth* 7:6; *M.T., Hil. Rotzeach u-Shmirath ha-Nefesh* 1:9; I. Unterman, *Resp. Shevet mi-Yehudah* (Jerusalem: 1955), p. 26; M. Zweig, in *Noam 7* (1964): 49-53.
12. *Sanh.* 72b; *J.T. Shab.* 14:4; *M.T., Hil. Rotzeach* 1:9.
13. The condom, for example, being the least acceptable generally (however, where necessary to prevent *sakanah*, see *Resp. Igroth Moshe: E.H.*, vol. 1, no. 63, pp. 152-63), and the oral contraceptive (its harmful side-effects notwithstanding), spermicidal, and diaphragm being the most acceptable. Determining the means of contraception involves rabbi, physician, and individual. For an exhaustive review, see F. Rosner, "Contraception in Jewish Law," *Tradition 13*, no. 1 (1971): 90-103.
14. B.Z. Uziel, *Resp. Mishpetei Uziel* (Tel Aviv: 1936), vol. 3, nos. 46-47.
15. I.M. Mizrachi, *Resp. P'ri ha-Aretz: Y.D.* (Constantinople: 1721), no. 21; N.Z. Friedman, *Resp. Netzer Mata'ai* (B'nai B'rak: 1958), vol. 1, no. 8.
16. See I. Jakobovits, "Introduction: Review of Recent Halakhic Literature," *Tradition 4*, no. 1 (1961): 96-97.
17. "Recent Statements on Jewish Medical Ethics," *Proceedings of the Association of Orthodox Jewish Scientists 3-4* (1976): 6. Note that throughout the remainder of this study I am not concerned with situations wherein the physical or psychological danger to the mother is caused by extraneous variables which the pregnancy happens to exacerbate; e.g., if a woman is threatened with mental

illness due to some organic brain syndrome—and happens to be pregnant. In such circumstances, many authorities would not be lenient—e.g., I. Lamprenti, *Pachad Yitzchak: Erekh N[e]falim* (Lyck: 1846), p. 79b; C.O. Grodzinsky, *Achiezer* (New York: 1946), vol. 3, no. 72; I. Schor, *Resp. Koach Shor* (Kolomyya: 1888), no. 20; Y. Weinberg, *Seridei Esh* (Jerusalem: 1966), vol. 3, no. 127 (end).

18. See the recent statements of major Orthodox rabbinic groups to follow in general circumstances the stringent view of *Rambam*, in J. David Bleich, "Sexuality and Procreation: An Address," pp. 1-11, In I. Franck ed. , *Biomedical Ethics in the Perspective of Jewish Tradition and Teaching: Proceedings of an Academic Conference* (Nov. 13, 1977) (Washington, D.C., 1980). *Rambam*'s view is also reinterpreted by R. Chayyim Ozer Gradzinsky in *Resp. Achiezer*, vol. 3, no. 72, who does not feel *Rambam* considers aborting a fetus to be murder; and also see Y. Weinberg, *Resp. Seridei Esh*, vol. 3, no. 167, who states that the majority of *poskim* do not hold with the *Rambam*. (Although he adds in a footnote that he has recently seen Rabbi Unterman's strict interpretation, he finds this view needing further clarification.)

19. *M.T. Hil. Rotzeach* 1:9; *Sh. A., Choshen Mishpat* 425.

20. M. Zweig, in *Noam* 7 (1964): 49-53.

21. *Sanh.* 73a.

22. Lev. 19:16.

23. Y. Bachrach, *Chavot Yair* (Lemberg: 1896), no. 31; *Resp. Koach Shor*, no. 20; *P'ri Megadim* to *Sh. A., Orach Chayyim* 328:1; Y. Landau, *Resp. Noda be-Yehudah: H.M.* (Vilna: 1904), no. 59; Y. Eybeschuetz, *Resp. Urim ve-Tumim*, 30:103; Y. Teitelbaum, *Resp. Avnei Tzedek: H.M.* (Sighet: 1886), no. 19; S. Zalman of Lublin, *Resp. Torath Chesed* (Jerusalem: 1909), vol. 2, no. 42; I.Z. Meltzer, *Even ha-Ezel to M.T. Hil. Chovel u-Mazik* 8:15 (Jerusalem: 1935). See esp. *Achiezer*, vol. 3, no. 72 [3].

24. *M.T. Hil. Rotzeach* 1:6.

25. Y. Teitelbaum, *Resp. Avnei Tzedek.*

26. Shlomo ha-Kohen, *Cheshek Shlomo*, in *Yedei Moshe* (Piotrkow: 1897), 8, no. 5. See also *Seridei Esh*, vol. 1, p. 307 and 315, note 18.

27. *Shevet mi-Yehudah* (Jerusalem: 1955), p. 26, and *Noam 6* (1963): 6-7.

28. "*Mitzvath Pikuach Nefesh u-Gedarehah*," *Ha-Torah ve-ha-Medinah 4* (1952): 22-29.

29. F. Rosner, "Tay-Sachs Disease: To Screen or Not to Screen," *Tradition* (1976): 108.

30. *Resp. Igroth Moshe: E.H.* (New York: 1964), vol. 1, no. 65.

31. Ibid., vol. 1, no. 65, vol. 3, no. 22.

32. *Resp. P'ri ha-Aretz: Y.D.*, vol. 3, no. 2, based on *Yoma* 82a-b.

33. *Ha-Torah ve-ha-Medinah 4* (1952): 29; *Resp. Tzitz Eliezer*, vol. 8, no. 15, chap. 13(5), "*... choleh ruach nikra choleh mesukan*": Y.Y. Weiss, *Resp. Minchath Yitzchak* (Jerusalem: 1969), vol. 1, no. 115, vol. 3, nos. 25(5)-26(2), permits abortion for threat of *teiruf da'ath*, and in vol. 4, nos. 8 (2-12) permits violation of the Sabbath for same reason.

I wish to entertain two interesting digressions at this point. The first concerns a serious error contained in an entry in the *Encyclopaedia Judaica* under the heading "Psychology," which cites the *Resp. Nachalath Shevah*, no. 83, as permitting violation of the Sabbath in order to spare an individual from "a state of emotional anxiety." In fact, the responsum cited refers to violating the Sabbath in order to save an individual who had left his *faith* ("*ha-yotzeh chutz l^e-dath l^e-hamir b^e-dath Yishmaeli*") and not one who left his *senses* (*da'ath*)!

The second digression concerns the issue of violating the Sabbath in order to prevent *teiruf da'ath*. First, *teiruf da'ath* is best translated as "psychological decompensation" since it does not refer to any specific condition, as do, for example, *kordiakus* and *marah shechorah*. Yet this means that *teiruf da'ath* must always be specifically qualified in terms of gravity, extent, and duration. The above-mentioned responsa—as well as others, such as *Resp. Tashbatz*, vol. 1, no. 54, and *Resp. Radbaz*, vol. 4, no. 66—who permit the violation of Sabbath norms to prevent *teiruf da'ath*, have as a basis for support the Talmud, *Shab.* 128b, which allows lighting a candle for a woman in labor in order to spare her similar psychic anguish (and see *Tur Sh. A., Orach Chayyim* 330). These responsa accept that the Sabbath may be violated even for *teiruf da'ath* which is not specifically related to the actual course of medical treatment (see esp. *Resp. Tashbatz*). Interestingly, *Rambam* addresses this need to prevent *teiruf da'ath* in three instances which indicate that he does not maintain unilateral leniency in this regard. In *M.T., Hil. Shabbath* 2:11, *Rambam* rules, following the Talmud in *Shab.* 128b, that one may light a candle for a woman in labor in order to spare her *teiruf da'ath* (and significantly requires, when permitting carrying oil to her labor room, that the act be done with a *shinnuy*). In *Hil. A.Z.* 11:11, however, *Rambam* permits snake-charming for a snake-bitten patient, even though he considers it useless, because it will nonetheless prevent *teiruf da'ath* in the patient. And the commentaries note that *Rambam* is permitting this act even on the Sabbath, when "meaningless chatter" is forbidden. Finally, in *Hil. Zekhiya u-Matanah* 8:2, *Rambam* permits validating the "contract" of a *shekhiv mera*, a deathly ill patient, even on the Sabbath, in order to prevent his *teiruf da'ath*, but only because the verbal instructions of the *shekhiv mera* are valid as contractual in themselves (and, thus, the additional "validation" is not truly a *melakhah* which would violate the Sabbath). Clearly *Rambam* differentiates between women in labor, sickness in general, and the deathly ill person insofar as the degree of otherwise forbidden activity that can be permitted in order to prevent *teiruf da'ath* is concerned. (See *Kesef Mishneh* and *Lechem Mishneh*, to *M.T. Hil. Shab.* 2:11.)

Y.H. Henkin, in a recent halakhic essay ("*Nokhachath ha-Ba'al be-Cheder ha-Leidah*," *Assia* 5, no. 3[1978]: 44-52), suggests in his own analysis of aspects of this issue that *Rambam* differentiates between *teiruf da'ath* which signifies threat to survival—the case of the woman in labor and perhaps even of *cholim* in general—and *teiruf da'ath* as a less dangerous consequence of not having one's instructions obeyed—the case of the *shekhiv mera* (as *Rambam* specifically states, "*keday she-lo titraf da'ato alav ke-she'yeyda she-ein dvarav kayamim*"). Thus, violation of prohibitions for such "*teiruf da'ath*" can only occur in limited circumstances, such as where the act in question would not be a true *melakhah* in any case. Also note that *Rambam* would not regard the pregnant woman (i.e., not in labor) as similar to the woman in labor with regard to being lenient in permitting *abortion* to prevent *teiruf da'ath*.

Finally, M. Briesh, *Resp. Chelkath Yaakov*, vol. 1, no. 72, and *Resp. Igroth Moshe: O.H.*, vol. 1, no. 127, permit violation of the Sabbath in order to prevent suicide—an interesting and important point inasmuch as the danger feared in this case is a probability rather than a surety. Thus, these responsa are permitting violation of the Sabbath for a *safek sakanath cholei ha-nefesh!*

34. See, for example, *Resp. Igroth Moshe: E.H.*, vol. 1, no. 22, where Rabbi Feinstein speaks of a mother threatened by *nerven brachen*, or "nervous breakdown." He makes it quite clear that "insanity threatens the life of the mother and of the people around her." See also *Igroth Moshe: E.H.*, vol. 1, no. 65; *Resp. P'ri ha-Aretz: Y.D.*, vol. 3, no. 2; M. Mizrachi, *Admath Kodesh* (Constantina: 1742), vol. 1, no. 6; M. Winkler, *Resp. Lebushei Mordekhai: H.M.* (Budapest: 1922), no. 39. That the laws of *pikuach nefesh* apply to mental health danger as well as to physical risk is restated by N.Z. Friedman, *Resp. Netzer Mata'ai*, no. 8.

35. See above, n. 10.

36. *M.T. Hil. Ishuth* 21:11. See also n. 68 below.

37. *Resp. She'elath Yavetz* (Altona: 1739), vol. 1, no. 43. See additional critique of his view in *Resp. Tzitz Eliezer*, vol. 9, no. 51(6).

38. *Or Sameach* to *M.T. Hil. Sanhedrin* 15:1, and see also *Resp. Chavot Ya'ir*, no. 191.

39. *Resp. Rav Pe'alim: E.H.* (Jerusalem: 1905), vol. 1, no. 4.

40. *Resp. Mishpetei Uziel: H.M.*, vol. 3, nos. 46-47.

41. Ibid., no. 47, though he does not permit abortion to an unwed and consenting mother; and see n. 37 above.

42. *Noam* 7 (1964): 47-48.

43. *Resp. Igroth Moshe: E.H.*, vol. 3, no. 12.

44. D. Sperber, *Resp. Afarkeseth de-Anya* (Satmar: 1940), no. 169.

45. I. Jakobovits, "Jewish Law Faces Modern Problems," pp. 74-76; E. Waldenberg, *Resp. Tzitz Eliezer* (Jerusalem; 1967), vol. 9, no. 237, permitted abortion only during the first trimester and in the absence of fetal movement. However, since he does *not* view lenient rulings on feticide as tantamount to permitting *retzichah*, he has recently reasoned that abortion, when the proper need arises, could be permitted until delivery of the child, but states finally that he only permits abortion up to the seventh month. See "Medico-Halakhic Aspects of Tay-Sachs," *Assia* 4, no. 1 (13) (1976): 8-10, and recently as a full responsum, "*Al Darkei Heter ha-Palath Ubar le-Tzorekh Gadol u-Meyuchad Biglal ha-Machalah ha-Nikreth Tay-Sachs*," in A. Steinberg, *Hilkhoth Rofeim u-Refuah al pi Tzitz Eliezer* (Jerusalem; 1978), pp. 33-46. See also S. Yisraeli, *Resp. Amud ha-Yemini* (Jerusalem: 1966), no. 32; M. Zweig, "*Al Hapalah M'lakhutith*," *Noam* 9 (1966): 193-215.

46. *Resp. Chatham Sofer: E.H.* (Vienna: 1855), vol. 2, no. 20, *O.H.*, no. 83. See also the comments of R. Meir Simchah, *Meshekh Chakhmah* to Gen. 9:7, and *Ket.* 83b, *Tos.*, s.v. *mitha shkhichah*.

47. I. Jakobovits to F. Rosner, May 24, 1968.

48. See *Resp. Igroth Moshe: Y.D.*, vol. 2, no. 57.

49. In *Noam 7* (1964): 47-48, based on *Shab.* 50b, *Tos.*, s.v. *bishvil.* In a more recent essay, Rabbi Jakobovits states that rape would not qualify as sufficient warrant for abortion because this would remove a substantial deterrent to sin: "Jewish Views on Abortion," in *Abortion and the Law*, ed. D. Smith (Cleveland: 1967), chap. 6. However, rape would certainly fall under the category of *bizyona.*
50. *Chag.* 3a-b; *Shab.* 105b; *Sanh.* 65b; *Niddah* 17a.
51. *M.T., Hil. Eduth* 9:9-11, and see *Kesef Mishnah* loc. cit; *Seridei Esh*, vol. 3, no. 35.
52. 1 Sam. 20:14-15; see M. Gorlin, "Mental Illness in Biblical Literature," *Proceedings of the Association of Orthodox Jewish Scientists 2* (1970): 43-62, for an excellent review of the Biblical view of insanity. See also chap. 1, no. 8, above.
53. *Resp. Chatham Sofer: E.H.*, vol. 2, no. 2.
54. R. Aaron Shimon b. Jacob, *Or ha-Yashar* (1902): p. 36. *Resp. Atereth Chakhamim: E.H.*, no. 17, rejects the opinion suggested by some that the *shtuth* which comes from *marah shechorah* (depression?), which he considers melancholia (*mel'anka'alia*), is not bona fide *shtuth*. He notes that under the heading "melancholia" are some full-blown mental disorders (*meshuga'im gemurim*), "as is known to anyone who has studied the texts on these matters." He notes that *Rambam* considers *kordiakus* a form of *ruach ra'ah* (see also chap. 9, n. 33, above) and that in *M.T. Hil. Shechitah 2, Rambam* compares the slaughter of a *shochet* who is a *cheresh, shoteh,* or *katan* to that of one who is overtaken by *ruach ra'ah.* It is also critical that *Rambam*, in *Peirush ha-Mishnayoth: Shab.* 29b ("*ha-mikhabeh eth ha-ner . . . mipnei ruach ra'ah*"), writes, "*Ruach ra'ah* is the name for many types of illness, and it is called in Arabic *malkuniya*," which, he explains, means the illness of those who desire no social company and who love solitude and darkness (*ve-tanuach nafsho hithbodeduth*). *Atereth Chakhamim* concludes that if melancholia reaches such proportions that one is also mentally disoriented (*me'turaf be-da'ath*), then, certainly according to *Rambam*, this is bona fide *shtuth*. Yet, he adds, simply dwelling alone is not sufficient; as *Rambam* stresses "*mi she-haytah ruach ra'ah meva'ato*," or that such melancholia must reach proportions of full mental disorientation. In a similar discussion of the role of *shtuth, Sedei Chemed*, vol. 5 (*Ma'areketh Ishuth 2*), pp. 119-29, cites the Mishnah in *Bekh.* 7:5, which refers to *ruach katzrith*, which is explained by the Talmud (44b) as *ruach ben nefalim* (falling sickness or epilepsy) and by Rashi as *ruach shtuth, al yedei sheid*, or, following *Rambam* and R. Ovadiah mi-Bartenuro, a type of disability caused also by *marah shechorah*, whereby one loses control of or sensation in one's limbs. Medini opines that *ruach ra'ah*, to qualify as bona fide *shtuth*, needs to satisfy the criteria noted earlier, and perhaps those in *Chagigah* or elsewhere in the Talmud, but that *Rambam*'s position would require that an individual exhibit such debilitation continuously, or at least three times (see *M.T., Hil. Eduth* 9:9, "*kol mi she-nitrafah da'ato ve-nimtzaet da'ato me'shubesheth tamid*"). Medini also notes that the case of interest would be an individual who is considered *me'shugah* but appears to be a *bar da'ath* in all respects except that his mind is disordered (i.e., irrational). According to *Rambam*, there is no need for this individual to also exhibit the symptoms noted in *Chagigah*. And thus the *kordiakus*, though he appears normal in every other way, would be considered a

bona fide *shoteh* despite the absence of the more conspicuous criteria cited in *Chagigah*. According to *Chatham Sofer* (*E.H.*, vol. 2, no. 2) anyone who "appears" normal in that he does not act bizarrely yet who still cannot respond appropriately to questions would be legally unfit as a *cheresh* even if, according to others, he could not be considered a *shoteh*. (This also challenges Hankoff's and Rosner's conclusions, in L.D. Hankoff, "Ancient Descriptions of Organic Brain Syndrome: The '*Kordiakos*' of the Talmud," *Am. J. Psychiatr. 129*, no. 2 (1972): 147-150; F. Rosner,"*Kordiakos* in the Talmud," *Isra. Ann. Med. Sci. 10* (1974): 278-281; see also M. Gordon, " '*Mi she-Achazo Kodiakos' be-Talmud u-be-Mada ha-Refu'i*," *Perakim 3* (1963): 117-130.

55. J.M. Tukachinsky, *Gesher ha-Chayyim* (Jerusalem: 1960), vol. 1, chap. 15; cf. *M.T., Hil. Sanhedrin* 18:6.

56. *Kid.* 81b.

57. Cited in *Pitchei T'shuvah: Y.D*: 345:2 and in Tukachinsky, *Gesher ha-Chayyim*, 1960, p. 273. Grunwald, *Kol Bo al Aveiluth*, vol. 1 (New York: 1973), p. 319, cites those who doubted the authenticity of this responsum attributed to the *Rosh*. However, see its use in *Arukh ha-Shulchan: Y.D.*: 345:5. Others who accept the view expressed in *Besamim Rosh* are J.S. Nathanson, *Resp. Sho'el u-Meishiv*, vol. 3, no. 217, *Maharsham, (Y.D.)* vol. 6, no. 49, *Beth Ephraim: Y.D.*, no.56. Curiously, *Resp. Chatham Sofer: E.H.*, vol. 1, no. 69 and *Y.D.*, no. 326, seeks to disprove the view of *Besamim Rosh* but upholds its essential approach in the references cited in n. 51 above (*E.H.*, vol. 2, no. 2). Additional support for the view that suicide represents a form of *non compos mentis*, relevant in this application as well as in others, comes from *Rambam*'s statement in *M.T., Hil. Sanhedrin* 18:6: "It is a decree of the Writ that *Beth Din* neither executes nor flogs an individual based simply on his own confession but rather through testimony from two witnesses . . . Sanhedrin does not execute or flog one who confesses a transgression *lest he happens to be deranged* [*nitrefah da'ato ba-dabar zeh*]; lest he be one of those troubled, bitter [melancholy] souls, who design to die, who thrust swords in their bellies and throw themselves from roofs; lest he [who comes to confess a capital crime] be one of these persons, and he says that he did something he did *not* do just so that he should be put to death." (Thus, it would also seem that a person who enjoys remission of a suicidal state is surely obligated to recite *birkath ha-gomel*.) Possibly, *Rambam* intended to differentiate between someone who is irrational in a specific domain (*ba-dabar zeh*), confessing to everything without regard to the consequences, and the more globally disturbed patient whose *teiruf da'ath* motivates him to self-destruction as an end in itself; no less *me'turaf* given *Rambam*'s equation of melancholia with *teiruf da'ath*.

58. Jakobovits, in the personal communication cited above in n. 47, states that "abortion would be acceptable . . . only on the basis of previous experiences of mental strain by the mother."

59. *Resp. Igroth Moshe: O.H.*, vol. 3, no. 53, and see *Rama* to *Sh.A., O.H.*, 325.

60. See R. Mester, "Requests for Abortion: A Psychiatrist's View," *Israeli Annals of Psychiatry and Related Disciplines 14*, no. 3 (1976): 294-99. Other psychiatric literature relevant to the psychological aspects of abortion and abortion requests

is: W.C. Brennan, "Abortion and the Techniques of Neutralization," *Journal of Health and Social Behavior 15*, no. 4 (1974): 358-65 (who examines the various defense mechanisms utilized by both givers and receivers of abortions); F. Dunbar, "The Psychosomatic Approach to Abortion and the Abortion Habit," in *Therapeutic Abortion*, ed. F. Rosen (New York: 1954), pp. 22-31 (where she introduces the notion of "postabortion hangover" and the ability of such guilt to cause spontaneous abortion of subsequent conceptions); N. Ekbald,"Induced Abortion on Psychiatric Grounds," *Acta Psychiatrica Scand. 1* (1955): 90-102 (who finds that postabortion guilt may motivate intentional or "unintentional" reimpregnation); N. Simon and A. Senturia, "Psychiatric Sequelae of Abortion: Review of the Literature—1935-1964," *Archives of General Psychiatry 15* (1966): 378-89 (who note that *pre*abortion psychiatric illness tends to continue after abortion!); J. Wallerstein, P. Kurtz, and D. Bar, "Psychosocial Sequelae of Therapeutic Abortion in Unmarried Women," *Archives of General Psychiatry 27* (1972): 828-32 (a discussion of postabortion effects in unmarried women); and an excellent discussion of the gross stress reaction to abortion in R. Weiss and H. Payson, "Gross Stress Reaction," in *Comprehensive Textbook of Psychiatry*, ed. A. Freedman and H. Kaplan (Baltimore: 1968), pp. 1027-31.

61. *Yev.* 65b; *Ned.* 66b; *Chul.* 141a; *Shab.* 116b; *Makot* 11a; *Suk.* 53b.

62. *Resp. Igroth Moshe: E.H.*, vol. 1, no. 63, p. 152.

63. Ibid., no. 67—N.B. the man in question in this case already had a child through a previous marriage.

64. Eccles. R. 12:5; *Yev.* 62b; *Eruv.* 100b; *M.T.*, *Hil. De'oth* 5:4, *Hil. Isurei Biah* 21:11; *Sh. A.*; *Orach Chayyim* 240:10, *Even ha-Ezer* 25:2.

65. *Shab.* 152a; see Rashi loc. cit.

66. *M.T. Hil. Ishuth* 15:1; *Resp. Igroth Moshe: E.H.*, no. 102.

67. Rabad, *Ba'alei ha-Nefesh: Shar ha-Kedushah* (Jerusalem: 1955), p. 131; *Menorath ha-Ma'or* (Jerusalem: 1961), *Ner* 3:4, v., pp. 369-71; *M.T. Hil. De'oth* 4:19.

68. A. Sofer, *Resp. K'tav Sofer: E.H.* (Pressburg: 1873), no. 26; S. Schwadron, *Resp. Maharsham* (Brezany: 1910), vol. 3, Introd.; A. Horowitz, *Resp. Tzur Ya'akob* (Jerusalem: 1955), no. 141. The central point is that *shalom bayith* rather than *sakanath n^e^fashoth* is the operative in the cases cited.

69. *Resp. Maharsham*, loc. cit.

70. See R. Hai Gaon in *T^e^shuvath ha-Geonim*, ed. A. Harkavy (Jerusalem: 1887); *Yev.*, p. 167.

71. Y. Ayas, *Resp. Beth Yehudah: E.H.* (Leghorn: 1746), no. 14; *Resp. Chayyim ve-Shalom*, vol. 1:40; *Resp. She'eloth Yitzchak*, no. 69.

72. *Resp. Shem mi-Shimon* (Satmar: 1932), no. 7. See also *Resp. Torath Chesed: E.H.*, vol. 42, no. 32 and *Resp. Tzitz Eliezer*, vol. 9, 51 (3).

73. *Resp. Igroth Moshe: E.H., vol.* 1, no. 64, p. 163.

74. *M.T. Hil. De'oth* 9:10.

75. M. Tendler, "Population Control—the Jewish View," *Tradition 8* (1966): 5-14.

76. *Taan.* 8b.

5

Postponement of Ritual Circumcision (*Brith Milah*) in Young Children for Psychiatric Reasons

[with Julian Gordon, M.D.]

I.

Brith milah, the ritual circumcision marking the entrance of the Jewish male into the faith-community of Israel, is a simple surgical procedure performed on the eighth day of life. Certain conditions of physical frailty understood by Halakhah to lead to adverse if not life-threatening consequences to the health of the infant allow one to postpone the procedure. The indications of physical frailty, such as a yellowish tint of the skin or eyes which corresponds roughly to the modern medical notion of jaundice, or a red color (*erythema neonatorum*), or abnormal breathing and low birth weight, are clearly described in the halakhic codes and are carefully studied by the ritual circumcisor (*mohel*) during his apprenticeship.[1]

When these contraindications are evident, or if a major illness or abnormality of any organ system exists (with certain exceptions[2]), the circumcision must be postponed until a halakhically defined improvement in physical status is ascertained. In some cases, such as where an infant had been preceded by two siblings who died as a consequence of circumcision, or has a genetic condition such as hemophilia or a congenital abnormality requiring surgical correction, ritual circumcision is postponed until such time as the individual is older, stronger, or the condition has changed.[3]

In the existing halakhic outlines of the legitimate contraindications for ritual circumcision, the central concern is the physical well-being of the infant.[4] Halakhah is extremely cautious in this regard, and will often require the postponement of *brith* in certain instances where there would be no formal medical contraindication or hesitancy in performing some other necessary surgery.

There does not, however, seem to be any evidence of a halakhic concern for negative *psychological* consequences of this procedure on the eight-day-old infant. Presumably, its effects at that time are appropriately repressed much the same as is the trauma of birth. Yet, in cases where ritual circumcision is performed on older infants and young children between the ages of 2 and 5 or 6, the question of possible psychologic trauma or adverse reaction becomes relevant. Examples would be infants whose circumcision was delayed pending subsequent physiological maturation, the cessation of an illness, the repair of congenital abnormalities (where it is impossible to perform the circumcision prior to other medical intervention), or children of converts to Judaism who, even if circumcised, would require a token incision and letting of blood *(hatafath dam brith)* for the express purpose of fulfilling the biblical obligation.

Currently, the opportunity of ritually circumcising young children who have not previously been circumcised (or whose circumcision is ritually unfit) is presented by the influx of Russian Jewish immigrants.* The families of these children are usually very recent immigrants who are experiencing the frustrations of socialization and acclimation to their new environment and language. They are assisted by various social service agencies; notably by certain chasidic organizations which introduce these families to Jewish customs and, among other things, to the need for ritual circumcision.

At Cleveland's Mount Sinai Hospital, older children who are to be circumcised are admitted to the pediatric floor of the urologic service. A physician-*mohel* (Henry C. Romberg, M.D.) and a urologist (JG) work as a team to complete the preoperative evaluation and perform the operative procedure. The surgery is

---

* In the authors' experience in the city of Cleveland, Ohio, 83 ritual circumcisions have been performed in the years 1979-1980 on this immigrant population. Twenty-three ritual circumcisions have been performed on children, ages 6 to 11 years; and 10 on adolescents, ages 15 and 16 years.

performed on an ambulatory basis, the child spending only part of one day in the hospital. The operation is usually performed under a general inhalation anesthetic after adequate premedication.

A specific concern is that surgical procedure on the genitalia, with the attendant general anesthesia, may elicit undesirable psychological reactions in young children who have reached the age of awareness of sex differences (about 2 years) and in preschoolers whose already burgeoning involvement with psychological themes of loss, castration, and disfigurement may be destructively exaggerated by this procedure or exacerbated by pre- and post-operative mishandling of these psychological issues. These concerns also exist for latency age children and are not uncommon among adolescents around the age of puberty.

When this issue is raised by medical facilities it is generally done in search for a policy which will satisfy both the Jewish community as well as the occasional pediatric or psychiatric professional who questions the advisability of performing this procedure on young children. In its extreme form, the question is: Can Halakhah accept the idea of categorically postponing the *brith* of young children to a psychologically more propitious time, perhaps after puberty, assuming that ritual circumcision may elicit adverse reactions? In its more conservative form, the question is whether Halakhah recognizes the need for a pre-operative counseling period of sufficient duration to mitigate the anticipated psychological reactions to this surgery in some individuals?

II.

There are three issues involved in responding appropriately to the problem. The first concerns the implicit assumption that *brith milah* is an elective and, hence, postponable procedure. The second involves examining the psychiatric literature generally taken to suggest the possibility of untoward consequences of such surgery, in order to determine under precisely what conditions adverse psychological reactions are elicited by surgery on young children. Finally, one must ask whether the types of negative consequences which have been reported constitute a danger or risk sufficient *in the eyes of Halakhah* to warrant the postponement of ritual circumcision.

According to Halakhah, *brith milah* cannot be viewed as elective surgery. The Talmud, expanding on a Biblical account,[5] relates that Moses himself was threatened with heavenly punishment for an inadequately justified delay of his son's circumcision.[6] In instances where ritual circumcision has been postponed for whatever reason beyond the eighth day of birth, the obligation to fulfill the Biblical commandment is incumbent daily, if not with each passing moment. This obligation is initially the father's and, if he is unwilling or unable to discharge this obligation—or if a now grown child is unwilling or unable to discharge his own obligation to have himself circumcised—it is transferred to the *beth din*, or the Jewish community at large, *in loco patrum*.

While practical considerations, duress, or lack of knowledge often preclude realizing this obligation immediately, the obligation remains. Each day of unjustified postponement of *brith milah* amounts to *bittul aseh*, an inappropriate nullification of a positive commandment. The eventual penalty for intentional failure to fulfill the obligation is *kareth*, excision at the hands of heaven from the Jewish community.[7] *Thus, ritual circumcision is in no circumstance an elective procedure* and its implementation cannot be constrained by anecdotal or intuitive apprehensions, or by statistical probabilities which have not been accepted by Halakhah.

The next task is to examine exactly what types of psychological or behavioral reactions have been reported following surgery on young children and then, to ascertain whether children's psychological susceptibility to trauma in such circumstances can find a place in the halakhic attitude toward postponement of ritual circumcision. As could be expected, there are disparate findings in the literature on the psychological effects of hospitalization and surgery on young children. There is unanimity that *any* surgical procedure and any hospitalization episode elicit *some* reaction in young children, but that persistent *traumatic* reactions are not inevitable.[8] Aversive reactions reported include enuresis, feeding disturbances, thumbsucking, restlessness, increased aggressive play behavior, aggressiveness toward siblings, nightmares, anxiety reactions, vague or specific fears of mutilation, attribution of pain to parental disfavor and punishment, and, occasionally, more severe regressions.[9] Schowalter[10] specifically examined the reactions of adolescents to surgery and illness and noted complications in stage-specific issues of self-esteem and ego-ideal formation as a reaction to bodily illness. Vernon et al.,[11] suggest a relationship between unfamiliarity of hospital setting, separation from parents, and post-operative psychological trauma, and between age, separation from parents, and traumatic reactions *during* hospitalization. They found ages 3 or 6 months to 3 years to be the most susceptible period. Interestingly, the variable of actual pain experienced during hospitalization did not produce systematic effects in this study. It is thus neither surgery nor hospitalization *per se* which may cause psychological complications, but rather other factors such as age, the method of handling post-operative pain, the availability of pre-operative counselling, and so forth.[12]

In fact, in every study where adverse reactions are reported, certain additional variables are common: hospitalization is protracted or involves a stay longer than two weeks, the illness requiring hospitalization and surgery tends to be chronic or, at least, complicated and there is separation from parents for considerable lengths of time, and, in some cases, parental mismanagement during the pre- and post-operative period.[13] In their review and replication, Davenport and Werry[14] point out the additional problem of numerous methodological flaws in studies such as Vernon's and others'. Davenport and Werry conclude that there is no significant evidence of psychological upset as a result of properly managed hospitalization, anesthesia, and surgery. They assert additional qualifications which are relevant for our problem. Favorable reactions are most likely when hospitalization is of short duration (2 weeks or less), post-operative discomfort is minimal and does not require extended periods of immobility, and anesthesia is explained to the patient and applied skillfully and compassionately. Their study amply covered children under 4 years old and the authors did not find evidence of marked psychological trauma within this subgroup.

With regard to the assumption that genital surgery itself causes traumatic reactions, consider Ozturk's study.[15] Ozturk specifically studied circumcision on young, Turkish (Islamic) children (30 subjects, ages $2\frac{1}{2}$-11 years; 46% were between ages 3-6 years), upon whom this ritual procedure is done without anesthetic. He found that though castration anxiety and nightmares of related content attend the period immediately preceding and following circumcision, upon follow-up 45 days later, only 8 children reported occasional nightmares or were observed to be slightly more aggressive in play. Ozturk concludes that while psychological reactions do occur at about the time of ritual circumcision, the cultural preparatory experiences and meanings attached to the ritual have far more impact upon the child than castration fears or stage-specific vulnerabilities. These findings are similar to findings with the Cleveland immigrant population. Any immediate anxieties are apparently resolved in three ways: (1) by compensatory mechanisms such as ritual fanfare, parties, gift-giving, the achievement of envied status; (2) by counterphobic mechanisms such as "not being afraid" or being able to make castration threats to other children; and (3) by, or contributing to an accelerated identification with the father and developing an attitude of submission to the father.

It would seem that there is little evidence that severe adverse psychological or behavioral reactions are inevitable with childhood surgery in the normal population. It also does not seem to be the case that genital surgery is necessarily traumatic even under favorable conditions. We, of course, recognize that operations performed on the penis *can* arouse castration fears, and that during the phallic phase of psychosexual development, whatever part of the body is operated upon *can*, by displacement, produce castration anxiety. However, the untoward aftereffects or severe reactions occasionally observed are usually due to accompanying factors not present in the routine ritual circumcision of young children as practiced in most hospitals by sensitive practitioners. Reactions of the modal sort described by Prugh, Davenport and Werry, Vernon et al., and others are readily preventable or manageable in a number of successful ways.

It would seem, however, that where there is valid evidence of severe psychiatric disorder in the child's personality profile, such as childhood schizophrenia or borderline psychosis or any other psychiatric disorder,* *and* where the ritual circumcision could not

---

* It is not clear whether a *shoteh*—who is typically viewed as Halakhah's most

be undergone without causing regression or exacerbation of symptomatology, Halakhah would subsume such conditions under its general rubric of *sakanath n^e^fashoth* or danger to life,[16] and would acknowledge that *brith milah* may be postponed. Should an individual with this severe degree of disorder be concurrently engaged in psychiatric treatment where, in the opinion of the professional mental health worker and the judgment of a competent halakhic authority, the advent of circumcision would constitute a serious obstacle to psychotherapeutic progress, or undo it, *brith milah* must be postponed.

Yet, one does not encounter such grave considerations with the majority of children and adolescents. Their reactions will be of the sort described by Davenport and Werry and Ozturk—e.g.,

---

paradigmatic case of psychiatric disorder—is Biblically required to be circumcised. The *shoteh* obviously cannot even as an "adult" circumcise himself, but the father of the *shoteh* may be obligated to ensure that his son does not remain in an uncircumcised state (however, this view requires construing the commandment in the negative). The *Minchath Chinnukh* addresses the issue of the obligation of the *suma* (blind person), who is exempted from certain *mitzvah* obligations, ruling that the *suma* is not biblically obligated, but may be rabbinically obligated to "not appear like a gentile." One might conclude that the *shoteh*, who is generally exempted from *mitzvah* obligations simply by virtue of being *non compos mentis*, is also biblically excluded from the obligation to be circumcised.[17] However, others maintain that the father of a *shoteh* must circumcise his son. Rav Pirutinsky notes the *Kli Chemdah's* argument that the *shoteh* is different from the *suma* and is similar to the *treifah* who must be circumcised.[18] Indeed, the *shoteh* "who might even be cured someday" is logically more strongly obligated. R. Pirutinsky also cites a ruling of Rav M. Feinstein that, like the normal child, the eight-day-old *shoteh* may be circumcised even on the Sabbath. The *Chatham Sofer* would also reason that *brith* must be performed upon a *shoteh* so long as it would not present a 'danger' to the infant![19] Elsewhere, the *Chatham Sofer* brings forward an argument which suggests that the father's obligation in this instance is "to prevent the 'ignorant' from stumbling on a prohibition," but cites others who disagree.[20] Apparently, the obligation to be circumcised falls upon any individual who can be halakhically defined as a living organism (*ben chai*) *regardless of intellectual or emotional capacity*. The exceptions would be the *sumah* and, more generally, where *brith* threatens to introduce or aggravate grave psychiatric danger. In fact, since *shoteh* is actually a description of a legal state of noncompetence rather than an exhaustive characterization of *emotional turmoil* (e.g., *mi she-nitr^e^fah da'ato*), it may not be the most instructive paradigm for disorders relevant to the postponement of *brith*. Psychiatric pain or *tza'ar*, rather than intellectual impairment alone, may be the more relevant criterion.

nightmares, temporary anxiety, increased aggressiveness in play, etc.—which occur under favorable circumstances and which can be readily managed if not prevented. One is primarily interested in avoiding truly aversive sequelae which may develop from even 'normal' reactions by explaining procedures simply and adequately, clarifying misunderstandings (e.g., circumcision is not due to illness and is not a punishment), training parents or relatives in proper post-operative management of the child's psychological and medical needs, and familiarizing the child with hospital surroundings and garb. It is of critical importance that one address any specific concerns of the child related to themes of castration, mutilation, sexual and gender confusion, parental punishment, and so forth. In this latter regard, Vernon and Schulman[21] have devised a useful, 27-item parental questionnaire which can assist in the process of preparing parents and children for ritual circumcision, as can a small primer by Geist, *A Child Goes to the Hospital.*[22] At the same time Anna Freud noted that too lengthy a preparation period leaves too much room for the "spreading out" of id fantasies, eliciting undue challenge to the child ego's defense system (Freud, 1952, p. 75n). Thus, it is advisable not to begin such preparations earlier than a few days prior to the actual surgery. Immediately before and after the procedure, it is vital that the parents be with the child. The encouragement of self-care is also helpful both with adolescents[23] as well as children who have reached the cognitive stage of concrete operations (approx. 7 to 11 years).[24] With preschoolers, play therapy and direct and simple communication, in addition to parental support, are also helpful.[25] In other words, for the child whose reaction to genital surgery under favorable circumstances would appear to be "normal," no categorical delay of such surgery to an indefinitely later date is especially warranted.

There are other occasions where a child's anxiety and confusion are greater and more pervasive than normal, where severe behavioral disorders (not of psychotic nature) follow being informed of the advent of circumcision, where parents are hostile to the procedure or appear to be too unsophisticated to prevent aversive reactions, or where family confusion (e.g., due to immigration) is severe enough to warrant, from the psychological viewpoint, postponing circumcision at least until these problems have been satisfactorily managed. Yet, we noted above that there is a halakhic premium on fulfilling the obligation of *brith milah* as soon as possible. Does Halakhah allow for a preparation period sufficient to avoid adverse psychological sequelae in such cases? (Actually, when the physician-*mohel* must perforce, and in obedience to the limits of admissions dockets and hospital service availability, etc., schedule *brith milah* for such children a week in advance, there is ample opportunity to properly counsel the child and family prior to the circumcision. The question raised in this paragraph assumes that one is capable at this given moment to perform the circumcision, but also wishes to psychologically prepare the child. Further assuming *arguendo* that such preparation would take more than a day, thus delaying the *brith* one full day, can one undertake such preparation?)

The response lies in the words of R. Shabbtai ha-Cohen in his commentary to *Shulchan Arukh: Yoreh De'ah*: "An infant who is in pain (*she-hu mitzta'er*) either because of illness *or because of anything else* is not circumcised until he becomes well."[26] *Nefesh Chayah*, no. 74, states, "The words of the sage [cited in *SHaKH*], 'or because of anything else' . . . mean that the child is in pain *because of something internal even though it is not caused by sickness*." This distinction of "pain" from physical illness is evidence of Halakhah's recognition of the role of psychiatric distress in causing damaging consequences—as is the case elsewhere where this distinction is made in halakhic literature.[27] The leniency factor of *tza'ar* in postponing *brith* applies to adults as well as children.[28] If the pain referred to here was the life-threatening sort discussed earlier, its role would not have necessitated additional comment. Thus, when conditions exist such that extensive (i.e., more than one day) prophylactic pre-operative counseling is necessary, Halakhah would also allow circumcision to be postponed for the shortest duration necessary to satisfactorily accomplish this task. This requirement must not be abused and its implementation is the dual responsibility of the mental health professional and the halakhic authority consulted on each individual case.

The practical problem presented here has not been directly addressed in the extant Halakhic literature. However Halakhah is equipped to address in a meaningful and constructive way the changing sensitivities and sophistications of different generations.

Indeed, the parameters for an appropriate response are ever those already established by halakhic precedent. I have stated that where severe psychiatric disorder exists or is somehow imminent, it would be subsumed under the existing category of *sakanath n^{e}fashoth*. Indications of such disorder would justify postponement of ritual circumcision. Apparently normal reactions to surgery under the most favorable pre- and post-operative conditions, on the other hand, cannot justify the postponement of this halakhically non-elective procedure, but can and should be managed in accordance with the principles of modern psychoprophylaxis. Where sufficient doubt exists as to the probable reaction of an individual child to such surgery, due to various unhealthy psychosocial prognosticators, ritual circumcision may be postponed for a ***minimum*** amount of time involving active pursuit of the modification or alleviation of such factors. As for the question of policy, we have seen that Halakhah cannot accept categorical and indefinite postponement of ritual circumcision in consideration of the average psychological reactions to such surgery.

Notes

1. *Sh. A., Y.D.*, 260-63.
2. See *Beth Yosef* to *Tur Sh. A., Y.D.*, 263.
3. *Sh. A., Y.D.* 263:2-3; *Resp. Nodah be-Yehudah: Tinyana Y.D.*, no. 165; *Arukh ha-Shulchan: Y.D.*, 263 (7). See also J. David Bleich's recent review, "Hypospadias and Ritual Circumcision," *Tradition 18* (1980): 295-304.
4. *Sefer ha-Chinnukh*, commandment no. 2; *M.T. Hil. Milah; Sh. A., Y.D.*, 263.
5. Exod. 4:24-25.
6. *Ned.* 32a.
7. *Rama* to *Sh. A., Y.D.*, 261.
8. Prugh, D., "A Study of Emotional Reactions of Children and Families to Hospitalization and Illness," *Am. J. Orthopsychiatr.* (1953): 23, 70-92;——. "Investigations Dealing with the Reactions of Children and Families to Hospitalization and Illness: Problems and Potentialities," in G. Caplan ed., *Emotional Problems of Early Childhood* (New York: Basic Books, 1955);——. "Clinical Appraisal of Infants and Children," in W. Nelson ed., *Textbook of Pediatrics*, (Phila.: Saunders, 1964);——. & Eckhardt, L. "Children's Reactions to Illness, Hospitalization, and Surgery." In A. Freedman, H. Kaplan & B. Sadock

eds., *Comprehensive Textbook of Psychiatry*, (Balt.: Williams & Wilkins, 1975 ed.); "Symposium: Observations on the Emotional Reactions of Children to Tonsillectomy and Adenoidectomy," pp. 97-156, in M. Sheen ed., *Problems in Infancy and Childhood* (New York: Josiah Macy, Jr. Foundation, 1949).

9. Bowlby, J., Robertson, J. & Rosenbluth, D., "A 2 Year-Old Goes to the Hospital," *Psychoanal. Stud. Child.* (1952): vol. 7, 82-94; Cansever, G., "Psychological Effects of Circumcision," *Brit. J. Med. Psychol.* (1965): 38, 321-331; Prugh, op. cit.; Vernon, D., Foley, J., Sipowicz, R. & Schulman, J., *The Psychological Responses of Children to Hospitalization and Illness* (Springfield, Ill.: Charles C. Thomas, 1965); Symposium, op. cit. (1949); Freud, A., "The Role of Bodily Illness in the Mental Life of Children," *Psychoanal. Stud. Child.* (1952): 7, 69-81.

10. Schowalter, J., "Psychological Reactions to Physical Illness and Hospitalization in Adolescence: A Survey," *J. Amer. Acada. Child Psychiatr.* (1977): 16, 500-516; also in S. Chess & A. Thomas eds., *Annual Progress in Child Psychiatry and Development* (New York: Brunner/Mazel, 1978).

11. Vernon, op. cit., 1965.

12. Compare this study with the unqualified statement of Bergman and Freud that circumcision after infancy is "inevitably" construed as a parental punishment. (Bergman, T. & Freud, A., *Children in the Hospital* (New York: I.U.P., 1965), p. 144. See also B. Spock, *Baby and Child Care* (New York: 1977 ed.), pp. 191-92, who considers the years 1-6 most susceptible to any possible psychological trauma following circumcision.

13. See Prugh, op. cit., 1953.

14. Davenport, H. & Werry, J., "The Effect of General Anesthesia, Surgery, and Hospitalization upon the Behavior of Children," *Am. J. Orthopsychiatr.* (1970): 40(5), 806-24.

15. Ozturk, O., "Ritual Circumcision and Castration Anxiety," *Psychiatry* (1973): 36(1), 49-60.

16. See Spero, M.H., "*Birkath ha-Gomel le-Achar Hachlamah mi-Machalath Nefesh*," *Assia* (1979): 23, 44-48.

17. Some additional comment may be relevant on this point. The *shoteh* (and *cheresh* and *katan*) is considered *non compos mentis* or *lav bar de'ah*, not possessed of judgment, which is almost always extended to mean that he is exempt from *mitzvoth*. (*Git.* 23; *Men.* 93a; *Yev.* 99b; *Chag.* 3a, Rashi, s.v. *Chutz*; *Yoma* 43a; *Shab.* 137a; *Arkh.* 3a,5b; *Yev.* 72b; *Eruv.* 96b; *J.T. Parah* 5:4; *M.T., Hil. Eduth* 9:9, 11; *Hil. Shechitah* 2:1; in *M.T.; Hil. Parah* 6:2, Maimonides gives no explanation). Controversy around the true extent of this exemption exists in the *rishonim* literature. Maimonides disqualifies the *shoteh* from bearing testimony since he is *patur min ha-mitzvoth*. A serious question raised by *Lechem Mishnah*, loc. cit., is why Maimonides did not mention the more logical disqualification: *shoteh lav bar de'ah*? Indeed, Maimonides himself cites the argument of *lav bar de'ah* elsewhere in disqualifying the *shoteh* from bearing agency (*M.T. Hil. Shiluchin ve-Shuftin* 2:2). Questioning from another avenue, *Resp. Shoel u-Meishiv* notes that the *shoteh*'s exemption cannot be understood categorically inasmuch as other authorities still forbad the guardians of a *shoteh* from allowing the latter to

come to transgression, implying at least some responsibility to *mitzvah* obligations. (*Tinyana*, vol. 4, no. 87, referring to *Resp. Maharil*, no. 196; also see *Resp. Chatham Sofer, O.H.*, vol. 1, no. 83). *Shoel u-Meishiv* explains that the *shoteh* is in fact exempt from *mitzvoth*, yet one must consider the possibility that the *shoteh* may become "cured" someday and, thus, care must be taken that he not be permitted to become habituated to inappropriate behavior (but cf. *Sh. A., O.H.* 266:4-5 which suggests that the *shoteh* cannot be expected to return to normal); at the moment, however, the *shoteh* will be exempt from *mitzvoth* because he is a *lav bar de'ah*. This response still does not explain the problematic rulings in the *Mishnah Torah*. Even more troublesome is that Maimonides quite explicitly exempts the *shoteh* from *mitzvoth* elsewhere in the *M.T.* without recourse to the principle of *lav bar de'ah* (*Hil. Chagigah* 2:4, *Hil. Chametz u-Matzah* 6:3), as do others (see *Turei Even* to *R.H.* 28b; *Mahartz Chiyos* to *Yev.* 62). The *Pri Megadim* in fact suggests that the *shoteh* is only exempted from positive, active *mitzvoth* but not from omissive *mitzvoth*. At the same time, if a *shoteh* causes damage or "transgresses" there is no earthly or heavenly penalty (*O.H.*, Introd., chap. 2; *P.M.*; *Mishbetzoth Zahav, O.H.*, 266: 4, s.v. *od; Resp. Pesach Devir*, vol. 3, no. 343 (12) rules that when the *shoteh* is "cured," he does not make recompense, but must try to experience some contrition or *t^eshuvah* for these deeds!) *According to this view, it would seem that the* shoteh *need not be circumcised unless one views the* mitzvah *of circumcision as also involving the prohibition against* being uncircumcised—*e.g., as to prevent the* shoteh *from accidentally eating the* korban pesach *when uncircumcised.* With regard to the problematic rulings in the *M.T.*, see *Urim ve-Tumim*, no. 35(6). The *Beth Yosef* to *Tur Sh. A., Y.D.* 264, s.v. *ha-kol*, explains that women and slaves can perform a *brith*, and so can the *katan* (minor) because "he is destined to become elligible to perform *mitzvoth*." *Arukh ha-Shulchan: Y.D.* 264:2 comments that it would seem from the *Beth Yosef*'s reasoning that a *shoteh* is not obligated *to be* circumcised and hence cannot circumcise. He demurs that wherever *katan* is mentioned, the *cheresh* and *shoteh* have the same status, and are frequently obligated in *mitzvoth*, and he suggests therefore that the rationale of "*klal mitzvoth*" is not a rigid one. He *implies* that the *shoteh* needs a *brith* but *states* that only a *katan* and not a *shoteh* is *deemed* a *bar milah*. Of course, one counterargues that a *katan* is actually not obligated to have a *brith*, but rather his father is obligated to circumcise him. Thus, *katan* is not "obligated"—save for the Torah's decree that he be circumcised—and the *shoteh* may be even less obligated. Nonetheless, I have already cited the authorities who demand that the *shoteh* be circumcised. (Rabbi D.S. Shapiro offers that *M.T., Hil. Eduth* 9 refers to the disqualification of "*lav bar mitzvoth*" in order to broaden the disqualification of the *shoteh*, including even the *shoteh* who does show some meager intellectual capacities—and who might therefore no longer be considered a "*lav bar da'ath*." Such a *shoteh* is disqualified nonetheless because he lacks the autonomous free-will to act, hence is exempt from *mitzvah* obligations, and is hence disqualified to issue testimony [see Shapiro's essay, "*Choleh be-Machalath ha-Ruach Im Yakhol le-Garesh?*" *ha-Darom 1*, no. 1 [1957]: 41-50].)

18. *Sefer ha-Brith*, chap. 260, no. 59; see also *Resp. Maharam Shick: Y.D.*, no.

243; see also *Resp. Chatham Sofer: Y.D.*, vol. 6, no. 64.

19. *Resp. Chatham Sofer: Y.D.*, vol. 6, no. 64.

20. *Resp. Chatham Sofer: O.H.*, vol. 1, no. 83; support for this view is also explicit in *Sh. A., O.H.*, 343 and in *Magen Avraham*, ad loc.

21. Vernon, D. & Schulman, J., "Hospitalization as a Source of Psychological Benefit to Children," *Pediatrics* (1964): 34, 694-96.

22. Geist, H., *A Child Goes to the Hospital* (Springfield, Ill.: Charles C. Thomas, 1965).

23. Schowalter, op. cit., 1977.

24. Neuhauser, C., et al., "Children's Concept of Healing," *Am. J. Orthopsychiatr.* (1978): 48(2), 335-41.

25. Prugh, op. cit., 1964, p. 179.

26. *Shulchan Arukh, Yoreh De'ah* 262(3).

27. *Rama* to *Sh. A., O.H.*, 328:17; *Resp. Igroth Moshe: O.H.*, vol. 3, no. 53; see also Spero, op. cit., 1979; see also I. Jakobovits, "*Tzar shel Adam be-Dinei Yisroel*, in M. Kasher, N. Lamm, & L. Rosenfeld eds., *Leo Jung Jubilee Volume* (New York: 1962), pp. 133-41, and *Resp. Chavoth Yair*, no. 191. Also see Rabbi M. Hershler's distinction to the effect that while one may not engage in *refuah* on the Sabbath merely for *tza'arah de-gufah*, one may violate other rabbinic decrees (i.e., not strictly *acts of healing*) for such *tzar*, in "*Din Mitzt'aer she-Hetiru bo Shevuth*," in M. Hershler ed., *Halakhah u-Refuah* (Jerusalem: 1980), pp. 109-12.

6
Toward a Halakhic Perspective on Radical Forms of Psychological Manipulation and Behavior Control

I.

The contemporary observer is witness to the ever-increasing extension of man's powers of influence and control not only outward but also inward in an intensified and sophisticated effort to eliminate randomness and variability in human behavior, in that portion of reality once considered the source of human uniqueness and individuality. This effort is manifested in many ways, including radical forms of psychological manipulation and behavior control: psychosurgery, or surgical manipulation of the brain (SMB), and electrical stimulation of the brain (ESB). Such procedures are aided by a complementary force which has taken the form of major and increasingly popular theoretical and philosophical revisions of the concept of man. These conceptual revisions, promulgated by some of the psychiatric professionals who advocate the rapid deployment of radical therapeutic procedures, are geared to making the eventual attenuation of human freedoms which can result from such techniques more assimilable in the minds of those individuals and societies who shall be its subjects. Eissler once expressed the problem in these words:[1]

> A new materialism, in the reprehensible meaning of the term, holds psychiatry at present in its sway. For example, as long as shock treatment and surgery are permitted to be used in the treatment of schizophrenias, almost no psychiatrist will undergo the burdensome task of struggling with the

> patient's mind for its recovery. As long as the prison is available as the final domicile of the delinquent and the criminal, why should society provide means of reorganizing the personality of the lawbreaker?

Eissler saw a danger primarily in the replacement of conventional psychotherapeutic modes by radical forms of behavior control which assume a less complex and creative image of man. It is, of course, conceivable—and even desirable—that future versions of radical behavior and psychological control will evolve more complex and subtle technologies even if these remain based upon relatively simple principles or models of behavior and will offer effective forms of behavior change which will render conventional forms of psychotherapy obsolete. However, it is also clear that moral and religious questions will have to be raised all along the road to such developments. Ethical imperatives must be asserted *before* we achieve some state of materialism where ethical obligations are no longer deemed relevant. And it is precisely at the current stage in the experimental development of ESB and SMB, when theory tends to be equal to if not more important than actual technology, that a shift in the theory of human behavior to a simple perspective which reduces personality to biochemical processes, cybernetic models, or operant reinforcement contingencies will have a far-reaching effect on preferred modes of psychological intervention, and vice versa.

The sense of concern, then, emanates primarily from the uncritical enthusiasm for and the directions and trends taken by this effort. More, we are made anxious by the awareness that there is yet an inexact comprehension of both the radical technology and its effects upon the subject and an unwillingness to constrain such progress by the ethical principles which have for so long guided other scientific endeavors.

At this point it would be wise to examine some radical forms of behavior control and psychological manipulation, and distinguish such forms of behavior control from conventional psychotherapy. Useful forms of radical psychological intervention must then be examined from the perspective of Jewish ethics. In so doing, I will propose and critically analyze a possible halakhic model for such forms of intervention.[2]

II.

Generally, one would separate two classes of behavioral or psychological control. One would be the use of positive and negative reinforcements, based on sensory or perceptual relations between ourselves and the environment which directly or indirectly effect or modify behavior. These reinforcements are evoked and rewarded in both subtle as well as gross forms and are mediated by fine gradients of symbolic communication through cognition, language, or body movements. This class includes social processes, all forms of verbal psychotherapy, hypnosis, education, and child rearing. The second class of behavior control is the use of chemical and physical agents to directly modify neurophysiology, which includes psychopharmacological intervention, psychosurgery, and electrical stimulation of the brain, including electroconvulsive or "shock" therapy.*

To be sure, there are differences among the types of modifications and influences within the two classes but these are less our concern than are the major similarities and differences between the classes themselves. Pharmacotherapy spans both groups, though the majority of its most critical characteristics necessitate its classification under the second group. In discussing the differences between these classes we will be able to gauge in exactly what respects electrical stimulation and surgical manipulation of the brain are more "radical" forms of behavior control than those techniques categorized under the first class.

III.

SMB (surgical manipulation of the brain) or psychosurgery, was attempted experimentally in the 1880s and was pioneered in the United States in 1942 by Freeman and Watts. The actual tech-

* Cf. Weiner ("Individual Psychotherapy," p. 336. In I. B. Weiner (ed.), *Clinical Methods in Psychology* [New York: John Wiley, 1976]) who would not consider these methods "psychotherapy" since they are not designed to engage the patient in the quest for increased self-understanding, but rather are interventions *done to* the patient.

nique generally involves surgical excision or ablation (by means of electrocauterization, cyrogenics, or radioactive signal) of brain areas related to emotion. An attempt is made to pinpoint the exact locus of the brain responsible for the unwanted behavior and hopefully to achieve the destruction of "only those tissues and nerve cells . . . leaving other functions and behaviors of the patient unaffected."[3] Since brain tissue does not regenerate, the gross effects of SMB are irreversible.

The limitations of the early, primitive radical lobotomies attempted between 1880-1930 were almost immediately recognized. Between that period and 1945, selective frontal lobe procedures were used for affective disorders, aided by improvements in the use of stereotaxic techniques of lesion placement and by the use of radio frequency and cyrogenics to produce lesions. However, by the 1950s the promise of new narcoleptic drugs and the popularity of electroconvulsive therapy decreased medical interest in this technique.[4]

Basically, the psychiatric target symptom is not removed through SMB, but a reduced concern about the problem on the part of the patient is achieved; e.g., the hallucination that disturbs a violent psychotic patient is not removed, but rather the patient's reaction to the hallucinatory experience is modified. SMB is not yet considered a specific treatment for any individual illness though its largest use has been associated with chronic depression, some schizophrenias (where pananxiety is a prominent symptom), and compulsive, violent aggressiveness. One practitioner, who uses SMB to modify the behavior of hyperkinetic children and for the management of mental retardates and schizophrenics, considers it "sedative neurosurgery."[5]

The goals of current SMB research are the replacement of lesions with more refined input for selectively changing the balance of activity in these regions (similar to the pacemaker innovation with cardiac patients) and to generate nondestructive pharmacological agents for use in these procedures (e.g., the direct application of procaine hydrochloride to frontal lobe "white matter" in the treatment of schizophrenia). In the present state of the art, unilateral temporal lobectomy has been found ineffective with seizures and schizophrenia-like psychosis associated with temporal lobe epilepsy. Bilateral lesions of the amygdala do appear to reduce emotional tension and affective responsivity, producing a relatively more stable patient, but also one with flattened emotional responsiveness and decreased spontaneity and productivity. In other instances, SMB seems to evoke diminished self-consciousness and an impaired sentiment toward all persons formerly evoking strong positive and negative emotions. SMB has also occasionally backfired and caused rage reactions which do not recede following the post-operative period.[6] In schizophrenia, the above surgical procedure may occasionally reduce aggressiveness, producing patients who are quiet and relatively cooperative, but who are also still deeply schizophrenic, hallucinatory, and capable of only poor emotional contact. Lesions elsewhere have been correlated with emotional-behavioral change, but not with curing mental illness or the restoration of qualitatively healthy personality organization.

Proponents maintain that specific sites in the brain are responsible for undesirable, usually violent or psychotic behavior, and that psychiatric relief should be obtained through techniques which deal directly with the "situational" anomaly. In a neat formula, Mark and Ervin asserted that violence is an expression of brain activity and that socially undesirable violent behavior is the result of a dysfunctional limbic system. Their hypothesis, as stated in their text,* supported the notion that SMB could be applied to tissue sites that were nonpathological in any observable way other than the patients' inappropriate behavior. In a sense, these sites were considered dysfunctional only in that they were designated as the *presumed* source of neurophysiological pathways causing a behavioral problem.

Advocates claim that this procedure is a potential relief for patients otherwise uncontrollable and dangerous to themselves and others. To be sure, aggressive, homicidal, and suicidal tendencies are well-documented in the case histories of the

---

* In all of their written work, Mark and Ervin assumed the existence of demonstrable temporal lobe disorder or brain lesion in addition to psychological disorder. On a later occasion, Dr. Vernon Mark stated categorically that as far as present evidence is concerned, one has no right to make lesions in healthy tissue when the patient suffers from rage attacks alone, and not some physical condition like temporal lobe epilepsy.[7]

subjects of and candidates for SMB. Proponents feel that while "the procedure may be experimental from our standpoint, from the patient's standpoint it is therapy."[8] In patients with less serious illness, increased social awareness and less distractibility and self-consciousness, *despite* an increased tendency for tactlessness and crudeness, flattened affect, and drive reduction, are considered to justify continued use of and experimentation with SMB.[9]

The irreversible nature of SMB cannot be denied even by advocates, but moderates offer the use of gradually progressing procedures which allow for continuous monitoring of what is in effect relatively more staged personality change (such as controlled multifocal frontal leucotomy). The strictly legal problem of obtaining appropriate consent from subjects *can* be safeguarded, and restrictive ethical standards have been proposed; e.g., not permitting SMB on persons under 21 years old, not on prisoners even for their treatment, always as a last resort, and so forth.[10] Yet, there remains the problem of obtaining informed and voluntary consent from persons with precisely the kinds of psychiatric illnesses typically considered the best targets for SMB.

Electroconvulsive or electroshock therapy (ECT) is another tool in the psychiatric armamentarium against mental illness, devised in approximately its current form in 1938 by Ugo Cerletti. There are three main techniques of eliciting the allegedly therapeutic convulsion in the patient: (1) via intravenously administered Metrazol, picrotozin, and triazol, (2) inhalation convulsion treatment (via Indokolon), which was erroneously believed to reduce post-treatment confusion and requires routine post-treatment medication with compazine, and (3) the application of AC current of 70-150 volts (50-60 cycles) for a duration of 0.1 to 1 second, usually three times a week but sometimes as often as several times a day. The third method is the preferred method in current use. During the actual convulsion, which the patient does not feel and has no subsequent memory of, there is a ten second tonic phase and a 30-40 second clonic phase. Partial suspension of breathing usually follows the actual convulsive movements; and when muscle relaxants have been administered to prevent bone breakage, oxygen must be given. Following ECT, there is a brief period of immediate confusion and retrograde amnesia which clears up within one to two hours. Memory loss, according to proponents, is rarely permanent, but does last longer and includes more material with continuous ECT treatment.[11] Untoward aftereffects have been documented, including painful and chronic states of emotional confusion, unremitting emotional bluntness, and long term memory impairment.[12]

ECT practitioners maintain that there are no contraindications for ECT except brain tumors and certain forms of cardiac sensitivity, and recommend it for affective disorders, involutional melancholia ("depression of old age"), the manic and depressive phases of manic-depressive psychosis, and wherever the danger of suicide exists in association with acute or chronic depressive reaction. It has achieved successful remissions in simple schizophrenia but there is invariably relapse. ECT has no proven efficacy in the treatment of neuroses or severe schizophrenia. Proponents are admittedly perplexed by ECT patients' fear of treatment. The initial, pre-treatment fear seems to center on the pain the patient expects to experience during ECT, which is relieved after treatment as he finds that there is no such pain. A more long-lasting anxiety occurs usually a week after ECT treatments and seems to be related to loss of identity or depersonalization.[13]

ECT is still not theoretically understood. Some maintain that the therapeutic element is a "biological antagonism" between epileptic-type states and the emotional states associated with schizophrenia and depressive psychosis. However, as Kalinowsky puts it, "Neither psychological nor organic theories [to explain ECT] have any basis in clinical or laboratory findings. Therefore, we must admit that we are very successfully treating conditions of unknown cause with treatments of an equally unknown mode of action."[14] Current studies have questioned the efficacy of ECT, and the increased sophistication in pharmacotherapy has certainly reduced ECT's popularity. However, it is still considered the "treatment of choice" for intractable, "drug resistant," and severely depressed suicidal patients.[15]

The use of neuroleptics, antidepressants, and other psychoactive pharmacologic agents to regulate, moderate, elevate and suppress emotional responsiveness is another technique of behavior control with roots in the prehistory of medicine. Both the noble and ignoble uses of this interventive approach are common knowledge and have been excellently documented elsewhere.[16] The morbid and toxic side effects (both drug- and mismanagement-related) are recognized by pharmacological firms as well as by the physicians who are proficient in their uses, though these tend to be deemphasized or rationalized as an unavoidable consequence of the best available treatment alternative. While pharmacotherapy does not in the short-range permanently damage or destroy brain tissue, its implementation raises the clinical issue of whether it is the brain itself or the ego which has undergone modification, whether the emotional change readily observed with most successful forms of pharmacotherapy is not merely enjoyed by the patient but is truly integrated into the personality.

One ready response to this problem has been that when one discontinues pharmacotherapy, there is regression to the pre-treatment state in the preponderance of cases where the patient is not concurrently undergoing psychotherapy. This strongly suggests that chemical modes of psychological intervention support such change during the course of treatment, but remain in a sense exterior to the patient's personality. Proponents of pharmacotherapy counterargue that (1) if the psychoactive chemical agent works efficiently, inexpensively and pervasively, then its implementation for the treatment of mental disorder should be likened to the treatment of diabetes with insulin therapy; (2) continuing with the diabetes analogy, the manifestations of mental health must be taken as an indication that the "ego" is also benefiting from such therapy and finally, (3) perhaps one should desist from talking about such hypothetical constructs as "ego," "unconscious personality," etc. whose existence has until now been inferred through relatively primitive clinical models. Such concepts can now be illustrated more materially through the success of pharmacotherapy, and are apparently the mentational or linguistic equivalents of the physiological processes concretely demonstrated during pharmacotherapy.

Technically SMB and ECT do not control behavior, but rather produce changes in behavior which are secondary to modification of emotional mechanisms. Electric stimulation of the brain (ESB), and pharmacotherapy to a lesser degree, more closely approximate what one would consider direct control of behavior. At the same time, the form of ESB which would fit the "direct control" model most precisely is still in an experimental stage. ESB involves the implanting of electrical stimuli directly in certain areas of the brain associated with either inhibitory or excitatory potential and to thereby achieve relative control of behavior through the eliciting of those centers' preprogrammed regulatory signals. The rudimentary experiments, including the introduction of electrical implants into the brain, began in the 1930's with W. Hess' work, and was applied to human subjects in the 1950's by Penfield and his associates. To date, practitioners have found that indwelling electrodes used in ESB are well-tolerated by the brain and that the organ seems to be able to tolerate the relevant trauma of the entire procedure. Radical proponents such as J. M. R. Delgado argue that ESB merely aspires to the role currently played by what we call "will" in triggering previously established brain mechanisms. ESB, in the radical view, merely supplants the will and, in certain applications, is perhaps more efficient than the will. Current research in both animal and human subjects confirms that ESB does activate and may influence some of the cerebral mechanisms involved in willful behavior.

ESB can elicit illusions, memories, emotions, psychical hallucinations, though nothing resembling "forced thinking" has yet been produced By stimulating the caudate nucleus of the reticular formation of the brain, ESB can elicit inhibition in the areas of food intake, aggressiveness, and territorial instincts. By stimulating the mesencephalon, changes in maternal behavior have been demonstrated.[17] Its inhibitory capabilities could be useful in treatment of Parkinsonian-type movements, intractable pain, epilepsy, anorexia, and a condition known as tradive dyskinesia, which is often a consequence of long-term treatment with some antipsychotic drugs and tranquilizers, and other neurologic syndromes induced by neuroleptic intervention. ESB, on an experimental basis thus far, can even simulate "sight" and "sound" for the blind and deaf, expanding their psychological orientation to the world.

A further refinement of ESB technology, perhaps with the greatest potential to challenge our notions of free will, is the use of "stimoceivers," already in use experimentally in animal and human subjects. Stimoceivers allow for the regulation and electric stimulation of behavior without interruption of social behavior. An epileptic seizure or schizophrenic episode could conceivably be detected by implanted electrodes, telemetered to some distant receiver and analyzed by a computer programmed to reorganize abnormal behavior patterns. The computer module would send back the appropriate signal to activate the patient's stimoceiver which would then emit an electric stimulus to the inhibitory area of the brain, thereby blocking the seizure or psychotic episode.

With ESB it becomes clear that cure may eventually be viewed not only as "implemented from without," but also from across great distances, emphasizing in a manner that is at once fascinating and foreboding the extent of man's increasing desire for and capabilities in psychological control and manipulation. It is imaginable that some of the conventional means of psychological influence (i.e., nonphysical intervention) could be employed to coerce and manipulate other persons to behave involuntarily, though such uses would for a long time remain highly impractical. However, it is precisely the potential for *impersonal* and *mass* control through SMB and ESB which makes these techniques stand out as uniquely different than conventional modes of psychotherapy, underscoring the *potential* for misuse. These potentialities, even if only imaginary, are part of what renders SMB and ESB "radical" forms of behavior control.

For other observers, such fears represent less concrete grounds for suspicion. And so, some concerned parties have chosen to stress *actual* abuses such as the dubious means of obtaining consent from some subjects of SMB experimentation or the untoward side effects of continuous psychopharmacologic intervention. From the standpoint of ethical analysis, however, there is no compelling reason to discount our fears and apprehensions about a phenomenon, so long as we can articulate these apprehensions in logical terms and in view of certain accepted principles and traditions against which the phenomena in question are found to be either in conflict or harmony. There is thus good reason to explore some of the senses in which SMB and ESB represent "radical" forms of psychological control and then to examine how much of their radical nature can be tolerated within current conceptions of ethical psychotherapeutic practice.

IV.

Conventional psychological interventions can be characterized by the absence of physical contact between subject and therapist as a necessary condition for the successful achievement of desired modifications. The efficacy of this class of interventions depends on: (1) the subject's perception of the therapist's authority, influence, 'rightness,' or 'wisdom'; (2) the subject's motivation or "willingness to change" (usually augmented by some amount of real or artifactual* deprivation); and (3) the mechanisms by which the brain internalizes the interaction between (1) and (2). Other factors may be involved as well. In some instances imparting insight positively augments the above factors; in some instances a maximally-directive therapist role may be more useful.

The balance of patients' responses to conventional psychotherapy suggests, among other things, that the 'brain' is not a passive participant in the psychotherapeutic process, and that input to it must somehow achieve a quality of ego-syntonicity and be sufficiently rewarding or promotive of adaptation before it can be integrated into personality. This characteristic is so critical as to be able to influence the therapeutic effects of even more direct forms of manipulation like behavior modification and pharmacotherapy. It seems that concepts like "will," "ego-syntonicity," "resistance," and so forth are relevant wherever the perceptual processes are considered the route to behavior change. In other terms, conventional psychotherapies seek to undo psychopathology by reversing the process by which pathology is believed to occur. This means, for most practitioners, utilizing methods which focus on intrapsychic equivalents of socio-perceptual antecedents, symbolic impressions of feeling, time, interpersonal process, etc.

Against this background, we can isolate several senses in which ESB and SMB are radical interventions. What seems most radical about such techniques is that their proponents are currently prepared to equate such constructs as personality, fantasy, desire,

* I.e., produced within the therapeutic environment as opposed to the pathogenic environment, such as the therapist's refusal at times to answer questions or the fact that the therapist cannot provide the patient with true "friendship."

will, and aspiration with discrete brain events. However, the notion that every mental event is causally related to *some* psychophysiological event, but is not *identical* with brain events (epiphenomenalism), is not the same as the notion forwarded by many extremists that every mentalistic aspect of personality *is* any *specific* brain event. At this stage in the art, even the first notion that every mental event is causally associated with some discrete brain event does not follow logically from the relatively few actual demonstrations of such apparent associations in *some* areas of brain-emotional activity. As Kety shows, there is yet no physiological argument which can explain consciousness—a necessary attribute of a major class of mental events.[18] Symbolic meanings, for another example, although they have to be learned, are not intrinsic to either the symbolized object or the brain's physiological mediating processes. Radical therapies have been criticized from an opposing direction. Many find it unconscionable that psychosurgeons are prepared to operate on brain matter that is physically undiseased yet is considered "dysfunctional" merely (1) by *assumption* of a relationship between the physical locus and emotional behavior and (2) by *inference* from disordered behavior (as postulated by Mark and Ervin).

It should be noted that conventional therapies also tend to define pathology or dysfunction by inference from behavioral omission or commission. Even without demonstrable tissue abnormality, psychology, and its equivalents through the centuries, has posited hypothetical entities to account for aberrant behavior: dybuks, demons, evil inclinations, libidinal deviations, S-R mediational engrams, etc. Indeed, the demonstrations in neurophysiology labs of a relation between emotional behavior and certain psychoelectric correlates tend to be more specific than anything modern psychology has offered.

However, as mentioned above, radical psychotherapists have been willing to posit unjustifiably broad and simple theories of behavior based on their inferences which bear unexplored implications for the understanding of normal and abnormal psychology, the limits of human potential, and the foci of treatment. Conventional therapies have tended to limit their lists of "unobservable" variables to those which appear to be amenable to change through the patient's willful participation in therapy (although obviously involuntary changes can also be wrought through manipulation of these variables). Somewhat paradoxically, then, the psychodynamic psychological "mythology" turns out to be sufficiently complex and discrete as a model as to *account* for correspondingly complex aspects of observable behavior. Psychophysiological models, on the other hand, cannot yet *account* for complex nuances in human behavior. Their accounts still consist of relatively gross explanations. So, for example, while no one has ever seen a "superego lacunum," it serves as a better explanation of why psychopaths typically have fears but no guilt, than does any extant, wholly physiologic explanation.

The difference in treatment focus, and the issue of physical versus nonphysical intervention, underscores the difference between conventional therapies' stress on the importance of the willful participation of the patient versus radical therapies' alleged ability to bypass the patient's voluntary participation. In conventional therapies, even a patient compelled to accept psychotherapy (e.g., a prisoner) can choose to resist, to waste his and the therapist's time, or to use the therapist as a stable mooring for self-discovery. With radical forms of behavior change, assuming knowledgeable consent was obtained prior to therapy, the patient's willful participation is irrelevant once the psychotherapeutic process has begun. During conventional therapy the ego is allowed to heal itself, while in radical psychotherapy, when successful, a patient is produced who is compelled to behave 'normally.'

Radical interventions as currently understood appear to have a truncated theory of human personality. The principles of conventional therapies, while often including certain deterministic tenets, are at least not incompatible with the principle of voluntarism, and tend to view involuntary behavior as significant of pathology rather than man's natural, most adaptive state.[19] The radical therapists' tendency to point out their successful management of heretofore unmanageable and unwilling patients merely underscores the *expedience* of their techniques. This very quality may also reflect inadequacies of technique or of their model of man rather than any truth to the belief that simplicity is more sound than complexity. As Nolan put it,[20]

> Regardless of whether science [psychology] is ethically neutral, a particular technology at any given stage of development will not be equally efficient at accomplishing all goals. In the absence of an independent basis for specifying goals, the technology is likely to dictate those goals which it can most efficiently accomplish. Such goals are not necessarily ethically neutral.

Thus, arguments of "superiority by virtue of expediency" or "simplicity" must also be carefully examined. At the same time there may be instances where ESB or SMB will be preferable to no therapy and times where no therapy is still the only ethically acceptable alternative for the patient. Such instances need to be distinguished as soon as possible.

Erwin argues that the dire consequences of radical forms of behavior control such as depicted in *A Clockwork Orange* are only outgrowths of behavior*ism* and radical learning theories which he feels are neither as empirially indubious as believed nor the equivalent of behavior *therapy*.[21] However, even in their current experimental forms, ESB and SMB and their theoretical models represent paradigms for social and behavioral control and assume an image of man which could popularize disagreeable norms of and expectations for human potential. As Gaylin wrote, "When behavior must be controlled for social living, the degree and direction of control will always be shaped and balanced by a view of man."[22] Obviously, a society may first surrender its current values in place of novel ones which then facilitate the attenuation of human freedoms through concrete measures. Delgado, for instance, notes that ESB does not closely resemble normal neuronal stimulation, but rather activates "and may influence" some of the already established cerebral mechanisms.[23] Yet, ESB is theoretically committed to and will soon be capable of accounting in ever more precise ways for the neurophysiological bases for complex behavior. It *is* inevitable, then, that under the influences of such a model, elements of personality would be equated with brain events and possibly substituted for by the delivery of electricity through external means or via the direct manipulation of brain tissue.

V. ———————————

We must also consider these issues in light of another matter. While few conventional therapists subscribe to the odious goal of the elimination of variability in human behavior, many more accept, at least theoretically or with a view to some ideal social state, the goal of maximum control of deviant behavior. Even the conventional therapist is called upon to offer therapy to incarcerated criminals and "unsocializable" adolescents. The therapist must often confront conflicting commitments to prevent private harm versus preventing public harm; e.g., using behavior modification or ECT to train an autistic child to be less self-destructive even though this will not likely restore or build a sense of free will in the patient.[24] Children, because they are "uninformed," are forced to adjust to school-required behaviors; prisoners, because they are 'unlawful,' must accept psychiatric rehabilitation, and psychiatric patients, because they are 'sick,' are sometimes forced by family or the state to participate in therapeutic efforts. In all such cases, the patient is truly an involuntary participant if only because the "consenting party" is concurrently the "damaged" or deviant party.[25] Thus, is not the implementation of *any* therapy on such patients radical? In addition to the problem of justifying radical therapy, *how does one justify the use of conventional psychotherapy in radical applications*?

The issue of forced or involuntary psychological intervention has been a matter of concern for the secular courts. While United States constitutional law allows the state to restrain, confine, or "contain" individuals deemed dangerous to themselves or others following the various legal commitment procedures, it is not legally or ethically clear whether the state may compel psychological intervention for the treatment of mental disorders. A practical illustration of this problem is the involuntary administration of powerful psychotropic drugs to prisoners or legally-committed psychiatric patients in order to alleviate hallucinations.

One point of view widely accepted within the mental health community is that mental illness robs patients of their autonomy and gives psychiatry warrant to override patients' wills with whatever confinement *or treatments* deemed necessary.[26] By analogy, the state has often presumed that it too has not only the power to confine, but also to treat.

Expressing another view, two important lower court decisions, not yet reviewed by the Supreme Court, have challenged these assumptions. In *Rogers v. Okin* (1979) and *Rennie v. Klein* (1979), it was ruled that the state does not, in fact, have the right to compel treatment of mental disorders in nonemergency situations and as long as there is no overbearing state interest in so doing.[27] Even in emergency situations, the state may have the right to avert physical injury, but only as a state interest and not merely to promote mental health.[28] The privilege of voluntary treatment, according to these decisions, is guaranteed both by the right of freedom of speech and by the right to privacy, which demands that the choice to accept psychological intervention be viewed as an "intimate decision."

The implication of these rulings is that even conventional therapies may not be involuntarily applied in the type of situations described above. A second important conclusion is that informed consent is a prerequisite in every instance of application of psychological intervention, whether or not the treatment method proposed is radical or merely conventional. And the effect is to sever the alliance between the state and the mental health profession, taking from both the power to impose involuntary treatment.[29]

Viewed from the standpoint of general society and secular law, then, the requirement for informed consent and for the protection of patients' rights to voluntary treatment can have numerous positive consequences. Speaking directly to Eissler's anxiety noted at the outset, these requirements will likely cause psychological professionals to practice more carefully, to rely more often upon conventional therapies, and to develop alternatives to radical treatments which have fewer ethically questionable or objectionable characteristics. This may initially strain current psychiatric conventions and ideologies but will, in the long run, preserve our ethical priorities and humanistic commitments.[30]

VI.

From the perspective of Halakhah, however, there are, in

principle, instances when what would appear to be "involuntary treatment" may be permissible, if not obligatory, and which do not on the surface involve the element of physical danger to self or bystanders.

The Talmud rules:[31]

> [The passage states] "And he *shall* offer it" [a sacrifice one vows to offer]. This teaches that we may force him to offer it. But could you mean that we force him against his will; did not the passage state "In accordance with his will" [Lev. 1:3]? Rather, we force him until he says "I am willing" [*kofin otho ad she-yomar rotzeh ani*].

For brevity, this will be called the *kofin*-model. The resulting law is that Jewish courts (*Beth Din*) may, under certain circumstances, exercise what appears to be coercion in order to elicit a "voluntary" fulfillment of religious obligations. Elsewhere, this law is applied to the granting of divorce, granting manumission to slaves, leaving appropriate funds to heirs, and fulfilling one's vows.[32] *Tosafoth*, in fact, rules that this power applies to all positive commandments at *beth din*'s discretion; while other authorities rule that all individuals may in some instances be required to compel a fellow to perform *mitzvoth* such as *chukim* and matters of *isur v^e-heter* (ritual prohibtions, *kashruth*, family purity, etc.).[33]

The paradoxical notion of "voluntary coercion" requires an explanation. Maimonides offers:[34]

> We only consider compelled one who is forced to do something that is not required by the Torah. . . . But one whose evil nature [*yitzro ha-ra*] convinced him to omit a religious precept or to commit iniquity, and was "forced" until he did that which he was obliged to do or until he refrained from that which he is forbidden to do — we did not *compel* him. Rather, he compelled himself [to do wrong] through his immoral intentions. Therefore, one who will not grant a divorce — inasmuch as he wishes to be [considered a] Jew and do all the *mitzvoth* and further himself from iniquity — but his conflicting inclination is compelling him [not to], once we rebuke [*she-hukhach*] him until his

> inclination weakens and he says "I am willing," he has [in effect] granted the divorce *willingly*.

Rabbi Joseph B. Soloveitchik has elsewhere distinguished between two levels of will: *ratzon elyon* and *ratzon tachton*.[35] *Ratzon elyon* represents the "I" that is the genuine center of personality, while *ratzon tachton* represents the surface, habitual personality. The halakhic efficacy of this distinction is seen in instances where we must assume for some reason that *ratzon elyon* was not involved in earlier actions or verbal utterances; e.g., *hatarath n^edarim*, *t^eshuvah*, and *asmakhtoth* ("conditional assurances"). In such instances, the earlier action may be considered "not I," and may be for all intents and purposes rescinded. It is presumably this same *ratzon elyon* which is the object of the *kofin*-model, the "true I" which Halakhah in such instances seeks to liberate and help reestablish in a position of autonomy over other aspects of self. Can one argue that society is justified in coercing the unwilling patient or subject to accept psychological intervention because such intervention is consistent with the individual's "deeper"—repressed, unconscious, physiologically confused, insufficiently reinforced—sense of normality and health?

Obviously, the *kofin*-model accepts this assumption. Thus, let us contrast the *kofin*-model to radical forms of psychotherapy. First, the *kofin*-model presumes to be merely a prod for the will rather than a *substitute* for the individual's self. The change in intent brought about following the *beth din*'s coercion presumably would then be integrated within the individual's overall personality. And, the individual *could* refuse to comply with the *beth din*'s wishes. However, following corrective SMB or ESB, it seems more precise to state that the individual is now behaving in obedience to a non-ego, physiologic manipulation. Indeed, using the example of granting a divorce, it is doubtful whether halakhah would accept as valid a divorce granted by a patient made to "want to" by ESB. It would view such external manipulation as exerting more influence than the individual's deeper convictions. In other words, what amounts to a momentary, corrective deprivation of free will in the *kofin*-model seems in the case of ESB or SMB to persist through to the post-therapeutic state.

Second, there is additional evidence, in each instance when the *beth din* may apply the *kofin*-model, of the individual's original intent to fulfill his religious obligations; the *beth din* merely seeks to readjust a *moral* lapse. Psychotherapy, on the other hand, can never hold an individual morally responsible for his failures and malapropisms or for failing to live up to his own or others' expectations. Thus, psychotherapists make no assumptions about the inherent desirability of the premorbid state, and would be loath to attempt to set up such assumptions as justifications for coercive treatment models.

Third, in applying the *kofin*-model, Jewish law assumes that, *ante facto*, the believer will be satisfied to have been coerced to do the will of God.[36] This assumption, however, is primarily a rationale for a religio-legal prerogative within a structure which happens to subscribe to a belief in man's "deeper" commitment to obey the Torah. Those seeking to justify radical therapy on these grounds would have to offer good evidence of their patients' post-therapeutic gratitude or at least some evidence that all individuals in their heart of hearts wish to be "normal." To date, such satisfaction can be demonstrated in the general population of less-disturbed patients, but in the population of these less-severely disturbed there is also no significant, interim compulsory state during psychotherapy. Too, it is doubtful that there are many recipients of "successful" ESB or SMB who are capable, even following treatment, of making adequate judgments about their new status. From the psychological standpoint, the patient's rationality *after therapy*, along with assorted other disruptive consequences of these procedures, may not be the equivalent of his rationality *in general*. This would seriously qualify the trustworthiness of the patient's report of satisfaction as an independent criterion by which to measure the worthwhileness or justifiability of radical therapy. However, it could be argued that even patients who cannot give adequate consent for such therapies may be "consented for" by *beth din*. This follows the view that *beth din* may provide for an insane individual's wife and children from his private funds, since *beth din* assumes that the individual would have consented had he been *compos mentis*.[37]

We are now in a better position to consider whether it is ethically justifiable to utilize radical techniques which by nature "bypass" human will and personal autonomy, even assuming one limits psychological intervention to situations where voluntary consent has been obtained. Of course, this issue is not likely to be resolved through a "yes" or "no" response, but probably involves determining the various conditions under which Halakhah would advocate, limit, or forbid the use of such procedures.

(1) It seems that Halakhah is not in principle opposed to techniques which are external to the will or which during their application circumvent free will. For example, although patients do not "participate" in the basic biochemical processes through which general medical or surgical treatment occurs, Halakhah accepts such intervention *per se* because both the pathological as well as normal operation of the biological processes, and their treatment, are not essentially voluntary mechanisms nor are these processes and related organs realistically viewed as the seat of human personality and intelligence. However, even when voluntary participation is relevant—such as in psychotherapy—Halakhah still accepts the possibility of involuntary treatment. One is therefore allowed to compel sick persons to obtain medical treatment since the "state" or *beth din* must indicate to persons that their obligation to physical health transcends their own self-interests.[38] And while the *rapoh y^e-rapey* model dictates that we may introduce treatment in emergency situations without consulting the beneficiary, the *kofin*-model further allows the direct contradiction of the patient's wishes if necessary. Based on similar reasoning, Rabbi G. Rabinowitz has recently ruled that one may in fact compel a person to obtain psychological therapy.[39]

(2) Halakhah would surely allow the use of any effective procedure in situations where risk to life is present or probable or where potential danger to bystanders exists, but only so long as the possibility of harm without such intervention persists. In this analogy, the psychiatric patient might be likened to the halakhic concept of *rodef* (the pursuer) and, if necessary, parts of the patient's own emotional apparati—*even* his will—may be viewed as *rodfim* with regard to his overall emotional well-being. When alternative and equally effective procedures to radical therapy exist, however, one would be obligated to utilize only those alternatives; doing no more than is necessary to effectively restrain the "*rodef*."

(3) The problem of utilizing radical techniques which may in

fact deprive or bypass the will for indeterminate duration will need to be analyzed with two additional factors in mind. One concerns the halakhic status of the cognitive-emotional abilities of the individual following treatment with such techniques. Note, for example, that the *kofin*-model in the case of the laws of divorce and the laws of sacrifices requires that the "compelled" individual still state "I am willing." At the same time, this utterance is not required in other instances of Jewish law when one may be compelled to fulfill obligations (e.g., inheritance). This suggests that in some instances even "voluntary coercion" via *k^{e}fiyah* does not attain full halakhic equivalence as free will until the individual in some way consciously "consents" to what he is about to do.[40]

Thus, if we wish to view the state of mind following or during radical psychotherapy as equivalent to the "voluntarily coerced" state of willingness produced through *k^{e}fiyah*, this state may not be qualitatively identical for all legal applications. Indeed, the global level of reaction currently obtained through radical procedures, and the subsequent wide area of personality modification which the patient would presumably have to assimilate, casts a shadow across the fairly limited capacity of the *kofin*-model. Specifically, in the case of the nonendangering or endangered psychiatric patient would we want to argue, by comparison to this halakhic model, that we are prepared to force him to become *socialized*—"flogging him even until his soul departs," or achieving an analogous degree of emotional bluntness and personality change?

A second factor concerns the general problem of whether or not the fulfillment of *mitzvah* obligations requires specific intent: *mitzvoth tzrikhoth kavanah* (see chapter 2). In the case of the numerous biblical and rabbinic *mitzvah* obligations which do require *kavanah* or intent, would the state of mind following or during radical psychotherapy be considered capable of maintaining autonomous *kavanah*?

A complete response to this problem will require careful halakhic and professional examination and testing of the personalities involved during various stages of treatment and with different treatment modalities. Of relevance in this examination will be the halakhic precedents which state that if one is compelled to perform a *mitzvah* by another individual who himself maintains the appropriate *kavanah*, the performance still fulfills the compelled subject's obligations.[41] Other authorities disagree, reinterpreting the precedents cited in the previous view as *mitzvoth r^{e}shuth* which *ante facto* may not require *kavanah*.[42] Moreover, the argument of the previous view is based on the concept of *areivuth* (fellowship) which allows for a "transference" of intent. However, in the case of ESB, SMB, or other radical techniques, no relationship of *areivuth* could be presumed to exist between the subject and the chemicals, computerized stimoceivers, or other mediating mechanisms operating during therapy. Involuntary, "mindless" compliance resulting from such procedures would be viewed by Halakhah as *mith'asek*, or coincidental behavior.

Aside from considerations concerning the compulsive quality of the states of mind produced by radical interventions, one must also consider whether the specific cognitive and affective sequelae of such interventions—both during the course of treatment as well as during the immediate post-treatment and long-term post-treatment stages—are equivalent to the talmudic definitions of insanity or *sh^{e}tuth*. This consideration is relevant inasmuch as the halakhic criteria for disqualification on grounds of mental incompetence include, according to some authorities, the mere demonstration of poor judgment or, according to others, severe affective disorder even in the absence of formal thought disorder.[43]

Rabbi Y. B. Landau, in a rarely cited halakhic essay, posits that if the recipient of pharmacotherapy, electroshock therapy, or regressive hypnosis retains basically intact judgment (demonstrated through competent halakhic examination), even in the presence of affect disturbance (which Rabbi Landau does not adequately quantify), the individual may be deemed *compos mentis* for matters of divorce.[44] In forwarding this view, Rabbi Landau is adopting the opinion that severe affect disturbance alone is not necessarily a contradiction to *pichuth* (sanity). Yet, as stated above, this opinion is not unanimously accepted. Moreover, the sequelae at least during the early stages of treatment and the initial post-treatment stage often include serious intellectual impairments and memory lapses which may limit an individual's halakhic status as a *pike-ach*. On the other hand, once a proven effective psychiatric treatment associated with minimal impairments has been initiated and a return to competence (*pichuth*) is apparent, one would no longer need anticipate the return of disqualifying characteristics.[45]

Thus, by way of general conclusion, while Halakhah might not object to the procedure of radical interventive technique *per se*, and may in specific applications deem involuntary treatment acceptable, the subsequent emotional and overall personality states may not necessarily be viewed as normal in an unqualified way, or in all halakhico-legal applications.

In this sense we are left with the serious ethical dilemma that, while the *kofin*-model may help justify ESB or SMB on the grounds that Halakhah considers the compulsory restoration of normal behavior just as obligatory as restoring moral posture, this model may in some instances be redundant—and hence not allow us to discover the halakhic identity of radical therapy *per se*—and in other instances cannot guarantee the same conclusions as it does in the strictly halakhic precedents. At the same time, the implication in the *kofin*-model that the "state" can assume the power to involuntarily treat mental disorder in certain cases suggests that Halakhah might differ with the humanitarian conceptions established in the secular courts. Finally, and in admittedly more abstract terms, we are left with the problem of developing some way to differentiate between procedures which, in Rabbi Soloveitchik's terms, liberate the *ratzon elyon*, and those which provide a more predictable, more socialized, yet more distant and dehumanized *ratzon tachton*.

VII.

Contrasting Halakhah with Delgado's tenets for a psychocivilized society, one notes that Halakhah cannot accept the view that man is not born free but subservient to genes and education.[45] Jewish ethics recognizes these influences, and accepts the notion of relative attenuation of personal freedom in cases of pathology and during some stages of development, but cannot accept that man's creative *and* regressive potentials are exhausted by rudimentary psychophysiological endowments or environmental influences. It also considers education and training as ways to facilitate wise and prudent choices and the purposeful use of personal freedom. In certain ways, it subscribes to the view that "normal" means not merely "not ill" but also "not stupid." But it cannot equate being "not stupid" with being *coerced.*[46] It recognizes the need for balance between complete autonomy and dependence, but cannot accept continuously supplanting individual choice with external control.

Notes

1. K. Eissler, *The Psychiatrist and the Dying Patient* (New York: 1955), p. 121.
2. M.H. Spero, *Judaism and Psychology: Halakhic Perspectives* (New York: 1980), pp. 11-30.
3. V. Mark & F. Ervin, *Violence and the Brain* (New York: 1970).
4. L. Laitinen & K. Livingston, *Surgical Approaches in Psychiatry* (Lancaster: 1973), while Vaughen states that the procedure fell into disuse earlier than the appearance of antipsychotic medications, in "Psychosurgery and Brain Surgery in Historical Perspective," p. 43 in W. Gaylin, J. Meister & R. Neville, eds., *Operating on the Mind: The Psychosurgery Conflict* (New York: 1975).
5. In Gaylin et al., *Operating on the Mind*, 1975, p. 192.
6. Ibid. p. 193. See also M. Greenblatt, "Psychosurgery," pp. 1291-95, in A. Freedman & H. Kaplan, *Comprehensive Textbook of Psychiatry* (Baltimore: 1972).
7. Cited in P. Schrag, *Mind Control* (New York: 1978), p. 298, note 34.
8. J. Swazy, "Psychosurgeon and Patient: Partners in 'Experiment Perilous,'" *Roche Report* (1975): 5(1), p. 7.
9. Greenblatt, "Psychosurgery," 1972 and see also W. Sargant, E. Slater & D. Keely, *An Introduction to Physical Methods of Treatment in Psychiatry* (Edinburgh: 1972).
10. J. Older, "Psychosurgery: Ethical Issues and Proposals for Control," *American Journal of Orthopsychiatry* (1974): 11(4), pp. 661-74; F. Redlich & R. Mollica, "Overview: Ethical Issues in Contemporary Psychiatry," *American Journal of Psychotherapy* (1976): 133, pp. 125-36; S. Halleck, "Legal and Ethical Issues in Behavior Control," *American Journal of Psychiatry* (1974): 131(4), pp. 381-85; S. Burton, "The New Biotechnology and the Role of Legal Intervention," *American Journal of Orthopsychiatry* (1974): 44(5), pp. 688-96; E. Mearns, Jr., "Law and the Physical Control of the Mind," *Case Western Reserve Law Review* (1975): 25(3), pp. 565-603. Recently, the 1976 *Commission for the Protection of Human Subjects of Biomedical and Behavioral Research* decided that psychosurgery should not be categorically prohibited and advocated its use with children, the institutionalized, etc.; see *APA Psychiatric News* (1976): Nov. 5 and see D. Martindale, "Psychosurgery: Furor Over the Cuckoo's Nest," *The New Physician* (1975): 26(2), pp. 22-25.
11. L. Kalinowsky, "The Convulsive Therapies," pp. 1279-85 in A. Freeman & H. Kaplan, *Comprehensive Textbook of Psychiatry*, 1972.
12. Ibid., see also Schrag, *Mind Control*, 1978, pp. 155-60.

13. Ibid.
14. Ibid., p. 1285.
15. See Schrag, *Mind Control*, 1978, p. 292, note 7.
16. Ibid., pp. 106-47.
17. J.M.R. Delgado, *Physical Control of the Mind: Toward a Psychocivilized Society* (New York: 1969), pp. 153, 173-75.
18. S. Kety, "A Biologist Examines the Mind and Behavior," *Science* (1960): 132, 1861-70 and also see W. Penfield, "The Neurophysical Basis of Thought," pp. 342-49 in J. Howells, ed., *Modern Perspectives in World Psychiatry* (New York: 1971). The patient reductionism of equating mind with body, or psychology with physiology, is brilliantly trounced by Gordon Taylor, *The Natural History of the Mind* (New York: 1979).
19. See my "Psychological Determinism, Free Will and Halakhic Values," in *Journal of Judaism and Psychology* (1978): vol. 2 no. 2, pp. 5-18.
20. J. Nolan, "Freedom and Dignity: A Functional Analysis," *American Psychologist* (1974, March) pp. 157-60.
21. E. Erwin, *Behavior Therapy: Scientific, Philosophical, and Moral Foundations* (Cambridge: 1978).
22. Gaylin et al., *Operating on the Mind*, 1975, p. 11.
23. Delgado, *Physical Control of the Mind* (1969): pp. 150-53, cf. p. 176, "Human relations are not going to be governed by electrodes, but they could be better understood if we consider not only emotional factors but also the intracerebral mechanisms responsible for their reception and elaboration."
24. Erwin, *Behavior Therapy* (1978): p. 179 and see D. Robinson, "Harm, Offense and Nuisance: Some First Steps in the Establishment of an Ethics of Treatment," *American Psychologist* (1974, April): 233-38.
25. Gaylin et al., *Operating on the Mind*, 1969.
26. Peszke, M.A., *Involuntary Treatment of the Mentally Ill: The Problem of Autonomy* (Springfield, Ill.: 1975).
27. *Rogers* v. *Okin* 478 F. Supp. 1342 (D. Mass. 1979), *aff'd in part, rev'd in part*, 634 F. 2d 650 (1st Circ. 1980), *cert. granted*, 49 U.S.L.W. 3779 (1981); *Rennie* v. *Klein*, 476 F. Supp. 1294 (D.N.J. 1979), *modified*, Nos. 79-2576 and 79-2577 (3rd Circ. Jul. 9, 1981).
28. *Addington* v. *Texas*, 441 U.S. 418, 432 (1979).
29. White, M.D. & White, C.A., "Involuntarily Committed Patients' Constitutional Right to Refuse Treatment," *American Psychologist* (1981): 36, 953-62.
30. See W. Coryell & R. Wetzel, "Attitudes Toward Issues in Psychiatry among Third-Year Residents: A Brief Survey," *American Journal of Psychiatry* (1978): 135, 732-35.
31. *R.H.* 6a.
32. *Yev.* 106a; *Kid.* 49b-50b; *B.B.* 48a; *Arkh.* 21a; *M.T., Hil. Ma'asei Korbanoth* 14:16, *Hil. Rotzeach* 10:10, *Hil. Ishuth* 12:15, *Hil. Matnoth Aniyim* 7:10; *Tur Sh. A., Y.D.* 248:1; *SMaG*, Pos., no. 162, Neg., no. 331 (see also Num. R. 10:10).; *Sh. A., O.H.* 328, *Mishneh Berurah*, no. 6; see also *Arukh ha-Shulchan, E.H.* 154:18-22, 63; *Resp. Radbaz*, vol. 1, no. 349; *Sh. A., H.M.* 107.
33. *Ket.* 49b, *Tos.*, s.v. *akhfiyah*; *R.H.* 6a, *Tos.*, s.v. *yakriv*; see also *Chiddushei ha-*

RaN to *R.H.* 62. See also *Sha'arei Tohar* (1978), vol. 6, no. 29 and *Resp. Chatham Sofer: H.M.*, no. 177, who argue that all individuals, and not only *beth din*, are obligated to compel a fellow man to perform *chukim*, matters of *isur ve-heter*, and other *mitzvoth*—because of the principle of *arvuth* and the obligations which devolve from it—with the exception of laws in the category of *mishpatim*, such as divorce, monetary matters, etc. since such laws require the expertise of *beth din* (see *B.K.* 28a). In some applications, while one cannot compel an individual to fulfill *mitzvah* obligations, such as *kibud av va-em*, one can still compel him to comply with fundamental social obligations such as not to cause *tza'ar* or embarassment (*kofin oto al kalon aviv*); see *Rama, TaZ*, and *Arukh ha-Shulchan* to *Y.D.* 240:1; *Mishnah la-Melekh, Hil. Malveh* 4:4.

34. *M.T., Hil. Gerushin* 2:20; *Sh. A., E.H.* 134:7-8, 154:21; *Rama, B.B.* 48b. With regard to whether *Beth Din* is required to compel and, if they are not, whether they are punished or not, see *Resp. Rashba*, no. 945; *Birkei Yosef: Y.D.*, no. 248; *Chinnukh*, end no. 33; *Rama, Sh. A., H.M.* 97:16; *Resp. Chatham Sofer: H.M.*, no. 177. As an interesting aside, the Talmud (*Shab.* 88a; *A.Z.* 2a) states that God compelled the Jews to accept the Torah at Sinai by "holding the mountain over them like a tub." Thus, one sage offers this tradition as a "grand excuse" to be ever free of punishment for violating Torah laws since their acceptance was involuntary. The Talmud responds with the well-known concept of *kimu ve-kiblu*, that the Jews subsequently and voluntarily confirmed the Sinaitic revelation, retroactively conferring a determinate status upon the original event. Other explanations for this pseudo-problem have been offered. R. Moshe Sofer asks why the dilemma cannot be resolved simply by appealing to the *kofin*-model on God's behalf, as it were (*Resp. Chatham Sofer: O.H.*, no. 185)? He responds that the *kofin*-model can only be applied *after* the initial acceptance of the Torah, which presumably then serves as the *a priori* basis for the subsequent use of the *kofin*-model (similar to the "ear that heard at Sinai" model).

35. In A. Besdin, Reflections of the Rav (Jerusalem: 1979), pp. 93-95.

36. *Kid.* 50a.

37. *Mor u-Ketziah*, no. 328; *Resp. Melamed le-Ho'il: Y.D.*, no. 104.

38. Rabbi G.A. Rabinowitz, "*Hotza'ath Bath she-Yatzah le-Tarbuth Rah mi-Beth Horehah*," pp. 342-48, in M. Hershler ed., *Halakhah u-Refuah* (Jerusalem: 1980). *Beth Din* may be able to force consent in our case by using the argument of *Ket.* 48a, *Sh. A., E.H.* 71, where *Beth Din* assumes that the individual in question *would have* consented.

39. See *Or Sameach* to *M.T. Hil. Gerushin* 2:20.

40. See *Sedei Chemed*, vol. 4, p. 134; *RaM* to *Ket.* 86a; *Resp. Radbaz*, vol. 2, no. 34; and also *Chiddushei ha-RaN* to *Chul.* 31a, s.v. *u'le-inyan*.

41. *Imrei Binah: O.H.*, no. 14 (p. 116) and *Resp. Beth Yitzchak: Y.D.*, vol. 2, no. 168:1, who state that in any obligation where *shlichuth* is possible, then too, the *kavannah* of an *omed al gabo* is acceptable.

42. See *Resp. Divrei Chayyim: E.H.*, no. 77; *Arukh ha-Shulchan: E.H.*, 121:13; cf. *Resp. Atereth Chakhamim: E.H.*, no. 17; see also *Sedei Chemed*, vol. 5, pp. 119-29. For matters of *eduth* (testimony), most authorities are far more stringent. See also chapter 4, note 52 and Appendix II. See also D.S. Shapiro, "*Choleh be-Machalath ha-Ruach Im Yakhol le-Garesh*," *ha-Darom* 1, no. 1 (1957):41-50.

43. "*Diyun be-Peratiyoth be-Sugey Choli ha-Ruach ve-ha-Nirpa'in be-ha'Metza'uth Terufoth ha-Chadashoth*," pp. 377-85, in M. Amsel ed., *Sefer She'eloth u-T^e^shuvoth ha-Ma'or* (New York: 1966). In a recent responsum, R. Moshe Feinstein finds no reason to object to the general use of hypnosis, but does not discuss the relevant problem of the halakhic efficacy of acts produced under hypnotic suggestion, *Resp. Igroth Moshe: Y.D.*, vol 3. (1981), no. 44.

44. Landau, op. cit., pp. 380-81; see also *Resp. Emek She'elah: E.H.*, no. 76.

45. Which he terms "postulates of psychogenesis," in *Physical Control of the Mind*, 1969, p. 242.

46. E. Becker, *Revolution in Psychiatry* (New York: 1964), p. 209. Compare with "No man sins unless a spirit of folly overtakes him" (*Sot.* 32).

7
Halakhic Definitions of Confidentiality in the Psychotherapeutic Encounter: Theory and Practice

The psychotherapist's role as bystander to the client's innermost secrets and confidences devolves from the high degree of mutual trust each party must invest in the other so that their working alliance can operate effectively. At the same time, the right of privacy with regard to such confidences which the patient maintains and the therapist protects is a practical consequence of certain legal and moral commitments that are either implicit or explicit in the contractual relationship which exists between the two parties. No less than in medicine, where the physician commits himself to safeguard professional secrecy by taking the Hippocratic oath, the mental health worker, too, commits himself through his professional code of ethics (which does not necessarily contain an oath) to safeguard the privacy of all information about the client whether directly pertinent to the client's problem or derived indirectly through the course of their relationship (e.g., diagnostic tests, referring notes, etc.). There are occasions, however, when it is morally imperative that the professional share his confidential knowledge. Yet, in between the unambiguous indications for either professional confidentiality or prudent disclosure of confidential material are grey areas where the professional is left to apply whatever ethical principles he abides by in order to determine where his priorities lie and what posture is most appropriate to the given situation.[1]

Confidentiality as an Ethical and Social *Desideratum*

The principle of professional secrecy is based on the notion that everything the patient says to the practitioner is actually the private property of the patient which he or she shares with the practitioner for the express purpose of facilitating the achievement of certain goals, or which comes forward during the course of their relationship even when not specifically related to the achievement of such goals.[2] The patient who elects to undergo psychological assessment, psychotherapy, or marriage counselling does not relinquish "ownership" of his private property, but instead, allows the therapist to share this property, *conditional upon* the therapist's guarantee that no further sharing of this property will occur with any other person with whom the patient has not struck a similar contract.

The privilege of confidentiality is closely related to the basic notion of secrecy. Implicit in the term "secret" (from the Latin *secretum*) is the connotation "something which is one's duty to set apart or conceal from the common knowledge of men." Objectively, a secret is a hidden thing; subjectively, it is the knowledge of something hidden with the obligation of not revealing it.[3] The right of privileged communication refers specifically to a legal right which protects the patient from having confidential information about him revealed in public, which includes his own family, or in court without his permission.[4] This right is presumed to generally, if not always, supersede all other incumbent obligations a therapist may have *qua* citizen to bring forth testimony relevant to civil or criminal proceedings. At the same time, this notion of the secret as private property has a complementary aspect which is that should a patient forfeit his right of privacy—such as by becoming a real or potential threat to others—the professional's unique obligation to the patient becomes secondary to his obligation to the common social good and welfare. However, when therapists have taken oaths of confidentiality not to testify in court regarding patients without their consent, the issue of revealing necessary information becomes complicated by the need to weigh the community's interests against the sanctity of such oaths.

Finally, what is "private" about the therapeutic relationship is that it is a dialogue which transpires solely between the two participants (or more, if such is the contract, as in family therapy or marriage counselling).[5] This notion of privacy also means that the patient will not discuss his relationship or the content of his therapeutic sessions with any other parties. In psychoanalysis, specifically, this dual-direction of privacy is discussed at the outset of analysis so that subsequent breaches of this rule can be explored from the standpoint of "resistance," "transference reactions," and so forth in the effort to understand the dynamic motives for trespassing the privacy of the therapeutic relationship. We shall see in a later section that practitioners working within closely-knit Jewish communities encounter particular difficulty safeguarding this commitment where violations of confidentiality on the part of therapists, patients, and the general community are prompted by both neurotic motivations as well as by ethnic attitudes which in *other* circumstances would be halakhically praiseworthy, such as *areivuth* or fellowship.

An additional moral principle underlying the preservation of confidentiality is that protecting a patient's good name and reputation is an important control or motive for good living; and that, within limits, minimizing public attention to deviant behavior promotes social peace.[6] Moreover, a necessary condition for persons to wish to seek the assistance of others is the assurance that one will not be betrayed, and thus find one's problematic condition made worse.[7] Frustration of this willingness to seek help would lead to hopelessness and despondency and would eventually disrupt social relations.

Thus, by basing the ultimate value of individual privacy upon the preservation of social as well as individual peace, we are also able to derive that an individual's right to a confidential relationship is subordinate to the rights of his fellows and of society in general. This is the basis for advocating the discreet revelation of professional secrets in the oft-cited example of the therapist or physician who discovers that his patient, who happens to be a school bus driver, is an epileptic or a poorly-maintained borderline psychotic.[8] In such cases, ethicists generally agree that it is insufficient for the therapist merely to give the patient the choice of either informing the necessary authorities or terminating his relationship with the therapist; but rather, *must* himself notify both his client and the authorities as soon as possible.[9]

The theologian Vermeersch, echoing Aquinas, states the moral principles here as follows:[10]

> Since both extremes must be avoided as sinful, namely, failure to tell the truth when it ought to be told and indiscreet revealing of the truth, the means of virtue is to be followed. This is obtained by observing the law of sincerity, which induces discreet manifestation of the truth, and by the law of secrecy, which prohibits indiscreet manifestation of the truth.

This double-edged principle is the basis of the "holy" fiduciary responsibility to preserve professional confidentiality as expressed in the Hippocratic oath,[11] the professional codes of ethics of the American Medical Association, the American Psychological Association, and the National Association of Social Workers. Each code recognizes not only the right of the patient to privileged communication, but also that this right cannot be absolute.[12]

To be more specific, each of the professional organizations mentioned above holds its diplomates or licensees to the following basic commitments: (1) The patient has the right to confidentiality. (2) This right extends beyond the period of professional services and even beyond the death of either party. Under this clause is included the careful disguise of all identifying characteristics of the patient during research or when using the patient's case material in public or professional reports. (3) The professional must state and guarantee this right. (4) If the patient's manifest or anticipated behavior may cause harm to individuals or society, the professional may be obligated to divulge the minimum information necessary to avert harm and only to the least number of persons necessary for achieving this goal.

In explicating these guidelines, Moore-Kirkland and Irey suggest that the therapist's role be viewed as that of a *mediator* of knowledge and not merely as a protector of secrets.[13] According to this perspective, both parties are cognizant that under certain conditions—not specified adequately by these authors—it will be incumbent upon the therapist to *mediate* certain knowledge gained from or about the patient to others outside of the therapeutic dyad. This perspective may have a certain appeal within the larger social work intervention model where the worker as broker is often expected to mediate otherwise confidential information among others such as agencies, relatives, support institutions, social service providers, etc. However, it does not really modify the dual obligations of the therapist: to preserve secrecy in the absence of mitigating circumstances or without the patient's consent to reveal confidential information to others, on the one hand, and to disclose confidential information in other circumstances when such disclosure is for the greater common good. More useful in this regard are Promislo's four conditions for determining whether the privilege of confidentiality can be guaranteed:[14] (1) All communication begins with the patient's belief that it will not be disclosed. (2) Confidentiality promotes a full and satisfactory relationship between therapist and patient. (3) Such relationships *ought* to be fostered, although this supposition would not be commonly accepted if it were learned that therapists generally held back information bearing on public safety. (4) The injury a therapeutic relationship would suffer by disclosure must be greater than the benefit such disclosure would produce for the protection of others or for the speedy disposal of litigation. Many of these principles are implicit in the halakhic scheme.

In actual civil law, most states have specific statutes which strictly subject the physician-patient relationship to a privilege of secrecy. These statutes specify, among other things, that the professional will not be compelled—and is not permitted (unless the patient waives his rights)—to testify in court regarding confidential knowledge.[15] However, in the recent decision of *Tarasoff v. Regents of the University of California*, the Supreme Court of California ruled that therapists who have determined that their clients pose a dangerous threat to the safety and welfare of others are obligated to protect the "intended victims" against such danger.[16] In such instances, disclosure becomes essential to the public good. In contrast with this ruling (which so far is law only in California) is Siegel's and Breggin's radical position that the psychotherapist should under *no* circumstance disclose confidential information, which, according to Breggin, includes even situations where commitment to confidentiality may appear to threaten the well-being of an innocent bystander. They believe that such an absolute commitment is vital to the institution of therapeutic trust.[17] On the one hand, practical experience informs us that unqualified confidentiality is not as vital as Siegel, Breggin, and others sympathetic to this view suppose. Indeed, it may be critical to the therapist's ability to represent some sort of model of morality that he or she be able to convey to a patient that there are reality-imposed limitations to absolute secrecy in certain instances. Moreover, such absolute libertarianism runs the risk of endangering the welfare of other citizens, impinging on society's right to enjoy peace and safety from harm. Yet neither *Tarasoff* nor the A.P.A. or N.A.S.W guidelines makes adequately clear the conditions under which confidentiality or disclosure is the proper ethical response, and guidelines such as Promislo's have not been applied to specific, practical situations. The professional is thus no further along in resolving the ethical dilemma of "when to tell and when not to tell."[18]

Halakhic Conceptions of Secrecy and the Value of Confidentiality

I. ————————————

In his most recent review of Jewish medical ethics, Chief Rabbi Immanuel Jakobovits briefly comments that in halakhic literature, "professional secrecy was never enjoined on physicians with the zeal with which it is now regarded by the medical profession because it was covered simply by the general injunction against talebearing."[19] In fact, there are numerous references in the midrash, Talmud, and codes to the significance and parameters of confidentiality—though not always strictly related to the medical profession and certainly not the psychological profession. Rabbis J. David Bleich and Alfred S. Cohen have recently reviewed some of the pertinent responsa regarding the disclosure of secrets in medical practice and in business.[20] While some of their findings will be noted here, additional references are examined as well. There will be a specific focus on unexplored models applicable to problems which arise in clinical psychology and psychotherapy. A useful halakhic perspective will emerge from the existing rabbinic statements regarding the value of confidence-bearing and the destructiveness of tale-bearing and from the ethical guidelines provided in scattered codes and responsa. Finally, such guidelines will be most useful if related concretely to specific applications from the field of practice.

II.

For Halakhah the importance of confidentiality in the individual or professional encounter could be seen as devolving most basically from its social theory that the *mitzvoth*, at root, are designed to promote individual and social welfare (*l^e-tzaref bahen eth ha-brioth*).[21] Expanding this, confidentiality is not merely a specific contingency of a unique professional oath or contract, but must presume—and as we shall see, sometimes grant priority to—the underwriting structure of *kavod ha-brioth*.

The basic halakhic ethic can also be deduced from passages from the Prophets. "He that goes about as a talebearer reveals secrets; But he that is faithful, conceals a matter."[22] More specifically, "Confidence in an unfaithful man in time of trouble is like a broken tooth, and a foot out of joint."[23] Simply put, an untrustworthy confidant actually becomes part of the patient's problems and a lack of trustworthy professionals increases society's problems. Additional Biblical passages which serve as bases for professional secrecy are discussed in a separate section.

The Talmud expresses itself on this subject in characteristic fashion. "Seven things are hidden from man . . .[one of which is] what is in his fellow's heart."[24] In other words, perhaps the greatest secrets—those which deserve to be kept secret—are those matters which lie in the "heart" or personality, in that domain which represents man's ultimate bastion of individuality. R. Shimon Edels (*Maharsha*) interprets this aphorism to mean that without discretion the concept of privacy would be defeated.[25] That is, man is entitled to keep private his thoughts, feelings, and other knowledge about himself because this is an essential component of differentiating the self from others and for maintaining this distinction.[26] Invasion of privacy is tantamount to the abolition of selfhood.

Apparently more extremely committed to the value of secrecy is Hillel's remonstration, "Do not tell a thing which should not be heard, for in the end it will be heard."[27] Hillel's statement suggests that one's privacy is already compromised by the very fact that someone other than oneself is also privy to the secret. Of course, Hillel's point must be taken as intentional hyperbole since its literal interpretation would contradict the prevailing rabbinic attitude that there are times when a suffering person has no better recourse than to share his innermost problems and woes with a sympathetic listener—"Or companionship, or death."[28] R. Asi specifically instructs that confidential dialogue or counselling helps abate the destructive effect of woe or anxiety.[29] Or, as a later ethicist, R. Chunin Ibn Ashik, would put it, "The preservation of a secret [*in a confidential relationship*] is the basis of love."[30]

An excellent example of the extent of the fiduciary obligation in granting confidentiality is found in the following talmudic statement:[31]

> From whence [does one derive] that one who has been told something by one's friend is under ban not to [repeat what he has heard] until he is [expressly] instructed "tell"? The Writ says, "And God spoke to him from the Tent of Appointment saying" [i.e., God's instruction included the specific command to "Tell"].

This statement relates to the earlier mentioned ethic that by initially sharing "private property" in the confidential relationship, the teller does not relinquish his domain over such property. This view is actually carried over into daily halakhic living by Rabbi Abraham Gombiner (d. 1683) who rules, with reference to the above citation, "If one tells over something he heard without permission to do so, he violates an injunction."[32]

Nonetheless, in line with the wisdom of striking a mean between absolute confidentiality and wanton indiscretion is the following rabbinic interpretation of Solomon's couplet, "A time to be silent and a time to talk"[33]—"There are times when one receives reward for keeping silent, and times when one receives reward for talking."[34] This would seem to be the general attitude for the psychotherapist toward the material the patient shares with him, implying that there will be exceptional situations where divulgence of secrets will be justifiable in specific amounts, as warranted by the particular circumstances.

From the few references cited thus far it is quite clear that Halakhah considers the maintenance of general and certainly professional confidentiality more than a matter of prudence. Basic to these references is the important ethical commitment to preserve *kavod ha-brioth*, individual and social welfare and honor.[35] *This commitment calls for an almost paradoxical promotion of interpersonal* areivuth *(fellowship) precisely by maintaining a minimum of traffic regarding confidential matters among outsiders to the confidential relationship.* It is in this sense that "the preservation of a secret is the basis of love."

The Talmud also relates confidentiality to the highly valued attribute of trustworthiness, "All who conduct themselves in trustworthiness merit to sit in the partition of God, as it is written, 'Mine eyes are upon the faithful of the land, that they may dwell with Me; He that walks in the way of integrity, he shall minister unto Me.' "[36] And elsewhere, "All who conduct themselves in trustworthiness, are not given over to the 'One who extracts' [a reference to God's oath to extract punishment from those who violate their vows]."[37] A further indication of the strong censure of untrustworthiness is found in the talmudic account of a student of R. Ami who revealed what was actually a widely-known matter that had been discussed in the academy twenty-two years earlier. R. Ami expelled him, dubbing the student with the epithet, "the judge who reveals secrets."[38]

Later ethical tracts also emphasized the importance of securing or being a trustworthy confidant. Shlomo Ibn Gabirol (d. 1069) records two stories. They asked one scholar, "How do you conduct yourself regarding secrets?" He replied, "When someone reveals to me a secret, I dig a grave for it in my heart where it will lie buried forever." A story is related of another scholar who was entrusted with a secret by his fellow. His fellow then asked him, "Did you comprehend what I told you?" The scholar replied, "I have already forgotten what you told me!"[39] R. Isaac Aboab (d. 1492) states, "One who reveals secrets that his friend entrusts with him is called a talebearer."[40] R. Yonah ha-Chasid of Gerona (d. 1263) in his halakhic-ethical tract, supports the concept of confidentiality as an assurance and a motive for help-seeking when he rules, "One is obligated to conceal a secret that his fellow reveals to him in confidence . . . for in unwarranted disclosure of a secret there comes harm to its owner and may cause him to become distraught."[41] Finally, in the ethical will of R. Eliezer the Great one finds the instruction, "Be a trustworthy spirit to all men."[42]

Halakhic Legislation Regarding Confidentiality

Several fully Biblical positive and negative obligations and injunctions also are involved which more clearly regulate the proper balance between indiscretion and confidentiality. We will be able to distill from these sources specific halakhic procedures and policies regarding the management of confidential material in psychological and psychotherapeutic practice.

On the one hand, preserving secrecy devolves from the basic categorical imperative "Love thy neighbor" inasmuch as keeping secrets preserves the established social order.[43] More specifically—and as will be evident, more practically— professional secrecy stems from the prohibition against talebearing and slander, "You shall not go about as a talebearer among your people" (*Lo thelekh rakhil*),[44] echoed again in Proverbs by, ". . . reveal not the secrets of your neighbor,"[45] as well as in R. Isaac Aboab's and R. Yonah ha-Chasid's ruling that one who reveals secrets is called a *rakhil*, or one who violates "*Lo thelekh rakhil.*" Commenting on "He who goes about as a talebearer reveals secrets," R. Elijah Gaon rules explicitly, "One who reveals confidences and one who bears tales, their transgression is the same."[46]

The halakhic codes further clarify that the injunction of "*Lo thelekh rakhil*" subsumes a wide variety of indiscretions, including the revelation of any matter which would infringe upon another's reputation or cause him embarrassment.[47] The law precludes both men and women from either initiating or listening to defamatory tales, and this applies to tales about children and even the deceased.[48] As elaborated in R. Moshe Sofer's classic text, *Makor Chayyim: Shmirath ha-Lashon*, the prohibition against talebearing is not lessened in general circumstances by the fact that the tale is common knowledge. That is, one is still forbidden to repeat or transmit such tales given the human propensity to embellish the tale or inadvertantly to encourage further discussion of the matter in a manner which might eventually lead to character assassination or to embarrassment.[49]

An additional parameter of safeguarding secrecy will be mentioned briefly at this point since it will need to be qualified later. When one party vows either verbally or through written contract—and perhaps even by tacit commitment to a widely-accepted professional code of ethics—to maintain confidentiality, then breach of such contract would also be forbidden by the laws of vows.

III.

The above references establish the case for *categorical confidentiality* and say nothing specific about the possibility of or need for circumspect disclosure of secrets on certain occasions. Of course, without marshaling further references, it would be the case that the prohibitions against disclosing professional secrets and against breaching professional oaths to maintain absolute secrecy would be waived in circumstances involving even the possibility of *sakanath n^{e}fashoth* (danger to life), as are all other obligations and prohibitions in such circumstances, with the exception of the three so-called cardinal sins.[50] The principle that "danger to life is more stringent than prohibitions" (*Chamirah sakanta me-isura*) is sufficient to waive the *prima facie* obligation to secrecy when danger warrants its application.[51] An important perspective in this regard is that to the degree that the patient who threatens to endanger others assumes the halakhic status of an aggressor (*rodef*), it would be incumbent upon the bystander—the therapist or his more perceptive supervisor—to do whatever is necessary, but no more than is necessary, to avert catastrophe.[52] This is so, at least according to R. Elijah Gaon, even in the absence of demonstrable or conscious intent to cause harm.[53] Note however, that we have not yet discussed alternatives to disclosure of secrecy in the effort to avert harm; the above only establishes the maximum obligations as such.

In addition to the above application of the stringencies of *pikuach nefesh* and *rodef* to the obligation of confidentiality, there are other principles which specifically require the disclosure of or the preparedness to disclose information not just when life is at stake, but even when such disclosure will aid one's fellow in non-life-threatening monetary matters, or will prevent him from violating ritual prohibitions.

First, consider Rabbi N. Z. Y. Berlin's observation that the apparently unrelated clauses of the passage "You shall not go about as a talebearer among your people; do not stand idly by your brother's blood" (Lev. 19:16) indicate that when "talebearing" will prevent calamity, *hesitating* to disclose is tantamount to bloodshed.[54] This lends greater halakhic impact to the rabbinic interpretation of Solomon's couplet cited earlier. The Talmud and codes state in various places that refraining from disclosing information as testimony which may spare one's fellow from trouble violates three separate Biblical injunctions: (a) standing idly by one's brother's blood; (b) ignoring a call to bring forth material testimony (*Im lo yagid . . .*)—which according to some authorities includes not bringing forth relevant testimony even when not subpoenaed by the litigants or the rabbinic courts;[55] and (c) being afraid to testify and concealing material testimony (*lo taguru . . .*).[56] Others add that inappropriate restraint regarding needed disclosure violates the Biblical "*mi-d^e^var sheker tirchak*" (stay far away from falsehood) and "*u'biarta ha-ra mi-kirbekha*"' (chase out all evil from among you),[57] although these passages serve primarily as supports (*asmakhtoth*) rather than as full Biblical injunctions. Finally, according to R. Yaakov Briesh, failure to disclose when appropriate violates "not placing a stumbling block before the blind."[58] The obligation to disclose when necessary is, of course, also steeped in the philosophic notion or preserving social order.

Specific details of the above laws are relevant here. Note that Halakhah requires even a *single* witness, such as a therapist or psychological examiner privy to pertinent information, to testify in monetary matters or matters of ritual prohibition (*isurin*), unlike in matters of *n^e^fashoth*, since in the former instances even a single witness has rabbinic efficacy.[59] On the other hand, most codifiers add that even in these applications the single witness is not obligated to come to court unless he is actually summoned by either the court or the litigant.[60] However, whenever two persons bearing material testimony are available, all agree that both parties must come forward even without being summoned. Second, the single witness is not obligated, if he is not forbidden to publicly testify on matters of *isurin* if the ritual transgression or impropriety has already occurred and no further transgression is anticipated. Should he disclose his knowledge in such instances, he, too, violates the injunction against talebearing.[61] A third relevant aspect of testimony is that while a witness in general is not allowed to present his inferences and assumptions as fact, he may present his inferences and assumptions *as such* and leave it to the court to decide how to deal with his disclosures.[62]

Problems of Disclosure as Treated in Some Responsa

Some important aspects of the conflicting requirements to disclose or to maintain confidentiality emerge in detailed case analyses presented in select halakhic responsa. In the responsa to be discussed in this section, two important issues are addressed: (1) Does the underlying principle in preserving secrets, *kavod ha-brioth*, supersede the incumbency of "*lifney iver*" (not placing a stumbling block before the blind); e.g., when keeping silent would prevent a second party from taking appropriate action regarding a possible violation? (2) What is the halakhic status of professional oaths or tacit commitments to secrecy, and under what circumstances may such oaths be violated for the sake of some greater good?

The first issue is discussed in separate responsa by R. Ezekiel Landau[63] and R. Chaim Halberstam.[64] The presenting case involved the following peculiar circumstances: A young man had an adulterous relationship with the wife of a couple with whom he lived for several years. Subsequently, he recanted his sin and became a *ba'al t^eshuvah*. He then became engaged to the couple's daughter! The specific questions addressed to Rabbi Landau and also discussed by Rabbi Halberstam were whether the young man is obligated to inform his future father-in-law of his sexual transgression since the husband is forbidden by Jewish law to continue living with his adulterous wife, and whether the *beth din* ought to be informed should the husband refuse to accept his unfortunate obligation?

In introducing his response, R. Landau rephrases the issue: may the young penitent maintain passive silence in order to preserve the integrity and honor of the apparently well-known husband? The supposition in ruling leniently would be that *kavod ha-brioth* supersedes passive violations (*shev ve-al ta'aseh*), which would obtain in our case if the young man maintained his secret. The husband would then be erring *b^eshogeg* (inadvertently) at worse. Rabbi Landau compares the case at hand to the law regarding one who notices his fellow wearing *sha'atnez* in public: *Rambam* and *Beth Yosef* rule that as long as the potential *transgressor* has a direct act to perform to prevent transgression (*kum v^e-aseh*), others must inform him of the error immediately—even to tear off the forbidden garments in public—since the offender's embarrassment is secondary to the *chilul ha-Shem* which might otherwise occur. The *Rosh* and R. Moshe Isserles rule that one does not have to take such radical action and may allow the offender to reach privacy where he can remove the garment without shame. Radical action, according to the *Rosh*, is only required when *oneself* is the transgressor. After some discussion, R. Landau notes that the *Rosh* is lenient in the case of *sha'atnez* only because the offender was in transit and the error *could* be corrected momentarily, whereas in the present case, failure to inform the husband would result in continuous transgression. R. Landau accepts this as the definitive limitation to the *kavod ha-brioth* argument. R. Landau thus concludes that the husband must be told, adding that this is necessary at the very least so that the young man can obtain forgiveness [*m^echilah*] from the husband without which his *t^eshuvah* will never be complete. He also states, however, that *beth din* need not be informed in any case since appropriate testimony is lacking and the husband is, therefore, not technically obligated to believe the young man's account.

Rabbi Halberstam reviews R. Landau's analysis and argues that even *Rambam*'s stringency applies only to a fully specified Biblical prohibition. He then attempts to show that the prohibition against retaining one's adulterous wife is not a distinct biblical prohibition. R. Halberstam then concludes that the husband need not be informed, viewing the young man's passive silence as an appropriate application of the *kavod ha-brioth* principle, and also that the wife need not be instructed to confess to her husband since he is technically not obligated to accept her account.

The above two responsa make clear that serious consideration must be given to the potential cost and benefit of disclosing information when even serious violations may be averted. Rabbi Halberstam appears to allow a passive stance and the maintenance of secrecy in the case of less than fully Biblical prohibitions when damage to *kavod ha-brioth* will occur. Even according to Rabbi Halberstam, however, one cannot preclude the obligation to disclose information when this may avert a more serious catastrophe. According to R. Landau, even a single witness would be obligated to disclose pertinent information *in a discreet way* if this would prevent the persistence and certainly the initiation of *isur ("le-hafrisho me-isura").*[65]

Despite the significance of their contribution, however, neither responsum deals with the issue of disclosing necessary information in the highly relevant case where the person harboring such information has taken an oath not to breach confidentiality, which generally includes a refusal to produce testimony regarding such matters in court, or belongs to a profession generally presumed to subscribe to such an ethic, even in the absence of a formal oath. One must examine other sources to clarify this problem.

Rabbi Eliezer Waldenberg discusses this topic and reaches the following conclusions: (1) One may certainly not take an oath not to testify *after* one has been called to court.[66] (2) If one takes a prior *general* oath to preserve confidences absolutely, such an oath is valid even though this oath would include not testifying in court.[67] However, such an oath still represents a nullification of the obligation to testify on one's fellow's behalf; thus one can presume that a halakhically observant professional has also accepted a prior mental reservation not to include in such a vow material testimony which would be of value to avert calamity. In effect, professional vows of secrecy would not be originally intended to cancel one's halakhic obligations. Rabbi Waldenberg adds that on the "slight chance" one did intend such a vow to exempt one from testimony, one must nullify the vow before a *beth din* so that he may be permitted to produce testimony when necessary.

Addressing the same problem, Rabbi Barukh Rakover forwards the following practical conclusions:[68] (1) A professional commitment without an oath to maintain absolute confidentiality is not deemed the equivalent of an oath. And although some decisors would appear to require informed consent before such a "commitment" be violated, most accept that even a single witness enjoined against testifying merely by such commitment must bring forth relevant testimony when necessary without the consent of other parties.[69] (2) An oath not to testify *after* being called to court is generally invalid. (3) A *single* witness who makes such an oath even after being subpoenaed need not testify (without first nullifying his oath) since his testimony is only rabbinically valid and thus his oath has not violated any Biblical prohibition. It has been indicated above, however, that the obligation of a single witness to testify certainly supersedes oaths when *sakanah* is involved. It would appear, then, that professionals who have not taken oaths of confidentiality—or have, but are presumed to have mentally qualified them according to Rabbi Waldenberg—would be required to testify as per the demands of *beth din.*

A final consideration of this problem was reported by the *Beth Din* of Israel.[70] The case involved a woman whose husband's psychiatric illness was disrupting their marital and family life. She had requested pertinent information and records from the military psychologist who refused on the grounds that a policy of revealing confidential matter would eventually threaten military security. The *Beth Din* ruled that the psychologist's argument indeed waived his obligation to disclose the necessary information, but only because disclosure *in this particular case* could actually have far-reaching negative consequences such as a threat to the security of the army and even to the state. One may infer in cases of lesser threat, such as when disclosure may cast aspersions on the reputation of a single professional, that the obligation to aid one's fellow is sustained. However, Rabbi Alfred S. Cohen states that when disclosure threatens a professional psychologist with irreparable damage to reputation and possible financial ruin, disclosure would not be obligatory.[71]

Rabbi Cohen forwards two arguments in support of his conclusion which merit further examination. He first appeals to the principle that one is not required to spend more than one-fifth of one's income in fulfillment of *mitzvoth*. While this principle generally applies to positive commandments, there is a question whether it also applies to negative commandments (i.e., one may not violate a negative commandment no matter what the cost). Although R. Moshe Isserles agrees with several *rishonim* who rule that this principle does not apply to negative commandments, Rabbi Cohen adopts the *Chatham Sofer*'s view that the above principle does apply to negative commandments, provided the person does no forbidden action but merely fails to act to prevent violation (*shev ve-al ta'aseh*).[72] He notes that this qualification is apparently anticipated by R. Elijah Gaon and others.[73] Rabbi Cohen then adds, "our research shows that the majority of halakhic authorities accept the position that a person whose livelihood depends upon maintaining the confidentiality of revelations made to him need not jeopardize his position by telling these secrets" (p. 84), since the professional is not violating the *mitzvah* by *doing* any action.

The reader is not told whom Rabbi Cohen consulted in adopting this conclusion, and one must consider some objections to his first argument. (1) Several authorities rule that when the therapist's secrets bear on the ensnarement of a *rodef*, the professional *is* obligated to disclose his confidential information and thereby avert catastrophe. Certainly it is presumed by these authorities that news of a therapist's disclosure may have some discouraging impact on others, but that this impact is still deemed secondary to the obligation to aid one's fellow. (2) While Rabbi Cohen is correct that the fulfillment of *mitzvoth* is generally limited to expenditures of up to one-fifth of one's income, there are also numerous positive commandments which actually require any and every expense, such as purchasing wine for the *Seder*, Hanukah candles, *pidyon ha-ben*, and others. Rabbi Cohen offers no evidence that aiding one's fellow through disclosures of relevant secrets is not also one such *mitzvah*. The *mitzvah* of *pidyon sh^evuyin*, which is quite analogous to the case at hand, may also require expending more than one-fifth of one's total wealth.[74] Even if one were to correctly apply the one-fifth principle as Rabbi Cohen has presented it, one would be required to ascertain that disclosure would actually cost the professional one-fifth of his income and no less. Thus, appealing to the principle of one-fifth does not seem to adequately support Rabbi Cohen's conclusion. (3) When "failure to act" is itself the nature of the violation, e.g., *not testifying* or *not* coming to one's brother's aid, one cannot construe this as an instance of "*shev ve-al ta'aseh*" (note that the *SMaK*, no. 239 considers "*v^{e}-im lo yagid*" a *mitzvath lo ta'aseh*, contrary to *SMaG*, nos. 108-109; *Rambam*, nos. 178-179; *Chinnukh*, no. 122).

The principle one ought to evoke at this point is whether one is permitted to place oneself in jeopardy to aid one's fellow. While the Jerusalem Talmud actually demands placing oneself into *sakanah* (danger) if necessary in order to save one's fellow from *sakanah*, the Babylonian Talmud rejects this view, and thus rule the codes and subsequent responsa.[75] It is from this ruling that one might conclude that a therapist, who *clearly* is threatened with ruin should he disclose confidences, may indeed not be obligated to make such a disclosure.[76] Where such a threat is not likely—as is more generally the case since such disclosures are usually discreet and often readily understandable in the public's mind—there would be little to defend a failure to come to the aid of one's fellow. Moreover, the Babylonian Talmud is only forbidding one to endanger one's physical existence to save another, but does not include financial expenditures.

Rabbi Cohen's second argument posits that the public's "fear of exposure would preclude many persons from seeking help which they desperately need." This is probably an empirical issue, although Halakhah is sensitive to the need to guarantee society that privacy can be secured from certain professionals. On the other hand, it would be a definite detriment to society if persons believed that such privacy was generally deemed so absolute that they might conceivably carry out harmful intentions and escape justice under the protective cloak of a confidential relationship. It would appear far more important for citizens to understand that they can expect from their psychotherapists a completely confidential relationship *so long as* they remain committed to certain basic ethical constraints. This understanding, I believe, has been sustained since earliest times and has not resulted in adverse consequences to the public or lessened the willingness of most to avail themselves of psychological services when needed.

Practical Guidelines for Confidentiality in the Practice of Psychology and Psychotherapy

Several practical applications with regard to a halakhic definition of confidentiality can be drawn from the preceding principles, codes, and responsa. Before enumerating these, it is worthwhile to reiterate that from the standpoint of Halakhah, even if a therapist does not subscribe to a formal or written contract or code stipulating his obligations and the patient's rights, all of the forthcoming obligations and rights are deemed in full force by virtue of an *a priori* halakhic mandate.[77]

Generally, (1) the psychotherapist has a solemn halakhic obligation to maintain professional secrecy regarding his or her patients and their families. This obligation would obviously require keeping secret the very fact that a specific person has entered or even inquired about the possibility of psychological assessment or psychotherapy. It would also demand that psychotherapists procure appropriate work locations which guarantee privacy (i.e., not their own homes unless extreme precautions are taken). This obligation extends even beyond the termination of the professional relationship or the event of the patient's death. All of these obligations obtain *whether or not* the therapist has taken an oath to this effect.

(2) When a patient forfeits the right to confidentiality because he directly or indirectly poses a threat to the life or welfare of others or even to himself (e.g., suicide), the therapist is halakhically obligated, first, to expeditiously explore alternatives to frank disclosure in the effort to prevent calamity.[78] Lane and Spruill, for one resource, discuss several alternatives to actual disclosure, yet fail to mention the most obvious: informing the patient *cum rodef* that he must choose between his "dangerous" wishes or intentions and his desire for a guaranteed confidential relationship.[79] Should this tactic fail, the therapist must be prepared to initiate a series of graduated disclosures (e.g., to the intended victim, his family, police, or other protective services). In such instances, one is still required to utilize prudence to ensure that such disclosure does not exceed necessity.

(3) The therapist cannot appeal to his prior commitments (*sans* oath) to professional secrecy when his knowledge is

demanded by the court or by a litigant and when his disclosures will help prevent even less than life-threatening loss. However, with the exception of Rabbi Samson Raphael Hirsch, most authorities rule that a single witness is not required to come forward unless he is summoned (if the professional has taken a prior oath to privacy, see section 8 below). In legal proceedings involving matters of *nafshiuth* (capital law), the therapist as a single witness is in fact forbidden to disclose his knowledge since a single witness's testimony is invalid in such proceedings. Indeed, his disclosure in such cases would be considered talebearing. However, when a supervisor or a co-therapist shares identical knowledge of the therapist's secret (and does not merely know of such matters indirectly through supervision), the two become obligated by Biblical mandate to come forward and disclose such material when relevant both in *mamonoth* (monetary matters) as well as *nafshiuth* (capital offenses).

An example of weighing the merits of confidentiality *versus* disclosure would be the case of a marriage counselor whose former clients are currently entangled in "dirty" divorce proceedings in court or before a *beth din*. The therapist has learned that one of the mates is grossly misportraying and maligning the other and the costs to the "victim" include financial loss and character defamation. It is obvious that the antagonistic mate will not wish to release the professional from his commitment to secrecy. Yet, it seems that the therapist is obligated to come forward for three reasons: (a) he cannot stand idly by as his fellow is "pursued" by another, (b) he cannot allow the "aggressing" party to utilize the therapist's commitment to secrecy as a tool through which to cause harm to others, and (c) it may be a necessary deterrent to domestic *dis*harmony for society to understand that the marriage counselor's commitment to confidentiality under *most* circumstances will not prevent him or her from disclosing professional secrets in court if one of the partners acts unethically.[80]

(4) If the therapist becomes aware during his relationship with a patient or while gathering data pertinent to the case, of the unwilling or willful transgression of Biblical prohibitions (e.g., incest, adultery, rape, etc.), the obligation to share such information depends upon (a) whom he wishes to inform (e.g., R.

Landau's case), (b) whether the transgression threatens to continue or has already been committed once and for all, (c) whether the patient, desirous of effecting complete *t^eshuvah* regarding the transgression, is himself obligated to confess his sin or make recompense to any offended parties, and (d) whether there exist appropriate witnesses through which to prove that the act in question indeed occurred (i.e., *ein adam meisim atzmo rasha*). Transgressions "between man and God" (*bein adam la-Makom*) must be kept private.

(5) In writing and presenting evaluational, diagnostic, and process reports, the writer must bear in mind that while the patient may have freely volunteered to be evaluated or tested, all inferences and diagnostic hypotheses are in a sense extorted from the patient's manifest behavior or verbalizations; i.e., the patient's "reasonable ego" does not initially wish to tell even his therapist that the patient is plagued by incestuous fantasies, and so forth, but a skilled clinician may infer from characteristic test responses that this is so. Such indirectly acquired so-called natural secrets are also the property of the patient even though the patient does not know he has such property, and must be respected as such. Also, when diagnostic or prognostic inferences need to be disclosed as testimony, Halakhah demands that such data be presented as inference rather than as fact. The important principle here is that Halakhah cannot accept testimony based on presumption or inference (*ein danim al ha-umd^ena*).[81]

(6) The discussion of clinical material in a clinical team conference format or in the presence of students is appropriate because this is done for the ultimate benefit of the patient and is not designed for *g^enuth* or character defamation, although the standard practice of disguising nonessential identifying characteristics should be applied.[82]

(7) While Halakhah enjoins one to "stay away from falsehood,"[83] professionals are often confronted with the dilemma of whether a lie is permissible to protect confidentiality when mere silence would be tantamount to disclosure (as the Talmud itself says, "Silence is as an admission"[84]). Can one respond to unauthorized questions by stating, "I know nothing about the matter," *with the mental reservation*, "to communicate to unauthorized persons?"[85]

Resolution of this matter depends upon the legitimacy of the third party's query. Sometimes such inquiry is wholly illegitimate, such as when a third party inquires whether Smith is in treatment, "So that we can lend him support . . .", etc., or when some inquisitive gadabout confronts the professional with, "I *know* you're seeing Smith's son. I referred him to you. I just hope you can cure him." Do these questions merit false answers or denials when the usual "I don't discuss my professional activities" will be taken by others as a confirmation of their suspicions?

In the case of Smith's son, since both professional and third party already know that Smith's son *is* in treatment, the therapist's reluctance to confirm or deny reveals no new knowledge. In this case, it is sufficient for the therapist to merely reply that he does not discuss his professional activities. More generally, the professional is duty-bound to protect his patients from illegitimate or unlawful inquiry. When mere silence would violate this obligation, modification of the truth may be the acceptable alternative. Halakhah specifically condones modification of truth in the interests of preserving peace or staving off embarrassment—which are the ultimate goals of confidentiality. "Said R. Illayi in the name of R. Eliezer, son of R. Simon, 'It is permissible to modify the truth in the name of peace' . . . R. Nathan said, 'It is an obligation.' "[86] This statement is further supported by the fact that Halakhah in some instances validates mental reservations made at the time of an oath and does not consider such reservations a violation of the principle of staying clear of falsehood.[87] Thus, it would surely seem permissible to mentally qualify one's much less sacrosanct, noncommital responses to illegitimate inquiries in order to preserve peace.[88]

At the risk of moralizing, I would add to this point that the Jewish ethic of fellowship or *areivuth* is not without its neurotic and self-serving determinants. The popular conception that intrusions and inquiries into others' welfare are permissible because of *ahavath re'im*, or a therapist's belief that "sharing" professional secrets with patients' relatives, rabbis, *roshey y^e^shiva*, and so forth is similarly justifiable, are fine examples of rationalizing a basic disregard for the selfhood of others or a therapist's unresolved need for the respect and love of his religious community.[89] Such *areivuth* is essentially annihilative, and is frequently bestowed upon incoming *ba'alei t^eshuvah*, some of whom in reaction feel virtually denuded by the oversolicitous advising, sharing, referring, monitoring, and counselling that often occurs "for their sake." All such tendencies merit careful self-examination or, at the very least, a second look at the excellent psychoanalytic primer, *Shmirath ha-Lashon*!

(8) The process of amamnesis or history-taking often involves a patient's disclosure of information bearing on the actions and character of others or the professional's solicitation of information from the patient's parents, teachers, and associates. Such collection of confidential information does not violate the prohibitions against talebearing or listening to slander or "evil talk." (a) Many halakhists have stated that when previous errors or transgressions—or any other pertinent matter—are evoked in the effort to modify personal weaknesses, such endeavors in fact fulfill the biblical mandate to "remember the days of old."[90] Thus, by analogy, history-taking and evaluation function to eventually promote required remembrances designed to facilitate the eradication of disease or suffering. (b) One of the basic halakhic models supporting the healing endeavor is that the physician, or psychotherapist, functions by implicit commission as an agent of *beth din*.[91] Thus, the therapist's professional endeavors are analogous to those of an "agent of *beth din*"—to guide, socialize, and correct. In addition to role (a), the therapist, as an agent of *beth din*, is exempt from the prohibition against slander and talebearing, as is the law regarding *beth din* itself.[92] Finally, (c) one is obliged to obtain, and if necessary provoke others to disclose information when this bears on one's personal investment (*l^e-tovath atzmo*) in establishing a viable and productive business or domestic relationship.[93] It would again seem that the psychotherapist's evaluations operate under the same intent in the establishment of an effective therapeutic relationship. Note also that each of these three analogies dissolves the prohibition of "placing a stumbling block before the blind" which the professional would otherwise transgress in the process of involving other parties in the disclosure of confidential information.[94]

(9) If the mental health worker actually took a halakhically valid oath or vow to categorical secrecy, this oath would not supersede *pikuach nefesh* where indicated.[95] In other circumstances,

a prior, general oath to categorical secrecy would be inviolable, although the therapist is urged, even obliged, to come forward and offer testimony where necessary by first obtaining absolution from such oaths so that he can fulfill his obligations.[96]

(10) Should the need or demand for testimony represent a clear and present threat to the therapist's professional livelihood—all the above obligations withstanding—there is reason to believe that the therapist is still obligated to reveal professional secrets. However, this tentative conclusion needs further analysis. If, on the other hand, no such threat exists, despite the therapist's *concern* in this regard, and the solicited disclosure would spare his fellow from clear and present danger, then the obligation to disclose remains incumbent according to some authorities. As the *Arukh ha-Shulchan* warns: although we maintain that one is not obligated to jeopardize his life for the sake of another's, one should not be unjustly cautious in this domain.[97]

(11) In most jurisdictions, death terminates the privilege of confidentiality. Thus, psychologists may be called to testify about their deceased patients in order to determine the mental capacity of a person at the time a will was executed or whether a death involved suicide, circumstances which may result in the nullification of insurance benefits or other compensations. While Halakhah extends the privilege of confidentiality beyond death, it would defer in such cases to the *dina d^{e}-malkhutha* or the call of *beth din*.

(12) While statutes have not yet been clearly worked out to address the unique confidentiality problems which arise in the practice of group or conjoint therapy, it would appear that when there are more than two parties in therapy, each must be seen as "an agent" of therapy (at least according to theory) and accordingly is obligated to preserve the type of relationship deemed critical to therapeutic success elsewhere. The fact that Halakhah sometimes considers statements made in the presence of three persons to be subject no longer to the laws of *lashon ha-ra* (since it is technically common knowledge), this does not mean that a *confidence entrusted as such to three or more persons is any less inviolable.*

(13) Problems of confidentiality can also arise in mundane areas of professional practice such as the settlement of delinquent

accounts. Professionals occasionally are forced to go to court in order to collect delinquent fees which necessarily involves some disclosure about the patient to the court or a collection agency. Current statutes do not consider this an invasion of privacy. Halakhah would concur with this view, presuming ample warning had been made. However, some court cases have established that the psychotherapist is responsible if his collection agent makes unjustifiable disclosures (e.g., calling up a patient's employer in order to collect the debt). Here, too, Halakhah would presumably concur, although if the patient persisted in acting as a *rasha*, *beth din* could empower its agents to threaten to and, if necessary, actually shame the patient into resolving his financial problems. This would remain, however, a highly discretionary matter.

Conclusion

We have seen that from the perspective of Halakhah, the problem of striking a mean between professional discretion and disclosure is certainly not left to the intuitive judgment of the mental health professional nor merely to the professional's application of the principle that his fiduciary obligation is contingent upon the patient's desert of the right of secrecy. Rather, there are specific imperatives which, on the one hand, demand professional secrecy as an individual and social good, while also demanding disclosure in other circumstances. The professional will surely encounter circumstances which have not been addressed sufficiently by the above principles and conclusions and, as in all cases, he will seek the opinions and recommendations of competent halakhic authorities. It is hoped, however, that one will find here the essential source material and some initial considerations which should sensitize the worker to the scope of his halakhic obligations and to the issues he will need to consider in evaluating his responsibilities.

Notes

1. See P. Lane and J. Spruill, "To Tell or Not to Tell: The Psychotherapist's Dilemma," *Psychotherapy: Theory, Research and Practice* 17, no. 2 (1980): 202-9; S. Arnold, "Confidential Communication and the Social Worker," *Social Work 15*, no. 2 (1970): 61-67; M. M. Reynolds, "Threats to Confidentiality," *Social Work 21*, no. 2 (1976): 108-13 and "Privacy and Privilege: Patients', Professionals', and the Public's Rights," *Clinical Social Work Journal 5*, no. 1 (1977): 33-34; K. Levick, "Privileged Communication: Does It Really Exist?" *Social Casework 62*, no. 4 (1981): 235-39; E. Promislo, "Confidentiality and Privileged Communication," *Social Work 24*, no. 1 (1979): 11-15.
2. R. Regan, *Professional Secrecy in the Light of Moral Principles* (Washington, D.C.: 1943); B. Ashley and K. O'Rourke, *Health Care Ethics* (St. Louis: 1978); H. Davidson, "Professional Secrecy," in E.F. Torrey ed., *Ethical Issues in Medicine* (Boston: 1968); O. Ruebausen and O. Brim, "Privacy and Behavioral Research," *Columbia Law Review 65* (1965): 1184-1211.
3. *Secretum* is derived from the verb *secernere*: *se*, or "apart," and *cernere*, or "to sift." See also A. Vermeersch, *Theologia Moralis: Principa, Responsa, Consilia* (Bruges: 1924), vol. 2, no. 697.
4. S. Shah, "Privileged Communications, Confidentiality, and Privacy," *Professional Psychologist 1*, no. 1 (1969): 56-69.
5. T. Szasz, "The Problem of Privacy in Training Analysis," *Psychiatry 25* (1962): 195-207.
6. Regan, op. cit. (1943): pp. 18-20; see also the perspective expressed by the *Sefer haChinnukh*, nos. 236-240. See also Songs R. 1 and *Sanh.* 43b to the effect that God despises those who publicize defamatory accounts about Israel.
7. Regan, ibid.
8. Issues relating to confidentiality and privacy are discussed in several outstanding psychoanalytic papers, such as A. Watson, "Levels of Confidentiality in the Psychoanalytic Situation," *Journal of the American Psychoanalytic Association 20* (1972): 156-76; A. Mariner, "The Problem of Therapeutic Privacy," *Psychiatry, 30* (1967): 60-72; and Szasz, op. cit., 1962.
9. Davidson, op. cit., 1968 and H. Brody, *Ethical Decisions in Medicine* (Boston: 1976).
10. Cited in T. V. O'Donnell, *Medicine and Christian Morality* (New York: 1976), pp. 281-82.
11. Constantine's code also required physicians to keep secrets, as described in T. Moore, *Principles of Ethics* (Phila.: 1935), p. 338. See also note 20 below.
12. "Code of Ethics of the American Medical Association," *J.A.M.A.* June 7, 1958; American Psychological Association, "Ethical Standards for Psychologists," *American Psychologist 18* (1963): 56-60; and see generally J. Clapp (ed.), *Professional Ethics and Insignia* (Metuchen, N. J.: 1974).
13. J. Moore-Kirkland and K. V. Irey, "A Reappraisal of Confidentiality," *Social Work, 26*, no. 4 (1981): 319-322.
14. Promislo, op. cit., 1979.
15. E.g., the *N. Y. Civil Practice Act, Sect.* 352, and others cited in Regan, op. cit., pp. 120-21.

16. *Tarasoff* v. *Regents of the University of California*, 551 P. 2d, 334 (1976).
17. M. Siegel, "Confidentiality," *The Clinical Psychologist 30*, no. 1 (1976).
18. See note 1 above.
19. I. Jakobovits, "Judaism and Medicine—An Overview," *Assia 7*, nos. 3-4 (1980): 57-78. It is interesting to note that Maimonides' prayer for physicians does not contain any reference to professional secrecy (cf. Jakobovits, *Jewish Medical Ethics* [New York: 1975, p. 16, n. 109] who disputes the authenticity of this prayer, and F. Rosner, "The Physician's Prayer Attributed to Moses Maimonides," pp. 125-41, in his *Medicine in the Bible and the Talmud* [New York: 1977]). However, the physician's prayer of *Assaf ha-Rofeh* includes the specific statement, "*ve-al tegalu et sod adam asher he'emin lakhem*," cited in A. Steinberg, "*Tefiloth u-Shevu'oth shel Cholim ve-Rofim*," *Sefer Assia*, vol. 1, p. 257.
20. J. David Bleich, "Professional Secrets," *Tradition 17*, no. 4 (1979): 90-94 and Alfred S. Cohen, "Privacy: A Jewish Perspective," *Journal of Halacha and Contemporary Society 1*, no. 1 (1981): 53-102. Cohen then published, "On Maintaining a Professional Confidence," *Journal of Halacha and Contemporary Society 7* (1984): 73-88, subsequent to my publication of the original version of this present chapter in *Tradition 20* (1982): 280-326, discussing many of the halakhic sources mentioned here.
21. Mid. Ps. 18:25; Gen. R. 44:1; *Tosefta Shab.* 16; *Chinnukh*, no. 545; *Moreh* 3:27; see also *Abravanel* and *Ramban* to Deut. 22:6.
22. Prov. 11:13; similar to Prov. 20:19 and Lev. 19:16; see also *B.K.* 99; *Sanh.* 31.
23. Prov. 25:19.
24. *Pes.* 54b; Gen. R. 65:12; Eccl. R. 11:9.
25. *Maharsha* to *Pes.* 54b.
26. C. Schneider, *Shame, Exposure, and Privacy* (Boston: 1977).
27. *Avoth* 2:5 and see the commentary of Rashi and R. Yonah, citing Eccl. R. 11:20; see also *ARN* 28. Similar thoughts are expressed by "Any secret you would hide from your enemy, hide also from your beloved" (*Mivchar ha-Pnimim* 29, no. 1) and "The wise person will not reveal his secrets and will not ask others to reveal their secrets" (S.D. Ibn Falaquera, *Igereth ha-Mussar*, p. 32).
28. *Taan.* 23a; *B.B.* 16b.
29. *Yoma* 75a; *Sot.* 42b; *Sanh.* 100b; see also R. Yonah haChasid, *Igereth ha-Teshuvah, Yom 2*, p. 195; also, *Avoth* 2:13.
30. In *Musrei ha-Philosophim 2*, no. 13.
31. *Yoma* 4b; *Pes.* 42a; *Tem.* 7b; *Sanh.* 31a, 44b.
32. *Magen Avraham* to *Sh. A., O. Ch.* 156; *SMaG*, Neg. no. 8; see also *Sefer Chasidim*, no. 85.
33. Eccl. 3:7.
34. *Zev.* 115b; see also *Arkh.* 15b.
35. *Avoth* 4; *Ber.* 19b, 28b, 43b; *B.M.* 58b; cf. *Ket.* 17a.
36. See *Tamid* 28a, citing Ps. 101:6; also *Taan.* 8a.
37. *J.T. B.M.* 12b; see also *Tosefta B.M.* 3:7.
38. *Sanh.* 31a.
39. *Mivchar ha-Pnimim: Sha'ar Hastarath ha-Sether*; see also *Meiri* to Prov. 11:13.

40. *Menorath ha-Ma'or, Ner* 1:4, 2.
41. *Sha'arei T^eshuvah* 3, p. 129, based on Prov. 15:22, 20:19.
42. *Tzava'ath Geonei Yisrael* (I. Abrahams, ed., J. P. S., 1937), vol. 1, p. 44.
43. Lev. 19:18 and see note 31 above; see also *Lev Avraham* (1976), vol. 2, pp. 69-70. The selection of an appropriate location for conducting confidential business is taught by Rabbi Akiva, "[For three reasons] do I honor the Medians . . . for when they consult, they consult in the field" (*Ber.* 8b, and see Rashi).
44. Lev. 19:16.
45. Prov. 25:9, and see *Sanh.* 44b.
46. *Peirush ha-Gra* to Prov. 11:13.
47. See *Mekor Chayim: Shmirath ha-Lashon*, intro. and passim. It is also plausible to consider the obligation to preserve secrecy as falling under the category of protecting a *pikadon* entrusted in one's care (Ex. 22:6; *Sh. A., Ch. M.* 291:26, 292:7), except that the laws of *pikadon* deal specifically with items of monetary value (*B.M.* 57b). However, I would suggest the idea that confidentiality is included as an instance of preserving *pikdonoth* to the degree that the revelation of many types of secrets (such as copyrights, patents, military secrets) has palpable monetary consequences. This idea can also be supported by another interpretation which broadens an apparent *monetary* obligation to include the appropriate disclosure of "secretly" obtained information. I refer the reader to R. Barukh Halevi Epstein (*Torah Temimah*: Deut. 22:2), commenting on the phrase "And you shall return it to him," which the Talmud interprets to include "the loss of life," who adds, "And included in this is if one heard that persons were plotting evil against another person — it is a *mitzvah* to inform him." This would obligate a therapist to inform intended victims about harmful intentions expressed by or inferred from his patients when the therapist has cause to believe that he cannot prevent the patient from acting upon such intentions (see also *Resp. Chelkath Yaakov* cited in note 58 below).
48. *Ber.* 19a; *J.T. M.K.* 9a; *M.T. Hil. Talmud Torah* 6:12; *Sh. A., Y.D.* 243:7, 334:47, *O. Ch.* 606:2-3; *Mekor Chayim*, no. 8(9).
49. *Mekor Chayim* 1-4.
50. *M.T. Hil. Yesodei Torah* 5:1-5; *Sh. A., Y.D.* 157:1.
51. *Chul.* 10a; *Suk.* 14b; *Sh. A., O. Ch.* 3:28, *Y.D.* 118; see also *B.K.* 23a, *Tos.*, s.v., "*u'l^e-chayav*" and *B.K.* 27b, *Tos.*, s.v.,"*amai*, " to the effect that one may be even more obligated to protect others from harm than to protect oneself or his professional reputation.
52. *M.T. Hil. Rotzeach u-Shmirath ha-Nefesh* 1:6-16.
53. *Bi'ur ha-Gra: Ch. M.* 425:10.
54. *Ha'amek Davar*: Lev. 19:16 and see also *Torah Temimah*: Deut. 22:2 discussed in note 48 above.
55. *B.K.* 56a; see also *Torah Temimah:* Lev. 5:1, and see note 61 below.
56. Lev. 5:1; Deut. 1:17; *B.K.* 55b-56a; *Sanh.* 6b-7a; *Shev.* 31a; *M.T. Hil. Shevuoth* 9:3, *Hil. Sanhedrin* 22:2, *Hil. Eduth* 1:1; *SMaG*, Pos. no. 108; *Sh. A., Ch. M.* 28:3, *Y. D.* 228:33; *Chinnukh*, no. 237; also, see Rashi to Deut. 1:17 who translates "*lo taguru*" as "you shall not conceal," citing the usage in Prov. 10:5.

57. See *Torath Kohanim* 19; *Sanh.* 6b, 7a; *Shev.* 31a. R. Aron Soloveitchik has pointed out to me the view expressed by the *Ba'alei ha-Tosafoth* to Deut. 13:7-9 that even if one's friend confided his intentions to commit apostacy or idol worship or tried in stealth to convince his friend to do so, one must not feel bound to "*lo telekh rakhil*" and is obligated to disclose the matter. R. Soloveitchik wondered whether this view implies permission to disclose confidences only by the threat of idolatry. However, it seems more likely that the *Ba'alei Tosafoth* are merely innovating the idea that in such circumstances one should not regard the intimate conversation as a true confidence! In other cases, confidentiality may be broken in the presence of the types of considerations discussed in the text. *Resp. Chelkath Yaakov*, vol. 3, no. 136, citing *M.T. Hil. Rotzeach* 1:13 and *Sh. A., Ch. M.* 426:1, specifically opines that the law to disclose applies to one who is in a position to prevent any loss and not merely to prevent idolatry. (On this, see *Arukh ha-Shulchan: Ch. M.* 426:1.)

58. *Resp. Chelkath Yaakov*, vol. 3, no. 136, referring to Lev. 19:14. This responsum is discussed in more detail by R. Bleich in *Tradition 17*, no. 4 (1979): 90-94.

59. *B. K.* 55b-56a and see Meiri ad loc. If a single witness refuses to testify, he is "guilty in the hands of heaven" but is not punishable by earthly courts; see also *Tur Sh. A., Ch. M.* 28:1, 2, 5; *M. T. Hil. Eduth* 1:1, 17:7; *Sh. A. ha-Rav: Hil. Eduth* 1; *Arukh ha-Shulchan: H. M.* 28:1 and also *Sedei Chemed*, vol. 4, pp. 420-21 for detailed discussion of the instances where the testimony of a single witness is accepted.

60. The *Rosh* to *B.K.* 55b; *Kesef Mishneh* to *Hil. Eduth* 1:1 adds, "or if they are in court." See also *Chinnukh*, no. 122, while S. R. Hirsch to Lev. 5:1 seems to accept that even a single witness is obligated to appear in court even without being summoned. On this point, see *TaZ* and *Atzei Levonah* to *Sh. A., Y.D.* 239:7 who reject a similar implication in a problematic comment of *Rama*.

61. *Shev.* 33b; *Pes.* 113b; Mar Shmuel in *Kid.* 66a; see also *Resp. Tzitz Eliezer*, vol. 13, no. 104.

62. *Arukh ha-Shulchan: Ch. M.* 28:6.

63. *Resp. Noda be-Yehudah (Kama): O. Ch.*, no. 35.

64. *Resp. Divrei Chayim: O. Ch.*, no. 35. See also *Resp. Mishneh Halakhoth*, vol. 7, no. 285 confirming that a consultant does not have permission to reveal a murderer's private, otherwise unsubstantiated confession.

65. See *Rama* to *Ch. M.* 28:1.

66. *Resp. Tzitz Eliezer*, vol. 13, no. 81 (2), citing *Shev.* 29a; *M.T. Hil. Shevuoth* 5:14, 15.

67. According to the *Maharam* (*Ch. M.*, no. 5) cited by R. Waldenberg, such an oath is valid even if taken by two witnesses who are Biblically obligated to testify; see also *Shev.* 24a, *Tos.*, s.v. *ela hen.* See also *Chokhmath Adam* 95:9.

68. B. Rakover, "*ha-Mutar le-Rofeh le-He'id al haCholeh shelo be-haskamato?*" *Noam 2* (1957): 188-91.

69. *TaZ* to *Ch. M.* 28; the *Rama* implies that *hatarah* would be necessary, but see *Tumim* ad loc.

70. *Piskei Din shel Batei ha-Din ha-Rabbanim be-Yisroel* 5: 132-153, Case No.

5637-21, cited in *Sefer Assia 4*, p. 285. In the case of the military psychologist—and in other cases such as where a patient-defendant asks his psychotherapist to testify in court regarding his mental condition—the psychologist does have an alternative to disclosure; namely, to urge the court (or his patient) to appoint an independent examiner to make a professional assessment and judgment about the patient for courtroom use (see R. Slovenko, *Psychotherapy, Confidentiality, and Privileged Communication* [New York: 1966]).

71. Cohen, op. cit., 1981, pp. 82-84.

72. Citing *Resp. Chatham Sofer: Ch. M.*, no. 177, in contrast to *Rama, Sh. A., O. Ch.* 656. It is not clear to me exactly why Rabbi Cohen decided to favor the ruling of *Chatham Sofer* rather than the opinion of the *Rama* when, indeed, a review of the relevant literature reveals a tendency toward the view that the principle of *al yevazvaz yother mi-chomesh* does not apply to negative commandments, and also favors the view that one ought not to maintain a distinction between passive and active compliance with regard to negative commandments; see, for example, *Sedei Chemed*, vol. 9, pp. 7, 64.

73. Citing *Gra* to *Y.D.*, 157, no. 5, and *Pithchei T'shuvah: Y.D.* 157 (4); *Chinnukh*, no. 588.

74. See *Sh. A., Y.D.* 252; *Resp. Igroth Moshe: Y.D.*, vol. 1, nos. 143, 145; *Ahavath Chesed*, 20(2) citing *B.M.* 62a. Advocating a comparison between psychotherapy and *pidyon shevuyim* confronts the problem that such *pidyon* is generally limited to "*keday demeihem*," or the worth of persons on the slavemarket or the standard ransom (see *Resp. Maharam Lublin*, no. 15; *Resp. Radbaz ha-Chaddashoth*, no. 40). This would mean that even if the therapist's anticipated heroism is an effort to "redeem" a patient "captivated" by external circumstances, he is only obligated (though not forbidden) to expend a set amount. Indeed, some argue that the rabbinic *takanah* limiting the ransom-ceiling extends even when danger to life (*sakanath nefesh*) exists (see *Pithchei T'shuvah: Y.D.* 252 (4)). Let it be said in defense that many poskim have suggested that it is primarily the community that is protected by this all-unclusive *takanah* and that individuals may expend more than *kedai demeihem* when the captive is in danger (see *Resp. Chatham Sofer: H.M.*, no. 177). *Sedei Chemed*, vol. 1, p. 47 leans in general to the view that *sakanah* would take precedence to this *takanah*, citing the ruling of *Tosefoth* (s.v. *kol, Git.* 58a) as support. Medini also explains *Rambam*'s ruling (*Hil. Matanot Aniyim* 8:10, 12), in apparent support of the all-inclusiveness of the *takanah*, to only apply when there is the *assumption* of danger (*hezkat sakanah*) and not when there is real or anticipated danger. Thus, the general *pidyon shevuyim* model—notwithstanding the problem of a contemporary definition of "*kedai demeihem*"—may apply in some practical dilemmas of confidentiality but not in others.

75. See *Resp. Tzitz Eliezer*, vol. 8, no. 15 (10), vol. 9, no. 17 (5); *Resp. Radbaz*, vol. 3, no. 627.

76. See *Lev Avraham*, vol. 2, chap. 18, note 9; *Resp. Minchath Yitzchak*, vol. 5, no. 7 (11-19); *Arukh ha-Shulchan: Ch. M.*, 426:4.

77. Ex. 21:6, 34:27; *Kid.* 22b; *Ned.* 28a; *JT Kid.* 1:2; *JT Ned.* 3:1; Deut. 29:11-13; *JT Sot.* 2:5; *Shev.* 29a (*kimu ve-kiblu*); *Meg.* 7a; *M.T. Hil. Yesodei Torah* 9:3.

78. By analogy to *rodef*, one may not kill when maiming will accomplish the *mitzvah*, and so one may not disclose liberally when uncalled for (*M.T. Hil. Rotzeach* 1:13).
79. See Land and Spruill, op. cit., 1980.
80. *Kid.* 49b; *M.K.* 18b; *JT Taan.* 4:5; *M.T. Hil. Sanhedrin* 24:1-2; *Sh. A., Ch. M.* 15:5.
81. *JT Taan.* 4:5.
82. *Mekor Chayim* 4:10, 8:2, 10:1, 4 and 9:3; *B.M.* 57b; *Shitah Mekubetzeth: B.B.* 39a. In this, the therapist's report has the status of a judge's *pesak* (*Sh. A., Ch. M.* 19:1). See also *M.T. Hil. T*ᵉ*shuvah* 7:8 who specifies "*keday le-beisho*," which is essentially not the therapist's motivation. Students would also be permitted to be privy to confidential information in the course of their learning experiences (*Resp. Tzitz Eliezer*, vol. 13, no. 81[2]), e.g., observing therapeutic sessions through one-way mirrors, participating in diagnostic conferences, and so forth.
83. Ex. 23:7; *B.M.* 37b; *Sanh.* 92a, "*kol ha-machalif diburo ke-ilu oved avodah zarah.*"
84. *Yev.* 87b. Technically, should a professional appeal to silence in a *beth din* in response to questions which he is not yet sure he can or may answer, *qua* witness, his silence can not be taken as an admission (*Chiddushei Ritva* to *Kid.* 22b cited in *Torah Temimah* to Deut 19:15, although I am unable to find this *din* in the location cited).
85. See S. Bok, *Lying: Moral Choice in Public and Private Life* (New York: 1978), p. 156.
86. Deut. R. 5; Lev. R. 9; Gen. R. 100:8; *DEZ* 11; *J.T. Peah* 1:1; *Yev.* 65b; *B.M.* 23a, *Tos.*, s.v. *be-ushpizyoh*," 87a; *Suk.* 53b; *Ket.* 16:17; *Piskei ha-Rosh, Maharsha, Nimukei Yosef, Meiri*, ad loc.; *Menorath ha-Ma'or*, vol. 2, 2(1); *Resp. Pesach Devir* vol. 1, no. 1; *Chiddushei ha-Ritva* to *Kid.* 81a; *TaZ* and *Magen Avraham* to *Sh. A., O. Ch.* 565. *Sefer Chasidim*, no. 642 (citing *Yev.* 65b), states that one may modify the truth to save one from *bushah.*
87. See note 95 below.
88. See also the story of R. Akiva in *Kalah* 2.
89. See my discussions in "Countertransference in Religious Therapists of Religious Patients," *American Journal of Psychotherapy 35*, no. 4 (1982): 565-75 and "Casual Encounters for Off-the-Cuff Advice: Managing a Professional Problem," *Journal of Jewish Communal Service 56*, no. 2 (1979-1980): 190-92.
90. Deut. 32:7, and also Lev. 26:40; see also Deut. 24:9 and the role given it by *Ramban* in his *Esen ha-Nosafim le-Sefer ha-Mitzvoth*, no. 7. See also *Shmirath ha-Lashon: Sha'ar ha-T*ᵉ*shuvah*, no. 12.
91. *Mak.* 8b.
92. *M.K.* 16a; *Sefer Meiroth Einayim* 11; *Ba'er Mayim Chayim* to *Mekor Chayim* 2, no. 2; *Shmirath ha-Lashon: Sha'ar ha-T*ᵉ*shuvah*, no. 5.
93. *Shev.* 39 (Rashi): *Mekor Chayim* 4:11; *Arukh ha-Shulchan: Ch. M.* 7:20; *Resp. Chelkath Yaakov*, vol. 3, no. 136.
94. Ibid.
95. However, see the account related about R. Yochanan who swore to a matron not to reveal the secret of some medicinal procedure and then revealed it (*Yoma*

84a; *A.Z.* 28a). The Talmud resolves the dilemma by saying that R. Yochanan originally intended to reveal the secret and had this in mind as he took his oath. The problematic implication is that without such qualification, R. Yochanan would not have revealed the confidential matter even though risk to life was involved in his case! In fact, the *J.T.* version of the story does not say that R. Yochanan took an oath but merely that he "said" that he would not reveal it. R. Channanel explains that the problem was not revealing confidences, but utilizing a cure based in idolatry (see also *Maharsha* to *A.Z.* 28a). Meiri (*A.Z.* 28b; *Chiddushei ha-Meiri: Yoma* 84a) offers that R. Yochanan made his condition explicit, which presumably means that he explained to the matron that he would be obligated to reveal his secret knowledge in the event of an emergency.

96. *Sh. A., Y.D.* 228:33 (and see *TaZ*, no, 42 and *Bi'ur ha-Gra*, no. 95); *Sh. A., Ch. M.* 28:1 and *Arukh ha-Shulchan: Ch. M.* 28:5; *M.T. Hil. Eduth* 1:1, *Hil. Shevuot* 5:15.

97. *Arukh ha-Shulchan: Ch.M.* 426:1.

8

An Examination of the Halakhic Status of Homosexuality: Female Homosexual Behavior, and Homosexuality as *Oness*

A. FEMALE SEXUAL BEHAVIOR

I.

In the first section of the following two-part chapter, I intend to clarify the halakhic status of female homosexual behavior or lesbianism in specific, a topic which has been given relatively little attention in previous papers.

The prohibition against male homosexual behavior is contained in two explicit Biblical passages, "Thou shall not lie with a man as with a woman; it is an abomination,"[1] and "A man that lies with a man as with a woman, they both have committed an abomination, both shall surely die; their blood is upon them."[2] These passages determine that (1) homosexuality is a capital offense punishable by stoning or, in the absence of proper warning, by excommunication (*kareth*); (2) the act incurring such punishment is intercourse *per anus* or even *n^e^shikath evarim*,[3] which confines the applicability of the full Biblical infraction as defined by (1) and (2) solely to males.[4] Homosexual intercourse is subsumed under the class of illicit sexual relations, *arayoth*, making its violation subject to the grave stricture of *yehareg v^e^-al ya'avor*; i.e., that in most circumstances one must choose death over any alternative which involves committing homosexual acts.[5] Finally, as suggested earlier, Halakhah forbids not only the act of homosexual intercourse, but also considers abnormal or deviant the broader homosexual *relationship*, psychological orientation, and life-style.[6]

It would seem that female homosexual behavior cannot be included in the aforementioned passages since there can be no genital intercourse. However, a proscription against such behavior is derived from a third Biblical passage: "After the deeds of Egypt, where you lived, you shall not do; and after the doings of the land of Canaan, where I bring you, you shall not do; and in their statutes you shall not walk."[7]

The *Torath Kohanim* elaborates upon this passage, emphasizing the last phrase "... and in their statutes";[8]

> If [there only was the first part of the passage] "After the deeds of Egypt... you shall not do," one might [conclude] that one is not allowed to erect buildings or plant gardens following their fashion. Thus, the Writ states, "and in their statutes you shall not walk," [meaning:] I am only [forbidding] those *statutes* that they and their forefathers established. What [were these statutes]? A man would marry a man, and a woman would marry a woman, and a woman would marry two men, and a man would marry a woman and her daughter. Therefore [the Writ] states, "and in their statutes you shall not walk."

The illicit sexual union between "a woman and a woman" referred to in *Torath Kohanim* is approximately what the Talmud and subsequent literature terms *nashim ha-m^{e}sol^{e}loth zo b^{e}-zo*, or "women who enmesh with each other."[9] In at least two references an appeal is made to the view of R. Huna who rules that *nashim ha-m^{e}sol^{e}loth* are ritually unfit to marry a priest.[10] The Talmud and later codifiers reject R. Huna's view, arguing that female homosexual behavior is not tantamount to *z^{e}nuth* or *arayoth* which would render a woman unfit to marry a priest, but rather is "merely immodest behavior" (*p^{e}ritzuth b^{e}-alma*) which does not render a woman unfit for priestly marriage.[11] At the same time, many codifiers refer to this view in ruling that the behavior of *nashim ha-m^{e}sol^{e}loth* is nonetheless forbidden, and utilize the passage "After the deeds of Egypt" as the source for this prohibition even though R. Huna himself did not relate the two.[12]

II.

It remains unclear, however, whether or not "After the deeds of Egypt" imparts a Biblical or rabbinic prohibition to female homosexual behavior. Put in other words, is the passage "After the deeds of Egypt" a proof text for a Biblical prohibition, an *asmakhta* for a rabbinic prohibition, or an "elastic" category which can levy rabbinic *isur* upon any number of behaviors as determined by the sages?

Contemporary scholars express varied opinions couched in elliptic phrases about the exact halakhic status of lesbianism. Preuss generalizes, stating that "the Bible does not mention lesbianism at all,"[13] yet subsequently offers the qualification that lesbianism might at least have been under rabbinic sanction "as equivalent to the doings of the Egyptians."[14] Rosenheim states, "Male homosexuality is declared by the Bible as an 'abomination' . . . The Bible does not mention lesbianism, but rabbinical sources alerted against such practice."[15] In a later version of his paper, Rosenheim states, "Lesbianism . . . was later condemned by the rabbis," citing *Rambam*.[16] Schindler suggests that Halakhah viewed female homosexuality in a less severe light than male homosexuality since a woman cannot violate what Schindler considers the basis of the Biblical prohibition—the wasteful spilling of semen. In fact, it is genital intercourse, whether or not *hashchathath zera* occurs, which defines homosexuality. Schindler concludes that "since no transgression is done . . . [lesbianism] has the status of a minor offense."[17]

Norman Lamm states,[18]

> Jewish law treated the female homosexual more leniently than the male. It considered lesbianism as *isur*, an ordinary religious violation, rather than *arayoth*, a specifically sexual infraction, regarded much more severely than *isur* . . . However, the transgression does warrant disciplinary flagellation. The less punitive attitude of the Halakhah to the female homosexual than to the male does not reflect any intrinsic judgment of one as opposed to the other, but is rather the result of a halakhic technicality: there is no explicit Biblical prohibition against lesbianism, and the act does not entail genital intercourse.

Yet R. Lamm does not state explicitly whether lesbianism is rabbinically or Biblically *asur*. Most recently, R. J. David Bleich states,[19]

> Lesbianism is included in the Biblical admonition against participation in the deviant sexual practices associated with the Egyptians and Canaanites of antiquity, but it is not a capital offense.

Here again, cautious phraseology.

Indeed, *Rambam* states in his *Peirush ha-Mishnayoth* that *nashim ha-m^{e}sol^{e}loth* is *asur* but receives neither rabbinic nor Biblical punishment.[20] Surprisingly, *Rambam* likens lesbianism to the preceding discussion in his commentary of *hotza'ath zera l^e-vatalah* to the degree that both are *asur* but are not punishable by *malkuth* (Biblical flogging).[21] However, *nashim ha-m^{e}sol^{e}loth* cannot involve *hotza'ath zera* and thus would not appear to be similar to the aforementioned *isur*. In fact, the Talmud does state that wasteful spilling of semen is punishable by death at the hands of heaven and other consequences,[22] but no such punishments are described for lesbianism. Furthermore, the prohibition of *hotza'ath zera l^e-vatalah* is, according to the majority of opinions, amply grounded in Biblical tradition,[23] whereas the grounding of lesbianism is far less clear.

Among the few halakhic commentaries who discuss *nashim ha-m^{e}sol^{e}loth*, one finds divided opinion whether or not acts of female homosexuality are Biblically forbidden, or only rabbinically forbidden as suggested by the term "*asur*." The *Levush* maintains that *Rambam* views the derivation as fully Biblical, yet there is no flogging because the prohibition is implicit in a larger category (*lav she-bik^{e}laluth*).[24] R. Yosef Rozen also states that *Rambam* considers *nashim ha-m^{e}sol^{e}loth* an *isur Torah* as an aspect of "and in their statutes you shall not walk,"[25] though not an *isur* of *arayoth*. In a broad view, R. Barukh Halevi Epstein states that "and in their statutes you shall not walk" specifically includes anything related to immodesty and idolatry,[26] which *presumably* includes lesbianism, *presumably* as an *isur Torah*.

However, R. J. Falk, in his commentary to the *Tur Shulchan Arukh*, considers the act of female homosexuality to be rabbinic and that the Biblical prohibition applies only to the last perversity recorded in the *Torath Kohanim*; viz., one woman marrying two men.[27] R. A. Kalin also states that *Rambam*'s phrase, ". . . and there is no flogging because there is no distinct Biblical prohibition [for it]," does not mean that lesbianism is actually a *lav she-ein bo malkuth*. Rather, the Biblical prohibition itself extends to the other perverse foreign statutes, but not to lesbianism.[28]

The *Kiryath Melekh Rav* brings forward the innovative view that *Rambam* only considers Biblically forbidden an institutionalized or socially condoned contractual relationship between two women since this is precisely what is described in *Torath Kohanim*.[29] That is, the Torah only forbids behaviors which have become *statutes* or social norms.[30] Occasional acts of female homosexual behavior, however, are not the object of the Biblical ban, although they are rabbinically forbidden, and may merit *makath marduth* as well.[31]

Note also the following. R. Barukh Halevi Epstein, in the reference cited above, cites R. Yosef Caro who states that the specifics of the prohibition against adopting non-Jewish practices ("*u'v^e-chukotheihem*") are left to rabbinic determination.[32] Interestingly, according to *Rambam*, all violations of "*u'v^e-chukotheihem*" are punished by *malkuth* (Biblical flogging).[33] However, if *nashim ha-m^{e}sol^{e}loth* is considered to devolve from "*u'v^e-chukotheihem*"—according to R. Epstein, Rozen, and others[34]— then the fact that *Rambam* does *not* record an ordained punishment of *malkuth* for it suggests that he did not consider female homosexuality a fully Biblical *isur*, although "it is fitting that [such a person] receive *makath marduth*."

In fact, one notes that *Rambam* subtly alters the derivation as stated by *Torath Kohanim*, relating the *isur* of lesbianism specifically to the phrase "After the deeds of Egypt" rather than to "*u'v^e-chukotheihem*." Thus, we remain with two possibilities: (1) *Rambam* considered lesbianism a unique Biblical *isur* distinct from "*u'v^e-chukotheihem*," or (2) he considered lesbianism a *rabbinic* elaboration of "*u'v^e-chukotheihem*," and offers "After the deeds of Egypt" as an *asmakhta*.

III.

We have seen that female homosexual behavior is at the very least rabbinically proscribed and punishable by *makath marduth*. And even according to the view that lesbianism is indeed Biblically proscribed, there is consensus that it is not included in the severe category of *arayoth*. Certain practical conclusions can be derived from this discussion.

(1) If female homosexuality is not considered *arayoth* even according to those who consider it Biblically forbidden (and is presumably not even an *abizrahu d^earayoth*), then certain halakhic problems regarding treatment are lessened. Specifically, treatment procedures need no longer confront the problem of *yehareg v^e-al ya'avor*—other difficulties notwithstanding. This means that the standard halakhic "medical model" can be applied, and that certain prohibitions may be waived in the interests of inducing heterosexual behavior or gender satisfaction in the female homosexual patient; e.g., verbalization of female homosexual fantasies would not necessarily involve the *isur* of *hirhur arayoth*, and masturbation-based behavioral techniques may become less objectionable.[35] This advantage is certainly enhanced according to the view that sporadic homosexual behavior among females is only rabbinically forbidden.

(2) Since Halakhah cannot technically legitimize a "homosexual marriage" *per se*, the description in *Torath Kohanim* of a "woman *marrying* a woman" indicates that Halakhah would still consider any form of explicit or implicit, long-term commitment between two female homosexuals to be a Biblical violation.

(3) Inasmuch as the Biblical prohibition subsumes the effort to institutionalize deviant sexual orientations *whether or not they are also considered abnormal*, it would be forbidden to partake in civil activism which seeks to obtain acceptance into society at large for homosexuals as a class by themselves.

The preceding should clarify the halakhically-oriented therapist's professional opposition to the subtle assimilation into professional values of concepts such as "alternative sexual preference," "100% ambisexuality," and other examples of the trend toward de-pathologizing homosexuality.[36] From the Torah perspective such trends run the risk of reinforcing attitudes and eventually policies (e.g., the legitimization of homosexual "marriages" and "families") which are halakhically detestable "statutes." The halakhically-observant mental health professional cannot treat homosexuals who wish to be accepted as homosexuals or to have their sexual life-style "improved" or even condoned.[37] He also cannot refer such individuals to other professionals, Jewish or non-Jewish, who will accept the homosexual on such terms, as this violates the principle of "not placing a stumbling block before the blind."[38]

It has also been stated that conferring upon the homosexual the halakhic status of *oness* or "compelled" has definite limits and does not render acceptable or less sinful homosexual acts committed in a nonpsychotic state and in full awareness of the halakhic opinion.

On the other hand, Halakhah does accept in principle the value of psychotherapeutically modifying the homosexual toward heterosexuality or lessened homosexual behavior, certain ethical objections to some of the currently utilized techniques notwithstanding. Some of these treatment problems may be significantly lessened where the status of homosexual behavior is not exactly in the category of *arayoth* and is rabbinically forbidden, and as long as the treatment technique itself does not involve an unwaivable, Biblically prohibited activity. It remains important, however, in order for the halakhically-oriented professional to practice ethically with this particular type of psychopathology, that he maintain the Torah perspective and incorporate it as part of his halakhic-professional values. The fact that the halakhically competent professional maintains specific moral beliefs about homosexual behavior does not preclude *professional* attitudes of empathy and sensitivity when treating the homosexual, inasmuch as these attitudes have been consistently linked to positive therapeutic outcome.

B. HOMOSEXUALITY AS *ONESS*

I. ______________________

The clinical, social, and ethical dilemmas presented by the emergence of homosexuality from its proverbial closet have encouraged analysis of uniquely halakhic perspectives on the phenomenon of homosexuality and its politics.[39] Beyond review of traditional Biblical, talmudic, and later rabbinic sources on homosexuality, several halakhic analyses have sought to categorize this sexual orientation in terms of sin, sickness, and the halakhic concept of *oness*—acts committed in a state of compulsion or duress. The central question for many of these writers is whether homosexuality has the status of *oness* or, can homosexuality be viewed halakhically as the consequence of "compelling" psychosocial or psychodynamic variables? A second concern is: Does homosexuality, from the standpoint of the halakhic proscription, refer to a psychological state of mind or only to acts of homosexual intercourse?[40] And which is to be considered the main contributing factor to the status of *oness*?

The assumption underlying the desirability of classifying homosexuality as *oness* is that the condition of *oness* would in some way render the homosexual somewhat immune to the halakhic ascriptions of "sinfulness" or "immorality," and the homosexual himself somewhat less sick or perverse. This putative moral "immunity" or unaccountability follows from the usual interpretation of the halakhic maxim *oness rachamana patreh* ("the Merciful One exempts [from punishment] one who is compelled").[41] However, we shall see that homosexuality as a state of being and as an act cannot in fact be rendered less objectionable by virtue of categorizing it as *oness*, assuming it can even rightfully be considered *oness*. These possibilities have been neglected because of inaccurate appreciation of the halakhic principles evoked and incomplete understanding of the homosexual condition itself.

The salient issues which must now be examined more carefully are: (1) Is the category of *oness* applicable to homosexuality?; (2) To what degree is homosexuality a "psychiatric condition" rather than a moral one, and to what degree is it a condition whose significance lies beyond psychiatric or sociological categorization?; (3) What are the implications of any eventual halakhic classification of homosexuality in terms of individual responsibility? These issues are plainly important for developing halakhic policies and attitudes about homosexuality, whether one's interest is a purely clinical or scholarly search for understanding. In addition to the value of such analysis for non-homosexuals, correct placement of homosexuality along the continuum of individual responsibility will significantly affect the homosexual's search for self-identity and social role.

II.

There is no question that Halakhah designates the act of homosexual intercourse as sinful, as well as, though to a lesser degree, female homosexual behaviors. All previous writers have demonstrated this fact, with minor disagreements, through the appropriate Biblical and talmudic references.[42]

Of course, the halakhic sources do not specifically label homosexuality as a "sickness" or "psychological disorder" primarily because these are not the basic legal-moral terms of the halakhic system. However, this technicality of language does not necessarily preclude the possibility that some acts which are labeled "sick" or psychiatrically disordered may at the same time be deemed morally reprehensible in the halakhic system. In other words, having labeled homosexual acts sinful and even repugnant (*to'evah*) according to standard halakhic convention, Halakhah thereby indicates that such acts remain sinful or morally repugnant even if subsequent classification of the condition as "sick," "deviant," or, more correctly, "treatable" is not meant to impart moral judgment according to the alternative diagnostic system.[43] Halakhah may consider certain conditions "morally disordered" in the sense that such conditions merit intervention or modification, be it *via* medical technique, psychotherapy, or *t^eshuvah*. Halakhah may also consider certain behaviors "sick" to the degree that such behaviors represent deviations from halakhically proscribed norms of psychosocial well-being. Thus, inasmuch as Halakhah considers *hetero*sexuality psychosocially healthy, it may, from within its unique perspective, consider homosexuality unhealthy or sick. Homosexuality would be at once *sinful* inasmuch as it violates halakhic-moral norms, and *sick* inasmuch as it deviates from halakhic-psychosocial norms.

On the other hand, there are extenuating circumstances under which certain conditions achieve an additional or subordinating status which Halakhah itself views as an exemption from moral accountability—such as the status of *oness*. But the burden of proof lies upon us to determine whether the condition in question is truly one of *oness* and whether the concept of *oness* actually exempts the given condition from halakhic accountability.

III.

Most authors approach the problem by viewing the three categories of *oness*, sickness, and sin as representing a continuum of individual responsibility ranging from complete lack of moral accountability for acts committed in a true state of *oness*, through the problematic amalgam of purposive (e.g., functional) and circumstantial, and hence accountable and unaccountable aspects of psychological disease or sickness, to more or less complete moral accountability for acts labeled as sin. In fact, we shall see that these different categories are not discrete, and that the status of *oness* is not necessarily the terminus in the range of unaccountability.[44]

Hershel Matt, in his attempt to define homosexuality as *oness*, states that, "when forbidden acts are performed in the absence of voluntary choice . . . or, in the absence of other options [by which he means treatment options] the offenders are judged more leniently than otherwise."[45] While a stringent view would be in force for those homosexuals who "could change," Matt speculates that the lenient view should be in force for those homosexuals who "cannot change" or who thus are subjects of *oness* (*anusim*). Matt does not actually suggest we adulterate the negative halakhic judgment of wanton or willful homosexual behavior. He does state, on the other hand, that we might convey to those homosexuals who qualify as *anusim* that this very status "removes from them . . . all burden of blame and guilt—accepting them as they are. It avoids at least some of the negative connotations of "mental illness." It acknowledges that *unalterable* homosexuality remains theologically unaccountable."[46]

Matt, along with others, errs in heavily basing his interpretation of homosexuality as *oness* on the assumption that there are no treatment options available for homosexuals. This lack renders the homosexual "compelled" to remain in his present state. Unfortunately, Matt's review of the relevant psychiatric literature is less than cursory. Successful treatment is actually far more than a "rarity," with different therapeutic modalities reporting different types or levels of change, ranging from the mere elimination of heterosexual anxiety to complete orientation-reversal.[47] Of course, the viable treatment techniques are time consuming and involve a level of commitment and participation from the patient that is not easy to maintain. Thus, many of the so-called "unsuccessful techniques" or "untreatable" cases of homosexuality are in fact instances of incomplete or inadequate treatment.

Precisely who are those homosexuals, considered by Matt to represent the majority, who "cannot" change? Are they in fact homosexuals who bolted treatment when insight became too painful? Are they homosexuals who were misaligned with their particular psychotherapist or who lost interest in change following several unfortunate experiences with pseudo-therapeutic modalities? Or are they homosexuals who would have sought change had their homosexuality caused them sufficient psychological anguish and conflict, but who do not consider seeking change merely because homosexuality is religiously reprehensible and who would indeed never seek change so long as homosexuality is socially acceptable or religiously pardonable? Undoubtedly, many if not most of Matt's "cannots" would be eliminated from this category if they were able to examine more critically the nature of their "compelled homosexuality."

The remaining problem in Matt's analysis is his assertion that the "very status of *oness* removes from [homosexuals] all burden of blame and guilt." Matt is not alone in appealing to the category of *oness* in the hope of lessening the distinctly moral and pathological connotations of homosexuality. R. J. David Bleich also implies that those homosexuals who are truly compelled are *anusim* and hence would not have to seek treatment, although he admits that these are in the minority.[48]

R. Bleich seems to hold that it is the *act*, not the homosexual *condition*, which is the object of the Torah proscription—"The former is an act of free will, the latter is a state of being."[49] R. Bleich is suggesting that homosexual *behavior* is reprehensible when it is not the result of *oness*, and that the homosexual *condition* is not reprehensible because it is not behavior! Now if R. Bleich means somehow to distinguish between active and passive homosexuality or to argue for a halakhic distinction between so-called latent and manifest homosexuality, he has failed to do so. In fact, he introduces a psychologically as well as halakhically inaccurate dichotomy between fantasy and behavior.

Both Halakhah and psychology subscribe to the belief that fantasy—the stuff of dreams, "passive" homosexuality, or of homosexual "tendencies" inferred from projective testing and so forth—is also behavior. From the psychological viewpoint, fantasy and behavior are synonymous *to the degree* that each is but a different form of expression of psychodynamic impulses, wishes, or conflicts. It is correct that psychotherapists often attempt to help their patients recognize the important differences between and consequences of their thoughts or wishes and actual behaviors, but they do not assume in a blanket manner that fantasies are any less psychically or socially determined than "behavior" or less real products of personality. Halakhically as well,[50] fantasy, the realm of *hirhur*, is considered a basic tributary of behavior (e.g., *achar kavanath ha-lev hen hen ha-d^e^varim*).[51] In legal matters, of course, *machsh^e^voth ha-lev* may indeed be bypassed in favor of demonstrable and quantifiable physical behavior. But this does not support a view that fantasy or psychological *conditions* are not in their own way subject to halakhic accountability. Indeed, *hirhur* about content of illicit sexual nature (*hirhur arayoth*), such as homosexual fantasies, is considered an "appurtenance of *arayoth*" and is rabbinically, if not Biblically, forbidden in its own right.[52] According to some halakhic authorities, the stringent requirement that one accept death rather than any alternative which requires committing any of the three cardinal sins (*yehareg v^e^-al ya'avor*) extends even to *hirhur arayoth*.[53]

These considerations, in addition to others,[54] suggest that homosexuality as a state of being, while not punishable according to the express biblical criterion, is no less subject to halakhic accountability and to possible categorization as sin or sickness. To be sure, there are probably as many gradients of moral responsibility for homosexual fantasies as there are levels of consciousness or indirect derivatives of sexual and aggressive impulses. But it would also be incorrect to conclude that Halakhah does not obligate the homosexual to seek modification of his general sexual orientation as long as it is not expressed behaviorally. This would be further reinforced by Maimonides' ruling that "inappropriate personality traits" (*de'oth ra'oth*) are also objects of *t^e^shuvah* or any other intervention prerequisite for *t^e^shuvah*.[55]

R. Norman Lamm also addresses the problem of homosexuality as *oness*.[56] He draws the reader's attention to the fact that the category of *oness* may not apply in the case of male sexual transgressions since, beyond all considerations of predisposing psychosocial determinants, genital erection is considered a "token of willingness" inasmuch as the psychological mechanism of erection is based on emotional arousal.[57] Even those few authorities who would in principle mitigate the culpability of a male forced to commit a sexual act—arguing that in such circumstances the emotional arousal and subsequent physiological mechanism are actually the result of *oness*—would nonetheless agree that pleasure derived during the commission of the act increases the level of prohibition and accountability.[58]

R. Lamm thus limits the usefulness of the "homosexuality as *oness*" equation to evoking "pastoral compassion, psychological understanding, and social sympathy" in our dealings with homosexuals. In so doing, he accurately recognizes that acts of homosexuality (and, I would add, the condition itself) are *to'evah* whether or not they are also *oness*. Viewed technically, a homosexual act "remains a *ma'aseh aveirah*, whereas the person who transgresses [*in a psychotic state*] is considered innocent on the grounds of *oness*."[59] In a nonpsychotic state homosexuality remains an accountable behavior. The important point is that *oness* does not lessen the gravity of male sexual transgressions even when the conditions which conduce overall behavior in such instances are themselves considered compelling.

It was mentioned earlier that Matt's assertion that "*oness* removes . . . all burden of blame and guilt" from the homosexual is problematic from yet another standpoint. This view is based on the notion that the fullest meaning of homosexuality transcends "sin," "sickness," or even *to'evah*. On a basic level, viewing homosexuality as *oness* allows the homosexual at least to be certain of his halakhic status and thereby experience less marginality and anomie. However, we have demonstrated that many of the interpretations of *oness* that would be offered to the homosexual are inaccurate. Second, there is the danger that this approach will establish the normality of homosexuality for homosexuals. As McIntosh states (and Matt apparently accepts this view), viewing homosexuality as a "deviant role" (i.e., *oness*) rather than as an "abnormal condition" legitimizes the uniqueness of homosexuality; "it appears to justify the deviant behavior of the homosexual as being appropriate for him as a member of the homosexual category."[60]

This is also the logic of the perspective expressed in the current *Diagnostic Statistical Manual* (III) which distinguishes between "ego syntonic homosexuality," where the homosexual is satisfied with his sexual orientation and is *therefore* not considered pathological, and "ego dystonic homosexuality," where the homosexual experiences conflict with his sexual orientation or related problems and *is* considered pathological. That is, the "ego dystonic homosexual" is pathological not because he is a homosexual, but rather because he is unhappy that he is a homosexual.[61] By this rather unpersuasive logic, one could also conceive of a whole range of diagnostic categories such as "ego dystonic *hetero*sexuality," "ego-dystonic color-blindness," "ego-dystonic suicidal tendencies," and so forth. The upshot is that homosexuality, even as *oness*, would be considered normal as long as it is accepted and enjoyed by the individual without guilt. The homosexuality of an individual would acquire what Huges termed a "master status," subordinating his other religious obligations to his identity as an *oness-mensch*.[62] But this approach defeats Halakhah's goal, which is in fact to maintain the deviant and aberrant status of homosexuality and to prevent its institutionalization in the guise of an "alternative sexual role."

There is a third problem with homosexuality as *oness*. Halakhah surely shares in the desire to reduce *neurotic* self-blame and guilt where they stand in the way of productive living. However, anxiety and guilt operate on at least two levels. One must differentiate between *dynamic* conflict based on psychosexual issues relating to the development of homosexuality in an individual and as evidence of the incompleteness of the neurotic compromise represented by the homosexual orientation, and *religious*-spiritual conflict uniquely characteristic of an individual's awareness of the incompatibility between the homosexual preference and the halakhic ideal. The second type of conflict is, of course, also "dynamic" in the sense that it involves different levels of consciousness and internal disequilibrium. Yet it is uniquely a "religious" conflict in that the parameters of conflict are not merely the result of irrational superego tensions, but rather are characteristic of the primacy of halakhic values for such individuals. There is no *a priori* requirement that such conflict be labeled neurotic in the strictly clinical sense.[63] Such conflict may indicate that the individual's endeavor to distort the relationship between Halakhah and reality has begun to weaken. In this case, guilt and self-blame become halakhically desirable.

IV.

The professional opprobrium that is currently associated with maintaining baldly moralistic views of individual sexual behavior plays no small role in motivating what can only be viewed as a "flight" into adjusting the meaning of the term *to'evah* through the subtle language game of disguising homosexuality as *oness*. Those who attempt this reclassification have merely revived an argument once utilized by some rabbinic authorities in the effort to reduce the stigma of suicide.[64] The argument, stated in unvarnished form, would be: "Homosexuality is, of course, immoral but only when it is a voluntary act. Homosexuality, on the other hand, is causally determined by innumerable psychosocial factors. In view of this, homosexuality cannot be deemed a voluntary act. Hence, most instances of homosexuality are not the type of homosexuality forbidden by the Torah." A similar stance has in fact been taken by both McNeill and Pittenger who argue that the homosexual condition itself is given and irreversible, and hence in itself is not immoral, since an activity is immoral only if it is possible to have acted morally. If it were possible not to be homosexual altogether, then this would be the moral choice.[65]

In the case of suicide, however, the argument that self-inflicted death is the result of a disturbed state of mind, and hence *oness*, is only used after the fact to lessen stigma and perhaps the level of transgression. Nothing particularly contradicts the attempt in this application to retroactively confer the determinate status of *oness* upon dubious causal factors. In its application to the phenomenon of homosexuality, on the other hand, the *oness* argument is being wrongly utilized *before* and *during* the fact to lessen transgression and to alter an entire halakhic attitude toward sexuality, ignoring the fact that the category of *oness* does not apply to such acts. In fact, those homosexuals who might be willing to exercise the halakhically correct moral choice and opt for treatment of their condition might now bypass this option if they were convinced that accepting their "role" as *anusim* is an equally valid moral option!

To summarize: (1) Homosexuality is rarely if ever the result of psychiatrically or ethically significant compulsion; (2) *All* behavior and sexual orientation is to a large degree psychically and socially *determined*, in the psychoanalytic sense of the term (i.e., has specifiable causes and meanings) but is not thereby *compelled*; (3) If (2) is false, then even heterosexuality is *oness*, which runs against common sense; (4) Even if homosexuality could be classified generally as *oness*, subsequent sexual acts or fantasies continue to be reprehensible inasmuch as sexual pleasure mitigates the *quality* of *oness*, especially where such pleasure is viewed as "ego syntonic" with the "role" of homosexuality; (5) Difficulty in modifying homosexuality does not render the condition *oness* in the full sense of the term.

V.

If homosexuality is defined by psychiatric criteria and terms and is a condition which one *diagnoses* with an eye toward *treatment* or modification, then one has classified homosexuality as disorder and homosexuals as disordered. If homosexuality is not a condition in the above sense *and* is not a diagnosable entity, it may however remain sociologically or statistically deviant. "Deviance" was the preferred category for homosexuality—prior to its recent beatification—for those who sought to reject theological and moral connotations and who eventually accepted the current American Psychiatric Association's view that homosexuality *per se* is not a pathological entity. Deviance indicates only that homosexuality is statistically atypical, but does not imply that homosexuality ought to be modified.

Indeed, some professionals have rejected the "disorder" categorization precisely because of the implication that individuals thus categorized *ought* to be treated.[66] This, they suppose, would violate the rights of those homosexuals who do not wish to be treated and certainly of those who do not wish to view their sexual orientation as abnormal. But Halakhah does unabashedly label homosexuality perverse and morally repugnant. Even if Halakhah would not require *psychotherapeutic* intervention for homosexuality—that is, assuming that it did not demand an equation between *to'evah* and "psychiatric disorder"—Halakhah still seems to require the spiritual or moral modification of homosexual behavior. Thus, our halakhic examination must also confront the ethical problem of whether a homosexual ought to be compelled to seek treatment.

With regard to the "diagnosis compels treatment" argument, whatever its inherent moral logic, the voluntarists may have overreacted to the moral force inherent in psychiatric diagnosis. It is reasonable to argue that we *ought* to offer treatment opportunities to cancer patients, but no one has seriously argued that such persons be hauled off to treatment centers against their wishes. And arguing from the other direction, even if the suitably trained professional is himself morally obligated to treat diagnosed patients, he generally may not discharge this obligation without the voluntary consent of the patient. Similarly, those in the psychological-psychiatric community who consider homosexuality a treatable condition do not conclude that homosexuals be treated against their will. Thus, merely defending the notion that homosexuality is a condition that *ought* to be treated does not necessarily or practically mean that homosexuals' *right to refuse* treatment will be violated.

From the halakhic standpoint, however, there is a sense in which having labeled homosexuality as sinful, perverse, and *to'evah* it could then be subjected to compulsory interventive measures. That is, the Jewish community or individual mental health professional *qua* agent of *beth din* may be required to invoke the halakhic concept of *Kofin otho*, of "compelling" one (or one's reasonable ego) to remain obedient to Jewish law.[67] While generally invoked in specific applications, such as compelling the granting of a divorce or fulfillment of vows, the "*Kofin* model" can in fact be applied to any *mitzvah*.[68] On the one hand, R. Matt, Bleich, and Lamm have correctly noted that since Jewish courts can no longer enforce the capital punishment for homosexuality they may not need to involve themselves with active persecution of homosexuals. However, further analysis is needed regarding the teaching role of Jewish leadership. From the standpoint of the teaching role, one which devolves from the principle of *hokhachah*, there are still two obligations incumbent upon the Jewish community which it must continue to discharge: (1) to remove "stumbling blocks" from the path of the unknowledgeable—which includes disseminating halakhically and psychologically valid views on homosexuality;[69] and (2) to evoke the "*Kofin* model" to actively encourage appropriate interventions and preventative policies and attitudes.

VI.

There is another reason why homosexuality cannot be considered *oness* simply because it is a psychopathological condition. Halakhah generally views the sick person or *choleh* as an *oness* in the sense that (1) he is actually unable to perform incumbent *mitzvoth*, or (2) he is sometimes compelled to employ methods of cure that are ordinarily forbidden (e.g., to eat *taref*). In fact, since the *choleh* always desires to be cured, it is difficult to state that he is wholly compelled to accept a heretofore forbidden treatment as if there were no element of voluntary will or self-interest involved. Thus, in situations of sickness, the actual principle which permits utilizing forbidden substances or performing forbidden action is not really the mitigating status of *oness*, but rather the Divine decree *Vachai ba-hem*, "And you shall live through them."[70]

However, in the case of curative methods which involve violation of the three cardinal sins, the above decree (*vachai ba-hem*) not only does not apply; the opposite is expected. Thus, if one's illness were to somehow take the form of violating one of the three cardinal sins (such as the case of the love-sick individual recorded in the Talmud, *Sanhedrin* 75a), or if one derived therapeutic effects through violation of one of these three sins, these states would not be viewed as *oness*, even though Halakhah recognizes that the sick person has limited choice.[71] Finally, the factor of *oness* does not *necessarily* impart the status of *lav bar chiyuva* or complete disobligation from *mitzvah* observance, such as is the case in conditions of *shtuth*, drunkenness, or some types of life-threatening illness.[72] Thus, the homosexual, even as *oness*, is no less obligated to have children, to seek treatment for his condition, or to fulfill any other *mitzvah* obligation.

VII.

Should *to'evah*'s interpretation rest upon contemporary nosologic categories or sociological norms? The answer partly depends on how we understand the function of the term *to'evah*. If used as a clinical term—rewriting Lev. 18:22 as "and behold it is a *pathology*," the value of *to'evah* would be to indicate pathological status. Further, it would imply the need for intervention. This, despite contemporary psychiatric notions and irrespective of the regnant political views. As a descriptive term or as an emotive emphasis appended to a given sociological norm, "and behold it is *sickening*," the fate of *to'evah* would perhaps seem more closely tied to changing norms and attitudes. That is, it becomes a subjective matter in which if a condition does not *sicken* me, it just does not—unless I choose to force myself to develop an attitude of disgust toward the condition. Though Halakhah is intent on fostering certain attitudes in us, nonetheless, it seems that the term *to'evah* is more akin to a clinical judgment than a descriptive statement—*to'evah: to'eh atah bah*, "you err through it."[73] As a clinical term, the proscriptive and prescriptive values of *to'evah* are unaffected by contemporary views since *to'evah* stems from a unique psychological perspective.

Finally, *to'evah* may also be an existential statement which transcends the category of individual pathology or the rules and norms shared between the deviant and nondeviants in a given social system. Homosexuality is a sexual masquerade, indicating an erroneous or inauthentic state of existence (". . . and behold [homosexuality] is *bad faith*"). In this last sense, homosexuality is not merely pathology; it is an unheroic state of being which takes on new relevance along the sin-repentance continuum in addition to the psychiatric illness-psychotherapy continuum. Judaism recognizes that the problem of the deviance of homosexuality resides not solely in a pathology within the individual or society, but also in the complex relationship which exists between the individual who demonstrates behavior labeled as *to'evah* and the One who labels such behavior as *to'evah*. From the halakhic perspective, then, homosexuality is *to'evah* precisely because it represents the acceptance of a neurotic resolution of conflict with the oedipal father in a way which will eventually distort one's relation to the heavenly Father.

Notes

1. Lev. 18:22.
2. Lev. 20:13; *Sanh.* 82a cites Jer. 3:20, but cf. Mal. 2:11 and Jer. 6:15, 8:12.
3. *Sanh.* 55a and also *Yev.* 8a, 55b; *M.T. Hil. Isurei Biah* 1:14.
4. Lev. 20:13; *Sanh.* 54 a-b; *Yev.* 83b; *SMaG*, Neg. no. 94; *Tur Sh. A., E.H.* 24; *M.T. Hil. Isurei Biah* 1:14-15.
5. Even though *mishkav zakhor* is not enumerated in *M.T. Hil. Isurei Biah* 1:6-8, it must be considered *arayoth* inasmuch as it is punishable by *kareth* as stated in *Hil. Ishuth* 1:5; see also *Arukh ha-Shulchan, E.H.* 24:1; *M.T. Hil. Rotzeach* 1:11 to *Sanh.* 72b-73a.
6. E.g., *Torah Temimah* to Gen. 2:24; *Sanh.* 58a; *J.T. Kid.* 1:1.
7. Lev. 18:3; see also the insightful *Hamek Davar* loc. cit. who distinguishes between *ma'aseh*—an abnormality or immorality which happens at the whim of individual temptation—and *halikhah*, which represents the institutionalization of such deviance and the habitual commission of sin.
8. *Torath Kohanim, Acharei Moth* 9:6-8.
9. *Yev.* 76a; *Shab.* 65a-b; *Sanh.* 69b; and in *J.T. Git.* 8:8 as *soledoth*.
10. *Yev.* 76a; *Shab.* 65a-b.
11. *Tos.*, s.v. *ha-mesoleloth, Yev.* 76a, and see the *Rosh* and Meiri ad loc.; Sifra 9:8; *M.T. Hil. Isurei Biah* 21:8; but cf. *Tos.*, s.v. *pesuloth, Shab.* 65b and also *Yafeh Einayim* to *Shab.* 65a. Nonetheless, *nashim ha-mesoleloth* may not marry a high priest.
12. *M.T. Hil. Isurei Biah* 21:8; *SMaG*, Neg. no. 126; *Tur Sh. A., E.H.* 20; *Sefer Charedim*, Neg. chap. 7:23.
13. *Biblical and Talmudic Medicine*, F. Rosner (Trans.), "Legal Medicine," p. 492, (New York: 1978).
14. Ibid., p. 498.
15. Rosenheim, E., "Sexual Attitudes and Regulations in Judaism," pp. 1315-21, in J. Money and H. Musaph eds., *Handbook of Sexology* (Amsterdam: 1977).
16. ——."Sexuality in Judaism," *J. Psychol. and Jud.* 4 (1980): 249-60, p. 258.
17. Schindler, op. cit., 1979.
18. Lamm, op. cit., 1979, p. 203.

19. *Judaism and Healing: Halakhic Perspectives* (New York: 1981), p. 69, citing *Kiryath Sefer* to *M.T. Hil. Isurei Biah* 21.
20. To *Sanh.* chap. 7, 54a.
21. *Rambam* uses the term "*u-k*e*mo kein....*"
22. E.g., *Niddah* 13b to Gen. 38:10; see also *Sha'arei T*e*shuvah*, vol. 3, no. 112.
23. See *Otzer ha-Poskim*, vol. 9, to *E.H.* 23 (pp. 163-80).
24. Cited in *Atzei Arazim* 21:1.
25. *Tzafnath Paneach*, vol. 3, no. 164.
26. *Torah Temimah* to Lev. 18:3.
27. *Perishah* to *Tur E.H.* 20, no. 11.
28. *Cheker Halakhah*, no. 14, p. 53, col. 2, noting also that *Rambam* does not list *nashim ha-mesoleloth* in the *Sefer ha-Mitzvot*. On this problem, see the general comments of *Penai Yehoshuah*, vol. 2, no. 44 (p. 22b).
29. Vol. 2, no. 26 (p. 89).
7. See also *BaCH* to *Tur Sh. A., Y.D.* 178.
31. According to the observation of the *Netziv* (note 9 above), both types of homosexuality would appear to be Biblically forbidden.
32. *Beth Yosef* to *Tur Sh. A., Y.D.* 178, who cites *Maharik*.
33. *M.T., Hil. A.Z.* 11:1, 4.
34. Yet, *Sefer Mitzvoth ha-Katzar*, Neg. no. 21 does not mention *nashim ha-mesoleloth* to Lev. 18:3.
35. See chaps. 10 and 11 in my *Judaism and Psychology*, op. cit., 1980. Consider also that (1) the *isur* of self-masturbation by a woman would be viewed less severely by most authorities (see *Otzer ha-Poskim*, vol. 9, pp. 166-67), and (2) some even permit masturbation for males when faced with an alternative involving *sakanath nefesh*, even according to the view that masturbation in males is Biblically forbidden. However, regarding (2), (a) the *sakanath n*e*fashoth* argument will not hold if homosexuality is considered *arayoth*, such as is the case by male homosexuality, (b) *most* homosexuals are indeed severely troubled but are *not* involved in grave *sakanah*, and (c) the precedents utilized to permit masturbation in cases of *sakanah* may not apply in the case of homosexuality since here the "illness" does not directly involve a physical problem in the reproductive or genito-urinary systems. Note that in chapter 4, I argued for the power of psychological *sakanah* or *tzar* to waive the incumbent prohibitions involved in contraception and possibly even abortion within the view that neither involves the *isur* of *retzichah*. For those who do view abortion as a problem of *retzichah*, only the *rodef* argument can effect leniency. If homosexuality is to be viewed as involving the grave Biblical offense of *arayoth*, we must be more strict. Rabbinic levels of *isur*, however, permit more leeway, such as is the case with some of the treatment techniques which might be used to cure homosexuality (see further).
36. See Bayer, R., *Homosexuality and American Psychiatry: The Politics of Diagnosis* (New York: 1981).
37. See chap. 11 in my text, op. cit., 1980.
38. Lev. 19:14; *Tos.*, s.v. *la'avod, A.Z.* 15b.
39. Matt, H., "Sin, Crime, Sickness, or Alternative Life Style?: A Jewish Approach to Homosexuality," *Judaism 27* (1978): 13-25; Schindler, R.,

"Homosexuality, the Haiacha, and the Helping Professions," *J. Relig. and Heal. 18* (1979): 132-37; Bleich, J.D., "Homosexuality," in his *Judaism and Healing: Halakhic Perspectives* (New York: 1981), 69-72; Lamm, N., "Judaism and the Modern Attitude Toward Homosexuality," *Encyclopedia Judaica Yearbook* (New York: 1974), 194-205, and in M.M. Kellner ed., *Contemporary Jewish Ethics* (New York: 1978), 375-99, and in F. Rosner & J. David Bleich eds., *Jewish Bioethics* (New York: 1979), 197-218; Spero, M.H., "Homosexuality: Clinical and Ethical Challenges," *Proc. Assns. Orth. Jew. Sci. 6* (1980): 177-99, and in *Tradition 17* (1979): 53-73; Rosenheim, E., "Sexual Attitudes and Regulations in Judaism," in J. Money and H. Musaph eds. , *Handbook of Sexology* (Amsterdam: 1977), 1315-21, and "Sexuality in Judaism," *J. Psychol. and Judaism 4* (1980): 249-60.

40. See Bleich, op. cit., 1981, p. 71.

41. *B.K.* 28b; *Torath Kohanim* to Lev. 20:3; *M.T. Hil. Yesodei Torah* 5:4, *Hil. Sanh.* 20:2; *Tos.*, s.v. *ein, Yev.* 54a; cf. *A. Z.* 54a.

42. R. Schindler, for example, states that a lesbian is forbidden to "marry into the priesthood" (p. 135). In fact, a lesbian may marry a priest, since her wanton behavior is considered *pritzuth* (immodesty) rather than *zenuth*. However, a *high* priest may not marry a lesbian (*Tos.*, s.v. *ha-mesoleloth, Yev.* 76a; Sifra 9:8; *M.T., Hil. Isurei Biah* 21:8; cf. *Tos., Shab.* 65b).

43. Whether or not the "illness" or "sickness" label is truly a nonmoral category, see M. Moore, "Some Myths about Mental Illness," *Arch. Gen. Psychiatr.* 32 (1975): 1438-97; P. Sedgwick, "Mental Illness *Is* Illness," in R. Boyers ed., *Psychological Man* (New York: 1975), 178-207, and E. Becker, *Revolution in Psychiatry* (New York: 1964).

44. See the contrasting views of M. Wikler, "The Torah View of Mental Illness," *J. Jew. Comm. Serv. 53* (1977): 339-344, and my response, "Mental Illness as Sin: Sin as Neurosis," *J. Jew. Comm. Serv.* 54 (1977): 116-127.

45. Matt, op. cit., 1978, p. 17.

46. Ibid., p. 20.

47. The recent *Diagnostic Statistical Manual-III* (1980) states that "satisfactory heterosexual adjustment in individuals who previously had a sustained pattern of exclusively homosexual arousal is rare" (p. 281). Yet, the DSM does not define what "adjustment" means: through psychotherapy? faith-healing? spontaneous remission? Of course, the DSM is not a textbook of psychopathology and surely does not speak for every orientation of psychology and psychotherapy. Indeed, the view stated in DSM, and apparently favored by Matt, must be contrasted with the recent work of J. Hinrichsen and M. Katahn, "Recent Trends and New Developments in the Treatment of Homosexuality," *Psychother.: Theo., Res. and Prac. 12* (1975): 83-90; W. Masters and V. Johnson, *Homosexuality: In Perspective* (Boston: 1979); H. Adams and E. Sturgis, "Status of Behavioral Reorientation Techniques in the Modification of Homosexuality: A Review," *Psychol. Bull. 84* (1977): 1171-88.

48. Bleich, op. cit., 1981, p. 71.

49. Ibid., p. 71.

50. "The Halakhic Status of *Hirhur Asur* in Psychotherapy," *Assia 25 / 26* (1980): 67-52 and chap. 10 in my *Judaism and Psychology: Halakhic Perspectives* (New York: 1980).

51. *Meg.* 20a; Zohar Gen. 155.
52. *Ber.* 12b to Judg. 14:3; *Sefer ha-Mitzvoth,* Neg. no. 44, 353; *Sefer ha-Chinnukh,* no. 387; *A. Z.* 20b; *Ket.* 46a; *M.T. Hil. Isurei Biah* 21:2-3.
53. *M.T. Hil. Yesodei Torah* 5:6, 9, *Hil. Isurei Biah* 21:1; *RaN* to *Pes.* 25b; *Rama* to *Sh. A., Y.D.* 157.
54. E.g., see *Torah Temimah* to Gen. 2:24 on *Sanh.* 58a.
55. *M.T. Hil. T^e^shuvah* 7:3.
56. Lamm, op. cit., 1979, pp. 212-13.
57. The principle Rabbi Lamm refers to is *Ein kishuy ela le-da'ath* (*Yev.* 53b; *Sefer ha-Chinnukh* 556; *M.T. Hil. Sanh.* 20:3, *Hil. Isurei Biah* 1:9; see also *Arukh ha-Shulchan: Y.D.,* 185:29-33; *Chiddushei ha-RaN* to *Sanh.* 61b; *Resp. Chatham Sofer: Y.D.,* no. 133 and *O. Ch.,* no. 202). Problematic is R. Lamm's speculation (p. 212) that "the warped family background of the genuine homosexual is considered *oness.*" Some logical or halakhic proof is necessary to buttress such an assertion. If this assertion were indeed the case, then psychotherapy would be halakhically unnecessary in the case of nonpsychotic disorders inasmuch as these, too, have predisposing if not determinative "backgrounds." I am not even sure if the full halakhic status of the oft-cited category *tinok she-nishboh* ("... as a child captured by heathens"), actually means to render the individual to whom it is applied an *oness gamur.*
58. E.g., *Resp. Igroth Moshe: Y.D.,* vol. 2, no. 59, and also see *Mishneh la-Melekh* (8) to *M.T. Hil. Yesodei Torah* 5:8.
59. p. 213. *Pithchei T^e^shuvah* to *Sh. A., E.H.* 178(7) cites *Resp. Makom Shmuel,* no. 25 who states that perhaps even the female *shoteh,* unlike the *k^e^tanah,* can be considered culpable for sexual crimes since she exhibits "desire," and thus perhaps she also experiences "willingness" ("*kivan she-anu ro'im she-yesh lah ta'avah, chayshinan she-yesh lah ratzon gam ken*..."). Of course, this interpretation is not in accord with the usual ruling in the laws of *oness u-mefateh* that "*pitu'i ketanah havi oness.*" Indeed, *Pithchei T^e^shuvah* then cites *Binath Adam* (*Sha'ar* 25:35) who argues that *ta'avah* is not necessarily related to *ratzon,* and that *shoteh* can be compared to *k^e^tanah* in this regard (see also *Resp. R. Akiva Eger,* no. 218 [end]). Also see *Otzer ha-Poskim: E.H.* 7:11, no. 74 (s.v. *de-chayshinan*) discussing whether an act of sexual intercourse which begins in *ratzon* or willingly, even when in the overall context of duress, can be considered fully *oness* or compelled.
60. McIntosh, M.,"The Homosexual Role," *Soc. Probs. 16* (1968): 182-192.
61. *DSM-III* (1980): p. 282. See also *Meiri* to *A.Z.* 28b and *Chiddushei ha-Meiri* to *Yoma* 84a.
62. Huges, E.C., "Dilemmas and Contradictions of Status," *Am. J. Sociol. 50* (1945): 353-359.
63. See my "Clinical Aspects of Religion as Neurosis," *Am. J. Psychoanal. 36* (1976): 361-365.
64. Based upon a much debated responsum attributed to the *Rosh* in *Resp. Besamim Rosh,* no. 345, cited in *Pithchei T^e^shuvah: Y.D.* 345: 2 and also see *Arukh ha-Shulchan: Y.D.* 345:5, but cf. *Resp. Chatham Sofer: E.H.,* vol. 1, no. 69 and *Y.D.,* no. 326 and *E.H.,* vol. 2, no. 2.
65. McNeill, J., *The Church and the Homosexual* (London: 1976) and Pittenger,

N., *Time for Consent: A Christian's Approach to Homosexuality* (Suffolk: 1970).
66. Davison, G.C., "Homosexuality. The Ethical Challenge," *J. Consult. Clin. Psychol. 44* (1976): 157-62; and see also S. Mitchell, "Psychodynamics, Homosexuality, and the Question of Pathology," *Psychiatry 41* (1978): 254-63.
67. E.g., *R.H.* 6a; *Yev.* 106a; *Kid.* 49b-50b; see also chap. 7 below, notes 27-29.
68. *Ket.* 49b, *Tos.*, s.v. *"akhfiyah,"* and *R.H.* 6a, *Tos.*, s.v. *"yakriv."*
69. Lev. 19:14 and see *M. T. Hil. Rotzeach u-Shmirath ha-Nefesh* 11: 4-5, *Hil. Chovel u-Mazik* 5:1. This duty may also involve "And you shall put away the evil from your midst," Deut. 17:7 and Sifra ad loc.
70. See the essay of R. Moshe Shternbuch cited in *Resp. Seridei Esh*, vol. 1, pp. 303-8 and R.Y.M. Weinberg's comments following, pp. 308-16.
71. Lev. 18:5; *Yoma* 85b; *Sanh.* 74a; see *Or Sameach* to *M.T., Hil. Yesodei Torah* 5:6.
72. *Or Sameach*, ibid., and see *TaZ* to *Sh. A., O. Ch.* 108:1, *Y.D.* 341:5.
73. *Ned.* 51a (see also the mysterious comments of *Netziv* to Lev. 20:11).

9
Countertransference in Religious Therapists of Religious Patients

The slowly growing literature addressing itself to the unique problems of psychotherapy with religious patients contains few studies devoted to problematic countertransference.[1] Pattison focuses on transference and complementary reactions between the pastoral counselor and the religious patient,[2] and Pruyser suggests dynamics which are conducive to transference-countertransference with religious patients.[3] I have dealt with the distinction between distortive countertransference and the general ethical commitment to "brotherly love" in the therapy of religious patients.[4]

The therapist's ability to perceive the patient with an appropriate balance of professional enthusiasm and detachment requires ongoing self-examination. This task is especially relevant when encountering unfamiliar clientele. It is also relevant when dealing with clientele whose familiarity with or similarity to the therapist may interfere with the therapist's attention, sensitivity, and ability to convey genuine acceptance of the patient.[5] When therapist and patient share a commitment to religious belief or to specific religious affiliations, the determinants of the therapist's attitudes toward religious valuational material must be examined. Appropriate evaluation of these determinants will help reduce their potentially destructive influence on the clinical alliance.

This task also includes the therapist's competence in recognizing and managing the religious patient's unique range of transference distortions and his complementary reactions to them. The uniqueness of such reactions in the case of religious therapists and patients, beyond the actual dynamic process, is the particular religious content through which they are expressed and the interrelationship between the participants' conscious and unconscious levels of religious ideology. Thus the psychotherapist must optimally be knowledgeable about religious belief in general as well as about the specific religious beliefs and customs of particular religious patients. At the same time, the use of such knowledge is equally subject to the determinants of the therapist's general attitude toward religious belief and this may also be wielded in a destructive way.[6]

The Emergence of Countertransference

Therapists and patients of like religious beliefs represent a favorable alliance by virtue of shared language and ethos which would contribute to a minimum of perceived distance or strangeness between them. This would also enhance the therapist's ability to differentiate between legitimate and illegitimate uses of religion. However, this very belief can be used by a therapist to rationalize a disinterest in monitoring the negative potential of such familiarity. In such instances, the belief itself is a clue to countertransference distortion.

In fact, the sense of religious familiarity shared and acted upon by patient and therapist may be co-opted by neurotic and nonneurotic intrapsychic influences which generally determine their religious beliefs and mannerisms. In the case of Jewish religious identification, for example, Klein has reported the initially destructive effects among group members of like-ethnic identification based in latent hostilities and on unconscious identification with out-group myths and prejudices.[7] Healthy and unhealthy aspects of the Jewish therapist's and patient's manifest identities such as (1) self-perception as a member of a minority, (2) feelings of fear related to and induced by parental upbringing, (3) warm feelings and attachment to religious rituals, (4) an obsession with being better than other members of society, and (5) sensitivity to bias and themes of persecution may bind the two together.[8] The therapist's readiness to identify with and confirm his own religiosity and to help patients do the same would be the complimentary and complicating aspect of the above with significant transference and countertransference potential.[9]

Indeed, despite apparent similarities between patients' and therapists' religious beliefs, there are often idiosyncratic and conflicting differences between such beliefs based on personal religious needs. In the patient, such personal influences tend to be readily identified through the patient's psychopathology and through numerous countertherapeutic expectations and resistances which motivate destructive transference. These transference reactions, in turn, can evoke equally destructive countertransference responses, thus derailing the process and purpose of psychotherapy. When the therapist does not understand that the basis of his reactions may be the patient's transferences, there is the danger of the therapist accepting as valid his inappropriate reactions to the patient.[10] When consistently left uncorrected, the therapist may reinforce the patient's *reactive* transference-based behaviors; i.e., negative reactions provoked by the *realistic* perception of uncontrolled countertransference on the part of the therapist, secondarily elaborated upon by the patient's own psychic conflicts.

Generally speaking, the therapist of religious patients must monitor a continuum of transference-countertransference responses. These range from rescue fantasies to disdain brought on by projection of personal insecurity, guilt, or prejudice. On the patient's part, responses range from the need to replace loved objects and to obtain gratification through identification with the therapist's religious life to the expectation of magical cure. Many of these negative responses are evident in the religious patient's pretherapeutic expectations and fantasies, such as the belief that the therapist is determined to destroy the patient's religious beliefs or, alternatively, that the therapist will readily join the patient in warm and protecting friendship.

Though many therapists believe that strong feelings of love or disgust for any patient can be realistic, there are rarely sufficient grounds for such emotions to develop in a properly maintained therapeutic alliance. Evidence of strong emotional attitudes toward patients should in fact be taken as an indication of countertransference.[11] When such emotions arise in the encounter between the religious therapist and patient, it is most probable that a semi-conscious assimilation of their religiously-based mutuality has evoked, in the case of positive feelings, unsatisfied needs for love, nurture or, alternatively, neurotic fears, insecurities, aggressive feelings against the group or unresolved rebelliousness. In both instances, transference projections and displacements from the patient become difficult to distinguish from the therapist's own identification with the patient.

Some case illustrations will highlight the above points.

Case 1: A seventeen-year-old male, religious patient was being treated by a religious therapist, both of whom belonged to the same religious community and to families with close ties. The patient had recently returned to America from Israel where he had emigrated with his parents when he was eleven. He had been very unhappy in Israel, got along poorly with peers and teachers, and was prone to anxiety attacks alternating with depressive periods during which he often threatened to commit suicide. The therapist had initially been consulted several times by the patient's grandparents. Subsequently, he suggested that the patient be encouraged to seek psychotherapy and when the patient did, the therapist was asked to take his case.

The patient came to his initial session quite anxious and agitated, letting the therapist know that all the secular psychologists he had encountered thus far had failed to appreciate the importance of religion in his life, while the religious counselors and rabbis he had encountered failed to appreciate the extent of his psychological pain. In characteristic style, the patient demonstrated many obsessive-compulsive trends, with a defense tendency toward splitting and lapsing into deep depression. After a few sessions the patient was able to discuss his masturbatory compulsion and disturbing sexual fantasies, but not with any adequate relinquishing of his intellectualizing or isolation.

During this period the therapist was frequently contacted by the patient's rabbi (who was also the therapist's rabbi), the patient's teacher (who was at one time the therapist's teacher), and grandparents who, with good intentions, all inquired about the patient's progress. The therapist gave each various amounts of confidential information, rationalizing that each was in a position to need psychological perspective on the patient. While the therapist actually had keen insight into the patient's problems, this insight was being used to obtain narcissistic gratification from the patient's and therapist's infracommunity rather than solely for the sake of the patient's well-being. The therapist had technically and factually denied the patient's individuality and need for independence at the same time that he considered these vital therapeutic goals for the patient.

After a few sessions the patient suddenly announced that he had decided to return to Israel. The therapist superficially questioned whether this was a healthy decision but failed to recognize that this decision was an acting-out of negative transference evoked by the unrecognized countertransference reactions to the patient as well as by the patient's inability to tolerate his increasing dependence upon the therapist. They decided to terminate therapy. Three days later the therapist was contacted by the patient's worried grandmother who informed him that the patient had decided to remain in America. The patient asked if they could resume their therapeutic contract. The therapist consented to this without discussing either precipitous decision. It was not long before the patient again decided to return to Israel and then to change his mind again. The therapist's consistent failure to confront his own mismanagement of the patient, his anger with him, and his almost conscious relief at the thought of being free of the entangling alliance left him unable to deal with this final spate of acting-out behavior. When the patient commented that he had gained much from their work together, the therapist blandly agreed and wished him good luck.

Case 2: An Orthodox Jewish psychologist took on a patient from the yeshiva (rabbinical seminary) in their community at the advice of the patient's dean, who had been the therapist's dean. While the therapist made meaningful initial attempts to prevent their mutual religious commitments and loyalties from interfering with therapy, signs of such interference surfaced within the first month of therapy. The therapist allowed the patient to discuss their therapeutic work with the patient's dean and, as a result, had to deal daily with the dean's animadversions expressed by the patient through arguments and ruminative monologues. The therapist was spending much time engaged in philosophical debate and found himself exhausted at the end of the hour. He also found it increasingly difficult to deal with the patient's hostility and diffidence and with his own resentment against the patient and his former dean.

The therapist soon began coming late to sessions, offering the patient and his supervisor lame excuses couched in terms intended to protest his own religious commitment. For example, the therapist suddenly felt the need to rearrange his personal religious study hour to the hour just prior to his patient's session and blamed his tardiness on an inability to "tear himself away" from the exciting material he was learning. Such comments failed to have any appreciable "inspiring" effect upon the patient.

The therapist was unable to interpret his patient's resistance and rumination. He believed that the patient was poorly motivated and not psychologically-minded. This was only partially true. To be sure, the patient was well-defended behind intellectualizations, denials, and projections and would no doubt remain "unmotivated" to change until such defenses were adequately dealt with. Moreover, the patient's reactions included a realistic perception of the therapist's countertransference. The patient's fantasy that he was "protected" by his mentor's surveillance from the spiritual dangers of psychotherapy was reinforced by the therapist's own fear of not being approved of and of being considered dangerous by his co-religionists.

When confronted with these problematic behaviors, the therapist expressed a "sense of pressure" to handle the patient with kid gloves in order "not to disfavor the profession in the eyes of the primitive yeshiva community" and his dean. This moralizing was a projection of the therapist's own superego demand for perfection and compliance and of his own feelings of guilt brought about by his professional career and a negative self-image based on hostile attitudes toward college education which he had assimilated during his earlier years at yeshiva. He came to understand his sense of pressure as emerging from his own ambivalence toward intense religious commitment and, at the same time, his doubts about the superiority of psychotherapy over the "inherent" curative potential of religious belief. Whereas his previous professional endeavors evoked in him a healthy sense of efficacy and satisfaction, the current religious patient (an alter ego) evoked a sense of unlove, marginality, and faithlessness. The deeper significance of the therapist's doubts lay in unresolved conflicts related to paternal authority and to an intense and complicated identification with his religious dean who was in certain ways a father substitute. The curative role that the therapist had adopted as a professional identity was itself a substitute for "priestly" powers he had earlier sought through his magical identification with the dean and about which he was so ambivalent.

It was not easy for the therapist to resolve this ambivalence. However, through more careful attention to his reactions with the current patient he became less defensive about his patient's mistrust and rigidity and he regained his independent leadership capacity in therapy. The therapist met with his former dean and informed him in a respectful manner that it was important to preserve the dyadic relationship. It took some time to win a pact of noninterference from the dean; however, when this was accomplished it effectively reduced one significant source of the patient's resistances.

In the cases of these therapists, their professional and technical preferences have been surrendered in favor of personal preferences. The patient and therapist are seeking the more general and immediate rewards of monopolizing upon their unanalyzed religious familiarity. Such surrender indicates mutual collusion, stimulated by the participants' religiosity and elaborated upon by intrapsychic needs and influences in order to avoid exposing each other to the effortful work of exploring the deeper conflicts of the religious patient.

Another manifestation of distortive countertransference occurs when the therapist identifies too strongly with the religious patient's struggles. This can lead to excessive agreement with the patient's rationalizations, too much sympathy with the patient's attempts to blame others or to find fault with his own lifestyle on superficial religious grounds, too great or too little participation in the patient's anxieties, too little expectation of better adjustment or too strong an attitude of permissiveness regarding the satisfaction of neurotic needs. Fostering a gratifying atmosphere whereby the patient comes to believe that improvement is the condition of acceptance and love and a means of pleasing the therapist, or identifies too strongly with the therapist and experiences "flight into health" based on the fear of losing the therapist, is the result of unmanaged countertransference.

Case 3: Religious psychotherapists who have themselves recently become more religious or committed to their faith, which always involves some degree of personal psychosocial upheaval, may have particular blind-spots when working with patients whose current psychosocial crises are also enmeshed in recent religious conversion or increased faith. One newly religious therapist repeatedly viewed his religious patients' religious struggles as "primitive versions" of his own, more sophisticated and "well-resolved" religious awakening. He tended to bore quickly of attending to his patients' accounts of their social and emotional struggles. He would generally mitigate his patients' turmoil by telling them of his own religious path and by giving advice, reassuring and educating on "correct" versions of religious belief. This approach encouraged his patients to avoid anxiety and conflict-laden decisions or thoughts and did not allow them to learn by working-through such decisions.

During a reactive episode with one particular patient of almost identical past history and emotional tenor, the therapist arbitrarily refused to allow discussion of religious issues. He argued that these were all diversions from the patient's "real" problems. In fact, many of the patient's problems involved areas of interpersonal living that were problematic for the therapist as well and which had been "resolved" only by massive denial and repression. In due course, patient and therapist were locked in an unfruitful misalliance.

The religious therapist's fear of becoming the religious mentor or "ideal" for the religious patient always involves the patient's tendency to idealize the therapist. When unrecognized, this unmanaged fear can result in the countertransferential loss of independent leadership in therapy. An illustration of loss of leadership is seen where the religious therapist allows himself to be manipulated into resolving ideological or philosophical problems for the patient or to respond to apparently innocent requests for "correct" religious or personal views. Analysis of such requests always reveals the hidden agenda to entrap the therapist into making precarious extensions from which position he will be weakened or devalued by the patient.

Case 4: The following is an excerpt from the treatment of a young married couple, both orthodox Jews. Mrs. L. had recently become more Orthodox and had become infatuated with Mr. L. at a religious youth convention where Mr. L. was the leader of her group. Mrs. L. exhibited many hysterical and obsessive trends. On the other hand, while scrupulous in his observance of Judaism, Mr. L. was undergoing a temporary crisis which involved his taking on lenient views of many religious practices formerly so important to him. Mr. L. found himself increasingly frustrated by his wife's rigid, perfectionistic demands and rules and incapable of responding with love to her manipulative relationship. Mrs. L. was deeply invested in increasing her religious commitments and practices and was very mistrustful of her husband's current religious behavior which added to their acute interpersonal difficulties.

At several points during early therapy, Mrs. L. would cite specific examples of her husband's "religious laxness" and maneuvered the therapist, himself an Orthodox Jew, into the position of making a statement on the correctness or incorrectness of some of Mr. L.'s practices. From the strictly religious standpoint, some of his practices demanded redress. However, the therapist sensed that Mrs. L.'s hidden agenda was to supplant her husband with the therapist as her new religious ideal such that any alignment by the therapist with Mrs. L. would effectively drive a wedge between the three participants. Of course, beneath Mrs. L.'s "religious" concerns was a strong erotic transference to the therapist—which had previously surfaced unanalyzed with their earlier marriage counselors and therapists and which clearly played a role in Mrs. L.'s initial attraction to Mr. L. He was now the victim of her "grand disappointment."

The therapist correctly declined to answer her specific demands and suggested that she explore her need for a specific response from him. Mrs. L. became infuriated with the therapist and accused him of defaulting on his religious obligations. The therapist maintained his professional stance and asked Mrs. L. whether she in a sense had already decided on the matter by not giving her husband the benefit of the doubt? After a few moments' silence, the therapist wondered whether her earlier anger with him and her current hostile silence were similar to her anger with her husband: when in situations of doubt or lack of control, she felt weak and attempted to manipulate others so as to regain a position of power. This interpretation hit home. With Mrs. L.'s subsequent work on her deeper insecurities and shame, prematurely covered over by her rapid and intense religious crisis, and Mr. L.'s work on his reaction to her rigidity, therapy progressed to a successful end. By the therapist's maintenance of professional neutrality—despite religious affiliations with both patients—he effectively prevented mutual religious commitment from evoking a destructive misalliance.

Yet another form of collusion occurs between the therapist and the religious community in the manner and content of the community's requests for professional services and his management of such requests. In the case of the Orthodox Jewish community, for example, there are numerous social and religious occasions which provide one with ample opportunity for soliciting free advice, off-the-cuff consultation, and counterphobic teasing. One may purposely utilize such inappropriate occasions for consultation because they guarantee little time for a proper, and therefore too pathological assessment and diagnosis. This tactic preempts the anticipation that the therapist is thinking about the individual's "obvious" problems, while the atmosphere of "social banter" tends to nullify his need to adopt a true patient role.

The therapist's need for identification and familial approval may render him susceptible to entrapment on such occasions, especially when such needs are reinforced by a strong rescue fantasy and a lack of an appropriate threshold for delayed gratification. Entrapment is a generally unproductive process which begins with accepting at face value inadequate information conveyed by the party through the erroneous acceptance of others' "diagnoses" and perceptions of a problem, ending with giving inadequate advice and having to deal with subsequent challenges and devaluations from the same party.[12]

Such collusion can occur to any socially active psychotherapist, but the religious therapist needs to guard against attempts to reduce the "fee" of abstinence by indulgence in extratherapeutic contact even when such contact is considered socially important from the strictly ethical or religious perspective on fellow love and compassion. The trained psychotherapist knows that it is advantageous in certain circumstances to suspend or constrain his natural inclination toward fellow love in the interests of equally humanitarian therapeutic goals. In establishing the initial relationship with the religious patient, the religious therapist is well-advised to analyze rather than accept a prospective patient's insistence on needing a therapist of similar religious beliefs as this request suggests fear, poor motivation, and the potential for entrapment. As Pruyser puts it, such a request must itself be viewed as a presenting symptom.[13] In the specific context of the general therapeutic relationship the therapist must demonstrate to the religious patient that the illusion of sharing only religious familiarity rather than the roles prescribed by their technical relationship is a neurotic attempt to gain love without sacrifice.

Management of Countertransference with the Religious Patient

Management of countertransference reactions in the therapeutic treatment of the religious patient is enhanced through implementing the following principles:

(1) The therapist must develop a consistent conceptual understanding of neurotic and normal needs for religious practice and belief. The therapist must explore particularly those aspects of religious belief which potentially are of conflict-bearing nature, such as attitudes toward otherworldliness and this-worldliness, attitudes toward God, which often include distortions of early parental object relations, the effect of religious belief in coping with problems surrounding death and loss, superego and narcissistic aspects, ethics, and the connection between religious belief and the ability to cope with problems.[14]

(2) The therapist must be competent at discriminating between mature and immature or neurotogenic religious belief in terms of the degree of adaptive potential and autonomy from conflict such religiosity has achieved. This ability includes the therapist's sensitivity to the ways in which neurotically-based

religiosity can become autonomous of its neurotic genesis as well as the ways in which healthy aspects of religiosity can achieve autonomy in an otherwise disordered personality.

(3) The therapist must be willing to scrutinize his own religious attitudes or lack of them from the perspective of the above two factors.

(4) Work with the religious patient is fostered by developing a calm and benevolent attitude about one's anxiety, anger, and frustration which emerge when encountering such patients. This factor is stressed in view of the possibility that there are numerous *non*countertransferential responses of religious therapists to religious patients; e.g., the anxiety of seeing members of one's own faith succumb to the effects of pluralistic society, or identification with certain problems common to one's former or current level of religious belief. These, like the anxiety experienced when working with the suicidal patient, are dysfunctional only if not kept in perspective. Specifically, the therapist must accept that these feelings and attitudes are based in filial attitudes and needs which must be bracketed during the therapeutic alliance.

(5) Such perspective is safeguarded through the "as if" paradigm in psychotherapy.[15] Tarachow's paradigm recognized the existence of a normal, nontransferential or countertransferential object-need to take fellow persons as loved objects, which also includes the therapist's need to maintain relatively vulnerable ego boundaries. Tarachow warned that distortive object relationships between therapist and patient can develop from these normal needs. This is similar to the suggestion here that distortive transference and countertransference can develop from but are not identical with the ethical or religious commitment to brotherly love.

Tarachow suggests that therapy must be conducted through a "therapeutic barrier." He means that therapy must be conducted *as if* factors such as religious similarities were not a basis for any additional positive or negative appreciation of the patient. This does not mean that destructive reactions will not occur or that the patient's and therapist's religious beliefs will never enter the therapeutic atmosphere. Rather, if the therapist has maintained the "as if" situation, he will be in a position to focus on contaminating factors that have gained illicit entry to therapy at a given point and to bring these to his and the patient's attention.

(6) The therapist must recognize that when a patient and therapist are committed to specific religious values, a limit is imposed upon the goals that can be achieved during psychotherapy. This sometimes means that there is also a limit on the degree of change that is possible with a given patient. The nature of these limits depends partly on the specific values and ethical views of the patient's religion. The therapist must be able to distinguish when the commitment to values is being used as a defense and when such values must be accepted as constraints and as representing valid goals which the patient may be helped to achieve in a nondefensive way.*

(7) Finally, a therapist of religious patients must be able to tolerate the patient's normal need for an area of emotional and not necessarily rational commitment and belief—a transitional zone. The therapist must learn to contain his own need to impart insight into every aspect of the patient's life. The patient's religious beliefs are relevant to the psychotherapist only insofar as they cause or are involved in conflict and not simply because the patient has religious beliefs.

Countertransference reactions will be minimized if ground rules defining the therapist's approach to mutual religiosity are explained at the outset of the therapeutic alliance. As Pruyser

---

* A related issue is whether there are occasions when the therapist's feelings toward the religious client are not countertransferential. Spensley and Blacker,[16] discussing the issue of appropriate and inappropriate affects in the clinical encounter, note certain reality-based emotions that emerge in therapy that are clearly appropriate insofar as the therapist is concerned, such as the anxiety associated with unpredictable suicidal and paranoid patients or with termination sessions and the stress resulting from the double-bind of having to suppress personal conflicts and emotions while remaining "vulnerable" (i.e., open to feelings)[17] in order to be most helpful to a client. As the issue has been framed, the religious therapist has to maintain the "therapeutic barrier" but not totally suppress his ethnic feeling of identification with the client and his problems. This might lead, for example, to a sense of despair after seeing "yet another Jewish family representative of the overall breakdown of the Jewish family," and so on. If one follows Spensley and Blacker, stresses or anxieties stemming from *this* basis would not be countertransference.

notes, even the initial demand by a religious patient for a therapist of similar religious affiliation must always be analyzed as an aspect of the presenting problem. Such a request generally masks deeper resistances to full therapeutic involvement which can be expected to surface at several points during the early stages of therapy. Thus, an early confrontation is useful. The early establishment of a consistent therapeutic focus on the underlying reasons for apparently religiously motivated behavior will serve to attenuate the defensive appeal to sacredotal beliefs and norms, and is far less confrontative than the approach recommended by Lovinger.[18]

The "as if" approach should be explained to the patient in brief and simple terms, emphasizing essentially that all aspects of the therapeutic alliance are equally the objects of therapeutic attention, including mutual religious beliefs. On this occasion the therapist should also explain the relation he expects the patient to maintain with former advisors and counselors. He should note for the patient that commitment to confidentiality is a dual responsibility. The unchecked need of the patient to maintain a third party's involvement is an example of acting-in hostile feelings and doubts about the therapist and reflects lack of commitment. A therapist's unchecked need for approval may in turn motivate him to not attend to this clue to misalliance. Again, the need for early confrontation of such tendencies is a therapeutic desideratum.

As these ground rules are presented to the religious patient, the therapist should monitor the quality of his own reactions and associations to the patient's responses to these early expectations. He should check for tendencies to fill gaps in his understanding of the patient's behavior with presumptions about religious personalities in general as well as subtle tendencies to disregard religious mannerisms which he believes are nonrelevant to therapeutic work.

When countertransference reactions are recognized during therapy they are best managed in three steps: the therapist must (1) modify the underlying basis in himself for the difficulty, (2) correct the effects of the error or mismanagement in the session, and (3) determine and explore the patient's response to the therapist's error.[19]

Case 5: The destructive countertransference reaction in the case of the seventeen-year-old male (*Case 1*) actually resulted in both parties bolting from their misalliance. The patient did, however, attempt once again to establish a therapeutic alliance. By this time the therapist had become more experienced with his feelings and more aware of the negative influence of his own reactions. He had achieved a *modus operandi* whereby he was able to limit his need for narcissistic gratification through his professional involvement within his own community. In their new initial session, the therapist raised the issue of his discussions with the patient's grandparents and teacher and allowed the patient to express his resentment toward all concerned. Accepting the patient's anger and the validity of his need for confidentiality, the therapist explored the destabilizing effect of the patient's earlier decisions about Israel. He carefully raised the possibility that these decisions were reactions to the therapist's apparent disinterest in the integrity of their relationship. The patient was able to acknowledge this and began to recall his associations at the time of these precipitous decisions. The therapist was then able to use this work as an example of the value of expressing feelings verbally rather than acting them out.

Consider this additional illustration dealing with co-religious Jewish participants:

Dr. R. had been meeting twice weekly with his client, C., for five months for the therapeutic management of agitated depression associated with schizoid personality disorder. Progress, as could very well have been anticipated in this case, was sporadic; regressions occurred frequently as C. was unable to sustain a more intense or more frequent therapy schedule. Since the beginning of the fourth month of treatment, Dr. R. slowly took notice that he willingly allowed standard 50 minute sessions with C. to overlap into an hour or more, became increasingly annoyed with C.'s temporary setbacks, overanxious at the start of each session in anticipation of hearing about such setbacks, and was particularly piqued with C.'s now constant harping that if psychotherapy ever does accomplish gains for him, it would be due not so much to R.'s ability or even to C.'s own insight as it would be "to the credit of God, the Ultimate Healer."

Initially, R. was flattered that C.'s religious leader, with whom C. consulted prior to electing therapy, considered him "religious enough" to be entrusted with C.'s case. R. also allowed C. to periodically review his sessions with this religious leader who, in the absence of any instructions to the contrary, genuinely felt this occasional review of therapeutic material to be helpful to C. Although C. never asked outright for special attention, R. recalled feeling strongly that C. presented a unique need for encounter with a therapist of similar religious education and persuasion inasmuch as many of C.'s characterological aberrations could not easily have been divorced from his overall personality, with religious commitment serving as the superstructure for the disordered personality components.

How should a therapist react to a clear transference expression such as the statement that any cure must be credited to God? The client's remark here is not entirely valid from the standpoint of Judaism. The Jewish world view considers people also responsible and creditable for progressions and regressions and enjoins them to seek natural modes of intervention for states of dis-ease. Indeed, the remark is less an expression of the client's religiosity than it is a case of simple resistance, an expression of mistrust in the therapist. And yet, it would be countertransferential for a therapist to debate theology with the client if such debate were based in part upon hurt feelings or ire with such naive religious fundamentalism. On the other hand, it might not be countertransference if the therapist desires to achieve client realization of the defensiveness of such statements and an understanding of the impediment such thinking represents for healthy religious as well as therapeutic self-affirmation.

Handling this issue is a delicate matter. Consider two approaches to transference: the first illustrates an approach motivated by inappropriate countertransference.

Client: As you know, even if any cure comes about here, it will be due to God, the Ultimate Healer, not to you or any therapeutic tricks.

Therapist: It sounds like you don't trust me.

Client: It has nothing to do with trust and you should know as well as I that God is responsible for everything and there is nothing God does not know.

Therapist: Well, I must say, my understanding of Judaism—and I assume that we've had the same educational backgrounds—is that it grants us ample power to be the masters of our destinies, relatively speaking of course. It sounds to me like you're hiding behind that belief or using it in the wrong way.

Client: Well, that's just incorrect. In fact, it's heresy . . .

As a philosophical discussion or the bantering of friends, this dialogue would be harmless and imply nothing in particular. Precisely, however, because the therapist already knows there is deeper, independent conflict in this personality and because a committed Jewish therapist is capable of shooting holes in such unsophisticated religious interpretation, it is necessary for the therapist to safeguard his own reactions as well as dodge the client's transferential curves. In this light, consider a more appropriate approach:

Client: As you know, even if any cure comes about here, it will be due to God, the Ultimate Healer, not to you or any therapeutic tricks.

Therapist: Do you think we do tricks here?

Client: No, I do not mean it that way; just we know that all is in the hands of heaven and hence my destiny and success or failure here is predetermined and beyond our control.

Therapist: I notice now you said "our" control. Do you feel that we are in this to work together?

Client: Well, yes, I'm coming here to you to see if you can help me understand my troubles, but we do believe that God makes the moves.

Therapist: It sounds to me like you have a lot of faith in God's power to control things and I can very well appreciate that. I am just wondering whether we might try to do our best at this point, in the hopes that God has positive results in store for us. Would you agree that we can take a chance on this account?

Client: Yes, I think we can.

Countertransference can prevail in a college educated therapist who feels superior to naive or even transferentially-hostile yeshiva students, in the observant therapist who harbors derisive preconceptions about the "typical craziness" of religious penitents (*ba'alei t^eshuvah*) and feels a need to show ultra-religious Jewish clients that they too need occasionally depend on the indirect benefits of the therapist's college education, in the counselor or rabbi who becomes angry at or anxious with a client expressing masturbatory guilt. When such feelings prevail, therapy with religiously observant clients is probably not a wise choice of specialization for such therapists, until such time as they undergo further self-examination or control.

Conclusion

The therapist's ideological views on the neurotic or nonneurotic nature of religious belief are not the prime cause of countertransference reactions during psychotherapy of the religious patient. Rather, such distortions can be directly attributed to the therapist's and patient's conflicts with psychosexual and psychosocial themes which are manifest or latent characteristics of or are disguised by religious beliefs and commitment. Distortions are also influenced by the therapist's personal comfort or conflict with the transitional qualities of religious belief. The therapist cannot expect his general level of self-awareness to adequately prepare him for work with religious patients as long as he assumes that personal religious preferences and attitudes are not subject to the analytic focus.

One comes full circle from the early view which held that one could not be simultaneously free of neurosis *and* a religious devotee, as well as from the reactionary view which holds that psychological theory cannot adequately address religious issues. Somewhere in midstream is the view that religious belief can have either autonomous or dysautonomous qualities and that such qualities exert an observable influence during the psychotherapeutic interaction between religious therapists and patients.

Notes

1. Beit-Hallahmi, B., "Encountering Orthodox Religion in Psychotherapy," *Psychother.: Theo., Res. and Prac. 12* (1975): 357-359; Pattison, E.M., "Transference and Countertransference in Pastoral Care," *J. Past. Care 19* (1965): 193-202; Spero, M. H., "Implications of Countertransference for the Religious Therapist and Client," *J. Psychol. and Jud. 1* (1977): 39-51; Wikler, M., "Fine-Tuning: Diagnostic Techniques Used by Orthodox Jewish Clients," *J. Psychol. and Jud. 3* (1979): 184-194.
2. Pattison, op. cit., 1965; and see also G. Bychowski, "The Ego and Its Introjects: Origins of Religious Experience," *Psychoanal. and Soc. Sci.* 5 (1958): 246-79; Godin, A., "Transference in Pastoral Counseling," *Theol. Digest 9* (1961): 73-83.
3. Pruyser, P., "Assessment of the Patient's Religious Attitudes in the Psychiatric Case Study," *Bull. Menn. Clin. 35* (1971): 272-91.
4. Spero, op. cit., 1977.
5. Chessick, R., *The Technique and Practice of Intensive Psychotherapy* (New York: 1974) and Giovacchini, P., *Tactics and Techniques of Psychoanalytic Therapy* (New York: 1975), pp. 5-94.
6. Compare the attitudes of Beit-Hallahmi, op. cit., 1975 and R. Lovinger, "Therapeutic Strategies with 'Religious' Resistances," *Psychother.: Theo., Res. and Prac. 16* (1979): 419-427.
7. Klein, J., "Ethnotherapy with Jews." *Int. J. Ment. Heal. 5* (1976): 26-38.
8. Berl, F., "Jewish Identity: Its Use for Clinical Purposes." *J. Jew. Comm. Serv., 52* (1976): 344-354.
9. Hofstein, S., "Integration of Jewish Commitment into the Treatment Process," *J. Jew. Comm. Serv. 52* (1976): 259-269.
10. Langs, R., *The Therapeutic Interaction* (New York: 1976), vol. 2, p. 549.
11. Marmor, J. "The Seductive Psychotherapist," *Psychiatr. Digest 31* (1970): 10-16.
12. Spero, M. H., "Casual Encounters for Off-the-Cuff Advice," *J. Jew. Comm. Serv. 56* (1980): 190-192.
13. Pruyser, op. cit., 1971.
14. Bychowski, op. cit., 1958 and see also S. Lorand, "Psychoanalytic Therapy of Religious Devotees," *Int. J. Psychoanal. 43* (1962): 50-56.
15. Tarachow, S., *An Introduction to Psychotherapy* (New York: 1963).
16. Spensley, J. and Blacker, K., "Feelings of the Psychotherapist," *Am. J. Orthopsychiatr. 46*, no. 3 (1976): 542-545.
17. Winnicott's term; see D. Winnicott, "Countertransference," *British Journal of Medical Psychology 33* (1960): 17-21. R. M. Lesser ("Sibling Transference and Countertransference," *Journal of the American Academy of Psychoanalysis* 6 [1978]: 37-49) suggests that there is a relationship between the therapist's birth order (i.e., only child, firstborn, middle child, etc.) and the way in which he focuses on the emotional themes of siblings seen in therapy. Lesser finds that only-child therapists tend to focus on the vicissitudes of patients' relations to authority figures—perhaps to the exclusion of other, equally salient aspects of their

personalities; firstborn therapists tend to be sensitive to patients' manipulative attitudes; and youngest-child therapists stress issues of emotional deprivation. Given the reality of a relationship between personal issues in the therapist's life and similar themes in the lives of his patients, could one not also assume an analogous dynamic in the case of the Jewish therapist and his Jewish client? Would a Jewish self-image as scapegoat possibly predispose a Jewish therapist to heightened sensitivity to such issues in his patients? Could this dispose the therapist to a peculiar myopia in counselling married couples where one of the mates scapegoats the other or both scapegoat their children? Would a Jewish therapist be less alert to true paranoia in his patients because of his own belief that Jews may "need" to be a little suspicious in current society? Would a similar dynamic occur with the issue of persecutory complexes? These questions surely deserve empirical study.

18. Lovinger, op. cit., 1979, and also see the further discussion here in chap. 13.

19. Langs, op. cit., 1976.

10

A Clinical Note on the Therapeutic Management of "Religious" Resistances in Orthodox Jewish Clientele

The continuous exploration of the therapeutic interaction with religiously committed Jewish patients is intended to create an ever-narrowing gap between the technical constraints imposed by a patient's religious beliefs and practices and the attitudes and goals of contemporary psychotherapy. Specifically, one of the purposes of such exploration is to develop halakhically appropriate techniques of intervention which simultaneously preserve the integrity of the clinician's practice procedures, his halakhic obligation not to place a "stumbling block" before the patient and which at the same time respects the value of both the therapist's and patient's healthy religious beliefs.

Workers who have had experience with the Orthodox Jewish patient in psychotherapy or casework are aware of the tendency of such patients to make direct or indirect appeals to their religious beliefs and to specific laws and customs in an effort to avoid certain topics or content.[1] Frequently, there will be direct appeal to, or confrontation with, the mutual religious beliefs shared by therapist and patient in the effort to draw some pact of nonbelligerence from the therapist. And as has been stated, the Orthodox religious therapist may have numerous neurotic and non-neurotic motivations to allow such collusion to occur. However, such collusion will always be counterproductive. Indeed, the very process of resisting is an element of the patient's pathology inasmuch as it tends to preserve conflict and oppose the development of a therapeutic alliance. The manner in which the therapist manages his patient's initial resistances is often decisive.

By specifying "religious" resistances we are denoting resistances couched in the language of normative or idiosyncratic religious attitudes and beliefs.[2] In the case of the alliance between a religious therapist and patient, the patient's appeal to dogma as a shield against the free associative process, for example, actually involves the patient's *and the therapist's* normal religious beliefs (e.g., that rabbinic law forbids wanton fantasizing about illicit sexual content[3]), as well as those aspects of the religious parties' personalities currently in conflict. This latter category refers specifically to the neurotic ways in which normative beliefs are coopted in the service of the ego.

No less than other resistances, "religious" resistances must be managed in ways which reflect how the therapist will interact with the patient and his technical approach to their shared or conflicting religious beliefs. Management of resistance represents an opportunity to interpret magical hopes and fantasies or deep-seated mistrust and hostility and other elements which have unique implications in the case of religious individuals and may contribute to uniquely complicating forms of transference and countertransference.[4] The religious therapist, on the one hand, wants to free his patient of pathologic inhibition yet, on the other hand, does not wish to arbitrarily denounce religious beliefs or laws which *in the case of his patient* are utilized for conflict-based purposes. In other words, the halakhically-committed psychotherapist is in search of a halakhically valid distinction between psychologically healthy uses of religiosity which cannot be challenged and unhealthy uses which he can and perhaps must challenge. At the same time, while resistance is usually viewed as a behavior of the patient,[5] any display of resistance calls into play the therapist's personal dynamics, and his management of resistance is carefully monitored by the patient's ego. Thus, the strength of the "religious" resistance partially rests on the therapist's manner of response.

Typically, "religious" resistances are initially displayed during the beginning phase of psychotherapy at which time the therapist and patient are endeavoring to establish the therapeutic alliance. At this stage such resistances bear the tacit message, "If you are truly religious, you, too, will accept my religious interpretations and allow me to avoid certain topics or content."

The excerpt which follows illustrates a religious patient's initial resistance to treatment and one productive management approach to such resistance. This approach is productive in that it keeps the two participants' mutual religious beliefs in the proper perspective during this beginning phase of psychotherapy.

The patient, an intelligent nineteen-year-old obsessive-compulsive male, with depressive trends, had just recently graduated high school and elected therapy to deal with depression and "certain fears and worries about death and punishment." His concerns included frequent rage reactions and emotionally violent outbursts during class and with his family and an inability to suppress "certain disturbing thoughts." The patient belonged to a religiously observant family and had attended yeshiva for several years. He informed me after our first encounter that the rabbis with whom he had earlier discussed his problems managed to temporarily assuage his depression and anxiety but he soon found them unhelpful. He then turned to psychology to find "relief from some typical problems of adolescents" but soon felt that psychologists did not express concern for his religious sensitivities.

The illustration is taken from the third therapeutic hour during the evaluation stage. The patient has been hinting that his outbursts might be in some way related to "certain things which perhaps occur prior to the outbursts." After a few moments' struggle with this thought, the patient muttered that when he was alone he often "found" himself "doing certain things that" he "would later regret . . . things that, uhm, I find very hard to, uh, talk about." As the therapist I continued to support the patient's efforts to bring out clearly what was on his mind, the dialogue proceeded as follows:

Therapist: It seems that whatever is on your mind is very difficult for you to talk about with me.

Patient: Yeah, uh . . . yes, you might say so.

Therapist: Why don't you try to pick up the trend of thought again?

Patient: [Shifts uncomfortably in his seat] Well . . . I, uh, was saying that there are certain thoughts that I have and certain things which, uh, happen that, uhm, are pretty troublesome to me.

Therapist: Certain thoughts?

Patient: Yes, and I have been assured by my teachers that these thoughts are normal, but they still bother me.

Therapist: I'm still unsure of what you mean by "certain thoughts" and "things that happen." Do your own expressions here not have a distant tone about them?

Patient: Well, maybe so . . . I mean, uh, by "thoughts," uhm, I mean having to do with certain sexual matters and, uhhm [voice trails off] . . .

Therapist: Are you referring to things that happen between you and some other person, or when you are alone?

Patient: [leans forward] Uuh, yes . . . [clears throat] yes, that's essentially what I mean.

Therapist: Essentially, but not exactly.

Patient: That's really about all I wish to say about the matter.

Therapist: Is there any more detail to what you are thinking about?

Patient: Uh, you know that there are specific laws, and, uhm, morals about talking about such matters. You understand the main thing so, so that's all I need to say.

Therapist: You are very uncomfortable with discussing your obviously troubling thoughts.

Patient: I can discuss that I'm upset about these types of things, but I don't see why we have to dig for details.

Therapist: Yes, it is hard to see why I am interested in details, especially about such a sensitive topic.

Patient: [Looks distantly out of the window.]

Therapist: I have the following impression. I'm getting the sense that while you are trying valiantly to maintain a "pure tongue" as we talk to each other here, the thoughts in your head are not what you would call "pure." Is that about right?

Patient: [Laughs self-consciously] Yes.

Therapist: Then it seems that your mind doesn't wish to accept the *halakhoth* that you live with in everyday life.

Patient: Maybe. But I'm trying to have my mind, uh, co-operate, OK?

Therapist: Is the problem that the thoughts are, let's say, sinful, and yet talking about them in order to get help may be just as sinful? Yes?

Patient: Yep, that's just how it is. Now you understand?

Therapist: I think I appreciate the difficulty. Now, you came to me to get some help, which means I'm going to soon be facing the same problem in our work as you are. But let me suggest something which may help us both. You know, in my own efforts to place my professional work somewhere within Halakhah, I have found it helpful to view it as something like *vidduy* or *t^{e}shuvah* in the sense that you wish to rid yourself of thoughts and feelings which cause you to sin, as you have expressed it to me. Can you see this?

Patient: That's a *chiddush* [novel exposition]! But, uhm, I mean, I am admitting that there are things which bother me. Every day I say all kinds of special *t^{e}filloth* [prayers] for this problem.

Therapist: [Recognizing that the patient has accepted the halakhic paradigm, but is interpreting the model of "therapy as *vidduy*" literally.] Perhaps I'm less concerned in having you "admit" things. As you have said, this alone hasn't been of much help to you. I am, however, interested that you feel free to allow your thoughts and feelings to unfold here—and nowhere else—so that you and I can explore them and confront them. You may recall that this is exactly what Halakhah demands in *vidduy: pirut ha-chet*, the requirement that one specify every detail of one's sin and the intensity of his involvement with sin. Whatever is held back is kept out of *vidduy*. Here, too, whatever you hold back does not benefit from therapy. We call this holding back "resistance." It is my job to point out this holding back and label it as "resistance" whenever I notice it. What do you think about all this?

Patient: [Thoughtful for a moment] Well . . . you put it rather clearly, uhm, so what can I say. I have thoughts about sexual matters, sometimes in dreams, too, and I do certain, uhm, things that I regret.

Therapist: "Sexual matters," "doing things"; Is this how you experience it or is this how you talk about it to a *rosh yeshiva* [dean]?

Patient: [Suppresses a smile] OK, uh . . . I, uhm, a couple of times, uh, what they call, masturbated.

Therapist: You masturbated a couple of times.

Patient: [Obviously relieved] Yes. Uh, it was probably more than occasionally that I did it while I was having these thoughts.

Therapist: "Thoughts?"

Patient: [Leaning back in chair] Ohh . . . uh, I think of people in positions of sexual intercourse . . . There.

Therapist: It is still uneasy for you to be able to express these facts. However, we are now really talking about your experience in the way that it happens.

Patient: [Looking almost exhausted] Yes.

The patient went on to discuss troublesome sexual fantasies and other compulsive habits. The patient's problems included the obsessive manner in which he used words and ideas in a futile attempt to control sexual fantasies. Thus, encouraging him to disinhibit the associative process was a significant early step in bringing him closer to the conflict-laden content which lay below the surface.

This brief case selection illustrates one approach to dealing with so-called religious resistances which avoids unproductive confrontation between the therapist and patient over dogma and faith. I attempt as early as necessary to introduce the patient in a forthright and simple manner to the conceptual scheme which governs my work and to the demands it imposes upon both of us in much the same manner as the psychoanalyst or other specialist briefly introduces the patient to the "fundamental rules" with which the patient is expected to comply. I do not "lecture" the patient on *vidduy* or *t^eshuvah per se* as these are not the immediate functions of psychotherapy and because I do not wish to encourage the patient to adopt compulsive breast-beating or intellectualization as substitutes for psychotherapy. Contrary to the approach suggested by Beit-Hallahmi and Lovinger, I stay clear of challenging the patient's religious interpretations and beliefs with my own formulations.[6] Such challenge unnecessarily and unproductively reveals the therapist's personal religious preferences. Like any other aspect of the professional's personal life, knowledge of the therapist's religious beliefs beyond the degree unavoidable due to extratherapeutic or communal familiarity, only provides the patient with additional material for rumination and manipulation. Revelation of personal religious beliefs—and certainly offering religious advice—generally elicits from the patient additional contentiousness and argumentativeness and encourages disdain and mistrust for the therapist's presumptuous attempt to wear two hats.

Of course, my imparting to the patient my conceptualization of therapy as *vidduy* may be considered an "interpretation" and the reader will perforce call me to account for failing to follow my own recommendations. In response, I would first assert that the analogy between psychotherapy and *vidduy* is readily established in halakhic literature,[7] and as such I present it to the patient as an *a priori* rather than as something I wish to debate. Second, and more important, I am essentially utilizing this analogy as a springboard to introduce the patient to the general concept of resistance *in language he or she can readily understand.* For this reason, even when I do consider it beneficial to mention the *vidduy* analogy, I do not present a detailed halakhic discourse, but rather, through the suggestion of analogy, emphasize the disvalue of holding back and the cost of mistrust. In the illustration offered here, the breaking of resistance actually began with the pointing out to the patient of the paradox between his "pious tongue" and "impious mind."

I recognize that presenting the patient with a religious framework for psychotherapy is only one approach to managing resistance, perhaps best utilized when the worker is reasonably sure that the patient will not offer too much resistance to the analogy itself. On other occasions, a more oblique approach should be used, one which addresses the same concepts and points out resistance but does not make any mention of the therapist's halakhico-psychological framework. That is, while the therapist still operates with the *vidduy* format in mind, this framework itself is not directly appealed to during dialogue.

The following illustrates the oblique approach. The material is excerpted from the second hour of therapy with an eighteen-year-old, devoutly religious *ba'al t*^{e}*shuvah* (penitent) whose presenting problems were general unhappiness in his studies at yeshiva, deeply conflicted feelings about his irreligious parents (who lived out of town), inability to form friendships and complaints of generalized anxiety, headache and other somatic symptoms. The patient was referred to me by a close but not religious relative acting *in loco parentis*. The relative advised me that the young man had of late been exhibiting various "primitive religious beliefs and practices." The patient's religious practices were in fact not pathological, but the well-intentioned relative had actually reacted to the contrast between the affected or "protested" quality of this *ba'al t*^{e}*shuvah*'s newly adopted faith and practice and its inability to make his life any more conflict-free or productive.[8] The patient, however, did have distinctly negative attitudes toward psychotherapy, partially reinforced by the views of his religious community, partially by his teachers' and peers' mistrust of psychotherapy over other home-spun "approaches" to unhappiness, and of course partially motivated by his own conflicts.

In the dialogue the patient attempts to manipulate the psychotherapist into granting a "no pain contract," thereby rendering the therapist nonthreatening and ineffective.

Patient: What are we going to do today?

Therapist: I prefer to leave this up to you.

Patient: . . . Well, I already discussed the types of things that are bothering me. But, uhm . . .

Therapist: But . . .?

Patient: Well, I frankly don't know if this whole business is such a good idea, because I don't think we share the same *hashkafoth* [religious-philosophical views].

Therapist: Do your problems involve these *hashkafoth*?

Patient: [Defiantly] No, no, there is nothing wrong with my *hashkafoth*. . . . I'm very satisfied, thank God, with being religious and everything, but how can I be sure that you won't do something to, uh, change these *hashkafoth*?

Therapist: You seem very concerned that I might subtly attempt to influence your *hashkafoth* and perhaps introduce you to some unacceptable *hashkafoth*.

Patient: Well, yeah. I mean, you know that psychologists have many *farkrumpt* [distorted] ideas about *hashkafah* and they reject the validity of God.

Therapist: Is this true of every psychologist or only of some who have gained infamy in our circles?

Patient: Well, OK, uhm, I'm sure many psychologists are quick to assume that *ba'alei t^eshuvah* are crazy.

Therapist: I'm aware of rabbis and other *frum* [religious] people who would jump to the same erroneous generalization.

Patient: True, but it's certainly true of psychologists.

Therapist: Why so, do you think?

Patient: [Reflects] . . . maybe because they see many who do have some slight problem or difficulties.

Therapist: Uhm. Perhaps you are afraid that I'm deeply concerned about your sanity?

Patient: [Laughs] Maybe.

Therapist: Maybe.

Patient: OK, yes, I've been warned about that possibility.

Therapist: Well, you said earlier that your *hashkafoth* are not the cause of your problems. So maybe your problems have to do with troubles or feelings that preceded your new religious commitments? Maybe these earlier troubles actually prevent you from enjoying a less conflicted religious life? Is this possible?

Patient: Uhm, no, I'd have to say that most of these problems have surfaced since I've been at the yeshiva.

Therapist: Then are you yourself pinning the blame on your new religiosity?

Patient: [Looks pained yet thoughtful] I don't know if I want to say that . . . but then . . . Maybe they've just surfaced now because of all the new things I've been experiencing . . . or because my parents and I no longer see eye to eye on a lot of things we used to.

Therapist: This sounds like a very realistic perception. If we could explore it in more detail with the same openness you've just demonstrated I could learn more about your *hashkafoth* and perhaps help you to separate these from the things that are really problems to you.

Patient: ... But what about my Torah beliefs?

Therapist: I think that everything that is meaningful to you should be shared here in complete confidence and explored by us without reservation. The fact that you are a *frum* yeshiva student cannot influence me positively or negatively about your problems for which you are paying me to help you resolve, the same way that *your* being religious has not helped you to eliminate your troubles, and the same way that my personal *hashkafoth* will neither help nor hinder your emotional pain.

Patient: ... I think I am feeling a little more comfortable with your approach now. Maybe a little cautious but more comfortable.

Therapist: Let's explore this feeling of caution and see where it takes us.

From this point therapist and patient enjoyed a very useful and successful alliance lasting for twelve months at which point therapy was terminated. At various points during the early weeks of therapy, "religious" resistances surfaced but were readily resolved. For example, during the third week, as the patient neared some very significant sexual topic, he requested to be allowed to review our sessions with his religious mentor. This request was not flatly denied, but rather was painstakingly analyzed in the manner illustrated above. The patient was helped to see how this request could undermine the fundamental trust necessary for an effective therapeutic relationship and was itself an indication of hesitancy to approach the dangerous but critical source of his problems.

Religious Resistances to Psychological Testing

"Religious" resistances may emerge prior to the actual work of psychotherapy. Religious patients' ideologically-tinged resistances are often used to reduce the anxiety of or impede diagnostic assessment and psychological testing. Such reactions may stem from more or less typical unease and anxiety about our "mysterious" tests, more general, hostile attitudes common in certain Orthodox Jewish communities toward testing and psychologists, severe difficulties with establishing a trusting or dependent interpersonal relationship or frank paranoia. In chapter 11, section IV, are presented the particularly contentious objections to psychological testing of a 23-year-old yeshiva student referred for psychological evaluation by his parents and rabbi. The subject challenged at several points the relevance and validity of psychological tests which "come from college" and are applied to the Jewish *n^e^shamah* (soul). It was clear in this case that aside from the subject's belief that he was merely expressing an ideologically valid critique of the products of a secular science, the patient was in fact severely troubled and was emotionally threatened on many levels by the test stimuli. As such, his reactions are not so much normative ideology, but examples of pathological behavior.

Since some of these reactions emerge during the testing process itself, it is important to deal with them in a way that is both effective and expeditious, minimizing the opportunity for undue contamination of the testing atmosphere through the introduction of too many of the examiner's beliefs, religious views and certainly his own negative countertransference reactions. The examiner's appeal to the patient's reasonable ego at such times ought to be limited to statements concerning the psychologist's responsibility to carry through his testing or that the patient needs to cooperate in order to get the help he desires.

Some colleagues have stated that in the case of extreme or persistently negative reactions against testing, it may be advisable to temporarily discontinue testing, and invite the subject to seek the advice of a trusted rabbinic authority regarding the desirability of psychological testing. Offering, with the patient's permission, to explain the testing process to the rabbi may succeed in reducing the patient's suspiciousness. This direct approach may elevate the patient's concern about his privacy and succeed in indirectly frustrating further questioning of the examiner and the test process.

However, this approach may also be inadvisable since it admits into the therapeutic relationship the opinion and authority of a third party. This effect may be less troublesome if the examiner is not also going to be the particular subject's therapist, but introduces a confounding parameter in cases where the psychologist is both examiner and therapist. My view here should not be misconstrued as supremacism. Subservience to halakhic authority is an integral component of the therapist's professional identity and development and as such is not rightfully an area one examines with or defends to the patient. Once a therapeutic alliance is entered into, the therapist can no longer allow his authority to be challenged or manipulated by encouraging the patient to maintain the surveillance of third parties.

On the assumption that a given religious psychotherapist has achieved both halakhic as well as professional competence in his line of work, which ought to provide an ample basis for a trusting relationship, the encouragement of third party approbations is generally a resistance on the part of the therapist and the search for such approbations is a resistance on the patient's part. If trust has not been established, then this must be dealt with from the standpoint of trust/mistrust, rather than by exchanging tokens of faithfulness. Again, however, this objection may be less significant prior to initiating the working alliance or during testing when all else fails, since at this point the offer is in the nature of a simple recommendation that the patient decide whether or not he truly wishes to cooperate with the professional.

Below is a selection from the verbatim record of the 23-year-old yeshiva student mentioned above which illustrates how "religious" resistances to testing can be successfully managed.

Patient: [During the Draw-a-Person task] To tell you the truth, this is very odd. . . . I mean, why do I have to draw a woman? It's disgusting to say the least! You know, at first, I didn't mind, but what do these tests have to do with me? These are tests that you probably got from your college background which have nothing to do with the *n^eshamah* of a Jewish person.

Therapist: You are concerned that these tests aren't relevant to the uniquenesses Jews have. Yet these tests are not tests of *frumkeit* [religiosity] nor do they in fact have much to do with your *n^eshamah*. But they do tell us about some of your other, everyday skills and feelings. These tests will help me to know a little bit more about you in a relatively short amount of time. You will have time after testing to express yourself as a Jew and to add anything that you wish me to know about you. . . . Does this seem sensible to you?

Patient: But, uh, to me these tests are like *gornisht* [absolutely nothing]. I mean, I'm not here for this . . . I'm here to get some advice about my, uh, problems, some depression, uh . . . to learn to get some social *finekeit* [finesse]. These things aren't really *noge'a* [relevant] to me, to say the least.

Therapist: It does seem like a one-way street at this stage. But before I can advise you or talk with you about your problems, I need certain kinds of information. You spoke on the phone and during our first meeting of several other problems. These can be due to many different things. Sometimes, these can be treated with medicine and sometimes not. My tests help me make this kind of decision.

Patient: [Reflects] . . . OK, OK—fine. . . But then why doesn't Dr. XYZ in Israel give such tests to the yeshiva *bochrim* [students] that talk with him?

Therapist: I really cannot tell you why other professionals do not use tests. I can tell you, however, that it is a standard procedure among most clinical psychologists to test persons who come seeking their help, especially when we don't know the person very well. You have the right after testing to ask me what I have found through such tests and how that might relate to your specific needs. You also have the right to seek out another professional who does not wish to use such tests. I suggest—since you are paying for this time—that you think about this choice.

Patient: . . . No. Uh, let's go on. I mean, OK, I just wanted to know.

Later discussion during the post-diagnostic sessions dealt with a few more resistances of this subject, but it also became clear that he had responded favorably to my directness and honesty.

Subsequent to testing, some religious patients may initiate additional resistances to psychotherapy itself by renewing their criticisms of the previous testing experience. The following steps might be followed in managing such resistances.

(1) Explore the patient's preconceptions or distortive myths concerning testing, their source and the individual's tendency to generalize or to admit qualifications of his views. Note also to what degree or other characteristic ways the patient invests his perceptions in such distortions. One patient, for example, eventually mentioned that he had "actually known" a yeshiva student who committed suicide "because he went to see a psychologist." Knowing about such an experience could easily cause anxiety about psychologists, but the experience as stated was not accurate. It was possible in this example to explore the facts with the patient, only to discover that while his friend had indeed committed suicide, this unfortunate event transpired following a major trauma which occurred *after*, and unrelated to, his *single* session with the rabbi *cum* psychologist! It was also possible to enable this patient to admit that a suicidal patient is a significant challenge to any adviser—psychologist or rabbi. This discussion did not totally eliminate the individual's concerns, but did allow the opportunity to experience the present psychologist as understanding, explorative and unanxious about his role and his responsibilities.

(2) Accept the patient's hypervigilance about the therapist's religious *hashkafoth* and those criticisms which the patient feels are "proven" by the testing he has just undergone or by some negative experience with another professional. Superior intellectual rejoinders by the therapist—especially those which only thinly mask the therapist's hurt—will almost always be unappreciated and only intensify the felt distance between patient and therapist.

At the same time, one may begin to demonstrate that although the patient really knows very little about testing or the therapist, he has chosen to fill in the gaps with negative rather than positive or neutral judgments and imputations. This method may help the patient understand the mechanism of "defense through offense," demonstrate its destructive effects and also introduce the patient to the concepts of defense and resistance.

(3) By allowing the subject to reflect on some of his own test products (the *DAP*, *TAT*, and *MAPS* are best for this purpose), he may be able to come up with a few "deep" insights about himself drawn from the test product. The subject can then be introduced to the notion that there are many levels and meanings to the things one does or says.

(4) Allow the subject who so wishes to ventilate the differences between himself, "Jews," and "*Goyim*." Yet, make clear that the tests used deal with the basics of human nature and that it is not presumed that either the examiner or the patient has yet fully explored the relationship between the patient's religiosity and his current problems. If the opportunity lends itself, one may also express to the patient that some of the traits he finds objectionable in "*Goyim*" sometimes occur among Jews without making such persons less Jewish.

(5) Throughout, one wishes to reinforce the patient's ability to speak freely, even to criticize the therapist, and to demonstrate the therapist's nonjudgmental and nonretributive attitude. Should a now "contrite" patient seek the therapist's *m*^{e}*chilah* (forgiveness) or to qualify that he "didn't mean" the things he said, one must emphasize: (a) that the patient need not ask for the therapist's forgiveness, since he does not deal with the patient's behaviors as in the normal interpersonal setting. Rather, the focus is on increasing the patient's ability to see the many sides of a thing and the effects of his behaviors on others. The therapist helps the patient learn these things without extracting the types of interpersonal costs customary in that sphere (e.g., a *m*^{e}*chilah* following an "insult"). At the same time, (b) the therapist discourages the patient from disclaiming his behaviors or intentions, helping him to see that he did indeed mistrust the therapist and his tests, but also is perhaps now more capable of surrendering some of his mistrust.

(6) Some workers attempt to dissolve resistances and reduce "strangeness" by utilizing Torah statements and concepts expressed in the common vernacular of the patient and therapist in the hopes that this vehicle will better communicate basic psychological concepts. In choosing this technique, the following points should be borne in mind: (a) the patient may suspect the therapist of disingenuously playing rabbi (which is sometimes an

accurate perception); (b) these concepts, when expressed in their original form, may invite the patient to debate their "real *peshat* (meaning)" with the therapist; and (c) the therapist has the burden of utilizing each concept consistently and of not confusing these concepts with his other technical terms and procedures.

Conclusion

Two examples of successful management of "religious" resistance have been presented. Such resistances are "religious" primarily by virtue of their expression through superficial or even intensely held religious beliefs or mannerisms. Their counterproductive potential lies in the combination of general psychodynamic factors and the religious therapist's neurotic and non-neurotic motivations for collusion with his fellow religionist. "Religious" resistances are almost always encountered during the beginning stages of therapeutic involvement with the religiously committed patient. However, once these resistances are appropriately managed and the therapeutic alliance is firmly established, the patient's resistances should no longer take a uniquely "religious" form. If such resistances persist, one must assume that basic trust has not been successfully established or that countertransferential distortion has interfered with the practitioner's ability to appropriately resolve the latent motivations behind such resistances. If managed appropriately, on the other hand, the psychotherapist prevents one major opportunity for misalliance with the religious patient.

Notes

1. See Wikler, M., "Fine-Tuning: Diagnostic Techniques Used by Orthodox Jewish Clients," *Journal of Psychology and Judaism 3* (1979): 184-194; Ostrov, S., "A Family Therapist's Approach to Working With Orthodox Jewish Clientele," *Journal of Jewish Communal Service 53* (1976): 147-154; Spero, op. cit., 1980, chap. 3 and also Spero, M. H., "Countertransference in Religious Clients of Religious Therapists," *American Journal of Psychotherapy 35* (1981): 565-575.
2. The term "religious" resistance was coined by R. Lovinger, "Therapeutic Strategies with 'Religious' Resistances," *Psychotherapy: Theory, Research, and Practice 16* (1979): 419-27.
3. In fact, even such forbidden fantasies or *hirhurim* can be incorporated in a halakhically valid way into psychotherapeutic practice, following an approach I have suggested elsewhere; see Spero, op. cit., 1980, chaps. 10 and 11, and also my "Homosexuality: Clinical and Ethical Challenges," *Proceedings of the Associations of Orthodox Jewish Scientists 6* (1980): 177-199, and chapter 3 here.
4. Spero, op. cit., 1980, chap. 13.
5. Greenson, R., *The Technique and Practice of Psychoanalysis* (New York: International Universities Press, 1967), pp. 132-39.
6. Beit-Hallahmi, B., "Encountering Orthodox Religion in Psychotherapy," *Psychotherapy: Theory, Research, and Practice 12* (1975): 357-59, and Lovinger, op. cit., 1979, p. 424.
7. E.g., Maimonides, *Mishneh Torah: Hil. T'shuvah* 7:3: and *Shmoneh Prakim*, end chap. 3 to Prov. 4:19; and see also Spero, op. cit., 1980, chap. 1.
8. See Spero, M. H., "The Penitent Personality: Diagnostic, Treatment, and Ethical Considerations," *Journal of Psychology and Judaism 4*, no. 3 (1980): 131-90.

11

Idiographic Responses of Orthodox Jewish Subjects on Diagnostic Psychological Tests

I.

This paper will report some observations and clinical understandings gathered over several years from the psychodiagnostic test protocols of Orthodox Jewish subjects, mainly children and adolescents. They are intended to illustrate that the "uniquely Jewish" or "religious" material often included in the responses of Orthodox Jewish subjects during testing may be rich in diagnostically useful implications which can and should be drawn and reported by the mental health professional. In other words, such material represents for the concerned mental health professional more than a mere nuisance variable or fortuitous by-product of testing Orthodox Jewish subjects that should simply be expected rather than be subjected to diagnostic analysis. I wish to emphasize that while it is valuable during testing and evaluating to remain attuned to behaviors which may on the one hand be considered normative for the particular subgroup, such subgroup expectations or norms cannot be allowed to dull our sensitivity to evidence of conflict, pathology, or other idiographic departures in such material from either subgroup or standard norms. I have asserted a similar thesis regarding the emergence of "religious" or "Jewish" valuational material during the course of psychotherapy proper,[1] and in this paper I will examine this issue more specifically with regard to psychological testing.

The reader should perhaps pause to consider two qualifications at the outset. First, many of the clinical interpretations to be offered conform to the ego psychological and psychoanalytic points of view, and may have limited relevance for professionals of other orientations. Second, there is in fact no such entity as a single, homogeneous Jewish or religious Jewish population or test response pattern, a fact frequently overlooked in studies of Jewish personality and any chosen dependent variable. Jewish populations vary in cultural heritage, intensity of religious commitment, and the degree to which Jewish mannerisms, argot, beliefs and attitudes influence and gain expression in everyday behavior. Subtle familial, emotional, and cognitive uniquenesses may differentiate among religious or "tradition-oriented" Jews, such as chasidic and non-chasidic Orthodox Jewish background, patients with yeshiva background and those without yeshiva background, the nouveau-Orthodox *ba'al t^eshuvah* and one who has moved beyond the initial crisis stage of religious development. Thus, some readers may impute different significance to the clinical examples presented here. Second, the illustrations are not exhaustive of the types of manifestations of religious valuational material during psychological testing. However, the type of sensitivity and attention to clinical material I am recommending should remain valuable regardless of the reader's orientation, and can be calibrated by each professional in accord with his or her theoretical stance and the specific qualities observed among one's own particular clientele.

II.

The appeal and rationale for Jewish subcultural test norms and stylistic patterns for widely used psychometric and projective test instruments was first presented by Boris Levinson in 1961.[2] Currently, the psychological test literature contains a few reports which seek to distinguish such norms (a few other studies are reported in unpublished doctoral dissertations), but on the main this clinically important topic has remained undeveloped.

The most salient rationale for such norms is that the diagnostic significance of Jewish subjects' responses ought to be examined against both their subcultural context as well as against standardized or national norms. For example, Levinson,[3] Levinson and Block,[4] Dershowitz,[5] and Dershowitz and Frankel[6] have pointed out in various related studies the consistent and stable pattern of relatively low scores among Jewish subjects on several *WAIS* (*Wechsler Adult Intelligence Scale*) and *WISC-R* (*Wechsler Intelligence Scale for Children-Revised*) sub-test items (e.g., Picture Completion, Picture Arrangement, Object Assembly). This suggests subcultural weakness in spatial tasks or, according to an alternate explanation, in tasks requiring a maximum degree of psychological differentiation. Specific factors in "traditional" Jewish upbringing and family, education, and social systems may actually reinforce a cognitive-intellectual "quality" which hampers successful execution of the tasks required by such subtests. An implication of this finding is that alleged Jewish intellectual superiority may not be characteristic for every component of the overall factor of intelligence. In an attempted application of the above rationale, Rosenschein has argued that "underachieving" yeshiva students characterized in the yeshiva environment as dull normal, or even borderline, in fact may actually fall within the average range when their achievements or intelligence test scores are compared to national standards.[7] Such information may be valuable in the formulation of therapeutic or educational recommendations in psychological test reports. Additionally, this may help modify the well-known negative effects of labeling upon teacher or parental perceptions.

However, ethnic subcultural test norms and patterns cannot fully supplant the important and useful qualitative perspectives gained by comparison of the individual subculture member's test responses against standardized, nationally or multiculture-based norms, or the need to report the findings of such comparisons. To report only the differentially-ranked subcultural performance (and certainly to attempt *ad hoc* modifications in the difficulty of test items to favor religious subjects) would defeat the design and function of nomothetic testing.[8]

Consider, for example, the case of an extremely isolated eighteen-year-old yeshiva student who did not know the date of Washington's birthday (*WAIS* Information item no. 14), or how many senators there are in the United States Senate (Information item no. 21), but in fact knew the exact birthdate and lifespan of several important Jewish kings and leaders, and was reputed to be able to offer a person-by-person list of the uninterrupted chain of tradition from Moses to the Men of the Great Synod. In deciding whether to substitute this subject's "equivalent" knowledge *in place of* the knowledge sought by psychometric tests, or whether to merely indicate this discrepancy in knowledge in the form of an "actual" and an "alternative" score, the examiner must, I think, bear in mind the basic functions of the psychological tests he is utilizing. From the standpoint of one essential function of the test and its typical use in American educational and occupational systems, it would seem important to indicate deficits in the types of general information considered typical of the range of information utilized as a criterion for successful assimilation within these American institutions. This is particularly so when a subject's responses indicate wide scatter among different subtests, or when markedly inferior performance on psychomotor subtests or perceptual tests (such as the *Bender-Gestalt* of the *Benton Visual Retention Test*) suggest real deficiencies for which the subject's apparent acumen in culturally normative areas of knowledge may be a mask or compensation.

From this perspective, the educational conclusion from the viewpoint of a secular educational system alters little when a five-year-old Orthodox Jewish child can name every item on the Passover *seder* plate, but cannot name at least two items of clothing (*McCarthy Scales of Children's Abilities* Verbal Fluency item no. 2) or cannot give an age-appropriate response to "What is a house made of?" (*Stanford-Binet* Year IV-6). That is, when intelligence testing is construed as "testing for *specific* knowledge" rather than "testing for *any* knowledge," accepting the subject's "equivalent" knowledge becomes a contradiction in terms. At the same time, it would be appropriate if not necessary that the examiner record what the subject *does* seem to know in order to fairly indicate the subject's ability to learn and retain the type of information to which he has been exposed. That is to say, the subject may lack some kinds of specific knowledge, but is at the same time quite knowledgeable about the world he or she lives in.

On the other hand, when reporting on the intelligence test performance of the above-mentioned five-year-old or eighteen-year-old to an institution which values primarily the types of knowledge such subjects in fact displayed, such as a *cheder*, then an alternative score—if not an altogether unique score based on normative "Jewish" or "religious" knowledge for specific age groups of students in such institutions—is of much greater relevance.

The diagnostic relevance of this discussion was actually anticipated by Rapaport, Gill, and Schafer, and was illustrated in their discussion of the diagnostic significance of the Picture Completion subtest of the Wechsler-Bellvue (the forerunner of the *WAIS*):[9]

> How a query for information replaces concentration and defeats the subject is clearly illustrated in an obsessional patient of Orthodox Jewish rearing who on no. 6 (a picture of a pig missing a tail) asked, "Do pigs have tails?" Apparently he had discovered that the missing element was the tail; but instead of relying on the result of his scrutiny, as a good obsessive doubter he wanted the approval of authority— which probably due to his rearing he did not have.

In other words, since it is doubtful that this subject truly lacked knowledge of such generally available information, his obsessive style became even more apparent, as it evidently was on other test items as well. Diagnostically, the subject's doubt cannot be excused merely as veritable lack of knowledge, and this is so despite the possibility of cultural influence. I might add, tangentially to this particular example, that among young children from very Orthodox Jewish homes, it is common that even nine- or ten-year-old subjects in fact do not know "from what animal we get bacon" [*WISC-R*, Information no. 9]. Of course, the failure of this item *alone* will not significantly alter such an individual's Verbal Subscale IQ or Full Scale IQ score, or the import of the score. It is quite another matter, however, when the child *does* seem to have this information, but appears embarrassed to produce such knowledge, or adds derogatory comments, and so forth, as will be illustrated below. (This item is deleted on the Hebrew version of the *WISC-R* currently used in Israel.)

One can state briefly that consideration for subcultural norms does not replace standard national norms, but (1) provides a normative base for intergroup comparison (e.g., between chasidic and non-chasidic groups) on the variables measured by psychological tests, and (2) provides the clinician with an additional context against which to measure a subcultural group member's idiographic and possible pathologic responses. Following (2), *characteristic* deficits and other nuances in the individual's response pattern can be significantly differentiated from other responses which are influenced by pathognomic factors.

The following examples from intelligence and projective test protocols obtained from Orthodox Jewish subjects will illustrate the above perspective.

A fifteen-year-old subject (IQ = 102) failed to respond within the time limit to *WISC-R* Comprehension item no. 16, "Why is cotton often used in making cloth?" In the middle of responding to the next item, the subject blurted out an obviously belated response to no. 16: "So we can wear it on *Tishah be-Av*!" *Tishah be-Av*, the ninth day of the Hebrew month of *Av*, is an important fast day commemorating the destruction of the First and Second Temples. Throughout the fast, observers also abstain from wearing leather shoes as a ritual form of "affliction." This custom, in fact, does not preclude wearing other leather garments (e.g., belts). Thus, despite the response's religious content, even a religionist would have to consider it a relatively impoverished and inaccurate association.

Consider at the same time the response of a ten-and-a-half-year-old to *WISC-R* Similarities item no. 5, "How are an apple and a banana alike?": "You make [the blessing] '*boreh pri ha-etz*' on the apple and a [blessing] '*boreh pri ha-adamah*' on the banana."*

In both examples, the ethnocentric reference might be viewed as "normative," but one cannot ignore that the response offers a highly concrete attribute instead of a more general or abstract quality or consensual significance, and may indicate not yet adequate reasoning and judgment. The response of the ten-and-a-half-year-old was, of course, incorrect for the obvious reason that a *difference* rather than a *similarity* was offered, which can be handled in the usual way ("Yes, but how are they *alike*?"), assuming this is

---

* "*Boreh pri ha-etz*" refers to the blessing "Blessed are you, King of the Universe, who creates fruit of the tree," and "*Boreh pri ha-adamah*" refers to "Blessed . . . who creates fruit of the ground."

the first such error on this subtest. More importantly, this response represents failure to grasp the basic similarity that both an apple and a banana are *fruit*, regardless of which particular blessing Jews recite for each fruit. While the knowledge that fruit from plants is blessed with *boreh pri ha-adamah* is an important and subtle distinction, the subject's response may merely indicate successful memorization rather than categorization. Second, it indicates a failure to disregard functional or attributary differences so as to be able freely to subsume both apple and banana under the abstract category of "fruit." An important convergent operation would seem to be absent from this subject's response.

Actually, it would have been useful to inquire further into the ten-and-a-half-year-old's response to determine whether the subject intended as the *common* property of apple and banana the fact that a blessing is recited over both fruits—as he might respond to *WISC-R* Similarities item no. 6 ("How are beer and wine alike?") even if he happens to note that beer and wine have different blessings. If the latter is the case, the response still represents a relatively inferior level of categorization, similar in quality to the response, "Both are to eat." Note also that in the case of the ten-and-a-half-year old illustrated above, the level of abstraction demonstrated is more or less developmentally normal, assuming a rigid timetable for the emergence of formal operations thinking (approximately 11 years). However, this developmental allowance cannot be applied in the example of the fifteen-year-old ("*Tishah be-Av*"), whose response reflects not only exceptionally concrete thinking, but perhaps also impulsive tendencies.

In another example, a bright twelve-year-old male responded to *WISC-R* Comprehension item no. 12, "Why is it better to give money to a well-known charity than to a street beggar?": "It *isn't* better! You're supposed to give *tz^edakah* (charity) to any poor person you see!" This response is laudable from the standpoint of Jewish ethics and may someday become a conflict-free attitude in this subject. At present, however, it was merely another example of angry obstinacy in a pre-adolescent hellion as demonstrated throughout his test responses: e.g., ("Why does oil float on water?") "Who says it does? I wish *you* were floating on water!"

("From what animal do we get bacon?")* "Why should a Jew know *that*, you piggyologist!"

Another example is provided by the case of a seventeen-year-old yeshiva student whose presenting problems included compulsive twitching, stealing, and fighting with dormitory fellows. During testing this subject eventually correctly completed each item of the *WAIS* Object Assembly subtest, but just under the time limit per puzzle. (His Block Design and Digit Symbol test efforts were similarly effected.) Because scoring of this particular item takes into account speed of execution as well as accurate perception and manipulation, the subject's low-weighted score indicated that his approach and manner of execution actually impeded complete success and compromised autonomous function.

Careful examination of this subject's verbalizations during his execution of the Object Assembly task revealed numerous "Jewish" references which actually assisted characteristic defense mechanisms of externalization and projection, and a pugilistic suspiciousness which suggested psychopathic tendencies: [While assembling the "Person" puzzle] "What's this?... (10") Oh! ... Hey, where's the *yarmulkah*?** Why don't you have a man with a *yarmulkah* for Jewish people? (mutters as he tries to force a piece into place)... Stupid business." [During "Elephant"] What's this?... (15") Oh, a *grobber, treifeneh* elephant. What's the meaning of an elephant?... (40") None of these pieces are cut right, you know." [During "Hand"] "What's this?... A bunch of sticks, what's the connection?...(70") A hand! Like those stupid *kabbalah* necklaces you see. So why do you use this? Does this have a meaning?... Here! It was easy!"

In this material, the subject's excessive moralizing and use of projection suggested the existence of a primitive, hypercritical superego which, along with the subject's vigilant attention to the examiner's motives, actually defeated the remnants of a "good" obsessional character defense. Indeed, the subject's difficulty in

---

* It may be useful to substitute "People" for "we" when giving this item to certain subjects.

**"Skullcap," worn by traditional-Jewish males, generally at all times.

recognizing the puzzle items within the conventional amount of time indicates that his preoccupations actually interfered with reality testing.

Two additional examples of the emergence of ethnic teachings and values during psychological testing bear consideration. In the first, a ten-year-old Orthodox Jewish male (Full Scale IQ=110; Verbal Scale IQ=101; Performance Scale IQ=121) who had recently slacked off in school achievement gave the following response to *WISC-R*, Comprehension no. 2 ("What is the thing to do if you find someone's wallet or pocketbook in a store?"): "Well, is it an *aveidah mi-da'ath* [the talmudic term for property willfully abandoned which, according to Jewish law, does not need to be returned to its owner] and do we hold *yiush she-lo mi-da'th havi yiush* or not [the rabbinic debate whether property is considered forfeit if the owner does not know the property is lost but his "abandonment" of it is anticipated]? I just learned the *Gemorah* today and I don't remember what the *din* [law] is!" Since the subject was smiling gamely as he discoursed, I responded by way of a neutral prod, "Let's leave the *din* aside for the moment, and just tell me what you would think to do." The subject then answered correctly that he ought to check for ownership and return the wallet, and then added, "But if there was no *siman* [some identifying mark indicative of ownership] you really could keep it."

Assuming that this last remark is correct from the standpoint of Jewish law, which it more or less is, there would be no reason to consider the earlier response spoiled, and so the subject received maximum credit for his response. Would his deliberations be rightfully viewed as obsessive? Here again, I would say not, since from the standpoint of a young child who is beginning to assimilate the legalistic methods of talmudic scholarship, the line of his inquiry was appropriate. Had he been unable, however, to extricate himself from his own legalistic considerations and arrive at a definite plan of action, or at least several valid contingent actions (one in case the wallet had a *siman* and another in case the wallet had no *siman*), we might be more concerned. Indeed, one might suppose that this particular item of the *WISC-R* Comprehension subtest invites precisely this sort of deliberation: What *does* one do when one finds a wallet in the street? Does one presume it forfeit, or does one investigate further for identification, setting aside those motivations which may lure one into "neglecting" to make such investigation? In summary then, while the subject in this illustration offered a *form* of inquiry which is unique to his religious commitment, the *type* of inquiry was normative. While responding to *WISC-R* Comprehension no. 15—"Why should a promise be kept?"—the subject again appealed to rabbinic teachings, noting first that his rabbi had admonished his students "never to make promises." In this case, too, the author suggested that while the subject's rabbi had indeed expressed an important Jewish attitude, he might still be able to come up with a good reason why one ought to keep one's promises *if* one made a promise. Following this, the subject did offer an intelligent, two-point response.

The second illustration is taken from the record of a thirteen-year-old Orthodox Jewish male (*WISC-R* Full Scale IQ=123) who had been expelled from several Jewish day schools and was currently on probation in his most recent educational placement. An obviously bright child with twelve younger siblings, the subject was an extreme discipline problem at home and at school, given to disruptive wisecracking when he was not baldly delinquent. The subject had been cooperating well throughout testing, but began to "have fun" during the *WISC-R* Vocabulary subtest as the relatively open-ended demand to "tell what a word means" stimulated numerous humorous associations. For example, the subject defined "brave" as "someone who sits through Rabbi ....'s class and lives to tell about it!", after which he revelled in his laughter, and so on throughout this subtest. Nonetheless, he was able to also offer correct, two-point responses after each humorous routine. After two incorrect definitions on subtest items nos. 25 and 26, the subject was asked to define "amendment" (no. 27). Perhaps picking up on an association to the term "amend," the subject responded, "Repenting? To repent? [Begins to laugh.] The *goy* goes to church and slips the priest five bucks, maybe a ten, and the priest says, 'You're forgiven! You're forgiven!' "

The subject's response is, of course, incorrect. More important, the theme of guilt hidden in his jocular digression was understandable in the context of his recent probation. He had been caught stealing and had refused to either admit guilt or take responsibility for his actions even though he was aware that his acceptance back into school depended upon such admission. Thus, although the subject projects his guilty feelings onto the culturally popular, devaluated image of the "*goy*," the very parody he creates bespeaks an immature, unrealistic conception of personal responsibility. In fact, this slip had been portended two days earlier during initial assessment when, while discussing his predicament with the subject and his parents, the subject suggested lightly that perhaps the principal could be "bought off."

III. ___________________

Idiopathic responses also appear in projective test material, where the manifestation of "Jewish" content may be merely a framework for intrapsychic conflict. A fourteen-and-a-half-year-old male of dull normal intelligence described the two males in *TAT* (*Thematic Apperception Test*) no. 7BM as "two disgusting, creepy *goyim*!" This emotion-laden, devaluating response was consistent in a personality featuring unrelenting, hateful paternal "superego" introjects, a deeply-rooted sense of personal inadequacy, and a primitive defense structure mostly dependent upon projection and denial. The response also represented a reaction to the threat of emergent homosexual impulses, which the subject had actually acted-out in his yeshiva. In this case, as in the above, "*Goyim*" serves as a culturally-condoned, learned source for projection of threatening impulses. Moreover, for the Jew, describing something as "*goyish*" would be an ultimate disclaimer. Thus, the description of the two men in the *TAT* illustration as "*Goyim*" also enabled the subject to more effectively distance himself from his impulses and devalued aspects of self.

For another example, an oppositional nine-year-old male (IQ=115) responded to the popular "crying person" illustration (*TAT* no. 3BM) as follows: "This is a girl whose cat got . . . whose cat died, and she's crying and what will happen is that she'll get a new one. [Inquiry: "What type of person is this?"] A good person, but someone I shouldn't play with. [Inquiry: "Why not?"] Because a Jew shouldn't play with *goyim*. [Inquiry: "How do you know she's a *goy*?"] Because Jews don't keep animals or pets in the house." As in the preceding case, "*Goyim*" is used to represent devaluated aspects of self or experience. In this story, as well as subsequent ones, one sees the projecting of devalued parts of the self (naughty, irresponsible "*goyim*") by this child of perfectionistic parents.

Finally, consider the following response of an eleven-year-old female to the "man climbing a rope" in *TAT* 17BM. "Well, here we have *Yosef ha-Tzaddik* [Joseph] who was stuck in a deep, dark and very scary pit for many years. He was put there by his mean brothers. Now we see him climbing out the rope [*sic*] to take revenge on his mean brothers. In the end, he will become the leader of Egypt and get his revenge." This material illustrates a slightly hysterical response to an overtly masculine, "phallic" stimulus, the impact of which may account for the curious departures from the facts of the well-known account (Joseph never frees himself from the well or the Egyptian dungeon). A vengeful, phallic fantasy is weaved in this subject's story which also expresses negative oral imagery. The subject's fantasy may express phallic envy as well as dissatisfaction with her gender role, or merely sibling rivalry, but probably both. More important, this response further illustrates that although an eleven-year-old Orthodox Jewish subject can be expected to be aware of Biblical stories such as the one created here, the clinically significant facts are that the subject associates this particular story to *TAT* 17BM and the manner in which she modifies the facts of the story in accordance with her object-relational needs.

The *Make A Picture Story* method (E. S. Shneidman, *The Make A Picture Test* [New York: The Psychological Corporation, 1949]), widely used as part of the diagnostic battery and as a therapeutic tool with children and adults, is a relatively good example of a culturally-fair projective test with relevance to the present topic. The *MAPS* consists of 22 "background" tableaux against which the subject composes a scene and a story using any of 67 paper figures. These figures include male and female adults and children, legendary characters, silhouettes, and minority group figures such as blacks, orientals, and Jews.

Of interest are figures *N-7* ("pious Jew with skullcap and beard") and *N-8* ("Jewish merchant with vest"). Of the two, only *N-7* is conspicuously Jewish looking. When using this projective method with Orthodox Jewish subjects, it is always useful to observe how these particular figures are utilized, how they are described, and how they are worked into the story, etc. One sixteen-year-old female child of former concentration camp inmates placed *N-7* on the "raft" background and told the story of an ailing Jew expelled from a boat bringing immigrants to the United States and set off alone on the raft. The subject included a rather lengthy description of anti-Semitic treatment of Jews by the United States Immigration Service. While her story was heavily weighted with the influence of stories told to her by her parents and her own understanding of Jewish history, all of her stories, in fact, featured a solitary figure or "hero," and the stories she related about each scene were permeated with themes of loneliness and vulnerability. Against this context, her use of the Jew in the "raft" scene only partly reflects a particular cultural sensitivity, and cannot therefore be isolated from its dynamic or psychosocial significances.

I would also note the practice of some examiners to add their own "backgrounds" and figures to the set for use with select populations based on the types of "pull" they deem likely to elicit useful projections (e.g., firemen, soldiers, more contemporary-looking blacks). It would seem that additional Jewish figures, or a "synagogue" background, might occasionally be useful with certain subjects. However, it would be important that any additional materials be introduced only following the standard administration, so as not to lose the opportunity to observe such persons' ability to deal with the "ordinary" world in terms of their ethnic perspectives, and how "general" stimuli are transformed into "religious" ones.

IV.

Devoutly Orthodox religious patients may also react contentiously to their need for psychological testing by aggressively questioning the applicability or validity of such tests, or by questioning the religious integrity of the examiner. Generally, contentious reactions will be sprinkled with allusions to deeper doubts or disrespect for psychology as a science and profession. Sometimes these reactions are expressed only after testing has begun and upon experiencing some unease with a particular test. In the case of religious Jewish patients, as demonstrated in the following examples, such reactions are ensconced in terms of the subject's interpretations of Jewish morals and beliefs. When this occurs, the clinical approach becomes complicated, because it is not clear whether these reactions are in fact valid arguments designed to protect authentic moral sensitivities, or pseudo-religious ones which mask neurotic disturbance. When the examinee directly questions the examiner's moral and religious scruples—if inappropriately understood and managed—the examiner may experience a host of negative countertransferential feelings which may cloud his clinical perceptions and render him unable to work effectively with the particular patient. Following the illustration below, I will discuss a rationale which allows one admission into the clinical picture of the immature, neurotic, or otherwise disturbed qualities of such reactions, despite their superficial appearance as normative moral or religious objections to psychological testing.

The subject to be discussed is a twenty-three-year-old male who since high school had been a student in an intensely Orthodox, so-called "black hat" yeshiva in Israel. He attended this institution for four years prior to referral. The patient left Israel ostensibly due to a clash with fellow students whom he felt did not respect his privacy or his unique religious perspectives. While the subject's parents maintained a kosher home and were moderately observant of the Sabbath, the young man described himself as more "*frum*" (observant) and knowledgeable than they.

Upon returning home from Israel, the patient described himself as "perhaps a bit depressed and indecisive," but also adamant about not going to college. He wanted very much to return to yeshiva studies. In filling in other details, the parents added that the "episode" in Israel appeared to have been akin to a manic reaction, that the patient had recently begun grimacing in a strange way, and that the young man's father's brother was hospitalized for schizophrenia. The patient was indeed withdrawn though polite during the initial interview. However, he also added that he was only carrying through his parents' and rabbi's request that he seek psychological help because his rabbi had assured him that I was a "*ben Torah*" (Torah scholar). He added that a well-known rabbinic luminary he had consulted while yet in Israel insisted that he only seek the help of a "*chareidi*" (a pious Jew), since "psychologists in general are *mekalkel* and *mekulkal*" (corrupting and corrupt). A brief discussion of these sentiments made it abundantly clear that this subject would be vigilant for any possible difference between my religious outlooks and his own. Although I knew well enough that it was neither true nor reassuring to guarantee the patient that my religious perspectives would not enter the picture, I did offer to evaluate his problems through "some standard procedures," present him with my findings, and allow him to choose at that time whether he wished to continue to undergo counselling with me. After some further discussion, wherein psychological testing was presented as a way to learn about the subject's likes and dislikes and skills, he agreed to participate.

I administered first the *Bender-Gestalt* which went without major difficulty and with no signs of organic disturbance. However, I noted one serious rotation and also that the subject experienced unease when copying the elongated, crossed, sharp-edged design (item no. 7), making numerous erasures and redrawings, which is sometimes suggestive of anxiety concerning sexual stimuli. The *Minnesota Percepto-Diagnostic Test* was then administered, again with no major difficulties although the same difficulty with sharp-edged designs was observed, and the overall score lay in the neurotic disturbance range.

I then administered the first set of instructions for the Draw-a-Person task (See Figure 1). The subject first drew a figure identified as a male. The "male" had no facial features, and even following my testing-of-the-limits, the subject felt his rendering needed no modification. I then instructed him to draw a female. The subject hesitated and became visibly upset. After 40 seconds of blank staring at the paper, the subject looked at me very seriously and exclaimed, "To tell you the truth, this is very odd. . . . I mean, why do I have to draw a woman? It's disgusting, to say the least! You know, at first, I didn't mind, but what do these tests have to do with me? These are tests that you probably got from your college background which have nothing to do with the *neshamah* [soul] of a Jewish person." The subject further

Figure 1

questioned what could possibly be learned by having him draw a woman, and did I feel that this request was "*tzniusdik*" (modest). I responded merely by saying that I need to sample different aspects of his life, and that in order for me to do my job, it would be important that he try to follow my instructions as best he could.

The subject hesitated for a few seconds, acknowledged that he was no artist, and proceeded to draw a female. The picture he drew was essentially identical to the male figure, with long hair and an outline of a dress alongside the body. He did not attempt to erase the "male" figure beneath the dress. Note also that the female figure had facial features. When next asked to draw a picture of himself, the young man responded that the first figure was himself. In describing the "persons" he had drawn, the subject remarked that the male "lacked character" which he explained only by comparison to the female who had "more personal strength . . . as you can see from her face." The subject still made no changes on the first drawing. And again, on the Draw-a-Family task, he drew two males with no facial features, while the females had facial features. There was now the stronger suggestion of inadequate sexual differentiation, the possibility of depersonalization, and a disturbed quality of object representations. The concrete way the subject described the figures' characters also bore the grim spectre of schizophrenic process.

The *WAIS-R* (*Wechsler Adult Intelligence Scale-Revised*) was administered next. In summary, the subject's scores were: *VIQ*=120; *PIQ*=92; Full Scale IQ=108. The significant discrepancy between the *VIQ* and *PIQ* subscales, seen in the light of observations drawn from the entire test protocol, is most probably due to anxiety rather than depression, since depression tends to lower all performance subtest scores rather uniformly, which did not occur here.

During the *WAIS-R* Information subtest, the patient responded in the following way to item no. 18 ("What is the main theme of the book of Genesis?"): "Well . . . it tells the story of creation through the development of the Jewish people." This response is correct, and the inclusion of specific reference to the Jewish people is appropriate in the present context. Further, there was no other indication of a tendency to overinclude or overelaborate in the subject's responses throughout the remainder of the test, which gives one additional reason to be unconcerned about this specific response.

On the Picture Arrangement subtest, the subject completed the tasks in a tedious but correct fashion, until the cards for item no. 7 were laid out before him (this item, new in the *WAIS-R*, depicts a man helping two women in succession up a small hill). The patient fumbled with the cards, put them in their correct sequence, and then sat back. He once again began an onslaught against the examiner, referring pointedly to his obligation to be treated by a pious Jew. At this point, I wondered aloud whether the subject felt he had been incorrectly advised about seeing me in particular. This he denied, but railed now against the validity of "tests made for *goyim* and for people whose minds are more attuned to the stuff on these cards. If you want to know about my feelings and *hashkafoth* [religious perspectives], ask me and I'll tell you. I can tell you right now that I won't come if this is the stuff we're going to discuss. Dr. XYZ in Israel would never give such tests to a yeshiva student. Even the *goyisheh* psychiatrist in [his home town] that I went to once didn't *bother* with such tests! I resent the whole thing."

I tried through analogies (e.g., do Jews require separate driving tests?) and in other ways to make it clear to the subject that the tests were merely a baseline of skills common to all persons, and were not intended to tap his spiritual beliefs or alter them in any way. I assured him that he would have ample opportunity to share these with me in a direct fashion—and that at that time the differences between himself and non-Jewish persons could be emphasized if he so desired. The subject seemed to collect himself, but then added that "if the [rabbinic luminary] knew I was taking these tests, he would yank me right outa here!" To this I remarked that I would be more than happy to explain my tests and their rationale to this rabbinic authority so that he could perhaps better advise the subject whether he could indeed participate in these specific tests. Surprisingly, the young man responded, "No. Let's just get on with the testing."

The subject then executed item no. 10 of the Picture Arrangement subtest, which features a man carrying the bust of a female mannequin into a car. After completing the item in a one-point (SALMUE) rather than maximum quality manner, he exclaimed, "This one is just impossible, to say the least . . . he's carrying half a woman!" This misrecognition of the bust for "half a woman" has pathological portent, suggesting regressed object relationships and a momentary slip in reality-testing.

I will conclude this detailed case illustration with some material drawn from the subject's Rorschach protocol. (The location scores included in the verbatim quotations follow Klopfer's system.) On Card III, the subject broke the gestalt into several large detail responses: "[35′] This reminds me of *Mishnath ha-Mapeleth* in *Masekheth Niddah* [the *mishnah* in talmudic tractate *Niddah* which deals with miscarriages from the standpoint of the laws of family purity]. . . . [12′] Here [D5] is a *nefel* [a dead child or fetus], you know, a child that, *rachmanah litzlan* [Heaven forfend!], uh . . . here [tiny, lighter shaded area in upper third of D5] is its eye. This [D3] is the *shilyah* [placenta] that came out with it. . . . This [D6] is, uh, these are two dead, I don't know, *k^emin oaf* [an abortus that has the appearance of a chick]. That's all. . . . Oh, to, uh, do something with these [D2], this is blood, the *chatikhath dam* [clump of blood]." This treatment suggests color shock, both in the way the blot is broken into details and how the color and shading are dealt with. "Blood" verbalizations and fabulized imputations of symbolic forces at work occurred in other of the subject's responses. Thus, from the clinical standpoint, the erudite talmudic references on a card where most persons see human figures must be deemed gratuitous, and little modify the standard inferences that must be drawn from such a response.

On Card VI, the subject concentrated for a long time, frequently turning the card, and then responded, "[2′ 32″] A *nasty* mind would say that this [D1] looks like the *makom ha-ervah* [genitalia] of a woman. But practically speaking, it really looks like nothing. . . . [10″] I can't tell what the top is supposed to be. Maybe . . . No! It doesn't look like anything." Of course, this response is technically a refusal and cannot be formally scored, but again indicates that anxiety is just barely managed through projection and massive denial.

When testing was completed, I asked the subject which test he liked the most and which the least. He replied, "I liked the blocks [Object Assembly subtest of the *WAIS-R*, on which test, incidentally, he scored lowest with a scaled score of 6] the best, and this [indicating the Rorschach portfolio] the least. To say the least, it was disgusting. The colors were, well, beautiful, but eechy because, you know, they're unreal, you don't see colors like that often." Here again one sees dramatically the effect of the testing process on this particular subject, emphasizing the deteriorated description of color which occurred several times during inquiry (during the free association phase of testing, however, the use of color was limited to one *CF* and one *FC*′ response).

The question for the clinician at this juncture is whether to view the patient's reactions as somehow valid; i.e., that psychological tests are indeed provocative for persons of high moral caliber, whose sensitivities are so fine that even looking at the picture card drawings of the *WAIS-R* is in violation of their ethics. Should not the clinician in this case appreciate and respect these sensitivities and spare such patients the untoward effects that might be induced through his standard test battery?

The correct approach, it seems to me, lies first in recalling the salient moral of the well known myth of the examinee who self-consciously attributed his more lurid responses on the Rorschach to the provocation of "those dirty inkblots" shown him by the "unscrupulous" examiner. The import of this story is that all psychological tests are to one degree or another *projective* devices, which means that subjects' reactions truly stem from *their* moral conflicts rather than from the test stimulus itself. Moreover, I am aware of no widely-accepted instrument that could be considered explicitly licentious, or that involves any more of an affront to modesty than browsing through the pages of *Ladies' Home Journal* [which, I must admit, some Orthodox Jews would indeed not read!]. Psychological tests are far less embarrassing than many physical examinations, to which almost any devout Jew would submit if necessary. The religious examinee's reactions to psychological tests are for the psychologist merely a clue to the ways the subject deals with stimuli: those stimuli that the subject experiences as anxiety-provoking or intrusive are as relevant to understanding overall personality structure as are some milder stimuli which rarely elicit any negative reaction in any person.

This view can be further explicated. In the context of the yeshiva study-hall for example, the Jewish yeshiva student will discuss with apparent ease the intricacies of Jewish law dealing with sexual matters, husband and wife relationships, even perversion. He does so at such times partly because of the protective effects of the "safe" context and also because the libidinal charge latent in such material is absorbed or neutralized through sublimation and intellectualization. But this ability cannot be limited to specific places or to highly rationalistic discourse. The principles of ego psychology dictate that such impulse control remain intact even outside of "safe" contexts. One expects the normal yeshiva student to be able not only to discuss sexual matters when studying the Talmud, but also to experience no more than the normal amount of anxiety when going out on his first *shiddukh* (date), when talking to his mother, his *Rosh Yeshiva*'s wife, or his physician's nurse. One expects such an individual to be able to walk down a typical American street in the summer without decompensating. Otherwise, one has reason to suspect that something is amiss, that something is lacking in the degree of secondary autonomy achieved by the individual over his impulses.

This perspective is accepted by Judaism as well in its larger view of how one manages or harnesses for creative use one's *y^e^tzarim* or "impulses." The ***kohen*** who administers the ordeal of the *sotah* (the infidelitous wife) is expected to maintain control despite the potential stimuli on such occasion for the emergence of erotic or even sadistic impulses. The opposite pole is perhaps the nazarite who, upon witnessing the ordeal of the *sotah*, finds himself impulsively overcome, and needs the aid of a temporary period of self-imposed asceticism to restabilize himself.

When the clinician is called upon to assess the psychological difficulties of religious persons, this rationale holds. Psychodiagnostic assessment exposes the subject to a varied array of stimuli which allows the examiner to compare individual behavior against a normative reference. Given the shared perspective of Judaism and ego psychology on this account, it is expectable to find the healthy religious individual to be in far greater control of his reactions and impulses than the patient in the above example, exhibiting the quality of control that one indeed does find in the majority of other equally religious and modest persons who take such tests. It cannot be denied that with some extremely cloistered religious individuals, the achievement of good impulse control is dependent upon remaining wholly within "safe" contexts, and is at the constant expense of every effort to avoid any potential challenge to such control. In such cases, secondary autonomy has in fact only been achieved within a narrow range of stimuli and ideas. With such persons, even psychological testing represents a direct challenge, and may be practically impossible to undergo without great discomfort. As a general rule, however, modifying the test stimuli, or deleting them in the interests of modesty or maintaining one's rapport with devoutly religious clientele, is genuinely unwarranted.

V.

The emergence of Orthodox Jewish particularity can also be expected in the Draw-a-Person projective test, one of the important if not standard components of the diagnostic test battery. This is illustrated in the following examples.

Figure 2 is the human figure drawing (HFD) of a nine-and-a-

Fig. 2
C. M., Age=9.7
IQ=114
HFD/DS=3

half-year-old Jewish male whose family had become intensely Orthodox when he was eight. His drawing contains at least two obvious and significant indicators of emotional conflict: pronounced slanting of the figure and the severe truncation or practical omission of the hands. Additionally, one notes the conspicuous, heavy shading of the hair and the obvious skullcap or *yarmulkah*.

After completing the figure, the subject initially drew an outline of a skullcap which he then worked over for about 20 seconds, filling in the outline with heavy black lines. Following a second's contemplation of the finishing product, the subject proceeded to add more hair which soon "overtook" the skullcap. He then quickly colored-in a darker center, as if to reemphasize the skullcap, and then added an extension of the skullcap on top of the hair. This overworking and shading is a significant emotional indicator—as is heavy shading in general when it occurs beyond the age of seven or eight years—suggesting anxiety and conflict over heavy authoritarian influence, in this case paternal.[10] In fact, the lack of integration in the subject's home between newly-adopted religious standards and former ways of life had of late given rise to a surfeit of arbitrary parental regulations and demands, a radical mid-year change in school (which found the subject placed back one grade), and frequent parental appeals to dogma with which the subject was unfamiliar and could barely assimilate. Taken together with other indicators of conflict throughout the subject's test protocol, his approach to the skullcap represents far more than a fortuitous inclusion of "subculturally normative apparel."

Among the twelve Orthodox Jewish male children in my current practice—whose HFD's featured on the average two or three pathognomic emotional indicators (EIs) such as shading of body parts and face, gross asymmetry, disorganization, and so forth — ten patients depicted a skullcap or *yarmulkah* on their human figure drawings. In some illustrations (such as Figure 2), the subjects worked heavily on the boundary and darkness of the *yarmulkah*. In these instances the *yarmulkah* clearly served as a prop for the projection of emotional conflict. Similarly, considering Figure 3, an angry, compulsive, frequently punished five-year-old child of average intelligence depicted a rocket-like figure

Fig. 3
A. C., Age=5
IQ=101
HFD/DS=4

whose conical *yarmulkah* might well be the sharp-tipped head of a guided missile in flight or the helmet of a man-in-combat. The dark shading, the slanting, unsure angle, and the aggressive, impulse-ridden slash marks (eyes and hands) almost seem to find their logical terminus in the pointy *yarmulkah* which the subject added last with one quick flick of the the pencil. In discussing his HFD, this subject in fact described the figure as a "soldier." In Figure 4, a seventeen-year-old adolescent with many school behavior problems provided one of many HFDs which although developmentally inferior—i.e., missing two or more physical features "expected" for subjects of the same age [11]—still featured the *yarmulkah*. For a variety of reasons, this subject deleted the entire body, suggesting graphically the depersonalization which led him to psychotherapy. At the same time, the jauntily perched *yarmulkah* reflected the *bon vivant* image he sought to project at home and among his peers, but which was belied by the overall self-image depicted in the drawing.

Fig. 4
C. S., Age=17
IQ=103
HFD/DS=0

VI.

Given the frequency with which the *yarmulkah* appeared in the HFDs of my clinical subjects, I have attempted to collect some normative data regarding the frequency with which Orthodox Jewish males include the *yarmulkah* in HFDs when executing such drawings in a relatively standardized context; i.e., when performing per the specific instructions "Draw a picture of a person." My interest in such data was motivated partly by a diagnostic assumption commonly used in interpreting Draw-A-Person tests that the depiction of objects such as clouds over the head of the human figure reflects anxiety over authoritarian or other pressures, or even depression. Does the *yarmulkah*, as an object over the head, bear an equivalent "symbolic" interpretation? Or, is the *yarmulkah*, in fact, depicted so frequently by religious Jewish children as to be no more significant than any other article of clothing drawn on an HFD, except when depicted in such a manner as to suggest the possibility of emotional conflict?

In thinking about this issue, one notes that black children typically do not color their HFDs black in the effort to portray a "correct" picture of a black person (although they may depict Negro features such as broad lips, etc.). This is so typical, in fact, that Koppitz considers shading of the face in HFDs of black children to have the same clinical meaning it does for white children, and does not excuse it as "afrocanizing."[12] Even upon inquiry, black subjects who describe the completed HFD as a self-portrait (which clinicians assume in any case) do not seem troubled by the discrepancy between their "white" drawing and their own skin color.[13] Presumably, the black subject's "blackness" even at an early age has been internalized to a degree where a standard drawing can be conceived without cognitive dissonance as that of a black person. By analogy, our concern is whether the need to depict the *yarmulkah* suggests that it is somehow not as internalized into self-image as is skin color.

I conducted a small pilot study in which I obtained 129 HFDs from male children, ages four-and-a-half/five to eighteen, who attended two Orthodox Jewish day schools in Cleveland, Ohio. Seventy-nine subjects attended a large Hebrew day school which has a less homogeneously Orthodox population in that it includes many students of limited religious background. Fifty students attended a *cheder*-type school whose families are all intensely religious (for example, almost all of the *cheder* students wore the traditional long sideburns or *peyoth*).

Each student was asked to draw one picture of a person, as per Koppitz's manual of instruction. Each drawing was evaluated and scored on three measures: (1) HFD Developmental Score, (2) HFD Emotional Indicator Score, and (3) presence or absence of a *yarmulkah*. The specific questions of interest were: (1) Is there a specific age when the inclusion of the *yarmulkah can be expected*; i.e., occurs in at least eighty-six percent of the sample

HFDs of Orthodox Jewish males? (2) Is the presence or absence of the *yarmulkah* correlated with either a "normal" or "unhealthy" HFD (for which I presumed the presence of three or more EIs)?[14] Many of my original clinical questions were not directly answered by this study. It did, however, provide valuable normative data (although I was unable to obtain an adequate number of subjects with which to establish distinct norms for each year between the ages of five and eleven).

Some of the findings were as follows:*

(1) Among the total sample population (N=129), fifty-seven percent of the students featured *yarmulkahs* on their HFDs. According to Koppitz's percentage bands, one can state overall that the appearance of the *yarmulkah*, while not frequent enough to be *expected* (eighty-six to one hundred percent), is in fact *common* (fifty to eighty-five percent) among Orthodox Jewish males.

(2) The mean HFD Developmental Score was 3.8, with an average of 1 or 2 "unhealthy" emotional indicators per drawing, indicating that the sample population was indeed "normal" on an overall basis. There was an observed tendency for the *yarmulkah* to appear more often on HFDs with *higher* EI scores, but this tendency did not prove statistically significant. That is, there was no direct correlation between *severity* of emotional conflict and the appearance of the *yarmulkah*.

(3) Among the population eleven years and older (n=50)—at which age, according to Koppitz, persons are expected to include in their HFDs almost all developmental items on her scales—the *yarmulkah* occurred in only forty-four percent of the HFDs. According to Koppitz's percentage bands, this would mean that the inclusion of the *yarmulkah* on an HFD in children over the age of eleven is "not unusual" (sixteen to fifty percent), or is not truly "typical." Caution is recommended, however, in actually extending this finding to all adult populations. In the population younger than eleven years, sixty-six percent produced *yarmulkahs*.

---

* I appreciate the assistance of Dr. Allan Taub in developing appropriate statistical models for the sample.

(4) Among the forty-eight subjects with "unhealthy" HFDs (EI score $\geqslant 3$), the *yarmulkahs* appeared on HFDs seventy-five percent of the time, compared to forty-nine percent on the HFDs of the remaining population. The difference between the means of these two groups was significant at the .001 level on a *t*-test of significance. While caution is again recommended in extending this finding to the general population, it may indicate of the subgroup with "unhealthy" HFDs that the "need" to depict the *yarmulkah* may have been accentuated by the presence of other pressures or conflicts. The specific link, if any, between emotional conflict and its effect on the inclusion of the *yarmulkah* was not studied at this time.

Based on these statistics, one can conclude that the depiction of the *yarmulkah* was "common" among the sample population of Orthodox Jewish children, and may become increasingly "common" with increasingly intense Orthodoxy but not necessarily with age, and was not so common as to be "expected" in the HFDs of the average Jewish male at any age. Even in the more intensely religious *cheder* subsample, the *yarmulkah* was present only sixty percent of the time, which still falls into the "common" and not the "expected" category.

I believe that this data reflects the tendency in most Orthodox Jewish homes to begin mildly reinforcing the wearing of the *yarmulkah* by children at about three years of age, and certainly by age five years, at which time the child is usually expected to wear the *yarmulkah*. Unlike skin color, the *yarmulkah* has to be expressly introduced to the child and its wearing mildly to strenuously enforced. Thus, on the one hand, one might presume that although the instruction to depict a "person" evokes a highly subjective, inward-oriented process, the additional inclusion of the *yarmulkah* merely represents an objective decision to "complete" one's drawing, making it "Jewish enough."

However, this view underestimates the manner in which children become emotionally invested in and express themselves through such things as toys, pets, transitional objects, and clothing. As I have illustrated above, children's depiction of a *yarmulkah*—or *tzitzith* and *peyoth*—can often reflect qualities associated with emotional conflict. To be sure, I have found no intrinsic symbolic significance to the mere depiction of a *yarmulkah* in an otherwise "healthy" human figure drawing, such as one assumes with the depiction of clouds, vacant eyes, missing limbs, shading, and so forth. At the same time, symbolic significance can be lent to the *yarmulkah*, as it were.

The Talmud itself states that the wearing of a head-covering symbolizes "Fear of the authority of heaven."[15] Most religious Jewish parents attempt to impart this concept to their children in an age-appropriate manner. In still other Jewish homes, this significance may be emphasized in a heavy or uneven way, perhaps by appealing to heavenly punishment for the errant child who neglects to wear his *yarmulkah* or by referring to not wearing the *yarmulkah* as shameful, "goyish," or as feminine behavior.

In such cases, it is possible that the *yarmulkah*'s inclusion in an HFD indicates a particularly Jewish aspect of the awareness of parental or even Divine authority. The depiction of the *yarmulkah* may thus merit a developmental interpretation, indicating that the child is attempting to integrate the authoritarian forces in his life or to establish a sex-appropriate identification. When the *yarmulkah* has been introduced to the child younger than two-and-a-half to three years, it may even develop transitional qualities, aiding the child through the separation-individuation process, or representing arrest and fixation in this process. Perhaps the depiction of the *yarmulkah* is less frequent among older subjects because the integration of Jewish identity has at this point become more complete. At the same time, one wonders whether the results would be the same if this task were administered to an ultra-Orthodox adult Jewish population. In cases where the inclusion of the *yarmulkah* is taken as a confirmation of the child's acceptance of his Jewishness and of his distinctiveness from nonreligious Jews or non-Jews, or of his masculinity, the quality of depiction may inform about his success in this endeavor.

I mentioned above that these same clinical possibilities can be anticipated in the manner of depiction of *tzitzith* and *peyoth*. Some of my patients have produced HFDs that are of interest in this regard. In Figure 5, a ten-year-old Jewish male produced a self-portrait which projected his devalued aspects (the "lousy teeth," as he described it) as well as his wishful self-image as a macho-sportsman, with a hairy chest like his father. While the *yarmulkah* depicted in this HFD appears to be free of pathognomic value, the

Fig. 5
M. T., Age=10.6
IQ=109
HFD/DS=5

tzitzith (which no one in the patient's family, including himself, wears "out") appear to be laden with the same phallic significance as the hair on the chest and the interesting baseball bat. In this case, in fact, the *tzitzith* reflected an unfinished struggle between strong tendencies toward feminine identification, reinforced by an over-anxious mother, and an attempt at masculine identification with a passive and unavailable father. Additionally, the *tzitzith* were executed with sharp slashes in the same fashion as were the sharp teeth and the cleats on the figure's shoes, suggesting anger or aggression, and a potential for acting-out, as one would generally have inferred from such rendering of the teeth and shoes alone. Such latent anger, however, turned out to be an important asset in helping this child pull away from smothering maternal attention. Similarly, the eight-year-old male's drawing depicted in Figure 6 expressed feminine tendencies through the curvacious rendering, which were confirmed through other projective tests. This child's father died when the child was five years old. In the Draw-a-Family procedure, the child drew his mother and six older sisters as enormous, overbearing beings towering over a miniscule male figure "hiding" in the bottom corner of the page. In the Draw-a-Person figure (Figure 6) the conspicuously overelaborated *peyoth* could easily be interpreted as girlish pigtails, emphasizing the plight of a child whose oedipal fixations and need for more distinct male identification were beginning to complicate the tasks of latency.

Fig. 6
E. S., Age=8
IQ=110
HFD/DS=5

Summary

I have attempted to illustrate some of the diagnostic possibilities which emerge through the expression of "Jewish" verbalizations or symbolisms during the process of responding to psychodiagnostic tests. I have discussed in detail some preliminary normative and interpretive approaches to the inclusion of the *yarmulkah*, *tzitzith*, and *peyoth* in religious Jewish children's human figure drawings. My general perspective has been that such products may be clinically significant even when taken in the context of subcultural norms and expectations.

It can no longer be contested that the mental health professional must constantly recognize and deal with the uniqueness of the religious Jewish patient in order to be able to give full consideration to the unique meanings and values borne by religious expressions produced by such persons. At the same time, all aspects of individual behavior and belief can express both autonomous as well as dysautonomous or conflictual characteristics, and this holds true for the behavior of religious Jews on psychodiagnostic tests. If one wishes to maintain that religiosity on the ultimate level is a well-integrated and mature aspect of human personality, one must also be willing to focus on indications of the contrary. It follows then that an apparently "religious" response to a test question or projective stimulus—whether it is a blatantly tangential remark or comment or an elaboration upon an essentially correct or appropriate response or a behavior that might be atypical in the general community but normative for a religious individual—must always be scrutinized from the above perspective so that a more complete understanding may be gained about the total reactions, attitudes, and feelings of the examinee.[16]

Notes

1. Spero, M. H., "The Contemporary Penitent Personality: Diagnostic Treatment, and Ethical Considerations with a Particular Type of Religious Patient," *Journal of Psychology and Judaism* (1980): 4(3): 133-191; "A Clinical Note on the Therapeutic Management of 'Religious' Resistances in Orthodox Jewish Clientele," *Journal of Jewish Communal Service* (1981): 57 (4): 334-341; "The Use of Folklore as a Developmental Phenomenon among Nouveau-Orthodox Religionists," *American Journal of Psychoanalysis* (1982): 42: 49-58.
2. Levinson, B., "Psychology: Its Practice and Teaching in a Jewish College," *Religious Education* (1961): 21: 46-53.
3. Levinson, B., "Jewish Culture and WAIS Performance among Jewish Aged," *Journal of Genetic Psychology* (1962): 100: 55-68; "Cognitive Style of Eastern European Jews," *Perceptual and Motor Skills* (1977): 45: 279-83; "Cultural Pressure and WAIS Scatter in the Traditional Jewish Setting," *Journal of Genetic Psychology*: (1958): 93: 277-86.
4. Levinson, B. & Block, Z., "Goodenough-Harris Drawings of Jewish Children of Orthodox Background," *Psychological Reports* (1977): 41: 155-58.
5. Dershowitz, Z., "Jewish Subculture Patterns and Psychological Differentiation," *International Journal of Psychology* (1971): 6: 223-31.
6. Dershowitz, Z. & Frankel, Y., "Jewish Culture and WISC and WAIS Test Patterns," *Journal of Consulting and Clinical Psychology* (1975): 43: 126-34.
7. Rosenschein, J., "The Exceptional Failure: A Plea for Average Children in Yeshivot," *Jewish Observer* (1980): 14: 3-6.
8. Munday, L. & Rosenberg, G.L., *Social Concerns and the Stanford-Binet* (Illinois: 1979); Anastasi, A., *Psychological Testing* (New York: 1976); see also J. Sattler, *Assessment of Children's Intelligence and Special Abilities* (Boston: 1982), pp. 358-86.
9. Rapaport, D., Gill, M. & Schafer, R., *Diagnostic Psychological Testing* (New York: 1968), p. 133.
10. Koppitz, E., *Psychological Examination of Children's Human Figure Drawings* (New York: 1968), pp. 57-8; Goldstein, H. & Faterson, H., "Shading as an Index of Anxiety in Figure Drawings," *Journal of Projective Technique and Personality Assessment* (1969): 33: 454-56; Urban, W. H., *The Draw-a-Person: Catalogue for Interpretive Analysis* (Los Angeles: 1981).
11. Koppitz, op. cit., 1968, pp. 1-30, Appendices A-B.
12. Ibid., p. 65.
13. Stein, M., "Thematic Apperception Test and Related Methods," p. 219, in B. Wolman ed., *Clinical Diagnosis of Mental Disorders* (New York: 1978); Murstein, B.I., *Theory and Research in Projective Techniques* (New York: 1963), p. 206. Note that W. Dennis & A. Uras, "The Religious Content of Human Figure Drawings Made by Nuns," *Journal of Psychology '61* (1965): 263-266, found that "religious content" appeared in 74% of drawings made by 100 nuns!
14. Koppitz, op. cit., 1968, p. 65. Koppitz considers two or more emotional indicators as suggestive of "serious maladjustment" (pp. 41-42). I continue to find this convention clinically useful, despite the findings of Fuller, et al., "The

Validity of the Human Figure Drawings with Disturbed and Normal Children," *J. School Psychol.* (1970) *8*: 54-56. Bailey, B. & Green, J., "Black Thematic Apperception Test Stimulus Material," *J. Person. Assess, 41* (1977): 25-30, however, have recently observed that "ethnic" test materials may in fact elicit qualitatively improved or less-guarded responses.

15. *Kid.* 33a; *Shab.* 118b.

16. As this chapter was prepared for publication, Stuart Chesner submitted a paper to the *Journal of Psychology and Judaism* which examines the relative degree of self-disclosure among subjects who had a brief experimental contact with either a "therapist" who wore a *yarmulkah* or one who did not. Chesner's data suggest that the persons whose "therapist" wore a *yarmulkah* were significantly less self-disclosive than those whose "therapists" did not wear a *yarmulkah*. These results do not necessarily mean that the *yarmulkah* will actually influence the development of the therapeutic relationship, but is an important area for future study.

12
The Halakhic Validity of Psychological Diagnostic Tests in Assessing Mental Competence

The psychologist as *mumcheh* or recognized authority in his professional domain utilizes a wide range of psychodiagnostic and psychometric instruments or "tests" which are designed to give him specific kinds of information about the examinee's psychological behavior. "Psychological behavior," of course, refers broadly to a continuum of behavior, ranging from clearly demarcated phenomena such as verbal and reading skill, school achievement, and perceptual-motor abilities, through more complex characteristics such as intelligence and creativity, to emotional characteristics such as quality of interpersonal relationships, impulse control, and subtle intrapsychic dynamics, such as psychosexual fixations and regressions.

Some psychological tests observe and directly measure fairly objective phenomena, while others provide responses from which the examiner makes inferences in accordance with consensual methods of interpretation. The pool of psychological test instruments includes such tests as the *Wechsler Adult Intelligence Scale*, the *Wechsler Intelligence Scale for Children*, the *Wide Range Achievement Test*, the *Minnesota Multiphasic Personality Inventory*, the *Thematic Apperception Test*, the Draw-a-Person test, the *Rorschach*, and numerous other inventories, schedules, and profiles. Many of these tests have as their most noteworthy capacity the ability to measure quantitatively and qualitatively critical components of healthy or normal ego functioning, such as reality-testing, judgment, synthetic-integrative functioning, and so forth.

The psychological examiner will generally select particular tests in order to objectify his understanding of specific aspects of the examinee's abilities, dispositions, or conflicts. These tests are usually the backbone of good diagnosis and prognosis and help guide intervention. Not all of these instruments measure "rationality" in the popular sense of the term, but all operate on normative assumptions. Presumably, an *ab*normal person will perform non-normatively relative to the majority of people (or a significant percentage of his cohorts), but will perform in a fashion that can be considered typical or normative for abnormal persons. Of course, most dramatic or frank types of irrationality and other forms of deviant psychological behavior are noticeable even without such tests, but some tests, such as the *Rorschach*, are especially sensitive to psychotic processes not otherwise obvious.

There are instances when it is halakhically relevant to be able to make objective statements about personality, such as in order to determine mental competence and incompetence. The quality of mental competence (*pichuth*) or "rationality" is a prerequisite for executing legal writs and actions or entering into contractual relationships such as marriage, or divorce; for the appropriate fulfillment of religious obligations, such as *mitzvah* observance and testimony; and for waiving incumbent prohibitions in the absence of any threat to *physical* well-being.

The most well-known halakhic conditions of insanity or mental incompetence, such as the *shoteh* (*shtuth*) and the *m^{e}turaf be-da'ath* (*teiruf da'ath*), are classified in the Talmud and codes by certain criteria whose definition, enumeration, and application have been the topic of much discussion and debate in past and current halakhic literature.[1] Assuming that irrationality, self-destructiveness, compulsion, and faulty judgment are the essential properties of the state of *shtuth*—and there is a considerable body of opinion supporting this view—does Halakhah accept modern diagnostic tests as valid instruments for classifying such states? In other words, does Halakhah accept the psychological conventions upon which such tests are based, and does Halakhah accept the variables and terms of the typical diagnostic profile as equivalents to its criteria for mental competence?

There is evidence in the halakhic literature dealing with mental incompetence of two distinct standards: a relatively lenient one for application to matters of divorce and marriage, and a relatively more stringent one for application to the determination of competency to testify (*eduth*). Specifically, in cases involving the laws of divorce and marriage, many authorities accept the view that for any contemporary definition of mental incompetence to be sufficient *as an equivalent to the talmudic criteria* to establish mental incompetence, it must coincide with all of the four criteria of *shtuth* mentioned in the Talmud (e.g., one who sleeps in cemeteries, walks alone at night, rips clothes, loses items entrusted him).[2] Since no current psychological test measures these specific behaviors, such tests would be halakhically irrelevant according to this first view. However, in cases involving the laws of testimony, any single demonstration of insanity or irrationality by contemporary criteria is sufficient to establish mental incompetence.[3] Others, however, interpret the codes as implying that in all matters, any single indication (which occurs at least three times) of insanity, irrealism, or faulty judgment is sufficient as an equivalent to the halakhic concept of *shtuth*.[4] This same view holds that even if an individual evinced all four characteristics of *shtuth* noted in the Talmud, this only renders one a *shoteh* in the absence of contradictory evidence. However, if one were to obtain evidence of such an individual's competence in a specific area of *mitzvah* observance, he would then be considered competent in this area.[5] Expressing yet another viewpoint, R. Yosef Rosen (Rogetchover) opines that when *shtuth* has been established through the characteristics noted in the Talmud, then the individual is to be considered incompetent in all areas. However, when "incompetence" has been established through *beth din*, and by evidence of any *other* indication of insanity, such incompetence need not extend to all areas of ritual or legal performance.[6]

With these differences of opinion in mind, would Halakhah accept a statement about competence or incompetence, rationality or irrationality, as determined, for example, through the *MMPI* or the *Rorschach* projective test? Can one accept their indices of psychosis or schizophrenia, or any other diagnostic instrument's portrait of formal thought disorder, as equivalent to *teiruf da'ath*, severe *ruach ra'ah*, or *shtuth*? Or, perhaps more importantly, can we state that in the unlikely case that an individual displays the talmudic signs of *shtuth*, and at the same time completes a diagnostic test battery with no indications of irrationality, etc., that such an individual is indeed a *pike-ach*?

Logically, it seems that the talmudic criteria were intended merely to represent *behavioral illustrations* of irrationality, aiding diagnosis by providing concrete definitions of a state of mind which otherwise would have to be inferred intuitively. For surely not every *shoteh* displays only or all of these characteristics—as the Talmud itself recognized ("*Shoteh b^e^chada milsa lo sarikh*").[7] Moreover, not every rabbinically recognized affective disorder of psychotic proportions, such as *kordiakus* or severe *marah shechorah*, presents with the specific symptoms noted in the Talmud.[8]

Maimonides seems to support this view when he specifically offers additional characteristics of *shtuth*, including "extremely foolish persons, who do not perceive contradictions, and who do not comprehend matters in a conventional manner."[9] Maimonides, according to most interpretations of his rulings in *Hilkhoth Eduth* 9 and *Hilkhoth Gerushin* 2, has broadened the definition of *shtuth* to include *any* satisfactory indication of incompetence, provided that this characteristic is demonstrated reliably ("... *kol mi she-nitr^e^fah da'ato v^e^-nimtzeit da'ato m^e^shubeshet* tamid *b^e^-davar min ha-d^e^varim*").[10] This interpretation is used to support the general emphasis among halakhists that *shtuth* may be defined by any single bizarre or disruptive intellectual process, demonstrated on a continuous and pervasive basis. Thus, others, who have accepted this basic interpretation of Maimonides' view, add that if rationality is basically intact—or there are significant periods of time when competence and rationality can be demonstrated—then even an isolated demonstration of hallucination or paranoid ideation may *not* render the individual a *shoteh* (though perhaps a *choleh*).[11]

The question of "reliable" determination of incompetence directly concerns our discussions. The Talmud and codes speak of certain "diagnostic tests" or *b^e^dikoth* (Rorschach himself would have termed this a *versuch*, an "experiment") which are designed to determine mental competence in matri-legal matters. For example, when there is cause to doubt an individual's sanity and, hence, legal competence to issue a writ of divorce, the codes note that one might query the individual on topics of common knowledge: If it is winter, one asks the person if he wishes to glean fruits known to grow only in the summer; if it is summer, we ask whether the individual wishes to harvest fruits known to grow only in the winter.[12] As Rabbi Y. M. Epstein and others add, one may employ any line of question which will require use of fundamental psychological abilities that underwrite mental competence.[13] These abilities would seem to be judgment, orientation in time-and-space, attention, reality-testing, and so forth. Finally, while the choice of examination is left to the discretion of the *dayan* (judge), "reliability" demands that at least three demonstrations be given of the abilities or disabilities in question.

From what has been said up to this point, it would seem that any single direct behavioral characteristic or inferential indication of irrationality—and as detected by any valid diagnostic instrument—would be adequate for the halakhic determination of *shtuth* or incompetence if such irrationality were demonstrated through *verbal* behavior. If, however, the initial suggestions of insanity were demonstrated behaviorally, then some authorities would still require evidence of the four specific behaviors noted in the Talmud, or equivalents of these behaviors. Indeed, consider the following statements by Rabbi Y. B. Landau from a responsum published in 1966:[14]

> And regarding psychiatric testing, which seeks to establish insanity through the *Rorschach* projective test, and sometimes through various assumptions that are not based upon the signs mentioned in the Talmud, one is compelled to state that even according to the sages of blessed memory [these tests and assumptions are acceptable] if we see from the person's actions and speech that he is confused; and he is [judged] a *shoteh*. Appropriate here are the words of the *Maharsham* (*Da'ath Torah*, 1:40), who writes that these "signs" noted in the Talmud were intended in instances where the individual has normal speech, and we seek to prove from his actions that he is a *shoteh*. In such instances, the "signs" demonstrate that he is a *shoteh*—but in instances where the individual speaks incoherently and in a confused manner, all authorities would admit that such a person is judged incompetent, even without indication from the talmudic "signs."

In other words, at the discretion of a competent *dayan*, any contemporary indication of insanity may have halakhic validity, but its use would depend upon the type of religio-legal context, as well as the position one takes in the controversy regarding how many indications of *shtuth* are necessary to declare an individual incompetent. In a situation where the halakhic authority rules that any single indication of *shtuth* is sufficient, such indication may come from demonstrations of behavior similar to the illustrations noted in the Talmud, *or* from projective tests.

Two problems remain which need further clarification. The first concerns the requirement that indications of incompetence or irrationality need to be established "reliably," or through three consecutive demonstrations. Does this mean three indications of formal thought disorder or the like on any single diagnostic test (e.g., three contamination responses to a single *Rorschach* ink blot), or three distinct tests? The response may lie in viewing each demonstration on any single test as a discrete behavior, especially since any diagnostic test will have presented the examinee with at least three separate stimuli (e.g., three separate ink blots or three TAT cards or three different questions on the WAIS Comprehension subtest). Each sufficiently disordered response would then be considered the equivalent of a distinct query put to the individual by a *dayan*.

The second problem concerns the type of questions a *beth din* might pose to an examinee in order to adequately determine competence. That is, while conventional diagnostic instruments may, in fact, produce evidence of irrationality, faulty judgment and so forth, the *dayan* may wish to ascertain whether the examinee has retained certain types of competence or judgment despite his other disabilities or areas of incoherence and irrationality. I noted above that according to some authorities a demonstration of competence in a given area of verbal and mental performance—even in the presence of the characteristics of *shtuth* noted in the Talmud—is sufficient to restore the status of competence in that area.[15] According to this view, most of our diagnostic instruments would be of little value and would be superseded by the direct interview of the individual by the *dayan*. The inverse would also be true: i.e., when an individual has been declared competent by *beth din* in a specific religio-legal area, this status may be immune to subsequent *general* indications of irrationality, and certainly the mere evidence of irrational "trends"—based on diagnostic test performance. Finally, if a *dayan* chose to support his determination of an individual as competent through reference to a "well-retained" diagnostic test performance, this determination would appear to take priority even over subsequent indications (without further testing) of general disorder.[16]

Notes

1. See *Sedei Chemed*, vol. 5, pp. 123-30; D. Applebaum, "Mental Competence in Halachah," *Koleinu* 6 (1973): 48-57; Y.B. Landau, "*Diyun be-Peratiyut be-Sugey Choli ha-Ruach she-Nirpa'in be-ha Metzaut Terufah ha-Chadashot*," in M. Amsel ed., *Sefer She'elot u-T^{e}shuvoth ha-Ma'or* (New York: 1966), pp. 377-85.
2. *Chag.* 3b; also see *J.T. Git.* 7:1; *J. T. Ter.* 1:1; *Beth Yosef* citing R. Simha and R. Avigdor ha-Cohen; *Rashba; BaHaG; SMaG;* but cf. *Resp. Maharik*, no. 19.
3. That is, even according to the first view that in other matters all four talmudic signs must be indicated. See *Resp. Maharit: E.H.*, no. 16; *Noda be-Yehudah* cited in *Or ha-Yashar*, no. 30; *Even ha-Ezel: Hil. Eduth* 9:9.
4. *Arukh ha-Shulchan: E.H.* 121:13; see also *Sedei Chemed*, vol. 5, pp. 123-30; *Otzer ha-Poskim: E.H.* 1:1, no. 72(2); and see the discussion in Landau, op. cit., 1966.
5. See *Resp. Igroth Moshe: E.H.*, no. 120.
6. *Or Yesharim*, no. 14, who distinguishes between incompetence established according to Biblical mandate (*g^{e}zeirat ha-kathuv*) and according to *beth din*'s evaluation. The first type of determination, which requires the four talmudic signs, extends even to areas where the individual may have competence, but not necessarily to areas of law known as "*kinyanim*." Finally, even the first disqualification can be nullified should the individual *demonstrate* competence in some specific area.
7. *Git.* 68b; also *Git.* 64b, 70b.
8. See also *Pitchei T^{e}shuvah* to *Sh. A., E.H.* 178(7). The status of the disorder of *marah shechorah* has been discussed with differing views concerning whether such deep, and apparently psychotic-like depression or melancholia is bona fide *shtuth*. Rashi, s.v. *u'le-olam (Chag.* 3b) seems to imply that it is not, but compare this with *Rambam*'s statement in *Peirush ha-Mishnayoth* to *Shab.* 29b. See also *Resp. Rav Yitzchak Brisk*, no. 30 and *Resp. Atereth Chakhamim: E.H.*, no. 17, but cf. *Resp. Divrei Chayim: E.H.*, no. 77. There is also debate whether the *pethi* (fool), or someone who is feeble-minded (*da'ath kalushta*), is the equivalent of *shtuth*. *Resp. Maharit*, vol. 2, no. 17 states that *pethi be-yoser* is only disqualified for *eduth*, but in

other applications is not necessarily as disordered as the *shoteh*. See also *Rama* to *Sh. A., E.H.* 42:2; *Magen Avraham* to *Sh. A., O.H.* 199 (8); *Resp. Malbushei Yom Tov ha-Chaddashot*, no. 4; *Resp. Chatham Sofer: E.H.*, vol. 2, no. 2; *Resp. Ba'er Sheva* 1:51; *Sefer Me'irot Eiynaim: H.M.* 35:10. *Arukh ha-Shulchan: E.H.* 121:13.

9. *M.T. Hil. Eduth* 9:9.

10. *Kesef Mishnah* to *M.T. Hil. Eduth* 9:9—providing that such behavior is *darko be-kakh* (see *Derishah* to *Sh. A., H.M.* 35). See also *Arukh ha-Shulchan: H. M.* 35:7.

11. See D.S. Shapiro, "*Choleh ha-Ruach Im Yakhol le-Garesh?*" *ha-Darom* 1, no. 1 (1957): 41-50, p. 48 and B. Bak, "*Choley ha-Ruach be-Dinei Gittin ve-Ishut,*" *Noam 16* (1973): 161-179, notes that there is debate whether *marah shechorah* is *shtuth*, and ends by declaring that this must be determined by the *dayan*. Our diagnostic instruments would be able to measure *da'ath kalushta* in terms of intelligence quotient, or several oligophrenic details (*Do*) on the Rorschach, and differentiate this state from more severe irrationality. Other references which suggest that certain states of self-destructiveness, and infanticidal behavior, are tantamount to *shtuth*, without appealing to the four criteria of *Chagigah*, are *M.T. Hil. Sanh.* 18:6, and *Arukh ha-Shulchan: E.H.* 13, no. 13. Manic depression, according to R. Bak, may render one unfit for *eduth*, but qualified to issue a writ of divorce or marriage.

12. *M.T. Hil. Gerushin* 2:14; *Tur Sh. A., E.H.* 121 and *Beth Yosef; Arukh ha-Shulchan: E.H.* 121. Such a *bedika* is of no use with the *kordiakus* (*Oneg Yom Tov*, no. 153(5) to *M.T. Hil. Gerushin* 2:17).

13. *Perishah* to *Tur Sh. A., E.H.* 121.

14. Landau, op. cit., 1966, pp. 379-80.

15. *Resp. Igroth Moshe: E.H.* 120.

16. According to *Resp. Chatham Sofer*, no. 175, one *mumcheh* is satisfactory since he can be examined by the *Beth Din*, while *Resp. Shevut Yaakov*, vol. 1, no. 65, vol. 2, no. 76, requires the testimony and examination of two separate experts.

13
Emergency Psychiatric Consultation on the Sabbath

Much has been written in the halakhic literature regarding the treatment of patients on the Sabbath. This literature primarily has focused on interventions and related procedures which fall under the general rubric of physical medicine; e.g., blood tests, surgery, catheterization, prescribing medicine, and so forth. Neglected in this literature is discussion of emergency psychiatric consultation on the Sabbath.

There are specific applications where psychiatric intervention must be instituted without reservation, such as in instances where the presenting psychiatric symptoms involve obvious *sakanath nefesh* or even *safek sakanath nefesh*.[1] It would thus be entirely appropriate to utilize psychopharmacological medications, hypnosis, psychotherapy, or any other psychological intervention recognized as a *r^efuah b^edukah*—or even *possibly* effective psychotherapeutic procedures[2]—in order to prevent *teiruf da'ath* or, for example, to prevent suicide.[3] For another example, some halakhic authorities have ruled that run-away behavior is also to be considered at least *safek sakanath nefesh* for which even Biblical prohibitions may be violated on Sabbath.[4]

There is another range of emergency psychiatric consultation which is not as easy to classify at first glance, although it is analogous to a basic problem that has been discussed in the codes and responsa. I refer to the case where a *choleh she-yesh bo sakanah*, loosely translated as a gravely ill patient, requests the services of a psychiatrist, psychologist, or social worker because of some as-of-yet inarticulated need. Presumably, the patient is experiencing some sort of anguish or pain which may or may not be directly related to his physical condition and which he feels will abate if he has the opportunity to consult with some mental health professional. Often, persons who become seriously ill and who also happen to be psychiatric patients may demand to speak to their personal psychotherapist, such as when important decisions must be made relevant to their physical condition. Young children who resist hospital procedure or who are otherwise uncooperative may require the services of their psychotherapist if they are concurrently under such treatment, or may simply need the help of such a professional in order to raise their level of cooperation, ease pre-surgical anxieties, or to help them deal with the formidable psychological pain which accompanies long-term hospitalization, extensive and intrusive medical procedures, and so forth.

The specific question in these instances is whether the mental health professional may violate Biblical and rabbinic prohibitions on the Sabbath should this be necessary to comply with the wishes of patients who are considered *cholim she-yesh bam sakanah*?

As I noted above, an analogous paradigm exists in the codes and responsa. The *Shulhan Arukh: Orach Chayim* states that almost anything which a *choleh she-yesh bo sakanah* demands—and certainly anything which a professional considers necessary for such a patient—which in the patient's view will be of value in dealing with his illness is to be fulfilled, even if this involves violating Biblical prohibitions.[5] The reasoning here is two-fold: (1) Halakhah gives credence to the gravely ill patient's intuitive understanding of his own needs ("*Lev yode'a marath nafsho*"[6]), so long as the patient's understanding does not contradict sound professional wisdom;[7] and (2) such a patient may become psychologically distraught if he were to see that his needs are not taken seriously ("*Shema titraf da'ato shel ha-choleh*").[8]

A practical application of this paradigm occurs when a gravely ill patient demands to see a specific person who does not happen to be a physician, where this person would have to traverse a distance greater than the *techum Shabbath* in order to reach the patient. A second application concerns the permissibility of accompanying a sick person, or a woman in labor, to the hospital in the ambulance or in a vehicle driven by another party.

One finds the following divergent opinions regarding these applications. One opinion is that if the *choleh* demands such things which though relevant for his overall condition are essentially designed to address his mood or anxieties, these things may be procured only through violation of rabbinic prohibitions, or by requesting a non-Jew to perform prohibited activities, but not through violation by Jews of biblical prohibitions.[9] One authority adds that this stricture applies even if the patient requests the presence of a specific person.[10] Thus, according to this first point of view, a companion, a husband, or a mental health professional might well *walk* beyond the *techum Shabbath** in order thereby to be of assistance to the patient, or perhaps accompany the *choleh* in a vehicle driven by a non-Jew (or a Jew who is driving the vehicle expressly for the sake of the *choleh* already in the vehicle)[11]—but may not violate Biblical prohibitions such as driving himself to the patient or, according to some, using standard telephone equipment.

A second halakhic opinion, however, is that as long as needs such as expressed in the above cases have been demanded by a *choleh she-yesh bo sakanah*, then one may even violate Biblical prohibitions.[12] Support for this view is drawn from the Talmud which permits kindling a candle if demanded by a woman in childbirth,[13] or extinguishing a candle if demanded by a person afflicted with *ruach ra'ah* of grave proportions.[14] If, however, it is not clear that the patient is yet in a complete state of *sakanath nefesh*, such as a woman in early labor, Biblical prohibitions may be violated only through some recognizably unconventional manner (*shinuy*).[15] From the standpoint of this second opinion, it would seem that the mental health professional may violate Biblical prohibitions, such as driving himself to a hospital or bedside, if his presence is demanded by a *choleh mesukan. One would be arguing in accepting this conclusion that the* teiruf da'ath

* Only the 12 mile *techum* limit is Biblical, according to most authorities, and rabbinic according to a minority opinion. All authorities agree that the restriction against traversing distances *up* to 12 miles on the Sabbath is a rabbinic *g^ezeirah* (see *Mishnah Berurah* to *Sh. A., O. H.*, 397:1 and *Sedei Chemed*, vol. 4, pp. 536-37).

which might be caused by failing to fulfill the demand of the choleh she-yesh bo sakanah *will initiate further deterioration bearing directly upon the condition of* sakanah. It would further seem the case that if a patient *not yet* presently in a state of *sakanath nefesh* demands psychiatric consultation, and it seems reasonably evident in this particular case that failure to fulfill such a demand will result in either the exacerbation of existing psychiatric problems or the creation of new *teiruf da'ath* to such degree that *sakanah* becomes imminent (e.g., self-destructiveness, refusal to eat or take medications where involuntary compliance cannot be achieved)—then such consultation may be provided even through the violation of Biblical prohibitions via *shinuy.*[16]*

* Note also that the professional would not be permitted to return home following the completion of his services if this involved violating even the rabbinic definition of *techum*, unless he has warrant to believe that his services will be needed at home during the Sabbath by another *choleh she-yesh bo sakanah*. Some authorities are more lenient, allowing the physician to be driven home by a non-Jew, while other *poskim* would even permit the physician to violate Biblical prohibitions in order to return home *if* his services were needed at home *or if* there was some form of danger inherent in his remaining in the neighborhood of the hospital.[17]

Notes

1. I have discussed the development of the recognition of psychiatric disorders as bona fide *sakanath nefesh* in my *Judaism and Psychology: Halakhic Perspectives* (New York: Ktav/Yeshiva University Press, 1980). Some of the important sources are *Resp. Rashbah* cited in *Beth Yosef, Tur. Sh. A., Y.D.*, 228 (p. 147); *Resp. Netzer Mataai*, vol. 1, no. 8; *Resp. Tashbaz*, vol. 1, no. 54; *Resp. Radbaz*, vol. 4, no. 66; *Resp. Igroth Moshe: E.H.*, vol. 1, no. 22, 65; *Resp. Minchath Yitzchak*, vol. 1, no. 115, vol. 1, nos. 25-26, vol. 4, no. 8:2-12.
2. See *Sedei Chemed*, vol. 8, pp. 401-9; *Encyclopedia Talmudit*, vol. 13, p. 262; and see *Resp. Tzamach Tzedek he-Chaddash: O.H.*, no. 38.
3. *Resp. Chelkath Yaakov*, vol. 1, no. 72; *Resp. Igroth Moshe: O.H.*, vol. 1, no. 127.
4. *Resp. Netzer Mataai*, vol. 1, no. 8; *Resp. Admat Kodesh: Y.D.*, no. 6; *Ramban* to *Shab.* 30a; *Sh. A., O.H.*, 288:10; *Arukh ha-Shulchan: O.H.*, 288:17.
5. *Sh. A., O.H.* 328:10 and *Mishneh Berurah* no. 25.
6. Prov. 14:10.
7. See *Ba'er Hetev*, s.v. *ve-ha-rofeh* at *Sh. A., O.H.* 328:10 and *Pitchei T^eshuvah*, no. 4 at *Sh. A., Y.D.* 155; also *Resp. Radbaz*, vol. 1, no. 67, vol. 4, no. 15.
8. The same reasoning appears in *M.T. Hil. Shab.* 2:11, *Hil. A.Z.* 11:11, *Hil. Zekhiya u-Matanah* 8:2. Y.Y. Henkin draws distinctions between these cases, distinguishing the case of *yoledet* from *choleh*, in his "*Nokhachat ha-Ba'al be-Cheder ha-Leydah*," *Assia* (1978): 5, no. 3: 44-52.
9. *Sh. A., O.H.* 306:9 and *Mishneh Berurah* no. 41 and see also *Arukh ha-Shulchan: O.H.*, 306:20; *Resp. Tzitz Eliezer*, vol. 8, no. 15:9. The *Beth Yosef* argues (*Sh. A., O.H.* 328, s.v. *u-mah she' katav*) that Rashi's opinion in *Shab.* 129a is that one may not violate Biblical prohibitions even for a *choleh she-yesh bo sakanah* for needs *not* directly related to the condition of *sakanah*. *Beth Yosef* apparently reads Rashi (s.v. *omer le-akum*)—"*aval davar she-yesh bo sakanah Yisroel atzmo oseh lo*"—as meaning that one may violate Biblical prohibitions for a *choleh she-yesh bo sakanah* if these violations bear directly on the *sakanah*, but not if these needs do not bear directly upon the *sakanah*. Yet, Rashi, s.v. *hakiz dam*, implies that one may so do for a condition not involving *sakanah*. The *RiF* and the *Rosh* accept the general view that one may violate the Sabbath for any of the needs of a *choleh she-yesh bo sakanah*. The *Beth Yosef* s view is reiterated in *Kesef Mishneh* to *M.T. Hil. Shab.* 2:14, although the *Magid Mishnah* to *Hil. Shab.* 2:11 differentiates between the case of *yoledet* in early stages of labor, where the *Rambam* requires a *shinuy* for violating Biblical prohibitions, and the general case of *choleh she-yesh bo sakanah*, where the *Rambam* does not make mention of the requirement of *shinuy*. *Rambam* also rules in *Hil. Shab.* 2:14 that one does not make a *medurah* for a "*choleh*," which would seem to refer to a *choleh she-ein bo sakanah*, but others seek to interpret even this "*choleh*" as a *choleh she-yesh bo sakanah*. This interpretation is only consistent with *Beth Yosef*'s interpretation of Rashi.
10. *Resp. Shoel u-Meishiv: Mahadura Til ta'i* vol. 2, no. 180.
11. See *Igroth Chazon Ish*, vol.1, no. 141; *Kaf ha-Chayim: O. Ch.*, 306:9, no. 75; *Resp. Harei Besamim: Mahad. Tinyana*, no. 189.
12. *Resp. Chelkath Yaakov*, vol. 1, no. 64.
13. *Shab.* 129a.

14. *Shab.* 29b; see also *Sh. A., O.H.* 328:35 and *Arukh ha-Shulchan: O.H.* 328:45, and also *Tur Sh. A., O.H.* 278.
15. *M.T. Hil. Shab.* 2:11.
16. See *Ba'er Hetev*, s.v. *madlikin* at *Sh. A., O.H.* 330. If we assume that psychiatric consultation is at the very least not less helpful for the *choleh* who requests it than is the kindling of a *medurah* for a *choleh she-yesh bo sakanah*, then, with the exception of the *Beth Yosef* and the *Rambam* according to the interpretation of *Kesef Mishneh* and *Magid Mishneh*, most authorities would permit violating Biblical prohibitions through a *shinuy*, but where this is impossible or would somehow result in denying the needs of the *choleh*, one may rely on the *RiF*, *Rosh*, and others who permit violating Biblical prohibitions without *shinuy* (see *BaCH* to *Tur Sh. A., O.H.* 330; *Shulchan Arukh ha-Rav: O.H.* 328:24; *Mishnah Berurah* ad loc., no. 62; *Kaf ha-Chayim: O.H.* 330: 6, no. 36).
17. See the discussion in *Resp. Tzitz Eliezer*, vol. 8, no. 15(7) and vol. 11, nos. 39-40, who permits a physician to return home in a car driven by a non-Jew, and *Resp. Igroth Moshe: O.H.*, vol. 4 (*ha-Chaddashoth*), no. 80, who appears to permit even the violation of Biblical prohibitions for health care professionals who typically do not remain for long periods of time at the scenes of emergency to which they are dispatched. See also *Resp. Yaskil Avdi*, vol. 7, *O.H.*, no. 22(5); and R.H. Porush, "*Livui im ha-Choleh be Nesiyah be-Shabbath*," in R.M. Hershler, *Halakhah u-R^e^fuah* (Jerusalem: 1981), vol. 2, who permits violation of rabbinic *isurim* in the existence of psychological anguish.

14
Violating the Sabbath for Emergency Management of Threatened Suicide

The permissibility of transgressing the Sabbath for the emergency management of threatened suicide (herein: parasuicide) concerns physicians, mental health professionals, interns engaged in field placements or clerkships which require "on call" responsibilities even on the Sabbath, and related service providers such as emergency rescue squads, and so forth. Readers will already view with interest my raising this "problem" because of the apparently obvious halakhic response: since threatened suicide involves the probable termination of/or serious injury to life (*sakanath n^efashoth*) then one may violate as necessary even Biblical prohibitions, including Sabbath prohibitions.

While this problem can, of course, be resolved by appealing immediately to the halakhic decisors who in fact permit the transgression of the Sabbath in order to save the life of a parasuicide[1]— to be discussed below—it is actually a deceptively simple problem. Indeed, at least two authorities have ruled that one may *not* transgress the Sabbath in order to save the life of an individual willfully intent on *hit'abduth atzmith*, self-destruction.[2] There would thus seem to be some kind of halakhic "problem" with the application of the standing principle "*pikuach nefesh docheh Shabbath*" to the case of *me'abed atzmo l^e-da'ath*, and this problem merits detailed examination.

I. ——————————

An analysis of this problem begins with considering the talmudic debate whether one is permitted to personally transgress even a minor *isur* or injunction in order to save one's fellow from even a major transgression. The search for a definitive principle is discussed regarding the case of an individual who placed dough in an oven on the Sabbath, either by accident (*shogeg*) or intentionally (*meizid*).[3] The Talmud states that as long as the dough has not yet formed a crust (indicating the completion of *m^elakhah*) the individual himself may remove the dough from the oven. This permission is granted in order that, in the case of *shogeg*, he may not be required to offer a *korban chatath*, or, in the case of *meizid*, that he not incur the grave penalty of *s^ekilah* (stoning). However, bystanders are not permitted to remove the dough, establishing the principle that one is not allowed to transgress in the effort to prevent one's fellow from transgression.

Tosafoth addends two qualifications to this principle in the effort to resolve an apparent contradiction between the above ruling and the law permitting a slave owner to grant freedom to an individual who is "half-slave and half-freeman,"* even though this violates the Biblical statement, ". . . you may make them serve forever."[4] For it would seem from the case of the slave, and in other instances cited by *Tosafoth*, that one is indeed permitted to "transgress" for the sake of one's fellow. *Tosafoth* responds that the Talmud only forbids such transgressions when the other's potential transgression is the result of negligence (*p^eshiah*), and hence only the potential transgressor himself may remove the dough from the oven, but no one else.[5] *Tosafoth*'s second qualification is that when a great *mitzvah* (*mitzvah rabbah*) may be gained, one may transgress for another's sake—and thus the rabbis permitted the slave owner to free his slave so that the new freeman could fulfill the obligation to propagate (*p^eru u-r^evu*). The halakhic codes formally rule that one is permitted to incur a violation in order to prevent one's fellow from grave transgression

* That is, an individual was owned by two partners, one of whom had earlier granted freedom to the slave in the domain of the one partner's share.

so long as the transgression under focus has not been the result of *meizid* or *p^e^shiah*.[6]

The relevance of this discussion to our topic of parasuicide on the Sabbath (and even regarding other Biblical prohibitions of similar gravity which might need to be transgressed on weekdays) is that the parasuicide, in contemplating and certainly in successfully carrying-through suicide, transgress the Biblical prohibition against self-injury (*chabbalah*) and suicide, based on the passage "And surely your blood of your lives will I require."[7] That is to say, the catastrophic path selected by the parasuicide is inherently sinful, and is presumably the result of "ethical negligence" or willful disregard for Halakhah. Thus, applying *Tosafoth*'s first qualification, it would appear that one is not permitted to transgress in order to save persons from even suicide inasmuch as this is a consequence of their own *p^e^shiah*! On the other hand, the implication of *Tosafoth*'s second qualification is the opposite of the first: that in order to fulfill a *mitzvah rabbah—pikuach nefesh* in our case—one may surely transgress in order to redeem one's fellow. An important question, however, is whether *Tosafoth*'s second approach intended that even a *mitzvah rabbah* allows one to transgress in cases involving negligence. We shall return to this question.

A second major precedent relevant to the current problem concerns the permissibility of transgressing the Sabbath in order to save an individual who is being compelled to commit sins or apostacy. Here, again, apparently contradictory rulings further elaborate the extent to which one may transgress the Sabbath in order to save one's fellow from iniquity. Rabbi Moshe Isserles, in his emendations to *Sh. A.,. O. H.* 328:10, rules, citing *Beth Yosef*, that one may not violate the Sabbath in order to prevent an individual from transgressing even a relatively minor transgression. However, he also states in this location, "See [*O. H.*] 306 [:14]." At this second location, the law, in fact states that one is obligated to save an individual captured by heathens who are intent on apostacizing the victim; and here, too, R. Isserles refers the reader "to [*O. H.*] 328." Various halakhic commentaries have suggested that there are actually two distinct applications involved in these problematic rulings. One may not violate the Sabbath to redeem an individual who is being compelled to transgress a *single* transgression (*Sh. A., O. H.* 328), but one is obligated to transgress the Sabbath to save someone who is in danger of being compelled into apostacy for indefinite and possibly perpetual duration (*O. H.* 306). Relevant, too, is that in this second application, one may violate (a) even Biblical prohibitions, (b) even where there is merely a chance of success, (c) for any person (not just one's child as in the proof-case), and (d) even bystanders may do so.[8]

By analogy to this second ruling, parasuicide could be viewed as initiating "perpetual apostacy" in the ultimate sense, and thus the Sabbath could be transgressed in order to save the individual. However, additional observations attend this tentative conclusion. (1) The *Mishnah Berurah*, commenting on the stricter application of *O. H.* 328, opines that when heathens are compelling the individual to transgress one of the three so-called cardinal sins—in which case there is reason to fear that the victim will be prepared to die rather than transgress—one may ("*efshar*") be obligated to transgress in order to save the individual's *life*.[9] That is, in such a case one is not saving the victim from his transgression *per se* but rather from death. On the other hand, (2) according to many decisors, the lenient application of *O. H.* 306 does not apply to potential transgression resulting from negligence,[10] although some have wondered whether one may at least transgress rabbinic prohibitions even in cases induced by negligence. Indeed, we shall see that others permit even Biblical transgressions, *even* when negligence-induced, in order to redeem life.[11]

R. Moshe Feinstein, defending his ruling that one may in fact transgress the Sabbath in order to prevent suicide, states that the stringency of *O. H.* 328 does not apply to *pikuach nefesh* even in cases where potential death is due to ethical negligence.[12] Indeed, with the problem of negligence in mind, R. Eliezer Waldenberg rules that as long as the parasuicide is currently in a state of actual *sakanah*, one may transgress Biblical prohibitions even to save the *poshe'ah* or the *meizid* (e.g., he is now hospitalized but still in a self-destructive stae of mind). However, if this individual's negligence resulted in his being merely a *choleh she-eyn bo sakanah* (e.g., he attempted suicide but was unsuccessful and sustained only minor injury and is no longer in an antagonistic state of mind), then one may no longer transgress even rabbinic prohibitions.[13]

II.

It emerges at this point that an important factor in permitting transgression of the Sabbath to save the life of a parasuicide, still assuming that his actions or intentions are to be considered negligent or sinful, is whether the *mitzvah* of *pikuach nefesh* prevails over the general principle that one does not transgress in order to save another from transgressing as a consequence of *meizid* or *p^e^shiah*?

I mentioned that *Tosafoth*'s qualification of this general principle suggested that any *mitzvah rabbah* such as *pikuach nefesh* would prevail, allowing one to transgress for the benefit of one's fellow. Yet, in the cases referred to by *Tosafoth* there is also no evidence of wanton intent or negligence on the part of any party.

It seems, however, that there are two possible solutions to this problem: (1) to find precedent that *pikuach nefesh* does in fact apply even to negligently-induced *sakanah*, and (2) to suggest that suicide is not necessarily an act of willful negligence or *meizid*. There is ample material regarding the first alternative, while the second will be the author's modest contribution to the present issue.

A

Addressing the question of whether one can transgress the Sabbath in order to save an individual who had willfully fled to convert to Islam, R. Shmuel ben David Halevi refers to a responsum of *Rashba* who in a similar case declined permission to transgress based on the "negligence" principle.[14] The author then cites *Beth Yosef* who ruled that if such an individual were compelled to apostacy one must certainly transgress even Sabbath prohibitions, which again implies that if such catastrophe had been the result of negligence one would not have been permitted to transgress. R. Shmuel ben David then offers his own novelum to the effect that *Tosafoth*'s second qualification (*mitzvah rabbah*) means that *pikuach nefesh* or *pikuach da'ath* in fact prevails over even negligence-induced *sakanah*. While this ruling establishes an important precedent, it was also rejected by *Resp. Shevuth Yaakov*, and others would only permit transgressing rabbinic prohibitions in the case of negligence.[15] Nonetheless, applying R. Shmuel ben

David's ruling to the present case, since suicide potentially involves *pikuach nefesh* and *pikuach da'ath* it would be permissible to transgress the Sabbath to save such an individual even when such *sakanah* is a consequence of *p^eshiah* or *meizid*. This basic approach is also accepted by R. Waldenberg (and others) who adds, as noted above, that when negligence is involved *and* there is no actual or probable *sakanah*, then one may not transgress even rabbinic prohibitions.[16]

R. Feinstein also suggests that *pikuach nefesh* prevails over negligence-induced *sakanah*.[17] In support of this opinion, R. Feinstein notes that although one is rabbinically forbidden from electing a journey or surgical procedure three days prior to the Sabbath (since by so doing one initiates the possibility of *chilul Shabbath* either through the "pain" to be incurred or actions that will have to be performed on the Sabbath itself[18]) the prohibition implies that *post facto*, we would of course transgress the Sabbath if there was *sakanah* and even though this need to transgress the Sabbath was negligence-induced.[19]

B

Offering a third perspective on this problem is an aside in a recent paper by R. Shlomo Y. Zevin. R. Zevin observes that R. Joseph Babad (*Minchath Chinnukh*) rules that there is no obligation to save the life of the *me'abed atzmo l^e-da'ath*, which would also mean that one may certainly not transgress the Sabbath for this purpose.[20] R. Babad's reasoning is that since the parasuicide wantonly endangers his life, the obligation to save him is no different than in the law regarding one who willfully abandons his possessions in a place where these will surely become lost (*aveidah mi-da'ath*). In this case, as the Talmud and codes rule, the finder bears no obligation to return such properties.[21] In our case, since the parasuicide by his actions or expressed intentions has revealed that he considers his life forfeit, his fellows have no obligation to "restore him *to himself*" ("*v^e-hasheivotho lo*")!

Regarding the obligation to "not stand idly by the blood of your brother," which is the second halakhic rationale for saving life,[22] R. Babad would appear to accept the strict interpretation of "*rey'ekha*" ("your fellow"); i.e., one is only obligated to save the life of a fellow Jew who acts as one ought to under Jewish law. And the parasuicide does not.

R. Zevin rejects this ruling, and states that while the parasuicide's behavior may not *obligate* others to save him, we may still be obligated to "draw him away from transgression" (*l^e-hafrushei me-isura*).[23] However, R. Zevin does not discuss what we now know to be an important question: since the focus according to R. Zevin's interpretation of R. Babad is not to save life but to "avert transgression," does *this* obligation prevail when such transgression is negligence-induced? Rabbi Zevin may hold that since this particular transgression may have irreversible consequences, we are in effect following *O. H.* 306, sparing the individual from *pikuach da'ath olamith.*

R. Zevin offers another approach which directly challenges R. Babad's conceptualization of suicide as a case of *aveidah mi-da'ath.* R. Zevin notes that the obligation to return lost property can only be suspended when there has been legal ownership in the first place that has subsequently been renounced. However, Judaism does not truly consider man the master of his body and soul, but rather a caretaker.[24] Thus, one cannot forfeit any property "rights" over one's body, soul, or health. From this perspective, even wanton disregard for life demonstrated by a parasuicide cannot suspend the obligation of bystanders to save him.[25]

Motivated in part by R. Zevin's approach, I would suggest further qualification of R. Babad's view, drawing precisely from the analogy between parasuicide and the laws of *aveidah mi-da'ath*. Not every instance of apparent disownership is regarded as *aveidah mi-da'ath*. Specifically, the Talmud rules that the obligation "to return" is not suspended in the case of an owner who throws property from a roof in public domain, due to the following logic: since he assumes others know that there is a prohibition against unnecessary waste (*bal tash'chith*), he also assumes that others will realize that he does *not* intend to forfeit his rights of ownership.[26] Elaborating upon this rationale, Rabbi Joseph Dov Soloveitchik of Brisk explains that in this case the owner is indicating through his actions that he for some reason actually wants the property *to be broken*, and hence others may not automatically presume that he has forfeited his rights to the disposed property.[27] The parasuicide, of course, also can be considered intent on damaging his body, and quite literally does not relinquish ownership of his body and health *until* he succeeds in destroying himself. Precisely up until this moment, too, do others sustain an obligation to save his life.

Indeed, the Talmud also rules that parents who heap clothing or property on a coffin about to be buried (so as to accompany the deceased)—which would ordinarily as *tashmishei ha-meth* become forbidden to use—is not considered an instance of *aveidah mi-da'ath*. In this illustration, the actions of parents are clearly the result of psychological anguish.[28] Here, too, others are obligated to return these properties to their owner ("... *v^e-eyn alekha aveidah g^edolah mi-zu*"). When suicide *qua* cry for help occurs in public or following an effort on the victim's part to reveal his intentions, and so forth, one's obligation to save life can be devolved from either Rabbi Soloveitchik's rationale or by comparison to the law of *ha-zorek machamath tza'aro*.

———C———

Throughout the preceding analysis, I have not challenged the assumption that the parasuicide is to be viewed as having either negligently or intentionally transgressed the ban against self-destruction. I would now suggest an alternative view that might obviate the need to pit the concepts of *pikuach nefesh* and *p^eshiah* against each other. This approach is actually an amplification of the halakhic model of *ha-zorek machamath tza'aro* mentioned above.

First, one recalls that Halakha does not consider an act of self-destruction suicide *per se* unless there has been both a prior expression of suicidal intention as well as a linked witnessing of the suicidal act. *Until suicide has occurred, we need not yet describe the penultimate behavior as suicide* per se! Indeed, if there exists any basis upon which to dispute a causal relationship between prior statements or intentions and subsequent acts of self-destructiveness, such acts are not considered *me'abed atzmo l^e-da'ath*.[29] Further, full warning is necessary in Jewish law before an act can be considered fully reprehensible or punishable.[30]

More important, it is well-known that many authorities have accepted in cases of alleged suicide that one may exert every effort to attribute such behavior on even the slightest grounds to antecedent states of psychological disorder or other compelling influences, thereby eliminating the critical element of *da'ath*.[31] In halakhic literature, the list of such antecedent states includes fear, panic, depression, religious fanaticism (thinking that suicide will finally prevent one from committing sin), excessive pain, confinement,[32] and intoxication (and probably any delusional state).[33] Studies have also shown that the thinking processes of the parasuicide undergo a tendency toward concretization, and utilize one-sided, compellingly negativistic logic, making communication between the parasuicide and others particularly difficult.[34] This cognitive constriction might also be included as a "compelling" factor. This general approach is best expressed in the view ascribed to the *Rosh*, that self-destruction is by its very nature an act of psychological disorder or *tza'ar*, even in the absence of more dramatic indicators of mental illness.[35] And although this view is considered to suffer questionable authorship, its principle is widely applied.[36]

Further leniency is provided by the view which presumes that perhaps the parasuicide has had second thoughts about his intentions and has recanted.[37] Armed with both of these traditions in this area of Jewish law, it can be suggested that the obligation to save the life of the parasuicide, even if it involves transgressing the Sabbath, does not necessarily confront the principle which disallows bystanders from preventing negligence-induced *sakanah* or "transgressions." As in the case of one who runs away on the Sabbath while under the influence of "*ruach ra'ah*," an obligation to save life remains.[38]

A final issue: in categorizing the parasuicide as something akin to a *shoteh* as regards his psychological imbalance, does this not imply that he is excluded from the category of "fellow" (*rey'ekha*) and, therefore, from "*lo ta'amod*"? Two responses are suggested: (1) One is in fact no less obligated to save the life of even a complete *shoteh* or a *katan*, even if this necessitates transgressing the Sabbath,[39] and (2) Halakhah establishes in many instances that we may exempt an individual from the stigma of suicide, by viewing his behavior as due to *oness* or *teiruf da'ath*, while at the same time limiting this categorization to his intentions regarding self-destruction but not other *mitzvah* obligations.[40]

III. ———————

Summarizing the above, one may, according to most authorities, transgress Sabbath or any other prohibition in order to save the life of the parasuicide, and even if one must view such behavior as negligence-induced. In all likelihood, suicide need not be considered an act of negligence. According to R. Waldenberg, one may not transgress even rabbinic prohibitions on the Sabbath if the parasuicide has only brought upon himself non-life-threatening danger or has become through his actions a *choleh she-eyn bo sakanah*. In instances of *sakanah*, one would be permitted to violate (1) even Biblical prohibitions, (2) even if there were only a probability of *sakanah*, (3) even for a non-Jew or an apostate or "wicked" Jew,[41] (4) even for a child or a *shoteh*, and (5) even where such *sakanah* has been induced through negligence or wanton intent.[42]

Notes

1. *Resp. Chelkath Yaakov*, vol. 1, no. 72; *Resp. Tzitz Eliezer*, vol. 8, no. 15(4), vol. 9, no. 17(2): 14, vol. 10, no. 25(17): 13; *Resp. Duda'ei ha-Sadeh*, no. 39; *Resp. Shoel u-Meishiv, M.K.*, vol. 3, no. 127; *Resp. Maharil Diskin*, vol. 1, no. 34; *Resp. Igroth Moshe: O.H.*, vol. 1, no. 127, *Y.D.*, vol. 3, no. 90; *Birkei Yosef* 301:6; *Shiurim Metzuyanim be-Halakhah: O.H.*, 201, no.1 and in his *Kuntres Acharon*, vol. 2, no. 92(1), vol. 4, no. 201(1).
2. See *Kometz Minchah* to *Minchath Chinnukh* 237; *Chakhmath Shlomo* 329:1, and according to the superficial interpretation of *Magen Avraham: O.H.*, 248, no. 14 ("*ve-al pi zeh somkhin* . . ."), but cf. *Resp. Igroth Moshe: O.H.*, vol. 1, no. 127. See also *Iyun Ya'akov*, s.v. *ve-oto*, to *Yoma* 36b (*Hillel ha-Zaken*).
3. *Shab.* 3b-4a (R. Bibi bar Abayeh).
4. *Git.* 41b; cf. *Git.* 38b on Lev. 25:46.
5. *Tos.*, s.v. *ve-hki, Shab.* 4a; see also *Arukh ha-Shulchan: O.H.* 254.
6. Rashi, the *Rosh, SMaG*, Neg. 65; *Rambam, M.T. Hil. Shab.* 3:18, 9:5, 25:1; *Sh. A., O.H.* 254:6, and see *Mishnah Berurah*, no. 40.
7. Gen. 9:5; *M.T. Hil. Rotzeach* 2:3; *Sh. A., Y.D.* 345; *H.M.* 427:8; *Taan.* 22b to Gen. 2:7; cf. *Tur H.M.*, 420:21; also Tos., s.v. *u-she'mor, Shev.* 36a.
8. *TaZ* to *O.H.* 306, no. 5 and *Magen Avraham*, ad loc., no. 29; *Mishnah Berurah* at *O.H.* 306:14, no. 58; *Kaf ha-Chayim: O.H.* 306:14, no. 110; *Arukh ha-Shulchan: O. H.* 306:25.
9. No. 31; see also *Kaf ha-Chayim: O.H.* 306, no. 111, citing *Levush* and *Eliahu Rabba*.

10. Cf. *Mishnah Berurah* at *O.H.* 328:10, no. 31; *Arukh ha-Shulchan: O.H.* 306:25 and *Resp. Shevut Yaakov*, vol. 1, no. 16.
11. *Resp. Nachalath Shevah*, no. 83.
12. *Resp. Igroth Moshe: Y.D.*, vol. 3, no. 90 (end).
13. *Resp. Tzitz Eliezer*, vol. 8, no. 15(4), vol. 9, no. 17(2):14, vol. 10, no. 25(17):3.
14. *Resp. Nachalath Shevah*, no. 83; *Rashba* cited in *Beth Yosef* to *Tur Sh. A., O.H.* 306.
15. vol. 1, no. 16.
16. See notes 1 and 13. In yet another interesting responsum, R. Dovid Tzvi Hoffmann responds to the following question (*Resp. Melamed le-Ho'il*, vol. 1, no. 61): A child was ordered by his father to write on the Sabbath, but the child refused to do so. The child's mother threatened that if the child did not do as instructed by his father, *she* would kill herself! May the child violate the Sabbath in order to prevent his mother from suicide? Rabbi Hoffmann states that the Sabbath may not be violated to spare the life of an individual who wantonly ("*be-zadon*") embarks upon a self-destructive path. He notes that if he were to rule leniently, others might capitalize upon such threats in the effort to compel vulnerable persons into apostacy. Rabbi Hoffmann also refers to the *Resp. Yehudah Ya'aleh, E.H.*, no. 140 who ruled that one cannot permit a *chalutzah* to marry a *cohen* despite her threat that she would otherwise leave the Jewish faith. Rabbi Hoffmann extrapolates that if one cannot permit the transgression of Jewish law, even in the case of a *chalutzah de-rabbonon*, to prevent apostacy, then one surely cannot permit the violation of the Sabbath for *pikuach nefesh* which, according to his reasoning, represents *less* of a threat (see *Ikrei Dinim, O. H.* 10:22, who argues that risk to physical life is more stringent than risk to "spiritual" life). Rabbi Hoffmann ends by noting that although the individual in question could be instructed to write with his left hand, thus rendering his transgression of the Sabbath rabbinic rather than Biblical, one should not so recommend, and the Sabbath may not be violated in the case in question! In so ruling, R. Hoffmann takes an even more stringent view than accepted theoretically by *Resp. Shevut Yaakov*, vol. 1, no. 16.
17. See note 12.
18. *Shab.* 19a; *Sh. A., O.H.* 248 (for exemptions from this rule, see Bleich, J. David, "Elective Surgery Prior to Shabbat," *Tradition 17*, no. 4 (1979): 94-97.
19. *Sh. A., O.H.* 248:4, *Mishnah Berurah*, no. 27; see also *Resp. Maharam Galanti*, no. 110. Rabbi Feinstein reinterprets the words of *Magen Avraham* (*O.H.* 248, no. 14) as not referring to actual *sakanah*, for, as in R. Feinstein's view, we would certainly violate the Sabbath in such cases. Rather, R. Gombiner means that there are some characteristically anxious persons who may be prone to perceive exaggerated danger during their journey three days prior to the Sabbath, who might thereby put themselves into a position to have to transgress the Sabbath unnecessarily. *Magen Avraham* warns only that this tendency must be checked, so that, given certain other conditions, even such anxious persons may embark upon travel three days prior to the Sabbath.
20. "*Ha-Im Mutar Latet Reshut le-Acher li-Chbol Bo?*" in M. Hershler ed.,

Halakhah ve-Refuah, vol. 2 (1981): 96-97, regarding *Kometz Minchah* to *Chinnukh* 237.

21. (Although such property is not exactly *hefker*.) *B.M.* 25b; *BaCH* to *Tur Sh. A., H.M.* 273; *SHaKH* to *Sh. A., H.M.* 261:3.

22. *Sanh.* 73a to Lev. 19:16.

23. See Rashi, s.v. *isura*, *B.K.* 28a; *Tos.* and Rashi, *Shab.* 3a; see also *Turei Even* in *Avnei Miluim* to *Chag.* 13a.

24. Ezek. 18:4; see also *Radbaz* to *M.T. Hil. Sanh.* 18:6.

25. R. Zevin offers a brilliant interpretation of the term *edrosh* ("I will seek") in the passage upon which is derived the prohibition against self-destruction (Gen. 9:5). Generally, *poked* is the term utilized to indicate that God will "extract punishment" from transgressors, whereas the term *edrosh* suggests that the transgressor has abused something which is in fact not his.

26. Rashi, *B.K.* 26b; *Netivot Mishpat* 261, but cf. the *Rosh.*

27. *Beth Halevi*, vol. 1, no. 24.

28. Rashi, *Sanh.* 48a; see also *Drishah* to *Tur Sh. A., H.M.* 261; see also *Sh. A., Y.D.* 349:3. *Resp. Chelkath Yaakov*, vol. 1, no. 72, states that in addition to all else, until an individual actually carries through his suicide, the preliminary activities are not themselves to be viewed as equivalent (in terms of gravity of *isur*).

29. *Arukh ha-Shulchan: Y.D.* 345. *Resp. Chelkath Yaakov*, vol. 1, no. 72, states that in addition to all else, until an individual actually carries through his suicide, the preliminary activities are not themselves to be viewed as equivalent (in terms of gravity of *isur*).

30. *Darkei Mosheh, Y.D.* 345, no. 3; also *Resp. Tzapichit be-Devash*, no. 69 (p. 168a).

31. *Arukh ha-Shulchan, Y.D.* 345, nos. 4-5.

32. *Kol Bo al Aveilut*, vol. 1, pp. 319-20; *Gesher ha-Chayim*, vol. 1, pp. 272-73; *Chiddushei R. Akiba Eger, Y.D.* 345; *Shem Gedolim* (*Birkei Yosef*) 10:17; *Resp. Levushei Mordekhai: M.T., Y.D.*, no. 134; *Resp. Parashat Mordekhai*, nos. 25-26; *Sedei Chemed*, vol. 5, p. 54; cf. *Resp. Chayim She'al*, no. 46; see also *Resp. Even Shoham*, no. 44. Cf. also *Resp. Ya'bia Omer*, vol. 2, no. 24 and *Even Ya'akov*, no. 3, who state that suicide caused by *yirah* (fear) or *tza'aroth raboth* is still considered *ibud atzmo le-da'ath* (*unless* the "fear" in question was in the context of forced apostacy).

33. *Kol Bo*, vol. 1, p. 320. *Sedei Chemed* cites *Resp. Ma'asei Avraham: Y.D.*, no. 60 who rules that *shikruth* (drunkenness) only nullifies legal transactions but cannot exonerate an individual from the crime of taking his or her own life. *Sedei Chemed*, however, offers precedent indicating that the drunk is indeed exempted from punishment (e.g., *Eruv.* 65a) and then opines that self-destruction consequent to intoxication "on the level of Lot's drunkennness" would not be considered bona fide suicide.

34. Tripodes, T., "The Logics of Suicide," NIMH Contract no. 23-5120-1930, unpublished, 1968; E. Schneidman & N. Faberow, "Suicide and Death," in H. Feifel ed., *The Meaning of Death* (New York: 1959), p. 284; C. Neuringer and M. Levenson, "Time Perception in Suicidal Individuals," *Omega 2*, no. 4 (1971): 247-251 and *Omega 3*, no. 3 (1972): 181-186.

35. *Resp. Besamim Rosh*, no. 345.
36. *Kol Bo*, vol. 1, p. 319, not 31; *Sedei Chemed*, vol. 5, p. 54; *Resp. Chatham Sofer: Y.D.*, no. 326; *Resp. Shoel u-Meishiv: M.K.*, vol. 3, no. 217.
37. *Resp. Maharam Shik: Y.D.*, no. 346; *Resp. Duda'ei ha-Sadeh*, no. 39; *Resp. Shevut Yaakov*, vol. 2, no. 111.
38. *Sh. A., O.H.* 288:10; *Resp. Admath Kodesh: Y.D.*, no. 6; *Resp. Netzer Mata'ai*, no. 8; see also *Arukh ha-Shulchan: O.H.* 288:17.
39. *Resp. Tzitz Eliezer*, vol. 8, no. 15(3): 11-12, vol. 9, no. 28(11).
40. I.e., *oness* is not necessarily the equivalent of *lav bar chiyuvah*; and see *Or Sameach* to *M.T. Hil. Yesodei Torah* 5:6 and *TaZ* to *O.H.* 108:1, Y.D. 341:5.
41. Rabbi Waldenberg suggests saving the life of a non-Jew by intending primarily to prevent *chilul ha-Shem* or to ensure that one will not be persecuted, thereby rendering one's actions on the Sabbath a *melakhah she-eynah tzrikha le-gufah, Resp. Tzitz Eliezer*, vol. 8, no. 15(6), vol. 9, no. 17(1), (8):1, (10):3, vol. 10, no. 25(19):1.
42. Two remaining issues are whether one is obligated to place one's own life into danger in order to save another's life (see Rabbi M. Hershler, "*be-Din Im Chayav le-Hakhnis Atzmo le-Safek Sakanah Kedey le-ha'Tzil Chaveiro*," in *Halakhah ve-Refuah*, vol. 2 [1981]: 52-57), and whether one must recite *birkat ha-gomel* upon being saved from suicide (see *Resp. Tzitz Eliezer*, vol. 12, no. 18(8), but cf. vol. 10, no. 25(23), and M. H. Spero, "*Birkath ha-Gomel le-Achar Hachlamah mi-Machalat-Nefesh*," *Assia* 6, no. 3 (1979): 40-42; also *Resp. Lev Chayim*, vol. 3, no. 53; *Resp. Yechaveh Da'ath*, vol. 4, no. 14.

15

Emergence of and Flight from Self—The Experience of Shame in Genesis 3: A Psychoanalytic Developmental Perspective

I.

The Biblical narrative of the glory and fall of primal man in Eden satisfies many as a sufficient account of the origins of humanity. Indeed, the faithful Jew views the Biblical episode of Genesis 3 not as mythology, but rather as an outline of historical events and as an introduction to the role of moral imperatives in the dialogue between man and God. Equally relevant, however, as an additional facet of the quest for moral foundations is the need for psychological continuity and dialogue with the past, to enable one to empathize with historical persons' experiences, to understand how they perceived and related emotionally to their realities. By pursuing psychological continuity between Biblical man and modern man, we are seeking to repersonalize history by discovering in earliest man experiences similar to our own and kindred crises and struggles which might serve as grounds for identification.[1] We are engaged, in other words, in the search for a sense of psychohistorical closure.

Such a study presupposes that the struggles and crises of the Biblical hero were universal ones. However, the search for dialogue in psychological terms, as a therapist might seek to understand a patient, has lead some scholars to overextend the process and to posit unsupportable analogies between the psychological patient and the historical character. This is a serious methodological error, one which I will want to avoid.[2] The present analysis does not seek to limit the experience of the Biblical hero to contemporary terms, nor is it an attempt to reduce the *moral* scope of Genesis by reference to the elements of developmental psychology. Rather this type of analysis seeks to use modern conceptions to understand fundamentals implicit in the Biblical episode and to expand these into fuller insight capable of supporting the moral lessons others have derived from it. I will reinterpret Genesis 3 by focusing on the development of the sense of self, borrowing from the perspectives of psychoanalytic developmental psychology and existential psychiatry. The object of analysis is the role played by the basic experience of shame in the self's emergence from consciousness of nakedness and its development toward the psychological achievement of individuality.

II.

The experience of the discovery of nakedness recounted in Genesis 2:25-3:1-12 is understood by classical Biblical commentators as an ethico-moral tragedy, as the result of regression from spirituality to temporality, the transformation from soul-centeredness to body-centeredness.[3] From this perspective, Genesis 3 is a morality play, depicting the antithesis between sacred and mundane. The human or distinctly psychological experiences in this episode are also lent a primarily moral significance. Thus, Samson Raphael Hirsch (19th cent.) views Adam's shame as the consequence of "the condemning verdict of one's conscience . . . *the failure of moral energy*.[4] Death, the ultimate consequence of this tragedy, is also viewed primarily as morally relevant—"There is no death without sin."[5]

Yet, to view Genesis as relevant for human development, one needs to view it as more than merely an epic of moral weakness, a battle between soul and matter, or even of the conflicts inherent in our condemnation to free choice.[6] Theology may gain by an understanding of the roots of morality in individual psychological development, in that it can there discover the early manifestations of moral and social development. A link is needed between wholly theological evaluations of the fall and the psychology of human suffering, the discovery of self, and the continuous adaptive regressions which man must deal with throughout his development toward identity. The uniqueness of the approach to be suggested here is that it views the drama or dynamic of the fall *as a necessary stage in personality development which makes subsequent moral achievements possible.*[7]

Rashi (11th cent.) already contributed to this understanding by emphasizing that the consumption of the forbidden fruit did not produce man's first awareness that he was unclothed—this much is objective knowledge that "even the blind man knows."[8] That is, *before* "knowledge"—before man's dawning awareness of the outside world and his radical difference from it—man already *exists*, he *is*, but he is *arum*, naked (*arum=aartila'in*=divest[9]), *or without identity*. But he does not know that he has no identity. Rather, he is *arum* but it has no emotional significance for him. He is totally without anxiety about his exposed body not for lack of perceptual capacity, but for lack of ego interest in the experience of being naked. Without an established sense of privacy, there can be no sense of exposure. Man is not only without self-consciousness— he is yet without self. Following the sin, Adam "knew that he was naked." This "knowledge" is not merely the acquisition of intellectual or perceptual awareness, but rather is the unfolding of a new psychological experience—the discovery of self.[10]

This discovery emerges in the development of the sense of shame. The text does not at first explicitly state that man was ashamed of his nakedness, but suggests it through the following: "... and they knew that they were naked, and they sewed together fig-leaves and made themselves aprons ... and the man and his wife hid themselves ... *and I was afraid because I was naked* and I hid myself." A sense of "I" has emerged from an experience of the naked body as invaded privacy. There is recognition on a yet primitive level of an inner, *own* domain and an outer, distinctly *other* domain. A body-self has emerged. So long as the focus of distinctness remains on the level of body-self, however, the body is still confused with the entire experience of self. Thus, in a primitive attempt to undo their behavior, man and woman furtively hide their genitals with aprons, as if the exposed part itself was the source of shame (pudenda=*pudor* [Latin]=shame).

They quickly become aware that the sense of smallness and inadequacy emanates from their very being. They are each gripped with an inarticulate feeling of exposure and powerlessness which transcends specific possessions or organs and pervades that which we call the self.

Yet, this is an experience which can only emerge in the perceived or actual presence of an other, the one before whom the self is ashamed, feels exposed and powerless. I will now expand on this point.

Nuttin views shame as the "combination of the privacy and penetrability of human consciousness . . . the private interiority of psychological life, combined with its inherent possibility of exposure, constitute what we may call the functional conditions for the origin of shame."[11] Becker gives shame a more social meaning, "Shame arises in the moment of acknowledgement that the private is merely the 'inner pole' of the social. *It is the confession that one really has nothing private per se to oppose to someone's scrutiny.*"[12] Thus, while the self can be discovered in the experience of shame—because it becomes the center of focus—it also becomes subject during shame to powerful drives to suppress the self, to withdraw into nothingness, to surrender the sense of identity and uniqueness in the effort to end the sense of shame.[13] Too, shame may indicate that the self is struggling desperately to resist these tendencies, that it is trying to resolve estrangement by reasserting the self by saying, as it were, "*I am* the ashamed one, *I have and am entitled to a private world.*"[14]

Shame involves hiding the self *from the self* as well as from the other. It expresses the discovery of identity and the private as well as the struggle against the psychologically regressive withdrawal from identity. Thus do the man and the woman hide *themselves* from before God. That which earlier stood in no particular relation to the world is now the object of restraint and inhibition (*yithboshashu=mithkalmin*[15]). Hence the paradox of Adam's behavior: in shame he shows to the other precisely what he seeks to hide.

The characteristic sense of smallness and insignificance in shame, the "unableness" of the self, is expressed in the Midrash and Talmud. "Six things did God take from Adam after the sin . . . his glory and his stature."[16] "Said R. Judah in the name of

Rab: 'Man spanned from one end of the world until the other end. Once he became spoiled [*kevan she-sarach*], God placed his hand upon the man and made him small.' "[17] "As the sun set, Adam said, 'Woe is me, for since I have become spoiled, [the world has] darkened in my sake, and it will revert to null and void.' "[18] The debased self-image has extended to nihilistic anticipation of destruction and abandonment. The intense experience of an other participating in the shame experience is also suggested by the Midrash: " 'And they heard the voice of the Lord, God, [which was] walking in the garden'—They heard the voice of the trees saying, 'There is the thief who has beguiled his Creator.' "[19] The voice of God *was already* present; man's ego had but to recognize it as a significant object. In this epic, the Other is recognized in the moment of shame. These rabbinic elaborations do not speak in the terms of moral regression. They describe a psychological experience of debilitating force, of intense smallness, inferiority, and helplessness.[20]

From the moral standpoint, the pristine world of innocence has been shattered by the act of rebellion. From the psychological standpoint, the autistic, selfless, naive shell has been broken by the experience of shame.

III. ——————————

The discovery of self, in the emotional experience of shame, does require the prior operation of certain cognitive processes. The very recognition of a difference between self and non-self, the beginning of countless similar differentiations that will occur during life is a cognitive process which has important emotional implications.

The serpent, described in Gen. 2:25 as *arom*, cunning, resourceful, intellectually advanced (Onkelos: *arom=chakim*), represents knowledge of the difference between self and other. According to the *Midrash*, he has cast his lustful eye upon man's consort; he desires that which he is able to recognize is another's and experiences frustration.[21] He can *anticipate* and plan rebellion, for he knows that it is difficult to make as one's own that which is possessed by another. At this point, man is to be understood by counterpoint: as *arum*, naked, divest of *arom*-ness, unsuspecting, not able to anticipate treachery because he is as yet unaware of "mine" and "thine." Man is naive.* Without an ability to sense separateness, there can be no anxiety about the possible losses in life, and so man cannot anticipate loss. Thus, he cannot truly comprehend the impact of God's *pro*-hibition against eating of the trees of Eden.

Adam's so-called moral rebellion is almost inevitable. Man's transgression of the bounds set by his single moral obligation (to not eat from the fruit of a particular tree) was as inevitable as an infant's first physical step away from its mother. From the moral standpoint, this may be viewed as disobedience. From the psychological standpoint, this is a risk required by the drive toward individuation. With the first forward movement out of the womb-like shell of Eden, man's "eyes are opened" (Gen.

---

* Eldad also suggests that the juxtaposition of *arom-arum* in Gen. 2:25-3:1 stresses Adam's parallelism to the serpent: naivete.[22] Hertz comments on Gen. 3:1, "Simplicity is the weapon of cunning." His insight is emphasized by S. R. Hirsch, who roots *arom*-cunning in *armah*, a heap of tied-together single grains. The subtle person takes together individual elements, which alone have unrecognized import, and uses the new, subtle (*subtilis* [Latin]=finely woven) creation to accomplish his ends. Hirsch then suggests the root of *arum*-naked in *or*-skin, "with the underlying conception of being sensitive to external impression." This would nicely capture the psychodynamic ontogeny of shame as an oral, skin-oriented phenomenon. Hirsch relates *i-ver*, blind man (spelled: *or*), to this interpretation inasmuch as the blind man is dependent upon his sense of touch. In other words, the blind man is a "skin man." (This should mean that the blind man is capable of shame which, while this would seem obvious, is disputed by certain halakhic-talmudic opinion [see *Addendum*] and some clinical evidence.) However, Hirsch does not relate *arom*-cunning to *arum*-naked and he attributes too much of a moral capacity to the sense of shame. What he sees in shame is actually an aspect of guilt which, as I shall show, is absent from Genesis 3. Also note that aside from the Hebrew *arum-arom* pun—although I think it is more than a pun—there is an etymological similarity in Arabic as well. Indeed, the linking variable between *arom* and *arum* has been *bushah*, the sense of shame following differentiation. In Arabic, the equivalents of *arom*, *arum*, and *bushah* are related. *Arum*-naked=*a-rin* (to strip flesh from bones), *arom*-cunning=*a-ron* (tricky) or, in the colloquial, =*khopth* (knowledge to be ashamed about). Thus, knowledge of self arises in shame, which describes the fear of, and the repressed desire to exhibit the self. Beldstein also recognizes that in becoming aware that he is *arum*, man has become *arom*.[23]

3:7)—*va-tipakachnah*. This is the discovery of the self-as-initiator. Man senses that he, too, has become *arom*, but not primarily in a moral sense. He has differentiated himself from all that is non-self. Adam becomes reflective—*he knows that his eyes are taking internally that which is external and is shared by others*—and he becomes intensely self-conscious.

Man is now *arum* in two senses. He discovers that he is *separate* from all nature and utterly alone (*aartila'in*=stripped). Second, with the experience of independence comes *vulnerability* (*va-tipakachnah*=open). The awakening of uniqueness (*arom*) has stripped man of a primary defense against reality. With the discovery of self come the anxiety of loss and an equally omnipresent tendency toward regressive merger within the haze of undifferentiated experience. Only with the ontological experience of separateness can self differentiate, yet only with this radical experience of the distinction between self and other can a sense of loss emerge.

This anxiety over loss is seen in Adam's rush to clothe himself. Rabbi C. D. Rabinowitz writes in his commentary on Genesis, "The experience of the discovery of the body immediately created the impulse to acquire possessions."[24] This important insight needs explanation. In psychoanalytic terms, shame involves a sense of loss, a fear of abandonment, even a wish for self-annihilation. Clinically, the preoccupation with possessions, things or ideas, connotes the preoccupation with things that are actually outside the self but are symbolically experienced as inside. In other words, such preoccupation is an attempt to deal with fear of loss and emptiness by focusing instead on what "ought" to or could belong to me. Clothes, and money, in particular, are what Fenichel termed "deindividuated" possessions—they look alike no matter who owns them and, hence, are always losable.[25] The neurotic preoccupation with possessions is always over a fear of having possessions that are *common*, which then only increases the compulsion to acquire and hoard the ever-new, ever-unique possession.

In Adam's case, the advent of the first loss—the loss of the sense of security in the new world of differentiated existence and the threatened loss of God's love—becomes the paradigm for subsequent experiences of anxiety and shame. With these emerges the need for a defense against loss. Clothing, tangible and easy to amass, become substitutes or symbolic replacements for psychological loss. God subsequently fashions garments for man (Gen. 3:21) perhaps to stress that comfort must come from within, that the use of clothing to replace lost security or identity by denying human uniqueness is nothing more than a fetish.*

We can now address another curious aspect of this dramatic episode. There is no sense of guilt in Genesis 3. While shame and guilt occasionally manifest together, and can elicit one another, especially in the more structured and complex adult personality, shame is actually the precursor to the experience of guilt or "mature" conscience.[29] Adam has some sense of having done something that is causing him pain—but it is not yet a fully articulate moral sense. *There is a sense of weakness but not a sense of transgression.* Guilt is about some*thing*. What man experiences in Genesis is about *himself*. In guilt, there is an evaluation of the act for which the self is held responsible, while the self functions silently. The self-as-judge is absent from the experience. Adam, however, experiences the presence of an intensely personified "other," an acute sense of someone "there" before whom he is ashamed and must hide. "There is no guilt implied in shame, there is no forgiveness in shame."[30] Adam does not yet seek to repair; he seeks to hide.

From the developmental standpoint, there is no guilt in Genesis 3 because the requisite self-development has not yet occurred. Man has acquired *da'ath*, the cognitive-emotional maturity sufficient for the dawning of self-awareness as manifested in

---

* These new garments (*kothnoth or*) were in some way presumably superior for man's needs than the apron of fig-leaves he had fashioned for himself. There is debate in the Talmud between Rab and Samuel whether *kothnoth or* means "something which comes from the skin" (*mei-or*) or "that which benefits the skin" (*l^e-or*).[26] The Midrash notes that R. Meir spelled *or* with an *aleph* rather than an *ayin*.[27] Needing to keep to the plain meaning of the text, Barukh Halevi Epstein finds a usage of *or* with an *aleph* as herbs, or vegetation, or possibly something to be fashioned into clothing.[28] However, if we retain the literal meaning of *or* with an *aleph* as *light*, then we easily derive that clothes serve to cover "that which light has been harshly shed upon," that which shames man! Additionally, *skin* is rooted etymologically in the sense of *to hide, to conceal*. To know someone thoroughly is expressed in Latin as *ego tu intus et in cute novi* ("I know you inside and in your skin").

the shame experience. However, mature conscience (what is called superego), based on a set of fully internalized, depersonified standards, has not yet been consolidated. Adam has the rudiments of self-body-image, against which his behavior has elicited the experience of shame *after the fact*, but he has not yet developed conscience, against which anticipated behavior elicits inhibitory guilt (or even shame) *before the fact*. Mature conscience is a significant achievement because its regulatory demands have been internalized and function in an anticipatory capacity as the proverbial "voice within." The earlier anxieties over loss and separation are during later development contained by psychic structures which only *represent* the primitive, feared parental or external controls and the equally unrealistic, inflated, narcissistic self-image. Conscience at this stage becomes part of the self, replacing to a large degree the individual's dependence upon external control, threats of physical punishment, and the need for constant repetition of regulations.[31]

Adam and Eve are motivated to act but do not hesitate until they have actually consumed the forbidden fruit and are confronted by the pain of self-awareness. Anticipation does not cause anxiety or fear of punishment. When apprehended, each devalues and passes on the blame to the other. This is typical of the primitive ego. Man, in other words, is not yet sufficiently *arom*. Only when the voice of authority, earthly or Divine, is fully internalized does "the distinction between doing something bad and wishing to do it disappear entirely."[32] Only at this stage of self-development does man become capable of saying, "If we did not do it, we *thought* it."[33]

IV.

What of Adam's punishment? God warned that man shall "surely die" upon consuming the forbidden fruit (Gen. 2:17). I suggest that this is really a statement about the course of psychological development, an evaluation of the psychological experiences which follow the emergence of self.

Adam laments, "*va-okhel*—and I did eat." The Midrash understands this statement as premonitory, "It does not state *va-akhalti*

[I did eat] but rather *va-okhel* [I *shall* eat], meaning, 'I ate and I shall eat again!' "[34] R. Tzadok ha-Cohen interprets this to mean that once freedom enters man, the sensation of evil intermingled with good renders clear choice between evil and good impossible. Thus *va-okhel* implies resignation to moral destiny.[35] Indeed, this classical approach has found expression in contemporary thought. "Self-awareness and foresight brought, however, the awesome gifts of freedom and responsibility . . . Man knows that he is accountable for his acts: he has acquired the knowledge of good and evil. This is a dreadfully heavy load to carry. No other animal has to withstand anything like it."[36]

I would clarify the problems of "you shall surely die" and "*va-okhel*" with the following considerations. I noted that concomitant with the differentiation of self and other is the dread of loss, the anxiety inherent in separation and independence. Man's finiteness and littleness, which are aggravated as much by his independence as by his moments of abject loneliness, are irrepressible symptoms of his insecure existence.[37] Self-knowledge makes man unique, but his body consciousness can fill him with anxiety or bring him to disgust and shame. As Rabbi Joseph B. Soloveitchik once phrased it, "Adam has never forgotten that he is just a handful of dust."[38] Each step toward individuation places man in a radical position, in opposition to nature and society, which creates precisely the isolation he cannot tolerate.

One might say that Adam would *surely* die in that he would now become preoccupied with the ever-present anxiety over ultimate loss, over death.[39] The anxiety over death gives it its psychological impact. Death, in existential terms, has become for man a phenomenon "with meaning for being." The Midrash relates that Eve became conscious of the possibility of loss immediately upon eating the forbidden fruit. With her differentiation of self came the awareness of ultimate loss, of death, and the possibility that she could be replaced by another. And so she prompted Adam to share her fate.[40] We noted earlier that Adam's awareness of loss immediately stimulated a defensive denial of individuation and loss through the symbolic substitute of clothes.

The meaning of *va-okhel*—"and I shall eat again"—is to be explained through a parallel prediction by God to the heavenly hosts that man, having eaten of the tree of knowledge, *will now* (*v^e-atah*) eat of the tree of life (Gen. 3:22). Man is not seeking a second rebellion. Rather, a psychological cause and effect relationship has been posited. Because man is now *arom*, or foresighted, he will of necessity seek to quell the anxiety of death and the dread anticipation of loss by consuming of the tree of eternal life. Man and God know that after individuation, there will be more "eating," continuous attempts at denying the very identity and uniqueness that man has so painfully gained, more attempts to regress to a primitive, incorporative mode of existence (dare I say "oral") where the difference between self and other are barely recognizable. God in His benevolence cannot allow this. Merger with eternity, at this point in man's development, would be a pathological shrinking from growth.

The mechanisms of conscience, shame and guilt rest upon the capacity to experience loss, anxiety, and so forth. These experiences follow the emergence of self-consciousness. Yet, subsequent moral development depends upon evolution beyond these basic, other-directed experiences. And such development must achieve a state of self-regulatory operation. For this reason God never questions the serpent during this episode. The serpent, as some traditional exegetes have suggested,[41] actually represents man himself. The serpent—that which tends to be projected outward as "alien" in man—is also part of human potential and man must learn to accept this. Man can become aware that he *is* because he is capable of being *arom*; once he is *aware* that he *is* he becomes *aware* that he is *arom*. And he becomes increasingly dependent upon this quality for survivial. This quality of *arom*-ness inheres in man and must develop into a mature intra-psychic mechanism. With each advance in *arom*-ness, the sense of self achieves stability and structure. Psychologically, he has learned to distinguish self from non-self. Morally, man acquires the ability to stand back and judge himself. From the experience of shame man will learn to respect the private world of others. Adam will develop shame's crude inhibitory quality into discretion and prudence. From shame, mature social relations will evolve.

From this perspective, the "opening of man's eyes" (*va-tipakachnah*) introduces an experience upon which must rest all subsequent moral interpretations of the term. In the moment of shame, man's senses open to a psychological reality necessary for the emergence of self and the preservation of identity. Shame can represent failure, but can also signal the struggle to maintain identity, to fight abandonment and the tendency for withdrawal in the wake of moral or personal weakness. In Rabinowitz's perceptive words, "Man is created now, as it were, a second time . . . weaker, yet richer in additional understanding."[42] We might consider this "second creation" man's psychological birth.

V.

I have attempted to show that Genesis 3 outlines the development of self from an autistic, undifferentiated world through the rudimentary experiences of shame and anxiety toward the achievement of mature conscience and social relationships. The Biblical text provides an adult model or schematic from which we have inferred psychological-developmental issues typical of early infancy (occurring before the third year of life), but which man participates in throughout a lifetime. From the moral standpoint, it is appropriate to use adult models which presume psychological development to the point where morality obtains. For the psychologist, the moral layer must be momentarily peeled back in order to focus on the implicit developmental issues which make morality possible. Indeed, using the psychoanalytic metaphor for the origins of morality, Adam's story stresses developmental issues which presage the birth of *social* morality depicted in the psychological theme of the binding of Isaac.[43] Adam's growth, at least what we can glimpse of it in Genesis 3, highlights a relatively small unit of psychosocial development: the emergence of the ego itself. Genesis 3 is accordingly of different historico-moral significance than the psychological struggles of later national heroes such as Abraham and Moses where the individuals' resolution of so-called oedipal issues bears more directly on the development of monotheism and other socio-religious advances.

A final consideration: The moral perspective informs us that man's task after the fall is essentially reparative, that the human endeavor henceforth must be marked by *t^eshuvah* (repentance).[44] Has the developmental perspective contradicted this goal?

Clearly it has not. The psychological perspective merely focuses on those aspects of development which will later comprise the psychological and emotional components of moral process. As I have demonstrated elsewhere, *t^e^shuvah* itself is rooted in the emotional experience of loss and the anxiety of longing which, as I have shown here, are consequences of individuation.[45] The psychological capacity to long for another makes possible moral dialogue and the quest for "return." Halakhah also recognizes the role of shame as an implicit acknowledgement of the One before whom one is ashamed. It incorporates this awareness into the *t^e^shuvah* process in the formula of the *vidduy* (confession): "I have sinned... I have been ashamed and embarrassed..."[46] Maimonides considers shame in the context of penitence a lofty experience, "For all the time that [the penitent individuals] are ashamed by their iniquities and are embarrassed [*mithkalmin*, refrain] from them, their merit multiplies and their stature increases."[47] Hence, "One who sins and is ashamed, all his sins are forgiven."[48] Psychological readiness for *t^e^shuvah*—the self-differentiation requisite for the experiences of shame and guilt—takes on moral significance. Without a self and an other, "return" is impossible.

Shame can indicate the breakdown of the ability to maintain identity and a weakening of the struggle during the shame-evoking situation against the tendency toward identity diffusion. This aspect of shame underwrites the moral crisis of the experience of sin: Has the exposure of the "sinful" or "inauthentic" self been so painful and intolerable—has it revealed such a lack of stable core identity—as to evoke flight from the Other in the form of lack of faith or, worse, of the destruction of the self? Fortunately, the healthy "shame of *t^e^shuvah*" may also begin from this crisis. The shame of *t^e^shuvah* persists until one's ambivalence toward God and man is resolved and one has reconciled with one's own self. The Other, discovered in the moment of the shame of sin and experienced as so remote, can then be approached in dialogue.

We should expect to discover in Genesis 3 universal elements of human experience. For the psychologist, regression, recapitulation, and growth are basic components of human experience. Truly meaningful psychological understandings of shame have demonstrated that it is also an existential emotion in that it relates man to self and the struggle of being. The religious believer adds to this the moral element: Some regressions are characteristic of sin, and some reconstructive trends are characteristic of *t^eshuvah*. Halakhic morality expands upon the basic psychological determinants of well-being and, indeed, seeks to become one of these determinants. *T^eshuvah* can thus be understood as an additional facet of the psychological-existential drama. It is the moral analogue to the creative, integrative, and generally growth-oriented functions of the ego.

Notes

1. I have discussed this possibility in my *Judaism and Psychology: Halakhic Perspectives* (New York: Ktav/Yeshiva University Press, 1980), pp. 28-31. See also my approach in "Remembering and Historical Awareness," *Tradition* (1975): 15(3), 43-51 and "Remembering and Historical Awareness—Part II: Psychological Aspects of a Halakhic State of Mind," *Tradition* (1981): 19(1), 59-75.
2. Compare the approach of D. Zeligs, *Psychoanalysis and the Bible* (New York: Bloch, 1974) and the critique of F.E. Manuel, "The Use and Abuse of Psychology in History," *Daedalus* (1971 Winter): 187-213.
3. *Ramban* to Gen. 2:9; *Abravanel* to Gen. 3.; *Akedah* to Gen. 3:1; *Malbim* to Gen. 2:9; *Drashoth Ha-RaN: Drash* 1; M.H. Luzzatto, *Da'ath T^evunoth*, 127; *Ruach Chayyim: Avot* 3:3; *Pri Tzadik*, vol. 1, p. 8; E.E. Dessler, *Mikhtav me-Eliyahu*, vol. 2, pp. 137-38; Rabbenu Bachaya to Gen. 3. See also Nechama Leibowitz, *Iyunim ba-Sefer Bereishit* to Gen. 1-3.
4. *Hirsch Commentary to the Pentateuch* (I. Levy, Trans.), Gen. 2:25-3:1.
5. *Shab.* 55a; Lev. R. 37:1; Gen. R. 17:13; *A.Z.* 5a; With regard to whether death was caused by man's sin or whether his punishment was merely premature death, see *Ramban*'s commentary to Gen. 2:17 and 3:22. See also Gen. R. 8:11; *Eruv.* 18b; *Ber.* 33a ("*Ein ha-arud meimit elah ha-chet meimit*"); and Rabbenu Bachaya to Gen. 2:17.
6. *Meshekh Chakhmah* to Gen. 1:31.
7. It is an approach toward the achievement of a shared spiritual language in psychology and religion, a language wherein psychology talks religiously about religion. I have developed this problem in my text and in "Continued Problems at the Interface Between Psychology and Judaism," *Journal of Psychology and Judaism* (1979): 4(1), 32-48.
8. See Rashi to Gen. 3:7; Gen. R. 19:10-11; see also *B.K.* 86a, 87b; *Sanh.* 86a.
9. *Onkelos* to Gen. 3:7; see also Gen. R. 19:11.
10. Rashi to Gen. 3:7; *Moreh* 1:2 states "new knowledge." This would, of course, also include new perceptive experiences.

11. "Intimacy and Shame in the Dynamic Structure of Personality," in M.L. Reymert ed., *Feelings and Emotions* (New York: McGraw-Hill, 1950), pp. 344-45; see also L. Binswanger, "The Case of Ellen West," In R. May, E. Angel & H. Ellenberger eds., *Existence* (New York: Clarion, 1958), p. 337.
12. *Revolution in Psychiatry* (New York: Free Press, 1964), p. 190.
13. H. Lichtenstein, *The Dilemma of Human Identity* (New York: Aronson, 1980), pp. 175-89.
14. See C. Schneider, *Shame, Exposure, and Privacy* (Boston: Beacon Press, 1977) and Becker, *Revolution in Psychiatry*, 1964.
15. *Onkelos* to Gen. 2:25. Shame, as a reaction-formation, suggests this holding-back or restraint of the forbidden impulse. See also *B.K.* 86a, "When you rebuke a child and he *shrinks back* in shame."
16. Gen. R. 12:6; Num. R. 13:2.
17. *Sanh.* 38b.
18. *A.Z.* 8a. Note that even self-hating fantasies can serve to relieve shame by reconfirming self-other boundaries, as stated in H.B. Lewis, *Shame and Guilt in Neurosis* (New York: International Universities Press, 1971), p. 432.
19. Gen. R. 19:8, "*. . . she-ganav da'ath Boro.*" Cf. *B.M.* 60a which explicates "the treacherous one" (*ramai*, rooted in *arom*), "*she-ayno ela ke-gonev et ha-ayin.*"
20. Lewis, *Shame and Guilt in Neurosis*, 1971 and M. Mayman, "The Shame Experience, the Shame Dynamic, and Shame Personalities in Psychotherapy," Unpublished Paper, University of Michigan, 1977.
21. The serpent's frustrations and cunning are illustrated in *J.T. Kid.* 4:1; *Sanh.* 59b.
22. *Hegyonut Mikrah* (Jerusalem: 1967), p. 20. *Arom*, as cunning or prudence, appears in Prov. 8:5, 12; 12:16, 23; 13:16; 14:8, 15, 18; 15:5; 19:25 (" 'When thou smitest a scorner, the simple one will become prudent'—'And the simple one will become prudent,' this is Eve" [*Mid. Shmuel* 7:12]); 22:3; 27:12; Job 5:12-13. In other Biblical citations, *a'r'm* has the sense of "stripped" as in Gen. 30:37; Ezra. 31:8; Isa. 32:11; Chab. 2:15. The Talmud uses *arom*=prudence, cunning, in several references, but commentators have sometimes punned with additional meaning by interpreting *a'r'm* as *arum*=stripped; e.g., *Sot.* 21b (see Rashi); *Ber.* 17a; *Shab.* 14a; *Meg.* 32a; *Sofrim* 3:16; *Chul.* 5b; *Niddah* 45b; *TDE* 13.

I would explicate the Hebrew term for legal fiction or artifact—*ha'aramah*—by reference to the double meaning of the root *a'r'm*. Jewish law regards *ha'aramah* in practice as legally valid, within limits. In legal fiction, all parties are fully aware if the artificial nature of the *ha'aramah*; there is complete exposure of the fact that there is no substance to the act but rather the fulfillment of formality so that the stringency of the law can be avoided. *Ha'aramah* is thus a *deus ex machina* of all the participants' imaginations—it involves the capacity to be *arom*. However, when an intended *ha'aramah* is too blatant, it becomes *mirmah*, simple deceit. In the latter case, the design of *ha'aramah* has become *arum*, exposed (see also *Rambam, Peirush ha-Mishnayoth: Temurah* 5:1; *Resp. Chatham Sofer: O.H.*, no. 113).
23. A.J. Beldstein, "The Genesis of Humans: The Garden of Eden Revisited," *Judaism* (1977): 26(2), p. 197.

24. C. D. Rabinowitz, *Da'ath Sofrim* (Jerusalem: 1953) to Gen. 3:7.
25. O. Fenichel, *The Psychoanalytic Theory of Neurosis* (New York: W.W. Norton, 1945), p. 281.
26. *Sot.* 11a to Gen. 3:21; see *Niddah* 25a, *Tos.*, s.v., *she-eyn.*
27. Gen. R. 20:12.
28. *Torah Temimah* to Gen. 3:21, citing 2 Kings 4:39; Isa. 26:19.
29. Mayman, "The Shame Experience," 1977; D. Ausubel, "Relation Between Shame and Guilt and the Socialization Process," *Psychological Review* (1955): 62, pp. 378-90, stresses that while shame and guilt are distinguishable, they are not dichotomous or mutually exclusive phenomena. This is true, yet shame stands as unique (a) as the precursor to guilt, (b) as an affect whose origins are in reaction-formation, and (c) in the intense experience of "the other" in whose perceived or actual presence one feels ashamed.
30. Lewis, *Shame and Guilt in Neurosis*, 1971; T. French, "Guilt, Shame and Other Reactive Motives," in his *Selected Papers of Thomas French* (Chicago: Quadrangle, 1970), pp. 258-68; S. Hammerman, "Conceptions of Superego Development," *Journal of the American Psychoanalytic Association* (1965): 13, 320-55.
31. Reference to an early form of internalization, where the individual introjects a regulatory experience but has not fully depersonified it, is seen in the midrashic account of Joseph's struggles to resist the temptation of Potiphar's wife, "Why did Joseph refrain? He saw before himself *the image of his father*, Jacob (*demut de'yukono* [root=*icon*] *shel aviv*)," *PDE 39*; *Tanchumah Vayeshev 9; Sot.* 36b; see also *B.B.* 58a; *Chul.* 91b.
32. S. Freud, *Civilization and Its Discontents* (New York: Norton, 1960/1933), p. 72 and also see C. Malmquist, "Conscience Development," *Psychoanalytic Study of the Child* (1968): vol. 23, pp. 301-31.
33. *Shab.* 64a; *Meg.* 20a.
34. Gen. 3:13; Gen. R. 19:22.
35. *Pri Tzadik* to Gen. 3:13.
36. T. Dobzhansky, *Mankind Evolving: The Evolution of the Human Species* (New Haven: Yale University Press, 1962).
37. E. Becker, *The Denial of Death* (New York: Free Press, 1973), pp. 50-51; see also I. Progoff, *The Death and Rebirth of Psychology* (New York: Julian Press, 1956).
38. "The Lonely Man of Faith," *Tradition* (1965): 7(2), p. 25.
39. As Searles shows, even the schizophrenic cannot completely escape this ultimate anxiety, "Schizophrenia and the Inevitability of Death," *Psychiatric Quarterly* (1961): 35, pp. 631-65.
40. Rashi to Gen. 3:6; Gen. R. 19:8, 20:19.
41. Zohar Gen. 35; *B.B.* 16a; Malbim to Gen. 3:19; Abravanel to Gen. 3; even Cassuto (to Gen. 3) adopts this approach.
42. *Da'ath Sofrim* to Gen. 3:7. Freud also traces the beginning of sexual life and cultural development to the moment of the unmasking of shame during childhood, and notes our return to this realm in the fantasy of Paradise, in *The Interpretation of Dreams* (1965/1900), pp. 278-79.
43. See R. Kaufman and Z.E. Klein, "The *Akedah*: A Contribution to the Theory

of Oedipal Object-Relations," Unpublished Paper, University of Chicago, 1980.

44. The midrash notes that Reuven was the first to initiate repentance (Gen. R. 82:12; Gen. R. 84:18; Num. R. 13:17). However, the Talmud and midrash record that Terach, Ishmael, and Esau effected repentance before their deaths (*B.B.* 16b; see Rashi to Gen. 6:14, 15:15, 25:9). Judah, too, performed public penitance (*Sot.* 7b). However, the midrash also states that Adam effected *t*^e^*shuvah* after encountering Cain and learning that he, too, had done *t*^e^*shuvah* and it had been accepted by God (Gen. R: 22:28[12]; Lev. R. 10:5). This apparent discrepancy is resolved by noting that Adam and Cain offered repentance after they had been punished while Reuven offered his repentance prior to punishment ("*Reuven pasach be-t*^e^*shuvah* . . .").

45. *Judaism and Psychology*, 1980, pp. 82-98.

46. *M.T. Hil. T*^e^*shuvah* 1:1.

47. *M.T. Hil. T*^e^*shuvah* 7:8.

48. *Ber.* 12b; *Ned.* 20a.

Concluding Note

In the preceding chapters, I have discussed numerous practical applications of halakhic ethics to different aspects of psychotherapeutic procedure with the Jewish patient, to specific professional responsibilities and to some of the wider philosophical perspectives of emotional and behavioral modification. I think these various analyses have remained true to our original goal: the evolution of practical responses to key halakhico-ethical dilemmas inherent in psychotherapeutic values and interventive methodology. The product in most cases has been a perspective or a modified procedure which highlights the uniquely halakhic approach, rendering such perspectives and procedures at once halakhic as well as psychologic.

I have found no need to supplant contemporary technique with a so-called Torah psychology or some simplistic, homeopathic model. Instead, these chapters have demonstrated, amply I think, that the halakhic values of and goals for inter- and intrapersonal adjustment can be best achieved through the employment of modern interventive principles in the single manner available to the halakhically-committed practitioner: to organize, integrate, and practice his scientifically validated profession in accordance with halakhic models. Where such models have been implicit rather than explicit, I have endeavored to exposit models which are consistent with halakhic values and which are useful for the mental health practitioner. In this manner we have realized a second goal which is to synthesize psychological and halakhic values and practice, rather than to bifurcate the two or to suggest an approach which unnaturally counterposes halakhic values to psychological values.

Some of the issues that we have discussed in this *Handbook* merit further and continuous study. Any halakhic analysis of psychosurgery or electrical stimulation of the brain, for example, will need to be updated in consonance with the anticipated advances in these techniques, and the quality of their outcomes. At the same time, novel ideological approaches to human nature which evolve from such technical advancements will also need to be subjected to halakhic examination. The establishment and validation of norms for intelligence and projective testing of the Orthodox Jewish population—a subject I have only tangentially mentioned here—should be considered a worthwhile topic for investigation in that such norms will help the psychologist to place his patients' idiosyncratic responses within a proper subcultural perspective (although such norms cannot seriously be expected to supplant the value of placing the Jewish patient against the greater context of standarized national norms).

Finally, clinical psychotherapeutic techniques for treating and counselling particular types of religious Jewish patients, be they chasidic, *ba'alei t^eshuvah*, reactively anti-religious, or otherwise, must become a subject of ongoing investigation *and reporting* so as to improve the possibility of maintaining constructive therapeutic alliances between religious patients and therapists. The commonplace notion that such skill will evolve spontaneously with continued experience—or worse, that such recalibration is unnecessary—throws the development of our professional identity and practice at the mercy of chance, and, indeed, bespeaks an unjustifiable willingness to subject our clients to the professional's own confusion and lack of direction. Lack of leadership in psychotherapy will eventually force the practitioner into taking an authoritarian, dogmatic stand should he try to arbitrarily flatten or ignore the uniqueness of work with such patients or to deny his own negative reactions to unremitting patients and communal mistrust and therapeutic failure.

Of course, the professional community has no reason to allow its practices to be influenced or modified by the fears and manipulations of the wider Jewish community, or to be cajoled into offering a watered-down, ideologically-tinged form of didactic counselling which deceptively caters to the misconceptions of the population at risk. At the same time, the consumers' fears can be substantially reduced if not eliminated if the professional continues willingly to submit his values and ethics to halakhic scrutiny, and to accept the limitations and obligations imposed by halakhic ethics. The professional will be rewarded for such willingness and humility by finding that Halakhah condones his endeavors and, in fact, obligates him to maintain an incorruptible and unmanipulative stance with regard to those who wish to obtain his services.

Appendix I

Catalogue of Sources in Hebrew Scripture and Rabbinic Literature Relating to Mental Incompetence and Psychological Disorder

Note: I have made no attempt to annotate these sources since they vary so widely in their applications and definitions, and since I have appealed to or discussed many of these sources in a variety of ways in the different chapters contained in my texts. I have formulated this catalogue primarily as a handy reference to the literature, whose use will be determined by the reader.

I. Biblical

Peti (simpleton)
Prov. 1:4, 22,32
7:7
8:5
9:4, 6, 13, 25
14:15, 18
19:25
21:11
22:3
27:12
Ps. 19:8
116:6
119:130
Ez. 45:20

Tipesh (fool, simpleton)
Ps. 119:70

Ba'ar (ignoramus)
Prov. 12:1
30:2
Ps. 94:8
49:11
92:7
Ez. 21:36
Jer. 10:8, 14, 21
51:17
Isa. 19:11

Mithcholel (madman); *Cholelut*
1 Sam. 21:14
Eccl. 1:17
2:12
9:3
7:7,25
10:13
Job 12:17
Prov. 26:18 (*mitlahleah*)

Timhon (emotional disquietude)
Gen. 43:33
Deut. 28:28 (see Abravanel)
Zekh. 12:4
Job 26:11
Ps. 48:6
Chab. 1:5
Eccl. 5:7
Jer. 4:9

Meshugah, Shigaon (madness)
Deut. 28:28, 34
1 Sam. 21:15, 16
2 Kings 9:11, 20
Zekh. 12:4
Hos. 9:7
Jer. 29:26

Ruach ra'ah ("evil" spirit; melancholy)
Judg. 9:23
1 Kings 22:21 ff.
1 Sam. 16:14, 15, 16, 23
18:10
19:9

Ruach iv'im (vertigo)
Isa. 19:14

Kesil, Sakhal (foolishness)
Jer. 5:21
4:22
Eccl. 1:17
2:3, 12, 13, 14, 19
7:17, 25
10:3, 13 (see Rashi), 14
4:5, 13, 17
2:15, 16
5:2, 3
6:8
7:6, 4, 5 9
10:2, 12
Ps. 49:11
92:7
94:8
Prov. 1:22, 32
3:35
8:5
9:13
10:1, 18, 23
12:23
13:16, 19, 20
14:7, 16, 8, 24, 33
15:2, 7, 14, 20
17:10, 12, 16, 21, 24, 25
18:2, 6, 7
19:1, 13, 10, 29
21:20
23:9

II. Midrash, Mishnah, and Talmud

Nikhpeh ("falling sickness," epilepsy)
ARN 11:1
Pes. 112b
Ket. 60b
Git. 70a
Yev. 64b
Bekh. ff. 44b (5:4)
Lev. R. 16:1; 26:5
Kalah R. 1

Ruach ra'ah
Shab. 29b; 108b-109a
Eruv. 41b; 93b
Pes. 112a

Kordiakos
Yoma 83a
Eruv. 4:1
Git. 67b; 70b

Shoteh, Shtuth
Tosefta Ter. 1:1; 10:18
Tosefta Ket. 1:3
Parah 5:4
Sofrim 1:12
Chag. 1:1; 3b
Meg. 2:4
Zev. 2:1
B.M. 12a
B. K. 4:4; 8:4
R. H. 8:8
Kid. 31b; 42b
Men. 9:8; 93a
Bek. 7:6; 45b
Git. 2:5-6
J.T. Git. 7:1
23 a-b
51b
59b
64b
67b

Niddah 2:1
3a
13b
Sot. 4:1, 5
Arkh. 1:1
2a
3a
5b
Makhsh. 3:8; 6:1
Chul. 1:1
2a-b
3a
12b
13a
31a-b
86a
J. T. Ter. 1:1; 10:10
Yev. 4:6
39a
59a
72b
96b
99b
112b
113a
116b
Shab. 128b, 153a
Taan. 19a (see *RaN*); 22b
Toh. 3:6; 5:8
Ned. 81a
Shev. 38b
Eruv. 31b
Yadaim 1:5
Ket. 18a
60b
72a
Yoma 43a
Meilah 21a
Sanh. 25b

III. Codes and Commentaries

Abravanel to Deut. 28:28
Rashi to Eruv. 4:1
Peirush ha-Mishnayoth to Yoma 8:6, Git. 7; Shab. 29b
Chiddushei Maharatz Chiyos to Yev. 62
Beth Shmuel to Sh. A., E.H. 121:1
Beth Yosef to Tur. Sh. A., E.H. 119; *Sh. A., Y.D.* 228
Rama to Sh. A., E.H. 119:5, 154:5
Ba'er Hetev to Sh. A., E.H. 119:11
P'rishah to Tur Sh. A., H.M. 35; Sh. A., Y.D. 1
Pithchei T'shuvah to Sh. A., E.H. 121:2, 178:3
D'rishah and *TaZ* to Sh. A., Y.D. 240:10
TaZ to Y.D. 84, no. 24
Sefer Me'irot Eynayim to Sh. A., H.M. 35
Tur Sh. A., O.H. 55:8, 330
Sh. A., H.M. 1, 35, 96, 424:8
Y.D. 179:6
O.H. 266:3-4
288:10
328:35
339:4
475:5
554 (*Magen Avraham*, no. 8)
571:3

576:13
589:2
617:2-3
640:4

Sh. A. ha-Rav, Y.D. 1
Arukh ha-Shulchan: O.H. 278:1, 288:17; E.H. 121; Y.D. 84:96
Isur ve-Heter ha-Arukh, no. 59:35
M.T., Hil. Shab. 2:11
Hil. A.Z. 11:11
Hil. Eduth 9:9-10
Hil. Gerushin 2:14, 17
Hil. Mekhirah 29:4
Hil. Shilukhin 2
Hil. Shechitah 2
Hil. Chametz 6:3
Hil. Sanh. 18:6
Hil. Zekhiya 8:2
Hil. Mamrim 6:10

IV. Responsa

Resp. Shivat Tziyon, no. 4.
Levushei Mordekhai: H.M., no. 39, vol. 4, no. 68.
Resp. Netzer Mata'ai, no. 8.
Atereth Chakhamim: E.H., nos. 17,18.
Resp. Tashbatz, vol. 1, no. 54.
Resp. Radbaz, vol. 4, no. 66.
Resp. Shem Aryeh, no. 1.
Resp. Tifereth Yosef, no. 27.
Resp. Minchath Moshe, no. 1.
Resp. Tzitz Eliezer, vol. 4, no. 13; vol. 6, no. 42; vol. 8, no. 15 (13); vol. 9, no. 17; vol. 10, no. 25(19):1; vol. 12, no. 18(8), no. 59; vol. 13, no. 35.
Resp. Minchath Yitzchak, vol. 1, no. 115; vol. 3, nos. 3, 25, 26; vol. 4, no. 8(2-12), vol. 6, no. 144.
Resp. Chelkath Yaakov, vol. 1, no. 72.
Resp. Pri ha-Aretz: Y.D., vol. 3, no. 2.
Admath Kodesh, vol. 1, no. 6.
Resp. Igroth Moshe: O.H., vol. 1, no. 127, 132; vol. 3, no. 53; *E. H.*, vol. 1, nos. 65, 73, 80, 120; *Y.D.*, vol. 2, nos. 57, 59; vol. 3, no. 44; *E.H.*, vol. 4, nos. 36, 69, 74(3), 82, 97.
Resp. Chatham Sofer: O.H., no. 83; *E.H.*, vol. 2, nos. 2-4, 150; *Y.D.*, no. 7.
Or Yesharim, no. 14.
Resp. Maharit, vol. 2, no. 16.
Resp. Maharik, no. 19.
Resp. Noda be-Yehudah (M. T.): E.H., no. 147.

Seridei Esh, vol. 3 nos. 1, 2, 35; vol. 4, no. 148.
Resp. Mabit, vol. 2, no. 20.
Resp. Maharil, no. 196.
Resp. Havalim ba-Ne'imim, vol. 4, no. 13.
Resp. Divrei Chayim: E.H., vol. 1, nos. 52-53; nos. 74, 77.
Resp. Maharsham, vol. 1, no. 21; vol. 4, nos. 43, 54; vol. 7, no. 164; and *Da'ath Torah*, vol. 1:40.
Resp. Tevuout Shor, vol. 1, no. 49.
Get Pashut, no. 121:12
Torath Gittin, no. 5.
Resp. Rosh Mashbir, vol. 2, no. 69.
Resp. Ba'er Sheva, vol. 1, nos. 46, 51.
Resp. Moharim, 30.
Resp. Tzamakh Tzedek: E. H., nos. 2, 3, 153; *Y.D.*, no. 8.
Magid Ta'alumoth, vol. 4, no. 93.
Machazik Berakhah, no. 1 (15).
Resp. Mayim Chayim: E.H., no. 40.
Sedei Chemed, vol. 5, pp. 107-30; vol. 4, pp. 522-27.
Gesher ha-Chayim, vol.1, chap. 15.
Resp. Or Yisroel, nos. 1-36.
Resp. Rivash, no. 468.
Resp. Rashba, vol. 1, no. 765.
Resp. BaCH, nos. 20, 93.
Resp. Petach ha-D'vir, vol. 3, no. 343.
Resp. Rosh, no. 3 (43), no. 42.
Resp. Nefesh Chayah: E.H., no. 27.
Resp. Beth Shmuel Aaron, no. 9.
Resp. R. Yitzchak Brisk, no. 30.
Resp. Shoel u-Meishiv: M.K., vol. 1, nos. 118, 122; vol. 2, no. 180; vol. 3, no. 108; *M.Tin.*, vol. 3, no. 68; vol. 4, no. 87; *M. Tilt.*, vol. 1, no. 138.
Resp. Beth Meir: E.H., no. 121, 151.
Resp. Beth Efraim: E.H., vol. 1, nos. 89, 111.
Resp. Or Zaru'ah, vol. 1, no. 778.
Atzei Levonah, vol. 2 (*Nimukim al E. H.*), no. 119.
Resp. Noda ba-She'arim, Hil. Git., no. 121.
Resp. Devar Moshe, no. 39.
Resp. Chesed Avraham, no. 4.
Amudei Esh, nos. 4, 20.
Resp. Emek She'elah: E.H., nos. 2, 76-80.
Resp. Makom Shmuel, no. 25.
Resp. R. Akiva Eger, no. 218.
Resp. Beth Yitzchak (Shmekles): *E.H.*, no. 6; vol. 2, no. 4.
Resp. Yehudah Ya'aleh, no. 93.
Resp. Sefer Yehoshua: E.H., no. 71.
Resp. Kav Zahav, no. 14.
Resp. She'erit Yosef, no. 53.
Resp. Or Sameach, p. 163.

Ba'er Moshe, no. 18.
Resp. *Divrei Ta'am*, nos. 37, 43.
Resp. *Meishiv Davar: E.H.*, no. 46.
Resp. *Oneg Yom Tov*, nos. 143, 153.
Resp. *Torath Chesed: E.H.*, vol. 2, no. 23.
Resp. *Yad Yitzchak*, vol. 1, nos. 238, 239, 240.
Resp. *Maharsham*, vol. 7, no. 164.
Resp. *R. Yecheskel Abramski*, no. 2 (*Iyar*).
Resp. *Chelkath Yoav: E.H.*, no. 20.
Resp. *Ohel Moshe*, no. 2.
Resp. *Chazakah Rabbah: H.M.*, vol. 1, no. 3.
Resp. *Me'orot Nathan*, no. 102.
Resp. *Yabia Omer*, vol. 5: *Y.D.*, no. 22.
Resp. *Ish Matzliach: E. H.*, no. 17.
Resp. *Divrei Yosef*, no. 14.
Resp. *Zekher Yitzchak*, no. 23.
Resp. *Yad Eliyahu: P'sakim*, no. 90.
Resp. *Yad Yitzchak*, vol. 1, no. 238.
Yeshu'ot Malko, no. 77.
Resp. *Maharim mi-Padua*, no. 36.
Resp. *Maharash Moholover: E.H.*, no. 10.
Resp. *Maharash Engel*, vol. 1, no. 32.
Resp. *Olot Yitzchak*, vol. 2, no. 10.
Resp. *Ezrat Cohen* (Kuk): nos. 67, 68.
Resp. *Sadeh Yehoshua*, no. 49.
Resp. *Zikhron Yosef*, no. 6.
Resp. *R. Yaakov Veil*, no. 52.
Resp. *Givat Shaul*, no. 40.
Resp. *Yaskil Avdi*, vol. 7, *O.H.*, no. 22.
Sefer Chemdath ha-Nefesh, no. 1.
Chavalim ba-Ne'imim, vol. 4, no. 13.
Resp. *mi-Ma'amakim*, vol. 1, p. 45.

V. Articles and Texts

R. Aaron Simon b. Jacob, *Or ha-Yashar* (Amsterdam: 1769).
Amsel, A. *Judaism and Psychology* (New York:1969).
Appelbaum, D., "Mental Competence in Halacha," *Koleynu, 6* (1973): 48-57.
Bak, B., "*Holey ha-Ruach be-Dinei Gittin ve-Ishuth*," *Noam, 16* (1973): 161-179.
Bar-Zev, A., "Aberrant Behavior in Jewish Tradition," *J. Psychol. & Judaism, 1*, no. 1 (1976): 67-76.
Bleich, J. D., "Mental Incompetence and Its Implications in Jewish Law," *J. Halacha & Contemporary Society, 1*, no. 2 (1981): 123-143.
Bulka, R. P., "Rabbinic Attitude Toward Suicide," *Midstream, 25*.
Feinstein, M., "*Ha-Chiluk bein Shoteh le-Peti ve-Chiyuvei Mitzvoth ve-Talmud Torah l[e]-Peti*," *Am ha-Torah, 2*, no. 2 (1982): 10-12.

Gordon, H.L., "*Mi she-Achzo Kordiakos' be -Talmud u'be-Madah ha-Refui,*" *Perakim, 3* (1963): 117-130.
Gorlin, M., "Mental Illness in Biblical Literature," *Proc. Assoc. Orth. Jewish Sci. 2* (1970): 43-62.
Granek, M., "The Madman Concept and its Implications in the Talmudic Literature and its Exegesis," *Annales Medico-psychologiques 1*, no. 1 (1976): 17-36.
Gruber, M., "The Tragedy of Cain and Abel: A Case of Depression," *Jew. Quart. Rev., 64*, no. 2 (1978): 89-97.
Hankoff, L., "Ancient Descriptions of Organic Brain Syndrome: the 'Kordiakos' of the Talmud," *Am. J. Psychiatr., 129*, no. 2 (1972): 147-150.
Henkin, Y.Y. "*Nokhachath ha-Ba'al be-Heder ha-Ledah,*" *Assia, 5*, no. 3 (1978): 44-52.
Jakobovits, I., "*Tzar shel Adam be-Dinei Yisroel,*" in N. Lamm, M. Kasher, & L. Rosenfeld, eds., *Leo Jung Jubilee Volume* (New York: 1962), pp. 133-43.
Landau, Y.B., "*Diyun be-Peratiyot be-Sugey Choli ha-Ruach ve-ha-Nirpa'in be-ha-Metza'ut Terufah ha-Chaddashah. Dinam le-Gabey Gerushin u-le-She'ar Halakhoth,*" in M. Amsel, ed., *Sefer She'eloth u-T^{e}shuvoth ha-Ma'or* (New York: 1966), pp. 377-85.
Levin, A.D., "*Machaloth ha-Shoteh ve'ha-Shtuth be-Halakhah,*" *Halakhah ve-Refuah, 4* (1985): 203-209.
Preuss, J., *Biblical and Talmudic Medicine*, F. Rosner, Trans., (New York: 1978), chaps. 10, 11—pp. 299-321.
Preuss, J., "Mental Disorders in the Bible," F. Rosner, Trans., *Isra. Annal. Psychiatr. & Rel. Disc. 13*, no. 3 (1975): 221-238.
Rosner, F., "*Kordiakos* in the Talmud," *Isra. J. Med. Sci., 10* (1974): 278-281.
Rosner, F., "Suicide in Biblical, Talmudic and Rabbinic Writings," In F. Rosner, *Modern Medicine and Jewish Law* (New York: 1972), pp. 177-93.
Rotenberg, M. & Diamond, B. L., "The Biblical Conception of Psychopathy: The Law of the Stubborn and Rebellious Son," *J. Hist. Behav. Sci., 7* (1971): 29-38.
Rothkoff, A, "The Divorce in Cleves, 1766," *Gesher 4*, no. 1 (1969): 147-169.
Shapiro, D. S., "*Choleh be-Machalath ha-Ruach Im Yachol le-Garesh,*" *Ha-Darom 1*, no. 1 (1957): 41-50.
Spero, M. H., *Judaism and Psychology: Halakhic Perspectives* (New York: 1980), chaps. 4, 11, 12.
Tal, S. "*Ha-Get mi-Kleve,*" *Sinai 12* (1949): 152-167; 214-230.
Unterman, I. Y., "*Mitzvath Pikuach Nefesh u-Gedarehah,*" *ha-Torah ve-ha-Medinah, 4* (1952): 22-29.
Wikler, M., "The Torah View of Mental Illness: Sin or Sickness?" *J. Jewish Comm. Serv., 53*, no. 4 (1977): 339-344.
Wollstein, S. "The Attitude of the Ancient Jewish Sources to Mental Patients," *Isra. Annal. Psychiatr. & Rel. Disc. 2* (1964): 103-116.

VI. Psychological Pain in Infants and Children

Gen. 44:22, see *Sforno*, s.v. *lo yukhal.*
Ex. 1:15, see Rashi, s.v. *pu'ah.*
Ex. R. 1:1.
Prov. 19:18-19, see *Peirush ha-Gra.*
B.B. 20a, "*be-kalanita . . .*," and see *Meiri*, "*ve-ken she-hu me'saret . . .*"
B.B. 21a, "*ke-she'atah malkeh et ha-tinok . . .*"
B.M. 92b, *Tos.*, s.v. *lo.*
Yoma 78b, Rashi, s.v. *tiburei ma'anei.*
Yoma 84b, "*ra'ah she-ninalah . . .*"
Pes. 112b, "*ha-meshamesh mitasa . .*," see also Tur. Sh. A., O.H. 240:16, E.H., 25.
M.K. 17a, "*be-makeh beno ha-gadol . . .*," see also *Chiddushei Ritva*; Semachoth 2:6; M.T. Hil. Mamrim 6:8-9.
M.K. 14a, Rashi, s.v. *katan*, also see Sh. A., O.H. 531:6.
Ket. 8a; *Ritva; SHaKH* to Sh.A., Y.D. 265, no. 24; cf. *Mordekhai* to Shab. 19:422.
Ket. 57b.
Ket. 59b-60a, and see *Tosefoth RiD*, "*she-af al pi she-hu yonek . . .*",
Shab. 10b, "*le-olam al yeshanah . . .*"; 58b, "*hani mili tinok . . .*"; 66b, "*ha-banim yotz'eim . . .*," and see *Peirush ha-Mishnayoth*; 94a, "*ha-ishah madedah et banah . . .*"; 129b, *Tos.*, s.v. *kol*; 141b, Rashi, s.v. *be-tinok*, *Tos.*, s.v. *ve-nishdeneihu* (142a), *Meiri*, s.v. *ve-hayah etzlam nachash. . . .*
J. T. Mak. 4:4, "*Amar R. Yitzchak . . .*"
Sh. A., O.H. 309:1, 330:7, 550:1 (*Magen Avraham*)
Sh. A., Y.D. 240:20 (*Rama*), see also *Chiddushei R. Akiva Eger*, 262:2, 263:4, 345:3.
Tur H.M. 282:2.
Sefer Chasidim, nos. 231, 235 ("*mi she-yesh lo ben . . .*"), 919 ("*yeled katan . . .*").
Sh. A. ha-Rav.: O.H., 328:15 to *Yoma* 84b.
Sh. A. ha-Rav *Hil. Shmirath ha-Guf ve-ha-Nefesh*, 12: see also Kitzur Sh. A., 33:13.

Appendix II

Cognitive/Emotional Presentations and Halakhah: A Typologic Index in re Mental Incompetence

The following is a typologic index of possible psychiatric presentations, analyzed from the perspective of various halakhic definitions of *shtuth* (mental incapacity or incompetence).* The purpose of this index is not to suggest definitive rulings (*halakhah le-ma'aseh*), but rather to coordinate, in an organized format, various presentations of intellectual and affective disorder with some of the important interpretations and rulings that address the respective presentations. I have chosen to not simply list nosologic categories (e.g., *kordiakos, teiruf da'ath*, organic brain syndrome, psychosis, etc.) since, in the course of the various halakhic examinations of these entities, it has proven necessary to break down these entities into their component cognitive and affective qualities or "symptoms." However, I have included some of the opinions of halakhic codifiers and decisors who have attempted to identify certain nosologic categories or states with the category of *shtuth*.

I have offered generally complete text citations for the codes and responsa referred to, but in the case of longer essays, I have merely referred to the author's last name. These can then be located in Appendix I (*Catalogue*).

Finally, the reader will keep in mind that the essential discussion of *shtuth* is in the Talmud *Chagigah* 3b-4a and the Jerusalem Talmud *Terumoth* 1:1. Six important issues, not fully resolved in the talmudic discourses themselves, pertain to every ruling concerning the definition of *shtuth*:

(1) Are the 3 symptoms or characteristics in *Chag.* 3b-4a satisfactory for the determination of *shtuth*, or does one also

---

*The Soncino editor's translation of *shoteh* as "imbecile" seems misleading, and is probably a correct definition of the *pethi*, rather than the *shoteh*.

need evidence of the fourth symptom cited in the *Tosefta* and *J. T.*?*

(2) Whether the 3 or 4 symptoms categorize the *shoteh*, does one need evidence of all 3(4)—the view of R. Huna—or merely any single one of the 3(4) if exhibited in a "*shtuth*-like" manner—the view of R. Yochanan, according to most interpretations?

(3) Is it satisfactory to observe a single instance of all 3(4) symptoms, or does one need 3 demonstrations of all 3(4), or 3 demonstrations of any single symptom produced in a *shtuth*-like manner?

(4) Whether one holds that *shtuth* is demonstrated through the exhibition of all 3(4) or any single of these symptoms, and whether or not one requires a single incident of such behavior or 3 instances of such behavior—may *other* characteristics of mental disorder not specifically mentioned in the Talmud be considered for these purposes?

(5) Does the establishment of the status of *shtuth* render the individual a *shoteh* across all religio-legal applications, or are there different criteria for establishing *shtuth* in the applications of testimony (*eduth*), divorce, other *mitzvah* obligations, and so forth?

(6) Can a duly classified *shoteh* who demonstrates mental competence in some limited cognitive function retain legal competency or efficacy in acts which are dependent upon the competent function?

I have not attempted here to analyze each of these issues, but they are implicit in most of the halakhic examinations cited.

---

*__Chagigah__ lists: walks alone at night, sleeps in cemeteries, and tears his garments; __Terumoth__ adds: one who destroys all that is entrusted to him. R. Channanel rules that we follow R. Yochanan, accepting any single symptom, performed in a *shtuth*-like manner, as indicative of the state of *shtuth*.

Presentation	*Opinions in the Literature*
A. No evidence in either verbal or overt behavior of a bizarre mental state, and no evidence of impaired reality-testing, but there is behavioral demonstration of all 3(4) symptoms noted in the Talmud, 3 times each, in a *shtuth*-like manner:	*A. Rambam* according to Shapiro (1957): Such *shtuth* suggests insanity in all applications, even if competence is demonstrated. *Tos.*, s.v. *ve-ha, Yev.* 104b according to Shapiro (1957): not necessarily a *shoteh* in all applications, but may be considered "*da'ath kalishta*" in all applications. Rogotzover, *Or Yeshorim*, no. 14: when *shtuth* is determined through these 3 symptoms, incompetence extends to all areas, except *shlichut, shechitah*, and the act of writing a writ of divorce (with a competent *omed al gabav*). According to the following, as long as *shtuth* is determined via acts and through verbalizations, the 3 symptoms of the Talmud render one incompetent in all areas: *Resp. Chatham Sofer: E. H.*, vol. 2, no. 2; *Resp. Eyn Yitzchak*, no. 9; *Resp. Tzamach Tzedek*, nos. 153, 155 (cf. *Resp. Beth Efraim: E. H.*, no. 89); *Beth Meir*, 121; *Resp. Mayim Chayim*, no. 40; *Torath Gitten* 121. *Resp. Igroth Moshe: E.H.*, vol. 1, no. 120: such an individual would be deemed incompetent in most areas, but could prove competence through rabbinic examination. This possibility would not apply to matters of testimony (*eduth*).
B. No evidence in either verbal or overt behavior of a bizarre mental state, and no evidence of impaired reality-testing, but there is the demonstration of a *single* of the 3(4) symptoms, in a *shtuth*-like manner:	B. *Arukh ha-Shulchan: E.H.* 121 without all 3(4), *shtuth* is not established, unless with any specific symptom there is also recognizable lack of mental clarity. Meiri; *Rambam* according to Shapiro: not a *shoteh*, unless there was demonstration of a single symptom in *verbal* behavior, three times. *Resp. Rashba*, no. 768: not a *shoteh*

Presentation	*Opinions in the Literature*
(*B. continued*)	unless there is *shtuth be-diburo*. Meiri: even without evidence in verbal behavior, evidence of the single symptom of "destroys all that is entrusted to him" renders one *be-cheskat shoteh* in all matters. *Resp. Igroth Moshe: E.H.*: one would be considered a *shoteh* only with regard to the specific symptom and the aspects of personality and cognition affected, except in matters of *eduth*. *Rosh* (*Chulin*): *shoteh*. R. Channanel (*Chag.*): holds like Meiri, except other 2(3) symptoms would require demonstration in unison. *Resp. Eyn Yitzchak; Resp. Shoel u-Meishiv: Tinyana*, no. 87: one symptom renders one a *shoteh*, and in all areas. *Or Yesharim*, no. 14; *Maharit: E.H.*, no. 16: a single symptom may establish *shtuth*, but not in every application. By *gitten* and *kiddushin*, even *Rambam* admits one needs all 3(4) symptoms to establish *shtuth*. *Torath Gitten* 121: any single symptom may establish *shtuth*, and despite demonstration of *pikchuth*. R. Simchah, R. Avigdor ha-Cohen, *Rashba*, no. 768, *Resp. Rivash*, no. 468, *Maharik*: one symptom is insufficient to establish *shtuth*, but if one can establish *teiruf da'ath* in the capacities involved (where the symptom of *shtuth* was demonstrated), then one's acts have qualified legal status and efficacy. See also *Resp. Seridei Esh*, vol. 3, no. 35 (this responsum by R. Eliezer Berkowitz bears the approbation of his master, R. Weinberg). Bak (1973), citing *Resp. Sha'agat Aryeh* in the second responsum published in

Presentation	*Opinions in the Literature*
(*B. continued*)	*Or ha-Yashar*: any bizarre behavior or verbalization not mentioned in the Talmud may render one a *shoteh* as long as it is demonstrated in a *shtuth*-like manner, and cannot be rationalized as due to any other cause ("*imur* . . .").
C. No evidence of any of the 3(4) symptoms noted in the Talmud, but there is evidence of *other* bizarre behaviors, demonstrated at least 3 times:	*C. Or Yesharim*, no. 14: *Beth Din* may establish *shtuth* in this manner, but such "incompetence" would not necessarily extend to all areas. *Chatham Sofer: E.H.*, vol. 2, no. 2: we would accept alternate symptoms regarding competence for *eduth*; or generally, if there was also some verbal demonstration of insanity. *Maharit, Or Yesharim*: the *pethi, muvhal*, and *nichpaz* mentioned in *Hil. Eduth* 9:10 are only incompetent in matters of testimony *even* if they suggest competence through examination. But these are not necessarily *shotim* in other applications. On the other hand, *Rambam*'s statement in *Hil. Eduth* 9:9 regarding "*kol mi she-nitrefah da'ato . . . meshubeshet tamid* . . .," even though this category includes "other" pervasive symptoms of *shtuth*, may in fact be incompetent in all applications. *Resp. Maharik: E.H.*, no. 19: "other" behaviors can establish *shtuth*, if demonstrated 3 times, even according to R. Simchah and R. Avigdor ha-Cohen. R. Avraham Abush, cited in *Or Yesharim*, no. 27: "other" behaviors can establish *shtuth*, and such *shtuth* would extend to all applications.
D. Evidence of bizarre or "other" insane behavior is limited to verbalizations:	*D. Rashba*, according to Landau (1966), p. 379: even one such symptom would establish *shtuth*. Shapiro: *shoteh*. *Maharsham, Da'ath Torah* 1:40: *shoteh*.

Presentation	*Opinions in the Literature*
(*D. continued*)	*Chatham Sofer: E.H.*, vol. 2, no. 1: when *shtuth* is demonstrated verbally, it extends to all applications unless one discerns some evidence of *tzilul da'ath* (*ChS* does not extend this leniency when *shtuth* has been determined via *ma'aseh* alone).
E. Shtuth has been demonstrated in some areas of behavior and/or verbal behavior, but *pikchuth* has also been established contemporaneously in some areas:	*E. Resp. Igroth Moshe*: remains incompetent in matters of divorce, etc. Rogezover: if *shtuth* has been established via the 3(4) symptoms of the Talmud, *shtuth* cannot be qualified in matters of *din* (divorce) but could be in matters of *kinyan* (*shilchut*, with an *omed al gabov*). *Shtuth* determined by *Beth Din* through "other" symptoms may be qualified. *Torath Gitten* 121: *shtuth* is always extensive and without qualifiability. The individual who is termed in halakhic literature as "sometimes sick and sometimes healthy"—who *may* be deemed competent during his periods of relative health—is sick, *but not insane. Shtuth* casts its shadow even on episodic periods of mental clarity. *Chatham Sofer: pikchuth* demonstrated avails when *shtuth* has been determined through verbal rather than physical behavior. *Resp. Tevuot Shor* 1:57: *pikchuth* can qualify *shtuth* in most applications.
F. No evidence of the 3(4) symptoms, and there appears to be demonstrable reality-testing, etc., but there are episodes of delusion and / or hallucinations:	*F. Resp. Igroth Moshe: E.H.*, no. 120: "foolish thoughts" do not define *shtuth* unless there is also impaired reality-testing (or there are never indications of *pikchuth* in other cognitive areas). Shapiro, citing *M.T. Hil. A.Z.* 11:16: delusions alone are not *derekh shtuth*. Landau: during non-delusional states, such an individual is no less competent

Presentation	*Opinions in the Literature*
(*F. continued*)	than the *kordiakos* in his non-disturbed state (and see also *Sh. A., E.H.* 121, *Beth Yosef*, citing *Rambam*, that *kordiakos* is *ruach ra'ah*). *Arukh*, vol. 1, p. 157, and *Arukh ha-Shulchan: E.H.* 121: 1-12.
G. No evidence of the talmudic symptoms, and no obvious signs of impaired reality-testing, but there is evidence of marked affective disturbance, ranging from pervasive apathy and anhedonia, to severe depression, to non-psychotic melancholia (e.g. post-partum depression, involutional melancholia):	*G.* The *Rosh*, vol. 3, no. 43, cited in *Tur Sh. A., E.H.* 154: so long as at the very worst the individual can respond coherently to examination, he is not a *shoteh*. *Chatham Sofer*: examination would render such an individual competent regarding matters of divorce, but not in *eduth*. Berkowitz (*Seridei Esh*, vol. 3, no. 35): examination can determine competence, as long as there is no *ma'aseh shtuth*. *Atereth Chakhamim: E.H.*, no. 17: severe emotional withdrawal (see his definition: "one who sits still like a stone"...) includes many bona fide *shotim*; severe emotional withdrawal may itself be *shtuth*. *Rambam*, R. Ovadiah mi-Bartenuro, according to authorities cited in *Sedei Chemed, Ishuth* 2, 11: *ruach katzrit=ruach ra'ah="malenkuniya"=kordiakos*. (However, it would seem clear from *Rambam* and *Sh. A., E.H.* 121 that such affective disorders would not effect competence were one able to demonstrate *pikchuth*, unless there was also demonstration of verbal insanity.) *Arukh ha-Shulchan, Chatham Sofer, Resp. Divrei Yosef*, no. 15, *Resp. Maharash Engel*, vol. 1, no. 32, *Pithchei T^eshuvah* to *E. H.* 121: *marah shechorah* is not necessarily the equivalent of *shtuth*, especially if the individual can

Presentation	*Opinions in the Literature*
(*G. continued*)	prove competence through examination. *Atereth Chakhamim: marah shechorah* is *shtuth*.
H. None of the 3(4) symptoms of the Talmud, but evidence of "cloudy" sensorium, confusion, and memory gaps:	*H. Pithchei T'shuvah: E.H.*, 121, no. 3, *Resp. Maharit: E.H.*, no. 16: the *pethi* includes faulty memory and is disqualified for *eduth*, but may, according to some authorities, qualify himself for other matters through examination. See *Chelkath Mechokek* and *Pri Chadash* to *E.H.* 121: such a case is not worse than "*im haya ha-davar safek im higiya le-shikruto shel Lot* . . .," i.e., examination would help qualify one in matters of divorce.
I. Symptoms have been presented as an outcome of organic illness or disorder, but treatment has been instituted:	*I. Resp. Divrei Chayim: E.H.*, no. 77: if behavioral symptoms are remitted, even if some *atzvot* remains, one is *be-chezkath pikeach*. *Sh. A., E.H.* 121:73, *Resp. Bekhor Shor* 4, *Chatham Sofer: Y.D.*, no. 17: following the institution of treatment *and* examination for *pikchuth*, competence may be assumed. Landau: following *terufoth* which have been well-associated with symptomatic relief, *pikchuth* can be assumed once the established period for the achievement of primary remission has passed. *Beth Yosef, E.H.* 121, and Landau's other sources: some period of *pikchuth* must be established—either 3 periods of time in a single day, a single day of no symptoms, or 3 days with either no symptoms or established periods of *pikchuth*. Shapiro, Landau, and Bak (p. 171): one can assume that a patient with whom

Presentation	*Opinions in the Literature*
(*I. continued*)	treatment has been initiated, and *pikchuth* established, will continue to follow the therapeutic regimen.
J. Psychopathic tendencies (e.g., guiltlessness, etc.), paranoia (non-psychotic), or well-retained schizoid tendencies—with no impairment of reality-testing:	*J.* Landau: these are not the equivalent of *shtuth.* (I have seen no one discuss these specific disorders with regard to *eduth,* but it would seem that such persons lack the requisite *ne'emanuth* to profer valid or reliable testimony—viewing these perhaps as *shakranim,* and the anti-social personality type as a *rasha.*) *Resp. Tzitz Eliezer,* vol. 6, no. 42(2):9 permits a paranoid who demonstrates clarity to grant a divorce.
K. Following electroconvulsive ("shock") therapy, electrical stimulation of the brain, psychosurgery, or psycho-pharmacology—even with bland affect and some short term memory impairment—but no apparent impairment of reality-testing, etc.	*K. Landau,* citing *Rashba,* vol. 1, no. 765: following examination, *pikchuth* can be presumed. *Arukh ha-Shulchan* (not specifically dealing with these treatments): *tzilul da'ath* must be determined through examination, and there is even more reason for caution in matters of *eduth.*
L. A female demonstrates the 3(4) symptoms, and so forth, but she is deemed somehow capable of safeguarding her divorced status even though she cannot entirely provide for herself (*shomereth et gitasah ve-lo shomereth et atzmah*):	*L.* According to the basic law, such a woman may be divorced, but this is disallowed in accordance with the "ban" of R. Gershom (*Yev.* 113b; *M.T. Hil. Gerushin* 10:23; *Tur Sh. A., E.H.* 119). See also *Resp. Seridei Esh,* vol. 3, no. 1, *Resp. Achiezer,* vol. 3, no. 17, *Resp. Oneg Yom Tov,* end no. 143.

Arukh ha-Shulchan: E.H., 119:22-24: after the fact (*be-de'aved*), such a woman is considered properly divorced according to *Beth Yosef,* but not according to others. Debate concerns only a woman who is completely insane (but can somehow "preserve her *get*"). However, a woman who has alternating episodes of insanity and *pikchuth,* may be divorced, with her consent, during the period of *pikchuth.*

Resp. Tzitz Eliezer, vol. 6, no. 42(1), (2), discusses the possibility of forcing a schizophrenic woman to recite "I am willing" to grant a divorce.

Glossary

ACHRONIM: rabbinic scholars and authorities since the end of the 16th century.

AL TEHI RASHA BE'FNEI AZMEKHA: lit., do not be evil in your own self-estimate.

BA'AL TESHUVAH (pl. BA'ALEI TESHUVAH; fem. BA'ALAT TESHUVAH): one who "returns" or repents.

BE-DE'AVED: *post facto*, or in religious observance, what is acceptable after the fact.

BETH DIN: Jewish court of law.

BIRKATH HA-GOMEL: blessing of gratitude upon the deliverance from certain types of danger.

BITUL ASEH: the annulment by omission of a positive commandment.

BOSHET: a form of financial indemnity based on the shame suffered by the victim.

BRITH MILAH (or BRITH): ritual circumcision performed upon Jewish males at the age of 8 days old.

BUSHAH: embarrassment.

CHESED: the attribute of kindness, benevolence.

EMUNAH: faith, religious trust.

HALAKHAH: lit., the way, the corpus of Jewish ethical principles and normative practices, Biblical and rabbinic. *Halakhah* is the distinguishing characteristic of Jewish life.

HASHCHATATH ZERA LE-VATALAH: Spilling semen in vain; e.g., masturbation.

HATAFATH DAM BRITH: ritual letting of blood at the site of the circumcision. This is often performed as a distinct ritual to "correct" an improperly performed brith.

HIRHUR (pl. HIRHURIM): thought or fantasy.

HIRHUR ARAYOTH: thought of elicit sexual content.

HIRHUR ASUR: thought of any forbidden content.

HOKHACHAH (lit.: "proof"): ethical rebuke or counsel.

ISUR: prohibition, prohibited status (*asur*).

KAVANAH: intention or concentration required in *mitzvah* performance.

KEVISHATH HA-MIDDOTH: suppression or sublimation of personality traits, a re-channeling of such traits along ethical lines.

LE-KHATCHILAH: *ante facto*, or, in religious observance, what is required before the fact.

LO LISHMAH: see MITOKH SHE-LO LISHMAH ...

MAKATH MARDUTH DE-RABANAN: lashes for rebelling against rabbinic authority.

MATZAH: unleavened bread, consumed for ritual purposes on Passover.

MI'PNEI CHATAENU: "Because of our sins."

MITOKH SHE-LO LISHMAH BA LISHMAH: inappropriate or ulterior motives for *mitzvah* performance eventually develop into appropriate ones.

MITZVAH (pl. MITZVOTH): Biblical or rabbinic commandment, either positive (acts of commission) or negative (acts of omission) in nature.

MOHEL: ritual circumcisor.

MOKHIACH: ethical rebuker or counselor.

MUMCHEH: expert or authority.

MUSSAR: a 17th and 18th century religious movement dedicated to ethical perfectionism, still popular in many Orthodox Jewish circles.

NAFSHIUTH: pertaining to the soul.

NASHIM HA-MESOLELOTH: "women who embrace with each other"; i.e., lesbianism.

NEFESH: the soul.

ONESS: compulsion, duress.

PARDES: an acronym for *Peshat, Remez, Drush, Sod* — the four realms or levels of interpretation of the Torah; a mystical realm.

PERITZUTH: immodesty.

PIKE-ACH (PIKCHUTH): mentally competent.

POSKIM: halakhic decisors.

RISHONIM: rabbinic scholars and halakhic codifiers dating from the close of the gaonate (ca. 1000) until the end of the 15th century.

SAFEK: doubt.

SAKANATH NEFASHOTH: danger to life.

SEIRUS: castration.

SHEMA: the credo of faith, "Hear, O Israel, the Lord thy God, the Lord is One."

SHEVIRATH HA-LEV: "heartbreak."

SHLEIMUTH: the quality of wholeness or completeness.

SHOGEG: an act committed unwittingly or accidentally (distinguished generally from an act that is completely *oness*, or by compulsion).

SHOTEH: a fool, one who is legally incompetent and irresponsible to perform rituals.

TEFILLIN: phylacteries.

TESHUVAH: return, repentance.

TIKUN HA-MIDDOTH: correction or modification of personality traits.

TEIRUF DA'ATH: psychological trauma or decompensation.

TZAR: pain.

TZIMTZUM: the kabalistic notion of "contraction."

VIDDUY: confession of sin.

YEHAREG VE-AL YA'AVOR: the law that one must allow oneself to be killed rather than violate the three so-called cardinal sins: idol worship, murder, and the incestuous relationships. During times of forced, public violation of Jewish law, one must accept martyrdom rather than violate any law.

YETZER: translated as man's inclinations, but more correctly: human strivings or initiative.

YETZER HA-RA: lit., the evil inclination.

YISHUV HA-DA'ATH: calmness or settledness of mind, mental stability.

ZAKHOR: (imperative) remember, the commandment to remember.

ZEKHIRAH (ZEKHIRATH): the remembering, remembrance of.

Index